Instructors Resource Manual

UNDERSTANDING ABNORMAL BEHAVIOR

Seventh Edition

Revised by
Anita Rosenfield

David Sue
Western Washington University

Derald Wing Sue
Teachers College, Columbia University

Stanley Sue
University of California, Davis

HOUGHTON MIFFLIN COMPANY   BOSTON   NEW YORK

W9-DFG-050

Editor-in-Chief: Charles Hartford
Senior Sponsoring Editor: Kerry Baruth
Senior Development Editor: Sharon Geary
Senior Manufacturing Coordinator: Jane Spelman
Senior Marketing Manager: Katherine Greig

Copyright © 2003 by Houghton Mifflin Company. All rights reserved.

Houghton Mifflin Company hereby grants you permission to reproduce the Houghton Mifflin material contained in this work in classroom quantities, solely for use with the accompanying Houghton Mifflin textbook. All reproductions must include the Houghton Mifflin copyright notice, and no fee may be collected except to cover the cost of duplication. If you wish to make any other use of this material, including reproducing or transmitting the material or portions thereof in any form or by any electronic or mechanical means including any information storage or retrieval system, you must obtain prior written permission from Houghton Mifflin Company, unless such use is expressly permitted by federal copyright law. If you wish to reproduce material acknowledging a rights holder other than Houghton Mifflin Company, you must obtain permission from the rights holder. Address inquiries to College Permissions, Houghton Mifflin Company, 222 Berkeley Street, Boston, MA 02116-3764.

Printed in the U.S.A.

ISBN: 0-618-22001-1

123456789-CS-06 05 04 03 02

CONTENTS

Copyright © Houghton Mifflin Company. All rights reserved.

Copyright © Houghton Mifflin Company. All rights reserved.

Copyright © Houghton Mifflin Company. All rights reserved.

Copyright © Houghton Mifflin Company. All rights reserved.

Copyright © Houghton Mifflin Company. All rights reserved.

PREFACE

This Instructor's Manual is designed for instructors to use in conjunction with the Seventh Edition of *Understanding Abnormal Behavior* by Sue/Sue/Sue. It is meant to be both a guide to using the text and a handy reference, filled with numerous teaching aids and ideas for enlivening classroom presentations. Whether novice or expert, each instructor should be able to select material from these resources to suit his or her needs.

ORGANIZATION OF THIS MANUAL

Transition Guide for Instructors Switching from the Sixth to the Seventh Edition of Sue/Sue/Sue, Understanding Abnormal Behavior.   The guide describes the major organizational changes in the Seventh Edition and also details chapter-by-chapter additions, revisions, and deletions of material..

The Case of Steven V.   The Case of Steven V. as it appeared in the Fifth Edition has been reprinted in its entirety. A guide to using the Case of Steven V. is also provided, entitled "A Note About Steven V."

The Chapters.   This manual contains eighteen chapters that correspond to the textbook chapters. Each chapter in the manual is filled with teaching suggestions and resources designed to enhance teaching and learning.

CHAPTER-BY-CHAPTER ORGANIZATION

Chapter Outlines   Chapter outlines are one of the most important features in any Instructor's Manual. The outlines in this manual are very detailed and highlight critical information for student mastery. Instructors can follow the outlines and be assured that they will cover all the key material in each chapter, or instructors can edit the outlines to accommodate their own teaching objectives.

Learning Objectives   Learning objectives, intended to aid students' mastery of essential facts and concepts, appear in both the *Instructor's Resource Manual* and the student *Study Guide;* text pages corresponding to the objectives are also identified. In addition, multiple-choice questions in the *Test Bank* are keyed to the learning objectives. This interactive approach to learning is unique and designed to maximize students' understanding of text material.

Classroom Topics for Lecture and Discussion   At least three topics for classroom lectures and discussions are given in each chapter. We have chosen topics that are current, complex, and interesting to students—ones we hope will encourage them to connect abstract principles and theories to their daily lives. Also, throughout the chapters we have added topics that allow students to think clinically and

Copyright © Houghton Mifflin Company. All rights reserved.

make differential diagnoses. Internet annotations are included to support key topics in this section. These Internet annotations will allow you to have the most current information on a specific topic, thus enhancing your lectures.

Classroom Demonstrations Every chapter contains at least three classroom demonstrations, selected for their ability to draw students into many of the issues and challenges confronting abnormal psychology. Many of the demonstrations come with handouts that can easily be removed from the perforated manual and copied for classroom use. Internet annotations for the classroom demonstrations are also included in this section. These Internet annotations will allow you to have the most current information on the specific demonstration, thus enhancing your effectiveness.

Selected Readings A list of selected readings is supplied in each chapter to support text material and classroom discussions. The lists comprise many articles and books dealing with important issues in abnormal psychology.

Video Resources An annotated list of films and tapes, dealing with high-interest topics in abnormal psychology, completes each chapter of the Instructor's Manual. Instructors can use these resources to support classroom presentations or as discussion starters.

On the Internet Information is provided about web addresses for Internet sites related to abnormal psychology. Internet addresses are listed, with annotations about sites to visit for general topics presented in the chapter.

ADDITIONAL ANCILLARIES AVAILABLE

Supplements for Instructors:

PowerPoint Slides: Instructors can utilize this updated set of PowerPoint slides in preparing their classroom lectures. For each chapter, a slide show is provided featuring lecture topics, tables, and illustrations to help highlight the major topics in abnormal psychology.

HMClassPrep: Instructors can create their own course materials and presentations using the resources available on the HMClassPrep CD-ROM. Resources include the PowerPoint slides, lecture outlines, Instructors Resource activities and handouts, as well as the seventh edition transition guide.

Instructor website: Instructors can access the useful and innovative teaching tools, activities, and other resources that support Understanding Abnormal Behavior, 7/e by logging onto our website at http://psychology.college.hmco.com/instructors.

Test Bank: Features one hundred multiple choice questions per chapter. Each question is labeled with the corresponding text page reference as well as the type of question being asked for easier test creation. Also, the text bank includes three essay questions per chapter with sample answers.

Computerized Test Bank: Allows instructors to create their own exams from the test bank questions as well as integrate their own questions with those on the disk.

Transparencies: The 100, 4-color transparency set includes a balance of charts, graphs, and illustrations from the text to help highlight key concepts in abnormal psychology.

Copyright © Houghton Mifflin Company. All rights reserved.

Supplements for Students:

Study Guide: Provides a complete review of the chapter with chapter outlines, learning objectives, fill-in-the-blank review of key terms and multiple choice questions. Answers to test questions include an explanation for both the correct answer and incorrect answer.

Student CD-ROM Real Deal: Designed to aid in the review of the chapter material, the CD-ROM provides an additional study and assessment tool for students. Featuring study outlines with glossary terms highlighted, Net Lab interactive activities focused on the major concepts in abnormal psychology, and chapter quizzes, this resource will help ensure student success in the course.

Student Website: Students can access the useful and innovative learning tools, activities, and resources that support Understanding Abnormal Behavior, 7/e by logging onto our website at http://psychology.college.hmco.com/students.

Casebook for Abnormal Psychology: Written by Clark Clipson, California School of Professional Psychology, and Jocelyn Steer, San Diego Family Institute. This casebook provides 16 studies and can be shrink-wrapped with the text at a discounted package price.

Abnormal Psychology in Context: Voices and Perspectives: Written by David Sattler, College of Charleston, Virginia Shabatay, Palomar College, and Geoffrey Kramer, Grand Valley State University. This collection of over 40 first-person accounts and narratives can be shrink-wrapped with the text at a discounted package price.

Internet Guide: Manual introduces students to electronic mail, discussion groups, on-line journals, newsgroups, and numerous addresses and sites relevant to psychology

Copyright © Houghton Mifflin Company. All rights reserved.

TRANSITION GUIDE

A Guide for Instructors Switching from the Sixth Edition to the Seventh Edition of Sue/Sue/Sue, *Understanding Abnormal Behavior*

The Seventh Edition of *Understanding Abnormal Behavior* retains the most popular features of earlier editions, with important new elements added.

GENERAL CHANGES FROM 6TH EDITION TO 7TH EDITION

- Condensed *Schizophrenia coverage* from two to one chapter

- Stand-alone chapter on *Eating Disorders added*

- Chapter-opening *Focus Questions added*

- Chapter summary organized by *Focus Questions*- presented in an easy-to-digest bulleted form

- *Myth vs. Reality* feature added to help dispel students' preconceived notions of mental health issues

- *Critical thinking questions* added to key photo captions

- Palette and design revised and updated throughout text, art, and tables

- *Focus On* boxes renamed *Mental Health & Society* better reflecting content; selected boxes updated or replaced

- Updated *case studies and examples*, with easy to find design designation

- Deleted dated *First Person* boxes

- Updated material based upon DSM-IV-TR

SPECIFIC CHANGES FROM 6TH EDITION TO 7TH EDITION

Chapter 1 Abnormal Behavior
- Updated material based upon DSM-IV-TR
- New coverage of the Surgeon General's Report on Mental Health on mental health costs/burdens
- Update of health care costs in U.S. statistics
- Updated references
- New <u>Mental Health & Society Box</u>: Managed Care
- Updated statistics on diversity from U.S. Census 2000 report

Chapter 2 Models of Abnormal Behavior
- New section on Human Genome Project
- Changed Neo-Freudian Perspectives to Post-Freudian Perspectives
- Updated references

Copyright © Houghton Mifflin Company. All rights reserved.

- Deleted section, "Development of Personality and Identity Within the Family"
- Deleted section, "Family Dynamics"
- Updated <u>Mental Health & Society Box</u>: Problems in Using Racial and Ethnic Group References

Chapter 3 Assessment and Classification of Abnormal Behavior
- Updated references
- Updates (text and box) based upon DSM-IV-TR changes
- New <u>Mental Health & Society Box</u>: "The Diagnosing and Classification of a Disorder: Depression"

Chapter 4 The Scientific Method in Abnormal Psychology
- Updated references
- New case study: Rebirthing therapy
- New case study and coverage of dental phobia experiment
- New case study: Cultural misdiagnosis
- New case study: Eye movement desensitization
- New coverage on Human Genome Project
- New <u>Mental Health & Society box</u>: "Should Scientific Findings At Variance with 'Common Knowledge' be Published?"
- Updated <u>Mental Health & Society box</u>: "Cultural Bias in Research"

Chapter 5 Anxiety Disorders
- Updated references
- Added new case studies
- Updated data on Generalized Anxiety Disorder (GAD)
- Updated section on Biological Perspective (GAD, PD)
- Updated section on Biochemical Treatment (GAD, PD)
- Updated section on Behavioral Treatment (GAD, PD)
- Edited/updated discussion of Social Phobias
- New section on "Negative Information Perspective" [Phobias]
- New section on "Exposure Therapy" [Phobias]
- New section on "Cognitive Strategies" [Phobias]
- New case study: Obsessive Compulsive Disorder
- Updates/new information on obsessive-compulsive disorder [perspectives and treatments]
- Extensive updating, new data on Post-traumatic Stress Disorder (diagnosis and treatment)
- Updated Table: Clinical Examples of Obsessions and Compulsions

Chapter 6 Dissociative Disorders and Somatoform Disorders
- Updated references
- New case studies (amnesia – real/faked)
- New case study: dissociative identity disorder
- Updated/edited data on Dissociative Identity Disorder
- Updated section: Behavioral Perspective [Dissociative Identity Disorder]
- New case study: somatization disorder
- New case study: conversion disorder
- New section on questions to determine Body Dysmorphic Disorder
- New <u>Mental Health & Society box</u>: Culture and Somatoform and Dissociative Disorders
- Updated <u>Mental Health & Society box</u>: Factitious Disorders

Chapter 7 Psychological Factors Affecting Medical Conditions
- Updated references
- Deleted section on Psychological Consequences of Stress
- New coverage on Stress and the Immune System
- New section on Self-Efficacy and Optimism

Copyright © Houghton Mifflin Company. All rights reserved.

- Updated information on Coronary Heart Disease
- Updated information on Stress and Hypertension
- Updated asthma research
- New coverage to Cognitive-Behavioral Interventions (Treatment of Psychophysiological Disorders)
- Deleted Focus On Box: Do Psychological and Social Factors Contribute to the Development of Cancer?
- New <u>Mental Health & Society box</u>: Can Laughter or Humor Impact the Course of a Disease?

Chapter 8 Personality Disorders and Impulse Control Disorders
- Updated references
- Updated data on Borderline Personality Disorder
- Updated data on Antisocial Personality Disorder
- Deleted section on Eysenck (Autonomic Nervous System Abnormalities)
- Update on Pathological Gambling

Chapter 9 Substance-Related Disorders
- Updated references
- Added information on drug use/abuse
- Updated data on prevalence of drug/alcohol/cigarette use
- New section on tension-reduction models related to alcohol use
- Updated information on treatment outcomes, research
- Added new <u>Mental Health & Society box</u>: Club Drugs

Chapter 10 Sexual and Gender Identity Disorders
- Updated references
- Updated case studies
- New <u>Mental Health & Society Box</u>: Is Compulsive Sexual Behavior (CBS) Sexual Addiction?
- Added data from Merck Manual of Diagnosis and Therapy in diagnosing sexual problems
- Update on changing view of homosexuality by Chinese Psychological Association
- Added new information on Aging and Sexuality, AARP survey results
- Added new data on Sexual Dysfunction prevalence
- Updated coverage of Viagra
- Added new case study: Sex-change health coverage (Gender Identity Disorders)
- Updated data on Rape
- New Table: Some Possible Physical Causes of Erectile Disorder and Dyspareunia
- Deleted Focus On box: Viagra
- New Table: What Have You Been Told About Rape?
- New <u>Mental Health & Society box:</u> Warning: Date Rape Drugs

Chapter 11 Mood Disorders
- Updated references
- Added new data on Cultural Influences on Depression
- Updated information on The Etiology of Mood Disorders
- Added new coverage of Comparative Test of Beck and Seligman (Response Styles)
- Updated data on Biomedical Treatment for Depressive Disorders
- Updated <u>Mental Health & Society Box</u>: Should Electroconvulsive Shock Treatment for Depression be Banned?

Chapter 12 Suicide
- Updated references
- Added new case study: Suicide Bomber
- Added section on "Surgeon General's Call to Action to Prevent Suicide"
- Combined coverage of Children and College Students as Victims of Suicide

Copyright © Houghton Mifflin Company. All rights reserved.

- New <u>Mental Health & Society box</u>: College Student Suicides (pulled out and highlighted from previous placement in text)
- Updated general data and information on suicide research
- Added new section on Suicide in Jails and Prisons
- Updated information on categories of suicide warning signs
- New Table: Surveillance for Injuries and Violence Among Older Adults
- Deleted Focus On box: Suicide Notes
- New Table: Risk and Protective Factors in Suicide Assessment and Intervention

Chapter 13 Schizophrenia: Diagnosis and Etilogy

- Combined former chapters 13 & 14 into one chapter
- Updated references
- Edited, modified content, art, photos to create one chapter
- Added new coverage of cultural issues affecting schizophrenia

Chapter 14 Cognitive Disorders

- Updated references
- Added updated data on MRI
- Added data on aging and memory, dementia
- Added updated data on Alzheimer's disease
- Added updated data on mental retardation

Chapter 15 Disorders of Childhood and Adolescence

- Updated references
- Updated data on childhood/adolescence disorders
- Updated coverage of Autism
- Expanded coverage of Asperger's Disorder
- Expanded coverage of Rett's Disorder
- Data updates on diagnosis and treatment of developmental disorders
- Expanded coverage of etiology/treatment of ADHD and Conduct Disorders
- Added section on Reactive Attachment Disorder
- Expanded coverage of Mood Disorders
- Updated coverage of Elimination Disorders
- Deleted entire coverage of Eating Disorders (moved and expanded to a full chapter)
- Deleted Table: Other Childhood Disorders
- Updated <u>Mental Health & Society Box</u>: Are We Overmedicating Children?
- Deleted Table: Effect of Parental Criminal Record on Adopted Sons
- New <u>Mental Health & Society Box</u>: School Violence: A Sign of the Times?

Chapter 16 Eating Disorders

- New chapter to this edition

Chapter 17 Psychotherapeutic Interventions

- Chapter retitled from "Individual and Group Therapies"
- Updated references
- Edited coverage of Eysenck's Criticism of Psychotherapy
- Changed focus of section "Group, Family, and Marital Therapy" to "Groups, Family, and Couples Therapy"
- Deleted dated case studies
- Added section on Culturally Diverse Populations and Psychotherapy
- Updated Table: Drugs Most Commonly Used in Drug Therapy
- Deleted Focus On box: Culturally Appropriate Mental Health Services
- Deleted Focus On box: Some Types of Therapy Groups

Copyright © Houghton Mifflin Company. All rights reserved.

Chapter 18 Legal and Ethical Issues in Abnormal Psychology

- Updated references
- Updated case of Russell Weston
- Expanded discussion of Cultural Competence (name change) and the Mental Health Profession

Copyright © Houghton Mifflin Company. All rights reserved.

THE CASE OF STEVEN V.

A NOTE ABOUT STEVEN V.

Readers familiar with previous editions of *Understanding Abnormal Behavior* will notice that the extended case of Steven V. now appears only in Chapter 2. Recognizing that instructors may want to use all of the Steven V. material, the full text of the case from the Fifth Edition has been included here, as well as this guide to using the case in chapters throughout the current edition of the text.

GUIDE TO USING THE CASE OF STEVEN V.

Chapter 2 (Models of Abnormal Behavior): This condensed chapter describing six approaches to abnormal behavior is an excellent place to use the Steven V. case. Students can be assigned to use one or more of the approaches to explain Steven's behavior, thoughts, and feelings. Written assignments, panel discussions, and debates are activities that can engage students in the important process of analyzing this single case from different angles.

Chapter 3 (Assessment and Classification of Abnormal Behavior): Because this chapter surveys the many forms that assessment can take, it suggests that Steven V.'s strengths and weaknesses might have been assessed in many different ways. Each theoretical orientation emphasizes certain forms of data and using particular methods to collect them. Again, an assignment requiring students to describe, compare, and contrast assessment approaches taken by clinicians of different theoretical stripes reinforces the importance of flexible thinking. An integrative approach to assessment, using neurological, psychological, and observational techniques, could be emphasized here since most clinicians are eclectic rather than purist.

Chapter 10 (Sexual and Gender Identity Disorders): Some of Steven V.'s symptoms entail violent sexual fantasies. Sexual performance concerns and embarrassment with his genitalia are both relevant to the material in this chapter. His use of sexually violent videos in adolescence illustrates some of the points made in the text about a behavioral explanation for sexual disorders. His Oedipal relationship with his mother relates to the psychoanalytic explanation.

Chapter 11 (Mood Disorders): Bipolar disorder is one of the diagnoses Steven V. received. Here you can compare the diagnostic criteria for bipolar and major depressive disorder with the symptoms that Steven displays. Ask students which signs are missing, which are present, and which ones we must speculate about.

Chapter 12 (Suicide): Steven V. seems like a young man with a high potential for violent behavior directed either at himself or at others. Have students do a lethality assessment of Steven based on what they are told. Give them a reasonable amount of discretion in speculating on the circumstances in which he would become more and more suicidal. What kinds of suicide prevention efforts might have been put in place on his university campus? How might his parents have responded if they knew he was suicidal?

Chapter 15 (Disorders of Childhood and Adolescence): Steven V. is a late adolescent when he arrives at the university counseling service. Students are likely to see him as having adult disorders. But what disorders would have been diagnosed when he was eight or twelve or fifteen? Students can review the information on childhood depression, separation anxiety disorder, and conduct disorder to see if the symptoms and events in Steven V.'s traumatic childhood match. Ask students what interventions with his parents might have changed the trajectory of his personality development.

Chapter 17 (Psychotherapeutic Interventions): Here, as in Chapters 2 and 3, students have an opportunity to describe, differentiate, and critique the use of different theoretical approaches with one case. Written assignments, panel discussions, debates, or role-played "therapy sessions" can impress

Copyright © Houghton Mifflin Company. All rights reserved.

upon students how different therapies would highlight different aspects of Steven's behavior, thoughts, and feelings. Once again, you could ask students to design an integrative approach that would take the best of the many approaches described to effectively treat him and, perhaps, his family. Family therapy is a particularly intriguing option for Steven. The conflict between and among him, his father, and his mother may trigger some strong reactions from students who often face similar, if less intense, circumstances. An entertaining and thought-provoking activity is to have students role-play a family therapy session with the V. family.

Chapter 18 (Legal and Ethical Issues in Abnormal Psychology): Clearly, a key issue in the case of Steven V. is the dilemma faced by his therapist. Should the therapist take seriously Steven's threats and break confidentiality or keep these secrets? Students should see the links between the *Tarasoff* ruling and the case of Steven V. They can also think about the means by which a therapist attempts to predict dangerousness. Ask students what evidence from the past would indicate that Steven was prepared to harm his former girlfriend; have them assess the risks of overpredicting dangerousness versus the risks of underpredicting it. Finally, compare the list of exemptions from privileged communications given in the text and the situation the counseling center therapist found himself in when Steven discussed his plans to harm his girlfriend.

THE CASE OF STEVEN V.

Steven V. had been suffering from a severe bout of depression. Eighteen months earlier, Steve's woman friend, Linda, had broken off her relationship with Steve. Steve had fallen into a crippling depression. During the past few weeks, however, with the encouragement of his therapist, Steve had begun to open up and express his innermost feelings. His depression had lifted, but it was replaced by a deep anger and hostility toward Linda. In today's session, Steve had become increasingly loud and agitated as he recounted his complaints against Linda. Minutes ago, with his hands clenched into fists, his knuckles white, he had abruptly lowered his voice and looked his therapist in the eye. "She doesn't deserve to live," Steve had said. "I swear, I'm going to kill her."

The therapist could feel himself becoming tense, apprehensive, and uncertain: How should he interpret the threat? How should he act on it? One wheel of his swivel chair squealed sharply, breaking the silence, as he backed away from his client.

Until this session, the therapist had not believed Steve was dangerous. Now he wondered whether Steve could be the one client in ten thousand to act out such a threat. Should Linda or the police be told of what Steve had said?

Steve V. had a long psychiatric history, beginning well before he first sought help from the therapist at the university's psychological services center. (In fact, his parents wanted their son to continue seeing a private therapist, but Steven stopped therapy during his junior year at the university.) Steve had actually been in and out of psychotherapy since kindergarten; while in high school, he was hospitalized twice for depression.

His case records, nearly two inches thick, contained a number of diagnoses, including labels such as *schizoid personality, paranoid schizophrenia,* and *manic-depressive psychosis* (now referred to as bipolar mood disorder). Although his present therapist did not find these labels particularly helpful, Steve's clinical history did provide some clues to the causes of his problems.

Steven V. was born in a suburb of San Francisco, California, the only child of an extremely wealthy couple. His father was a prominent businessman who worked long hours and traveled frequently. On those rare occasions when he was at home, Mr. V. was often preoccupied with business matters and held himself quite aloof from his son. The few interactions they had were characterized by his constant ridicule and criticism of Steve. Mr. V. was greatly disappointed that his son seemed so timid, weak, and withdrawn. Steven was extremely bright and did well in school, but Mr. V. felt that he lacked the "toughness" needed to survive and prosper in today's world. Once, when Steve was about ten years old, he came home from school with a bloody nose and bruised face, crying and complaining of being picked on by his schoolmates. His father showed no sympathy but instead berated Steve for losing the fight. In his father's presence, Steve usually felt worthless, humiliated, and fearful of doing or saying the wrong thing.

Mrs. V. was very active in civic and social affairs, and she too spent relatively little time with her son. Although she treated Steve more warmly and lovingly than his father did, she seldom came to Steve's defense when Mr. V. bullied him. She generally allowed her husband to make family decisions.

When Steve was a child, his mother at times had been quite affectionate. She had often allowed Steve to sleep with her in her bed when her husband was away on business trips. She usually dressed minimally on these occasions and was very demonstrative—holding, stroking, and kissing Steve. This behavior had continued until Steve was twelve, when his mother abruptly refused to let Steve into her bed. The sudden withdrawal of this privilege had confused and angered Steve, who was not certain what he had done wrong. He knew, though, this his mother had been quite upset when she awoke one night to find him masturbating next to her.

Most of the time, however, Steve's parents seemed to live separately from one another and from their son. Steve was raised, in effect, by a full-time maid. He rarely had playmates of his own age. His birthdays were celebrated with a cake and candles, but the only celebrants were Steve and his mother.

Copyright © Houghton Mifflin Company. All rights reserved.

By age ten, Steven had learned to keep himself occupied by playing "mind games," letting his imagination carry him off on flights of fantasy. He frequently imagined himself as a powerful figure—Superman or Batman. His fantasies were often extremely violent, and his foes were vanquished only after much blood had been spilled.

As Steve grew older, his fantasies and heroes became increasingly menacing and evil. When he was fifteen, he obtained a pornographic videotape that he viewed repeatedly on a video player in his room. Often, Steve would masturbate as he watched scenes of women being sexually violated. The more violent the acts against women, the more aroused he became. He was addicted to the *Nightmare on Elm Street* films, in which the villain, Freddie Kruger, disemboweled or slashed his victims to death with his razor-sharp glove. Steve now recalls that he spent much of his spare time between the ages of fifteen and seventeen watching X-rated videotapes or violent movies, his favorite being *The Texas Chainsaw Massacre*, in which a madman saws and hacks women to pieces. Steve always identified with the character perpetrating the outrage; at times, he imagined his parents as the victims.

At about age sixteen, Steven became convinced that external forces were controlling his mind and behavior and were drawing him into his fantasies. He was often filled with guilt and anxiety after one of his mind games. Although he was strongly attracted to his fantasy world, he also felt that something was wrong with it and with him. After seeing the movie *The Exorcist*, he became convinced that he was possessed by the devil.

Until this time, Steve had been quiet and withdrawn. In kindergarten the school psychologist had described his condition as autisticlike because Steve seldom spoke, seemed unresponsive to the environment, and was socially isolated. His parents had immediately hired a prominent child psychiatrist to work with Steve. The psychiatrist had assured them that Steve was not autistic but would need intensive treatment for several years. And throughout these years of treatment, Steve never acted out any of his fantasies. With the development of his interest in the occult and in demonic possession, however, he became outgoing, flamboyant, and even exhibitionistic. He read extensively about Satanism, joined a "Church of Satan" in San Francisco, and took to wearing a black cape on weekend journeys into that city. Against his will, he was hospitalized twice by his parents with diagnoses of, respectively, bipolar affective disorder and schizophrenia in remission.

Steve was twenty-one years old when he met Linda at an orientation session for first-year university students. Linda struck him as different from other women students: unpretentious, open, and friendly. He quickly became obsessed with their relationship. But although Linda dated Steve frequently over the next few months, she did not seem to reciprocate his intense feelings. She took part in several extracurricular activities, including the student newspaper and student government, and her willingness to be apart from him confused and frustrated Steve. When her friends were around, Linda seemed almost oblivious to Steve's existence. In private, however, she was warm, affectionate, and intimate. She would not allow sexual intercourse, but she and Steve did engage in heavy petting.

Even while he and Linda were dating, Steve grew increasingly insecure about their relationship. He felt slighted by Linda's friends and began to believe that she disliked him. Several times he accused her of plotting against him and deliberately making him feel inadequate. Linda continually denied these allegations. Finally (on one occasion), feeling frightened and intimidated by Steve, she acquiesced to having sex with him. Unfortunately, Steve could not maintain an erection. When he blamed her for this "failure" and became verbally and physically abusive, Linda put an end to their relationship and refused to see him again.

During the next year and a half, Steve suffered from severe bouts of depression and twice attempted suicide by drug overdose. For the past six months, up to the time of his threat, he had been seeing a therapist regularly at the university's psychological services center.

A BIOLOGICAL VIEW OF STEVEN V.

How would a psychologist oriented toward biogenic explanations view the case of Steven V.? If Steve's therapist were so oriented, we believe that he or she would discuss Steve's behavior in the following terms.

Copyright © Houghton Mifflin Company. All rights reserved.

Before I interpret the symptoms displayed by Steven V. and speculate on what they mean, I must stress my belief that many "mental disorders" have a strong biological basis. I do accept the importance of environmental influences; but, in my view, the biological bases of abnormality are too often overlooked by psychologists. This seems clearly to be the case with Steven V.

Much of Steve's medical history is missing from his case records, along with important information about his biological and developmental milestones. We do not have the data necessary to chart a family tree, which would show whether other members of his family have suffered from a similar disorder. This lack of information about possible inherited tendencies in Steve's current behavior pattern is a serious shortcoming.

At age fifteen, Steve was given a diagnosis of bipolar affective disorder (formerly called *manic-depressive psychosis*). Pharmacological treatment was moderately effective in controlling his symptoms. After Steve's condition became stabilized, lithium carbonate treatment was instituted for a period of time, and Steve was free of symptoms during that period. Unfortunately, Steve apparently disliked taking medication and did so only sporadically.

In any case, evidence documents and supports a diagnosis of bipolar affective disorder. Steve displays the behaviors associated with this disorder, ranging from manic episodes (elevated mood characterized by expansiveness, hyperactivity, flight of ideas, and inflated self-esteem) to depressive episodes (depressed mood characterized by loss of interest, feelings of worthlessness, and thoughts of death or suicide). These symptoms are not of recent origin but probably were evident very early in his life. Steve's first contact with a mental health professional was with the school psychologist in kindergarten, who described him as "autisticlike." I believe the child psychiatrist whom Steve subsequently visited was correct in saying that Steve was not autistic. The chief symptoms described in his early years, which appeared to indicate autism (social isolation and unresponsiveness), are similar to those of depression. I suspect Steve was experiencing a major depressive episode as early as kindergarten, and it may not have been his first. Unfortunately, we do not have access to Steve's pediatrician, who may have observed even earlier signs of bipolar disorder. What we do have, however, are several statements from his parents indicating that "even at birth, Steve did not respond in the normal way."

Thus the following conclusions can be drawn: Steve's disorder was evident early in his life, and he suffered from a chemical imbalance. In spite of a shortage of information, there is some indication that some of Steve's relatives may have suffered from a similar disorder. The most defensible diagnosis is bipolar affective disorder. The most effective way to treat this disorder is through drug therapy.

These conclusions strongly support a biological interpretation of the patient's psychopathology. Heredity seems to have played a part; we have some evidence that relatives may have suffered a similar disorder. The precise biological mechanism that triggered the disorder is probably within one of the two major classes of neurotransmitters (catecholamines and indoleamines). If this diagnosis is accurate, the patient should resume taking medication. Of course, stressful life events may also be contributing to Steve's emotional problems, and I intend to continue psychotherapy with him. But I believe that many of Steve's depressive episodes would have occurred regardless of *psychological* intervention. And they will probably continue to occur unless Steve controls his biological problem with medication. I am not an M.D. and therefore cannot prescribe drugs, so I have arranged for Steve to visit a physician at the college medical center. Only when Steve's organic problem is under control can I or any other therapist begin to make headway with Steve's problems in relating to other people.

A PSYCHOANALYTIC VIEW OF STEVEN V.

Let us hypothesize again. Suppose that Steven V.'s therapist had a psychoanalytical orientation. Here is what we believe that he or she might have to say about Steve.

In Steve's case records, I see many possible explanations for his continuing problems. I will focus on four areas that I find particularly important: Steve's early childhood experiences; his repression of conflicts, intense feelings, and other impulses; the oedipal dynamics that seem to be at work; and the unconscious symbolism behind his relationship with Linda.

Copyright © Houghton Mifflin Company. All rights reserved.

Steve did not receive the love and care, at crucial psychosexual stages, that a child needs to develop into a healthy adult. He was neglected, understimulated, and left on his own. The result was that he felt unloved and rejected. We have evidence that he was prone to "accidents"—being hit on the head by a swing, burning himself severely on an electric range, numerous falls. I believe that these were not really accidents. They represented Steve's unconscious attempts to gain attention and to test his parents' love for him. Furthermore, I believe that his proneness to accidents was the forerunner of his attempts at suicide, a reflection of the death instinct and a desire to punish himself. Although Steve may not have been conscious of his feelings or able to verbalize them, it is obvious that he was deeply affected by his parents' negative attitudes. It must be an awful experience for a young child to believe that he or she is unloved. For many of us, it is easier to deny or repress this belief than to face up to it.

Steve may have been the victim of marital unhappiness between his mother and father. The records indicate that they lived rather separate lives and that Mr. V. kept several mistresses whom he saw on his frequent "business trips." In one therapy session, when Mrs. V. was seen alone, she stated that she knew of her husband's extramarital affairs but never confronted him about them. Apparently she was fearful of his dominating and abusive manner at home, and she avoided potential conflicts by playing a passive role. When Mr. V. belittled Steve, she chose not to intervene; secretly, however, she identified with her son's predicament. Unable to form an intimate relationship with her husband, she became physically seductive toward Steve. As you recall, Mrs. V. frequently caressed and kissed her son and even had him sleep with her. To a youngster still groping his way through oedipal conflicts, nothing could have been more damaging. Steve's sexual feelings toward the mother were no doubt intensified by her actions.

Mr. V.'s verbal abuse of Steve also aggravated Steve's problems. One of his father's common remarks to Steve was "You've got no balls." Abuse such as this deepened and prolonged Steve's oedipal feelings of rivalry with and fear of his father. Steve's oedipal conflict was never adequately resolved. His continued feelings of inadequacy and anger, and his sexual drives as well, have remained repressed and are expressed symbolically.

Steve's repressed anger is certainly present in both his fantasies and behavior. His violent "mind games" and his preference for sadistic pornographic films are an indirect expression of anger at his father, whom he continues to see as a powerful feared rival (he has failed to identify with his father in resolution of the oedipal conflict), and at his mother, who never came to his defense and suddenly withdrew his "bed privileges" when she became aware of Steve's sexual excitement. There also appears to be a strong relationship between Steve's anger and his depression. Steve's periodic bouts of depression are probably the result of anger turned inward. His frequent accidents, his episodic depression, and his attempts at suicide are classic manifestations of the death instinct.

Steve's early childhood experiences continue to affect his behavior with women. Note the similarities between his woman friend, Linda, and his mother. Linda is described as being active in student affairs; the mother was always involved in civic affairs. Linda seemed oblivious to Steve's existence in the presence of others, and he felt slighted by her friends; the mother seems never to have introduced Steve to her friends and relatives. Linda was "warm, affectionate, and intimate" in private; the mother, when "alone with Steve," was quite affectionate. Linda would consent to "heavy petting" but drew the line short of intercourse; the mother suddenly withdrew "bed privileges" when Steve showed incestuous sexual interest. It is clear that Steve continues to search for a "mother figure" and unconsciously selected a woman who is most like his mother. His impotence with Linda is additional evidence that Steve unconsciously views her as his mother. (In our society, incest is an unthinkable act.)

If Steve is to become a healthier individual, he must commit himself to intensive, long-term therapy aimed at helping him gain insight into his deep conflicts and repressed experiences. Resolving past traumas, overcoming resistance, and working through a transference relationship with the therapist will be crucial components of his therapy.

Copyright © Houghton Mifflin Company. All rights reserved.

xxii The Case of Steven V.

A HUMANISTIC-EXISTENTIAL VIEW OF STEVEN V.

A therapist who strongly endorses the humanistic or existential approach would see Steven V. quite different from the way a psychoanalyst or a proponent of the biogenic model would see Steve. If Steve's therapist were so oriented, we believe that he or she would consider the case of Steven V. very much as follows.

I must begin by stressing a point that is likely to be underemphasized by many other psychologists. Steven V. is not merely the sum of the voluminous case records I have before me. Steve is a flesh-and-blood person, alive, organic, and moving, with thoughts, feelings, and emotions. How could anyone hope to understand Steve by reading a pile of material that is static and inorganic and occasionally seeks to pigeonhole him into diagnostic categories? To classify Steve as schizophrenic, manic-depressive, or suicidal does not help me understand him. Indeed, such labels might serve as barriers to the development of a therapeutic relationship with him.

I intend to develop such a relationship with Steve, to engage him in a dialogue that will require no pretenses or self-justifications, and to travel with him on a journey whose destination neither of us will know until we get there. What makes me so sure that such a journey will be worthwhile? Almost everything I know of Steve, I learned from Steve himself. Here, for example, is an entry from Steve's diary, written when he was in his junior year in high school.

> Seems like I can't do anything right. Why does he always pick on me? Came home with top scores on my SAT. Mother was impressed. Showed Dad. Wouldn't even look up from his newspaper. All he's interested in is the *Wall Street Journal*. Make money, that's the goal!!
>
> Tried to tell him at dinner again. Got top score, Dad!! Don't you care?? Of course not! Said he expected it from me. Said he wanted me to do better next time. Said I should sit up and not slurp my soup. . . . Said I should learn better table manners. . . . Said I was an asshole!!! I am an asshole, I am, I am, who am I? Who cares?

Steve expresses strong feelings and emotions in this passage. Steve is deeply hurt by his father, he is angry at his father, and he seems to be seeking approval and validation from his father; he is also grappling with identity issues. These themes, but especially that of seeking approval from his father, are sounded throughout Steve's diary. His self-image and self-esteem seem to depend on his father's reaction to him. He clings to this perception of himself because he is afraid that without it he would not know who he is. This is illustrated in his questions: "Who am I? Who cares?" Until Steve knows who he is, he cannot understand what he might become. Now here is another diary entry, this one during his senior year in high school:

> Hello diary! Another do-nothing day! Parents won't let me do anything. Maybe I should jack off. . . . Got another good porno tape. This room's like a prison. Hello walls. . . . hello desk . . . hello fly . . . hello hell! Ha, that's a good one . . .
>
> > Every day's the same.
> > When you're in the well!
> > Every day's a game.
> > When you're in hell.

This passage reveals another aspect of what is happening with Steve. He feels trapped, immobilized, lonely, and unable to change his life. He has never recognized or accepted the responsibility of making choices. He externalizes his problems and views himself as a passive victim. In this way Steve evades responsibility for choosing and protects himself by staying in the safe, known environment of his room.

Steve needs to realize that he is responsible for his own actions, that he cannot find his identity in others. He needs to get in touch with, and express directly, his feelings of anxiety, guilt, shame, and anger. And he needs to be open to new experiences. All this can be accomplished through a free, open, and unstructured client-therapist relationship.

Copyright © Houghton Mifflin Company. All rights reserved.

A BEHAVIORAL VIEW OF STEVEN V.

Now suppose that Steve's therapist is strongly oriented toward the behavioral models. He or she would then discuss Steve's problems in terms very much like the following.

Let me start by drawing an analogy between behavior and music. In music, all the songs a performer has learned make up the performer's repertoire. Quite similarly, all an individual's behaviors — all the responses the person has learned to make in each situation — constitute the person's behavioral repertoire.

The roots of Steve's problems can be traced to his behavioral repertoire. Many of the behaviors he has learned are inappropriate (much like songs that nobody wants to hear), and his repertoire lacks useful, productive behaviors.

Many of Steve's troubles stem from his deficiency in, or lack of, social skills. He has had little practice in social relationships, and so has difficulty distinguishing between appropriate and inappropriate behavior. You can see evidence of these problems in his withdrawn behavior when he is in the company of relatives or his parents' or Linda's friends. Steve himself reports that he feels apprehensive and anxious in the company of others (for example, Linda's friends) and finds himself with no idea of what to do or say. While others seem to have no difficulty making "small talk," Steve remains silent. When he does speak, his statements are usually perfunctory, brief, and inappropriate. I think this deficiency stems from Steve's early social isolation, which prevented him from developing interpersonal skills, and from his lack of good role models. His parents seldom interacted with one another or with Steve. Recall that Mr. V.'s manner of relating to his son was generally antagonistic; he did not model effective and appropriate skills.

I am also interested in exploring Steve's bouts of depression, but I need to know several things: first, through what specific behaviors is Steve's depression made manifest? Does he withdraw from social contact? Lose his appetite? Weep? Make negative statements? If we are to help Steve change his behavior, we must know what behavior we are talking about. Too often terms such as *depression, passivity,* and *anxiety* are used without a common referent. For example, when a client calls himself "shy," we must be sure that both therapist and client understand the term in the same way.

Second, what situations tend to elicit his depression? If the events share common characteristics, then we may be able to control or alter them to Steve's advantage. Again, it appears that Steve experiences depression when he believes himself to be worthless: when rejected by his woman friend, when belittled by his father, and on becoming impotent in his first sexual encounter. Steve may be able to master such situations by developing more effective behaviors. He might benefit, for example, from learning to respond to his father's bullying by telling his father how hurt and angry he feels when his father belittles him. A behavioral program designed to enhance Steve's sexual functioning could also prove helpful in combating his depression. And Steve must learn to challenge his own irrational beliefs — for example, the belief that his father's failure to acknowledge Steve's academic achievements is somehow Steve's fault.

Steve's heterosexual anxiety and impotence must also be addressed. I believe that Steve has a conditioned or learned anxiety toward women and especially toward sexual intercourse. This anxiety not only blocks his ability to relate to members of the opposite sex but also directly affects his autonomic nervous system, so that his sexual arousal is impaired. We must teach Steve through classical conditioning how to subtract anxiety from the sexual encounter. Counterconditioning techniques seem to offer promise in treating Steve's impotence; relaxation could be used as a response that is antagonistic to his anxiety about sexual intercourse.

I have purposefully saved the discussion of Steve's delusions for last. Perhaps you find it difficult to imagine a behavioral analysis of delusions. But I am not concerned with the phenomena of Steve's imagination; my concern is with the behavior that are alleged to expressed a delusional system. Many people display inappropriate behaviors that are considered aversive, odd, or unusual but that may be somehow reinforced. Steve's repeated assertion that he is controlled by demonic forces and his continual thinking about Satanism disturb many people. But the people who call him crazy and are occasionally frightened by him may actually be reinforcing these behaviors.

Copyright © Houghton Mifflin Company. All rights reserved.

When Steve behaves in this way, he garners much attention from his parents, peers, and onlookers. Fully seven pages of a ten-page psychological report, prepared by a therapist two years ago, are devoted to Steve's delusions. I submit that by finding the topic fascinating and spending a lot of time talking with Steve about his delusions, the therapist thus reinforced the client's verbal behavior! I am not the only behaviorist who contends that psychoanalytically oriented therapists make this mistake. Many behavioral therapists believe, for example, that psychoanalysts elicit so much sexual material from their clients precisely because they unwittingly reinforce this concentration on sex. Is it possible that Steve's verbal and other behavioral evocations of Satanism would diminish if people ignored them? It is more than possible.

In sum, a behavioral program including modeling, role playing, and assertiveness training could be used to enhance Steve's social skills. I would use cognitive strategies and teach him behaviors through which he may more adequately control his environment to combat his depression. His heterosexual anxiety and impotence would be treated via counterconditioning methods and relaxation training. Finally, the use of extinction strategies might reduce his excessive concern with Satanism.

A COGNITIVE-BEHAVIORAL VIEW OF STEVEN V.

What if Steve were working with a cognitively oriented therapist? How would the therapist view Steve's problems and how would he or she help him?

In essence, it is important to show Steve that the psychological problems he is experiencing derive from the many irrational beliefs that he uses to judge himself and others. First, it is very easy for us to conclude that the problems he now encounters are a function of unrealistic and illogical standards that he learned from his family and significant others in his life. This would be simplistic, however, because the real problem is not the learned values in his childhood, but rather the many dogmatic, rigid "musts," "shoulds," and "oughts" that he has creatively constructed around these standards and around the unfortunate events that occur in his life. Second, as a practicing cognitive therapist, I would attempt to work with Steve in a highly didactic, cognitive, and behavior-oriented manner, stressing Steve's need to (1) recognize the role thinking and belief systems play in his problems; (2) identify self-statements, belief systems, or assumptions that are irrational and maladaptive and rationally dispute them; and (3) learn to replace irrational self-statements with productive ones. Let us use an example to illustrate this approach.

As you recall, Steve first came to the attention of the university therapist after a breakup with his woman friend, Linda. Initially, he became severely depressed and withdrew from almost all social activities. Most of us, including Steve, could easily conclude that the reason he became depressed was because of the breakup of a valued relationship. However, this simple cause-effect analysis negates the importance of Steve's internal cognitions. Ending a relationship is certainly unpleasant and unfortunate. Most people do not feel good about such an event, and the negative reactions we experience might even be normal and expected. Nevertheless, Steve's reactions to the breakup are too severe, intense, and prolonged to be considered normal.

The breakup with Linda must have other personal significance and meaning to him, contained in irrational beliefs he holds. Using Ellis's *A-B-C* theory of personality we might say that the breakup with Linda is the activating event *A* and Steve's depression and withdrawal is the consequence *C*. Steve's beliefs and interpretations *B* about *A*, however, cause his psychological reactions *C*. It is quite clear that Steve has irrational beliefs about himself and others that are the basis of his problems. He might be saying something like this to himself: "Linda's rejection of me shows me how inadequate and worthless I am. I'll never be able to find another woman again. I'm a miserable failure as a man. No one will ever love me again." These thoughts are very active in Steve and he keeps telling himself that they are true. Some of the irrational assumptions that seem to be operating in Steve's thought processes are as follows:

1. "I should always please my parents. I must live up to their expectations or I will be a failure as a son and person."

2. "If everyone doesn't love me and approve of me, it would be awful. I'm a worthless and miserable person."

Copyright © Houghton Mifflin Company. All rights reserved.

3. "I must be perfect in school. I must get straight A's. If I don't get good grades, I am stupid."

4. "A real 'man' would never be rejected by a woman. A real 'man' should always be able to perform sexually."

5. "I'm a prisoner of my past. No matter what I do I cannot change how screwed up I am. I can't help being crazy. My future looks bleak."

These irrational beliefs are at the basis of much of Steve's problems. He must be helped to distinguish between the real event and the unrealistic assumptions he makes about its consequences. Because human beings have the capacity for both rational and irrational thinking, I would utilize Steve's capacity for rational thinking to attack his belief system. Logic could help Steve recognize and dispute faulty assumptions and reasoning, using statements such as "Where is it written that one's self-worth is based on being universally loved?" He could be taught realistic and productive self-statements to replace irrational ones: "I'm catastrophizing again. It's okay to flub up occasionally. I'm a worthwhile person even though my father doesn't approve." Having Steve understand the cognitive source of his problems, helping him attack these irrational beliefs, replacing them with realistic values and standards, and correcting his faulty logic will go a long way to help Steve become a more productive and healthy individual.

THE FAMILY SYSTEMS MODEL OF PSYCHOPATHOLOGY

What if Steve were working with a family systems oriented therapist? How would the therapist view Steve's problems and how would he or she help him?

Steve's problem is not an isolated phenomenon. It resides in the family system, which should be the primary unit of treatment. Although Steve is manifesting the disorders, his father and mother are also suffering, and their pathological symptoms are reflected in Steve. Attempts to help Steve must therefore focus on the entire family. It is obvious that the relationships between Steve and his father, between Steve and his mother, and between his father and mother are unhealthy.

Furthermore, the relationship of Mr. and Mrs. V. can be characterized as isolative. Each seems to live a separate life, even when they are together in the same house. Each has unfulfilled needs, and each denies and avoids interactions and conflicts with the other. As long as Steve is the "identified patient" and is seen as "the problem," Mr. and Mrs. V. can continue in their mutual self-deception that all is well between them. I recommend that Steve's entire family be included in a program of therapy.

MODELS OF DIVERSITY AND PSYCHOPATHOLOGY

How would a therapist oriented toward the multicultural model of therapy view Steve's problems? What if Steve were working with this therapist? How would he or she help Steve?

Steven V. is not only a biological, feeling, behaving, thinking, and social being, but a person with a culture. The cultural context in which his problems arise must be considered in understanding Steve's dilemma. He is a European American of Scottish descent, born to an extremely wealthy family in the upper socioeconomic class. He is a male, raised in a cultural context that values individual achievement. All of these characteristics mean that many of his experiences are likely to be very different from those of a person who is a member of a minority group, economically indigent, or of female gender. One might argue, for example, that Steve's father values American individualistic competitiveness and achievement in the extreme. He has succeeded by his own efforts but, unfortunately, his success has come at the emotional cost of his family. To truly understand Steve, we must recognize that the many multicultural variables—race, culture, ethnicity, gender, religion, sexual orientation, and so on—are powerful factors. As such, they influence the types of social-psychological stressors Steve is likely to

Copyright © Houghton Mifflin Company. All rights reserved.

experience, the ways he will manifest disorders, and the types of therapeutic approaches most likely to be effective.

AN INTEGRATIVE APPROACH TO THE CASE OF STEVEN V.

I am the therapist who has worked with Steve throughout his college career. I've been asked to comment on our sessions and to give you insights into Steve's progress, but before I do so, it is important that I explain my therapeutic approach and goals.

I believe strongly that therapy should involve a blend of techniques aimed at recognizing that each client is a whole human being. Many current schools of psychotherapy are one-dimensional; they concentrate only on feelings, or only on cognitions, or only on behaviors. It is important to realize that each of us comprises all these and more. I also believe that no single theory or approach to therapy is appropriate for all populations and all problems. People are similar in many respects, but each is also different and unique. To recognize this difference means to use different strategies and techniques for each individual.

I have tried to organize my comments topically. This may give you the impression that I worked with isolated parts of Steve's makeup, but that impression would be wrong. I try always to work in an integrated fashion and to deal with all aspects of the client's cognitive, affective, and behavioral makeup.

Meeting Steve: The Initial Session   Steven V. first came to my attention during the early part of his junior year. A very "unstable" relationship with Linda, his woman friend, had just ended, and he seemed quite disturbed by it. As I found out later, his own private therapist was on vacation, and he did not like the therapist who was on call. As a result, he contacted the university psychological services center and was assigned to me.

During our initial contact, Steve appeared extremely suspicious, withdrawn, and reluctant to disclose his thoughts or feelings. I can recall the long periods of silence following my questions and his short but sarcastic responses. It was almost as though he were testing me to see what kind of therapist I was, to see whether he could trust me. Usually I try to be less active at first and to encourage the client to tell his or her own story. I employ almost a person-centered approach, listening and mirroring the client's thoughts, feelings, and perceptions. It was obvious, however, that this was not having the desired effect with Steve. It seemed to be alienating him and to be compounding a relationship problem.

Here is a portion of our first conversation.

Therapist: My name is Dr. S., Steve.—I wonder if we could begin by having you tell me what brought you here. (Long silence; Steve looks down, looks up at the therapist, looks down again, crosses his arms in front of his chest, and turns away.)
Therapist: It's hard for you to tell me what's on your mind.
Steve: Yeah (sarcastic tone, but does not change body posture). I'm not sure you can help me.— My therapist is on vacation, otherwise I would be seeing him. He's a psychiatrist, you know.
Therapist: It must be hard to begin a new therapy relationship again—to start all over.
Steve: Great, that's real perceptive.
Therapist: You sound angry right now.—Where is your anger coming from?
(Silence from Steve)

This type of interaction—or lack of interaction—was characteristic of nearly the entire first half of our first session. My attempts to get Steve to open up and to trust me didn't seem to work. It was at this point that I felt a change in approach was necessary. I took on an active and directive manner characteristic of the behavioral therapies.

Therapist: We don't seem to be connecting, Steve; something is blocking us from working together.
Steve: You're the therapist, so you tell me what it is!
Therapist: You want me to tell you what the answer is.
Steve: I don't need a damned parrot for a therapist!

Copyright © Houghton Mifflin Company. All rights reserved.

Therapist (raising voice): Look, Steve! If you want to waste this session in a tug-of-war, let's just end it now. I'm not going to sit here and be insulted by you. You respect me, and I'll respect you! — I know it must be difficult to trust a stranger. You'd rather be seeing your own therapist, but the fact is, he's not available. You're hurting enough to come for help. If you want to waste the session playing games, go ahead!
Steve (looking up and obviously surprised): I didn't mean to be disrespectful — I was only — only —
Therapist: Testing me — to see if you could trust me, to see where I'm coming from — to see if you could manipulate me.
Steve: Yeah, it was nothing personal.
Therapist: I know. Now suppose we start over again. — What brings you here, Steve?

As I look back, I believe this brief but heated exchange represented the beginning of our relationship. I think Steve realized that I was an authentic person who could get angry but would not let the anger become destructive. Clients like Steve often test the therapist with attempts at manipulation. They are ambivalent about this ploy because they want it to succeed (so they can "win"), but they also want it to fail (which means the therapist is perceptive and competent enough to see through their manipulations and thus to give them the help they need). In any event, this tactic changed the entire tone of our session. Steve became much more cooperative and open, and he lost the conscious antagonism and resistance of the early part of our meeting. It also became much easier for me to use a nondirective approach.

Gathering Information   Gather biographical information is very important to my understanding of clients, and I do much of it during the actual therapy sessions. I needed to know Steve V. Who is he? How does he see things? What are the important events and relationships of his past and present? What type of medical history does he have? Are there any biological conditions that have a major impact on his psychological or social life? What type of therapy has Steve had in the past, and how successful was it? The more information I have about a client, the better I can identify his or her problems and formulate treatment strategies.
   In some of our early sessions, Steve briefly mentioned how much he had hated physical education classes in high school. When I asked why, he referred to the "jocks" who were always exhibiting themselves in the shower rooms.

Steve: They strut around like Greek Gods, showing off their bodies. — They don't seem to have any shame at all.
Therapist: Shame of what?
Steven: I mean, I don't exactly mean shame. — Yes — they're trying to make the others feel ashamed of their own — well, you know.
Therapist: Tell me what you mean.
Steve: Just because they have bigger genitals, they're trying to show off and make the others feel bad.
Therapist: When they did that, how did it make you feel?
Steve: I didn't pay any attention to them. They're not worth it. — Let them strut around, I got bigger grades than all of them.
Therapist: But how did that make you feel?
Steve: I know what you're trying to imply. (Raising voice) You're trying to get me to say I felt inadequate!
(Silence)
Steve: The size of a penis is no measure of a man! Those dumb pricks — most of them barely made it out of high school. — I could outthink all of them.
Therapist: You sound very angry at them. What exactly did they do?
Steve: When I had to take a shower, they — they made fun of me.
Therapist: How did they make fun of you?
Steve: Nothing in particular — but I knew what they were thinking.
Therapist: What were they thinking?

Copyright © Houghton Mifflin Company. All rights reserved.

xxviii   The Case of Steven V.

Steve: I don't want to talk about it.
Therapist: I know it's difficult to talk about these things, Steve. — Maybe when you feel ready.
Steve: You'd laugh at me.
Therapist: Is that what you really think?
Steve (after a silence): I had this operation when I was young; they removed my left — I mean, I've only got one. And those bastards never let me forget it. They wanted to humiliate me.

When Steve was six years old, his left testicle was surgically removed because of a malignant growth. Apparently this incident and Steve's self-consciousness about it had haunted him throughout his life. I am not particularly psychoanalytic in orientation, but I believe that Steve did relate his sexual potency and his own masculinity to the absence of a testicle. His feelings of inferiority, low self-esteem, and periodic impotence may have evolved from his erroneous interpretation of this relationship. In this discussion Steve also made what might be labeled a Freudian slip (or a slip of the tongue) in describing his grades as *bigger* (unconscious equation of penis size?) when he probably meant *better*. (Steve's Rorschach responses also led the therapist who originally administered the test to infer a severe castration anxiety related to his surgery.)

Our discussions also revealed some potential areas for treatment. For example, cognitive strategies might be used to directly attack Steve's implicit equating the size and intactness of his genitals with the idea of masculinity. Perhaps strategies aimed at helping Steve get in touch with his feelings would be helpful; he continually avoided "feeling" statements in our conversations.

Using Tests and Formal Assessment   To gather information about my clients, I sometimes resort to more structured, formal assessment means. I may use homework assignments (asking the client to keep a diary of important events or to write an autobiography) or actual psychological tests. I rarely use projective testing but rely more on objective personality measures. (The use of tests is consistent with the behavioral, the cognitive, and even the psychoanalytic approaches. It is inconsistent, however, with the humanistic-existential school.) When I do use tests, I consider them mainly as a source of corroborating data. I try to demystify testing for the client by explaining what testing is, what its limitations are, and how we will use the results.

The computer interpretation of Steve's MMPI responses, for example, seems to reinforce what I have learned during our interviews. The interpretation suggests that Steve is moderately to severely disturbed. It indicates that he is defensive, is hostile, and has a tendency to blame others. (I saw many of these tendencies in our first interview.) The MMPI suggests that a more confrontative, direct approach might work best with Steve. Other problems that are noted, like Steve's poor perception of his social impact on others, difficulty in getting close to people, confusion of aggression with sexuality, and depression and suicidal tendencies seem right on target. The MMPI interpretation does note, however, that patients with Steve's profile are typically poor academic achievers. But Steve is an exception to this. He has consistently performed well in school, despite his emotional problems.

Steve keeps a diary, so I asked him to write a brief autobiography, emphasizing important childhood experiences, relationships with peers, relationships with his parents, current struggles, and future goals and aspirations. My intent was, first, to help Steve actively sort out his life experiences, away from our therapy sessions, and second, to help me understand his subjective world. The following portion reveals his reactions to our first therapy session; I believe Steve copied it out of his diary.

My first time with Dr. S. was very confusing. I thought I was in complete control. I'm still not sure what really happened. I know I was angry and resentful the moment I saw him. He was sitting there sipping a cup of coffee without offering me one. When I called the center, they told me I could only come in for an 8 A.M. appointment. I'm not even alive at that time of the morning. Usually Dr. J., the psychiatrist I've been seeing, sees me in the afternoons. I guess I was angry at Dr. J. for going on vacation and making me see another therapist who isn't even a psychiatrist.

I really wanted to talk to somebody about Linda. I guess I was pretty bad with Dr. S. I wasn't sure I could trust him, and I took out my anger on him. I tried to put him down and make him uncomfortable. I tried to make him feel defensive by saying he was only a psychologist and not a psychiatrist. It scared the shit out of me when he got angry back at me. I never had a therapist do

Copyright © Houghton Mifflin Company. All rights reserved.

that to me. It was like he knew what I was doing. He thinks I do it with other people too. Maybe he's right. He seems to be able to see through me, and I don't like that. I'm afraid to have someone really know what's going on inside. What is going on inside? I don't know! Why should I be afraid? Strange, I really don't like Dr. S. Or do I? Why am I seeing him now instead of my therapist? Mom and Dad are angry at me because I don't go back to Dr. J.

There are some very revealing elements in this passage. First, it supports my previous impression that Steve finds it difficult to trust people and behaves so as to push others away. Second, he is beginning to gain some insight into his behaviors—how he attributes his feelings to others and blames them for his troubles. Third, he has a long way to go. There is something that he is afraid to reveal to himself and others. When he expresses the fear that I can "see through" him, his writing becomes disjointed and fragmented. Obviously, this "dark secret" is deeply frightening to him. It affects not only his emotional state but his cognitive state as well.

What was encouraging was that, despite his discomfort with me. Steve decided to continue in therapy—and with me rather than with his previous therapist. A part of him didn't want to look at himself, but another part seemed to know that this was the only way he could ever get better.

Overall Objectives in Therapy   As I got to know Steve better and better, I was able to identify some treatment objectives that would benefit him. Again, let me emphasize that I saw Steve as I see each of my clients—as a complex individual who feels, thinks, experiences emotions, behaves, and is a social being. I had to deal with each of these aspects during the two years I worked with him. Here, though, I'll discuss only a few facets of Steve's self to illustrate my therapeutic approaches.

Dealing with Steve's Feelings   One theme that persisted throughout my work with Steve was his inability to get in touch with his feelings. He found it difficult to experience feelings or to make "feeling" statements. The autobiographical passage suggests that there is something he was afraid to acknowledge. He was ambivalent about therapy because it was forcing him to face frightening parts of his existence; he could no longer be safe and avoid taking risks.

It would have been a mistake to directly reassure Steve that he could trust me and that things would turn out well. Such reassurance would have been transitory at best, unless Steven ventured out on his own to take the risk and to confront his own fears. I saw myself as a guide who would use various strategies to help Steve confront himself. In this respect I relied on existential psychology, which places choice and responsibility clearly in the hands of the client. Here is an example, from one of our sessions.

Steve: My parents are upset with me for terminating with Dr. J. They think I should continue because he's a psychiatrist, and I've been with him for years.—I like him—and he really understands me. I feel comfortable with him.

Therapist: What made you decide to continue seeing me instead of Dr. J.?

Steve: I don't know, I mean—I'm not sure I even like you. Maybe it's just so much more convenient to go to a campus shrink than to travel across town.

Therapist: I don't believe that's the reason. You're hiding from yourself again! When are you finally going to start facing yourself?

Steve (angrily): That's what I mean. I don't know if I like you—you're always picking on me. —Shit!

Therapist: Say it again.

Steve: Shit! (Pounds the table.)

Therapist: Again and louder!

Steve: Shit! Shit!

Therapist: What are you feeling?

Steve: I'm pissed off at you!

Therapist: That's not a feeling!

Steve: I'm angry! (Yells at the top of his lungs.) Are you satisfied now?

Therapist (after a silence): That was real.

Steve: Yeah. (Exhales.) Funny how I felt like an overcooked artichoke crumbling just then.

Copyright © Houghton Mifflin Company. All rights reserved.

Therapist: I want you to close your eyes and become that artichoke. What are you feeling now?

Steve: I want to keep all the leaves from falling away so that no one will see my artichoke heart. I want to strike out at whoever tries to peel the leaves off.

Therapist: Imagine the leaves being peeled away—

Steve: No, I can't do it!

Therapist: You don't want to do it.—What are you afraid of?

Steve: I'm afraid you'll see me—what's really wrong with me.

Therapist: Become that fear and tell me what's going on now.

Steve: I've got to hide.—All the artichoke leaves help me hide, so others won't see.

Therapist: Can you peel off just a few of the leaves?

Steve: Yes, but it doesn't feel good.

Therapist: For each leaf you peel off, say what it is.

Steve: I'm peeling off my phony self—I'm peeling off my mask—I'm peeling off my rationalizations—I'm peeling off my anger.

Therapist: Okay, open your eyes. What's happening now?

Steve: I feel naked, I feel everyone can see how inadequate I really am. I don't like myself either.—I feel scared—scared you won't like me anymore. I feel ashamed because you saw a part of me that no one else did.

Therapist: I know. It's scary to let others see the real you.—But look at you. Before we began this session you were very uptight and defensive. Your fists were clenched; you were sitting bolt upright on the edge of your chair; you had a strained expression on your face; your voice was tight. Now your body looks more relaxed.—Can you feel it?

Steve: Yeah—

Therapist: Get into your body.—What is it tell you?

Steve: It's funny—I don't like what I see in myself, but—but—I hate myself but I feel relieved. I don't have to always hide from you.

Therapist: You mean you don't have to always hide from yourself.

Steve: Yeah.

Dealing with Irrational Thoughts I had to discover how Steve's feelings and many of his self-defeating behaviors were related to his cognitions. I had enough evidence to indicate that Steve created his own miseries through the thoughts and beliefs he held. My work with him in this vein tended to parallel cognitive behavior modification and rational-emotive therapy: in some way, Steve was feeling himself irrational and unrealistic assumptions. My task was to identify these irrational beliefs, show Steve that he was constantly reindoctrinating himself with these messages, and teach him how to challenge or dispute them.

Some of Steve's irrational beliefs are evident in these words of his, taken from another session:

I just feel like I'm a miserable failure. I've disappointed my parents. I know Dad wanted someone who was more athletic. I tried, but I'm not a jock. I did well in school and Mom is proud of that—but—I thought when I went to college and could do well at the university, Dad would come around. So far I have a 3.75 GPA, but I should have a 4.0. In several classes I missed an A by just a few points. When I told him [Steve's father] my grade point average last night, he told me Jeff, my cousin, has a 3.9 GPA. I guess I let him down again. I was so bummed out last night—I couldn't sleep—maybe it's not worth going on. Life just isn't worth it. Why should I keep trying? Maybe I should just take courses I know I'll do well in.

Several themes in this paragraph appear to form the basis for Steve's feelings of worthlessness and his low self-esteem. These absolutist themes are often punctuated with must, should, and ought:

1. "I must do what is necessary to please my parents, especially Dad. I must get my parents' approval, love, and recognition. If I fail to do this, I will never be able to value myself or feel I have succeeded. If they don't love me, I can't love myself. And life would not be worth living without their love and approval."

Copyright © Houghton Mifflin Company. All rights reserved.

2. "I must be at the top of my class. I must live up to the expectations of my professors, peers, and parents. I must be perfect. If I fail to attain straight A's, it means I've failed again and am basically stupid."

3. "I must be thoroughly competent in everything I do. If I can't, I'll avoid trying anything new. I cannot make mistakes because they will prove how deficient I really am."

After identifying these themes with Steve, I discussed with him how these thoughts and self-indoctrinations lie at the root of many of his problems. For example, he thinks his parents' lack of approval has caused him to feel unloved and unappreciated. I tried to show Steve that it is his belief about a real or imagined situation, rather than an actual situation, that is causing his difficulties. In therapy sessions, I confronted his belief system by having him respond to these following questions:

1. Who is telling you that you are worthless unless your parents approve of you?

2. Do you need to be loved and liked by everyone?

3. Do you want to spend the rest of your life in a futile attempt to win over your father?

This line of questioning was helpful in getting Steve to think, to challenge himself, and to decide—for himself—how he would live.

Learning New Behaviors One thing that I have discovered is that a client's insight into or understanding of a problem doesn't necessarily lead to a behavior change. The understanding that he feared rejection by members of the opposite sex because he equated rejection with his "worthlessness" would not have made it easier for Steve to interact with women. And from my work with Steve, it had become clear that he suffered from immense interpersonal anxiety, especially with women. Not only did he not know how to interact with others or to "make small talk," but he also engaged in inappropriate behaviors that put people off. When Steve was with his friend Linda, he had constantly tried to make her prove she "cared for him." He had accused her of not being faithful to him, of not caring for him, and of not including him in her extracurricular school activities. This continual "prove you love me" testing of their relationship never ended because no amount of reassurance seemed to be enough. In fact, it pushed Linda away from him.

This mode of interaction was characteristic of nearly all Steve's relationships. While he worked to combat this irrational belief ("I am worthless; therefore no one can like me"), I felt it was important to help Steve become more comfortable in interpersonal and heterosexual relationships. I attempted to help Steve subtract anxiety from his interpersonal encounters by using a behavioral technique: assertiveness training.

Here is Steve talking to me again:

The truth is I'm always afraid. I panic when I think about being in a group of people and having to talk to them. What am I going to say? Even if I could say something, who would listen? Last month I went to a party with Linda—it was thrown by her friends. —When she introduced me all I could say was "hi." I stuttered when I said anything else. It was like in class—I really felt inadequate. And one of the guys was trying to hustle Linda. He knew Linda came with me, but he ignored me completely. He asked her to dance, and I spent the whole evening sitting in the corner. I was really angry at him and Linda too, but I couldn't do anything about it. Then he came over and asked if I would mind if he took her home. I could only say, "Sure, go ahead." When I really wanted to say was "Go to hell." I feel like I'm a doormat for the world.

Obviously we had to work on Steve's assertive behaviors. What I intended to do was, briefly, the following:

1. Identify Steve's unassertive behaviors that were linked to specific situations (for example, withdrawing and sitting in a corner by himself and not being able to say no).

Copyright © Houghton Mifflin Company. All rights reserved.

2. Determine the specific skills he needed for assertion (saying no, introducing himself to strangers, asking Linda to dance, and so on). Then try to grade these skills from least to most assertive.

3. Re-create the problem situations, as vividly as possible, in the consultation room. Engage Steve in role playing and behavioral rehearsal with me or volunteers.

4. Get Steve to practice the assertive behaviors in actual situations, under my guidance and monitoring.

Our first use of the procedure will illustrate how we implemented it. Steve and I identified an upcoming event that was causing him considerable apprehension—a class assignment. He was to give an oral critical analysis of an assigned novel in his English class and then lead a discussion of the novel.

Steve needed to practice the assertive skills related to the oral presentation. First to desensitize him, I had him practice very low-level assertive skills in front of groups. For example, he practiced raising his hand in class in situations where he was sure he would not be called on—for example, when many other students raised their hands or while he was out of sight of the professor. To Steve, this act was an assertive one. After he became comfortable with that, I asked him to raise his hand and ask a simple question (a safe assertive skill), such as "Could you repeat that last point?" After his anxiety regarding this act was conquered, he proceeded to paraphrase what the instructor had said and finally to state an opinion. Each succeeding act represented an increase in assertiveness.

While he was practicing these classroom acts, Steve was finishing his book report. I then asked him to do his oral report for me. Next I asked another counselor and the two clerical staff members to be present while he repeated the report. After a second repetition, we simulated a question-and-answer session and then repeated that several times.

This systematic training helped Steve greatly when he finally presented his report to his English class. Although he was anxious throughout the presentation, he felt that he had the anxiety under control.

A similar program, which I developed for his heterosexual anxiety, proved only moderately successful.

Steve's Threat Against Linda   "She doesn't deserve to live—I swear, I'm going to kill her." Given the conduct in which it occurred, Steve's threat to kill Linda placed me in a dilemma. My conflicting feelings and apprehensions were, no doubt, similar to those experienced by any therapist whose client threatens to kill someone or to commit suicide. Today more than ever, we as therapists must recognize that our work does not occur in a social vacuum. What we do or don't do in therapy has not only clinical implications but ethical, moral, and legal ramifications as well.

In that particular session Steve was becoming increasingly agitated about his breakup with Linda; his expressions of anger were stronger and stronger. He was quite depressed at the time, and in my therapeutic judgment, his venting of feelings was healthy. I had been working on that with him when he blurted out his threat. The first thoughts that came to my mind were questions: Does he really mean what he's saying? How likely is he to carry out the threat? Is this just an empty threat characteristic of his anger and hostility? What should I do? Should I inform the proper authorities, breaking confidentiality, and risk losing Steve's trust?

I chose to go along with my clinical judgment to let Steve continue to express his feelings without cutting him off, while constantly assessing the strength of his anger and the likelihood of his acting impulsively. I made that decision for several reasons. First, in the time I had known Steve, he had made several suicide threats. In each case, when he was allowed to express his feelings, the suicidal ideation and threats diminished. I felt that his threat to kill Linda would follow a similar course. Second, despite his often bizarre thoughts and behaviors, I had never considered Steve to be a danger to others. He was more a danger to himself than to anyone else. Third, I felt that some other perspective was needed. There was still time to consult with colleagues about the case and to get their input. And last, I was prepared to cancel other appointments and extend our session if that became necessary. I felt that I could monitor Steve closely, and I even made an appointment for him to return the following day. In other words, after pondering all the issues, including the need to protect myself by informing the proper authorities or even Linda, I decided that the likelihood of his carrying out the threat was very low. Luckily this did prove to be the case.

Copyright © Houghton Mifflin Company. All rights reserved.

The dilemma for me as a therapist was not whether I should inform a potential victim or the appropriate authorities about a homicide that I deemed likely. I have no doubt that I would have taken that action if it were necessary. I was disturbed that I lacked the ability to precisely assess dangerousness and—even more—was unable to inform a client about the legal limits of confidentiality without adversely affecting our therapist-client relationship.

An Epilogue to the Case   Several years have passed since my sessions with Steve came to an end. He graduated from the university with a degree in English literature and went to a graduate school in the east. I did get the chance to see some changes in Steve that are definitely for the better. He relates reasonably well to people now, though I still consider him a loner. His bizarre behavior and ideation have eased off, but he still suffers from periodic bouts of depression. Whereas most clients need only brief periodic therapy to help them cope with life's problems, I'm afraid Steve is one of those people who will need some form of therapy for the rest of his life. He has chosen to work toward a doctorate degree and to become a teacher, doing research and writing. I think this is as good a vocational choice as any. Not only does it play to his strengths (writing, reading, and research), but the college environment seems to be one of the few in which Steve has done well and has felt sufficiently secure. Perhaps this is a statement about academic life as well as about Steve. Some perceive it as a protected environment that is structured and, in some ways, undemanding.

I don't know what has happened to Steve since he left this university. I am aware that he signed a release of information form so that his case records could be transferred to the university he now attends. I can only assume that he has chosen to continue therapy, and I wish him well.

Copyright © Houghton Mifflin Company. All rights reserved.

CHAPTER 1
Abnormal Behavior

CHAPTER OUTLINE

I. The concerns of abnormal psychology
   A. Describing abnormal behavior
   B. Explaining abnormal behavior
   C. Predicting abnormal behavior
   D. Controlling abnormal behavior
II. Defining abnormal behavior
   A. Conceptual definitions
      1. Statistical deviation: based on frequency but no distinction of desirable and undesirable
      2. Deviations from ideal mental health
      3. Multicultural perspectives
         a. Cultural universality: symptoms same regardless of culture
         b. Cultural relativism: abnormality defined by culture
   B. Practical definitions
      1. Discomfort (physical or psychological pain)
      2. Deviance (disorientation, hallucinations, and delusions)
      3. Dysfunction (gap between potential and performance)
   C. Integrated definitions
      1. Three vantage points (Strupp & Hadley, 1977): individual, society, professional
      2. Biological facts and social values (Wakefield, 1992): "harmful dysfunction" where social norm defines *harmful* and biological sciences define *dysfunction*
   D. The Surgeon General's and DSM-IV-TR Definitions
      1. Abnormal behavior: Before that departs from some norm and that harms the affected individual or others
      2. The Surgeon General's report on mental health (DHHS, 1999) and the American Psychiatric Association's Diagnostic and Statistical Manual of Mental Disorders (DSM-IV-TR, 2000); clinically significant syndrome associated with distress, disability, or increased risk of suffering
III. The frequency and burden of mental disorders
   A. Current research into the epidemiology of mental disorders
      1. Roughly 29 to 38 percent of the population has at least one DSM disorder
      2. No change in prevalence since 1980 Srole and Fisher study

      3. Gender differences: alcohol problems in 24 percent of men, 4 percent of women; depression and anxiety higher in women

      4. Age differences: substance abuse in younger groups; cognitive impairment in older groups

      5. Mental illness is more debilitating than malignant diseases such as cancer.

    B. Stereotypes of the mentally disturbed

      1. Easily recognized as deviant

      2. Disorder due to inheritance

      3. Incurable

      4. Weak willed

      5. Never contribute to society

      6. Dangerous

IV. Historical perspective on abnormal behavior

    A. Prehistoric and ancient beliefs

      1. Trephining: chipping away portion of skull

      2. Exorcism: prayers, drugs, starvation

    B. Naturalistic explanations (Greco-Roman thought)

      1. Hippocrates: brain pathology, classification

      2. Galen: role of brain and nervous system

    C. Reversion to superstition (the Middle Ages)

      1. Dark Ages: sinfulness

      2. Mass madness (thirteenth century): tarantism, lycanthropy

      3. Witchcraft (fifteenth through seventeenth centuries)

        a. Related to church under attack

        b. Pope Innocent VIII's papal decree (1484) to identify and exterminate witches

        c. Although some witches may have been mentally ill, most were not

    D. Rise of humanism (the Renaissance)

      1. Emphasizes human welfare

      2. Johann Weyer challenges notion of witchcraft (1563)

    E. Reform movement (eighteenth and nineteenth centuries)

      1. Moral treatment movement (Pinel in France, Tuke in England)

      2. American reformers

        a. Benjamin Rush insists on respect and dignity for patients

        b. Dorothea Dix campaigns for mental hospitals

        c. Clifford Beers exposes cruel treatment

V. Causes: early viewpoints

    A. The biological viewpoint

      1. Emil Kraepelin observes syndromes

      2. Emphasis on brain pathology

      3. Discovery of organic basis to general paresis

    B. The psychological viewpoint

      1. Mesmerism and hypnotism

Copyright © Houghton Mifflin Company. All rights reserved.

a. Anton Mesmer: treatment of hysteria; assumptions discredited, but spur debate about psychogenic nature of disorders

b. Hypnotism

2. The Nancy School

a. Jean-Martin Charcot: hypnosis produces and removes hysteric symptoms

b. Josef Breuer and Sigmund Freud: the cathartic method

VI. Contemporary trends in abnormal psychology

A. The drug revolution

B. Prescription privileges for psychologists

C. Managed health care

1. Health care costs in the U.S. have exploded

2. Managed health care: industrialization of health care

3. Fear of psychologists: decisions made for business reasons, not health reasons

D. Appreciation for research

E. Diversity and multicultural psychology

1. Social conditioning

2. Cultural values and influences

3. Sociopolitical influences

4. Bias in diagnosis

VII. Some closing thoughts

LEARNING OBJECTIVES

1. Describe the primary objectives of abnormal psychology, including description, explanation, prediction, and control of abnormal behavior. (pp. 3–5)

2. Identify and distinguish between the various kinds of mental health professionals. (pp. 5-6)

3. Identify four definitions psychologists use to define abnormal behavior and their assumptions, strengths, and limitations. (pp. 5–13)

4. Describe the multicultural perspectives in defining abnormal behavior including definitions of the terms *cultural universality* and *cultural relativism*. (pp. 9–10)

5. Distinguish between Szasz's views on mental illness and Wakefield's (1992) views of abnormal behavior, the textbook authors' definition of *abnormal behavior*, and that of the DSM-IV. (pp. 12–13)

6. Discuss how researchers determine the scope of mental disorders in the United States. (pp. 13–17)

7. Describe the most prevalent disorders and how mental disorders are influenced by age and gender. (pp. 14–16)

8. Discuss common myths concerning the mentally disturbed and the facts that refute them. (pp. 17–18)

9. Summarize the various explanations of abnormal behavior from prehistoric times through the Middle Ages. (pp. 18–20)

10. Describe the changes that occurred in the conceptualization and treatment of abnormal behavior after the era of witchcraft, including the rise of humanism and the reform movement of the eighteenth and nineteenth centuries until the present. (pp. 20–23)

Copyright © Houghton Mifflin Company. All rights reserved

11. Discuss the main assumptions of the biological and psychological viewpoints on perceptions of abnormal behavior. (pp. 23–25)

12. Discuss the contributions of mesmerism and hypnosis to the psychodynamic viewpoint. (pp. 24–25)

13. Describe the impact of the drug revolution and managed care on the mental health profession. (pp. 25–28; Mental Health & Society)

14. Discuss the rise of *multicultural psychology*, and explain how social conditioning, cultural values, and sociopolitical influences may account for apparent differences in abnormality in minority groups. (pp. 29–31)

15. Explain the term *biopsychosocial approach* and its use in conceptualizing the multiple factors underlying abnormal behavior. (p. 31)

CLASSROOM TOPICS FOR LECTURE AND DISCUSSION

1.   During the first class meeting, it is generally helpful to explain your grading policies, the number and types of tests to be given, and reading and research assignments. A detailed syllabus is an invaluable tool for helping students know what is coming and for preventing later confusion concerning what was expected. A detailed syllabus should give the dates for each reading assignment, test, paper, or other requirement and explain the policy on missed exams, grade cut-offs, and other such matters. Since most of the students will not have the textbook in time for the first class, it is best to spend time asking students what they think *abnormal* means. This word can be compared and contrasted with *mentally ill* or *deviant* or *in need of treatment*, all of which have their own connotations.

Internet Site: http://www.behavenet.com/capsules/disorders/dsm4Trclassification.htm. Contains terms and definitions of DSM criteria.

2.   This chapter gives students a good opportunity to compare and contrast the training experiences, qualifications, and work-setting roles of the various mental health professionals. On the blackboard the instructor can make four columns labeled *clinical psychologist, psychiatrist, psychiatric social worker*, and *marriage/family counselor* and then indicate the educational requirements, clinical and research training, certification requirements, and typical work settings for these major categories of mental health professionals. A sample handout is provided.

Students are likely to be interested in the career opportunities these fields present and the academic preparation necessary for each. A career counseling specialist in the college or university student services office may be helpful in this discussion. Even better is to invite a psychiatrist, a social worker, and a counselor to class to discuss their own experiences. At a minimum, the instructor can present his or her own training and clinical experience so as to establish credibility for teaching the course.

Internet Sites: http://www.psychologicalscience.org/American Psychological Society. Contains information on this organization, including schedules of conventions, teaching, research, and other information.

http://www.apa.org/American Psychological Association Contains information about the organization and its services.

3.   One way to probe the criteria that students use to define abnormality is to present a variety of small vignettes and ask students to rate them in terms of abnormality. The instructor can vary certain aspects of the stories to see whether perceived deviance increases or decreases. For example, a vignette might be

Copyright © Houghton Mifflin Company. All rights reserved.

Martin is a forty-year-old manager, husband, and father of three who works fourteen hours per day and brings work home on the weekends. His wife complains that he is more interested in work than he is in her and the children. Martin has trouble sleeping, is often irritated by small inconveniences, wishes he spent more time with his family, and has been diagnosed as having a stomach ulcer.

The instructor can ask students whether Martin has a mental disorder or is abnormal or needs psychological treatment. (The terms have important connotative differences.) Ask a person who is convinced that Martin has a mental disorder why he or she takes that view. Ask a person with the opposite perception for his or her reasons. (The case of Martin should emphasize problems with statistical rarity and personal distress.) Ask students whether their perceptions would change if they knew that Martin's boss forced him to work this hard, or that, in his corporate culture, managers were supposed to be relaxed about coming to work.

4. The risk of mental disorder varies with demographic groups. One of the fastest growing groups in the United States is people of Hispanic ancestry. A study (Shrout et al., 1992) compared epidemiological statistics on rates of mental disorders for adults living in Puerto Rico, and three groups of adults in Los Angeles—Mexican-American immigrants, Mexican-American natives, and non-Hispanic whites. The large samples (1505, 610, 488, and 1092, respectively) increase the reliability of the statistics given. Mexican-American immigrants had the fewest mental health problems of all groups. Puerto Ricans had more somatization disorders (0.7 percent versus almost 0 percent in the other three groups) but less affective and alcohol disorders than did U.S.-born Mexican-Americans or non-Hispanic whites.

These results underscore the need to consider cultural group membership when discussing the scope of mental disorders. If also shows the need to look at subcultural groups—Puerto Ricans versus Mexicans or immigrants versus second-generation individuals. Further, immigration may not have identical effects on different subgroups. Previous research showed no global differences in rates of depression between poor, island Puerto Ricans and economically similar Puerto Ricans living in the New York City area (Vera, M., et al., 1991).

Sources: Shrout, P. E., Canino, G. J., Bird, H. R., Rubio-Stipec, M., Bravo, M., & Burnam, M. A. (1992). Mental health status among Puerto Ricans, Mexican Americans, and Non-Hispanic whites. *American Journal of Community Psychology, 20,* 729–752

Vera, M., Alegria, M., Freeman, D., Robles, R. R., Rios, R., & Rios, C. F. (1991). Depressive symptoms among Puerto Ricans: Island poor compared with residents of New York City area. *American Journal of Epidemiology, 134,* 502–510.

Internet Site: http://www.psych.org/American Psychiatric Association. Links to sites associated with the psychiatric profession.

5. Students often have difficulty placing the changes in psychological thinking in a historical context. Try to make the point that explanations for mental disorders always come out of the social and intellectual atmosphere of the time. A timeline written in a handout, on the board, or on a transparency can help make links between psychological thinking and what was going on in the wider world at the time. A timeline for the last two hundred years could show how the American and French revolutions coincided with the advent of moral treatment. Both movements stressed the value of the individual and the virtue of personal freedom. Dorothea Dix's reforms and advocacy for institutions for the poor coincided with the great waves of immigration in the United States. Many people who came to the United States did not cope well with the stresses of a new culture and city life, and many recent immigrants were admitted to state hospitals. The rise of the medical model in mental health during the latter half of the nineteenth century coincided with the scientific discoveries linking microbes to diseases. Physicians such as Kraepelin and even Freud emerged from an era of boundless optimism that explanations and cures were just around the corner. The devastation of World War I altered Freud's

Copyright © Houghton Mifflin Company. All rights reserved

thinking, and he invented the death instinct in response. After World War II, when the veterans hospitals were filled with psychological war casualties, clinical psychologists exploded in numbers and influence. The civil rights movement of the 1950s and 1960s also coincides with a mental patients rights movement and the beginnings of the multicultural approach. Finally, you can point out the current discussion in managed health care related to the rapid increases in health care costs during the 1990s.

A sample handout is provided, but obviously you can choose from an infinite number of historical events and teach many economic, political, and social lessons. Regardless of the specific examples you use, this exercise should show students that wider forces were and are at work to influence the field of abnormal psychology.

Internet Sites: http://www.geocities.com/Athens/Delphi/6061/en_linha.htm. Contains information on the early history of psychology and has a timetable of significant events in psychology from 1846 to 1935.

Copyright © Houghton Mifflin Company. All rights reserved.

HANDOUT FOR CLASSROOM TOPIC 2:
MENTAL HEALTH PROFESSIONALS:
TRAINING AND PRACTICE SETTINGS

Profession	Degree	Training	Specialties	Settings
Psychiatrist	M.D.	Four years at medical school; internship; three-year residency	Prescribe medications; therapy	Private; hospitals; mental health centers
Clinical psychologist	Ph.D. or Psy.D.	Four years at university or professional school; internship	Assessment; research; therapy; prevention	Private; hospitals; mental health centers; universities
Psychiatric social worker	M.S.W.	Two years at university social work school; internship	Therapy; family and community advocacy	Private; hospitals; mental health centers
Marriage and family counseling	M.S.	Two years at university counseling department	Marital and family therapy	Private; mental health centers

Copyright © Houghton Mifflin Company. All rights reserved

HANDOUT FOR CLASSROOM TOPIC 5: TIMELINE OF POLITICAL EVENTS AND PSYCHOLOGICAL MILESTONES

1790	French Revolution	
1810		Pinel unchains patients in Paris; Tuke establishes York Retreat
1830		
	Irish immigration to United States	
1850		
		Dorothea Dix works for improved care for mentally ill
1870	Pasteur and others show impact of microbes on health	
1890		
1910	Muckraker journalists in United States expose corruption; World War I	Freud studies hysteria and hypnosis, Kraepelin develops diagnostic system, Freud writes *Interpretation of Dreams*
1930		Beers exposes brutality in mental hospitals
	World War II	Behaviorism begins
1950		
		Humanistic psychology; growth of clinical psychology
1970	Vietnam War	
	Reagan administration cutbacks on human services; health cost increases	Development of antipsychotic and antidepressant medications; behavior therapy; recognition of PTSD
1990		Rise of managed care

Copyright © Houghton Mifflin Company. All rights reserved.

CLASSROOM DEMONSTRATIONS

1.   An important function of the abnormal psychology course is to break down some of the pernicious attitudes that lay persons have about people with behavior disorders. One concern is the tendency to stereotype people who are different and thereby classify everyone into an "us" category (meaning "normal and good") or a "them" category (meaning "abnormal and bad"). During the first or second class meeting, hand out the survey questionnaire for Demonstration 1, the results of which can debunk the idea that behavior disorders happen only to other people. Make sure the students understand that they *should not* identify themselves on the paper. Tell them to turn the page face down when they are finished filling it out and when they pass it forward and that only group data will be reported back to them.

Over the course of several semesters, you can compile statistics on the average percentage of students who report family members or close friends with these problems. Data from roughly 270 students at a small midwestern university showed the following:

Problem	Family (percent)	Friend (percent)
Drinking problem	37.2	49.1
Depression	34.9	40.9
Stress-related illness (for example, migraine)	34.6	27.9
Alzheimer's disease	27.1	6.8
Anxiety disorders	13.8	13.0
Illicit drug dependency	10.8	35.7
Eating disorders	11.1	46.8
Mental retardation	3.3	6.3
Schizophrenia	2.6	5.2

After computing the percentages for the current class, you can put the class's data and the averages from previous classes on a blank questionnaire form. Before returning these data, you can ask students which problems they think are most common. The ensuing discussion provides an easy and thought-provoking entrance into the text material on epidemiology.

2.   Depending on your acting skills, you can use this exercise to clarify the differences in thinking that mark historical eras. First describe the popular explanations and treatments for abnormal behavior during the Greco-Roman period, the era of witchcraft, the moral treatment movement, and the early twentieth century (medical model). Then describe a deviant individual. Here is an example: a 55-year-old woman is suddenly unable to take care of her normal responsibilities—she no longer cooks or cleans. She talks to herself and seems to hear voices that no one else can hear. She is frightened easily and cries often.

Tell students that you will play, one at a time, the roles of several different people living in different historical eras. Students are to ask you questions about how you explain this woman's odd behavior and the treatments you think will address her problems. You should answer as if you lived in that era. For instance, if you were pretending to be a monk in the fifteenth century, you would discuss this woman's soul, her lack of religious devotion, her probable status as a witch, and the appropriate "cures" of exorcism or execution. Respond to the questions and comments as though everyone accepts your point of view. A goal of this exercise is to show that we are somewhat trapped in our thinking by the conventional wisdom of our day, including our own time.

Copyright © Houghton Mifflin Company. All rights reserved

For a more dramatic presentation, you might invite some colleagues to play the various roles, which will allow debate among the role-players and increase the enthusiasm for audience participation. Be sure to give colleagues adequate preparation concerning the thinking of each historic era. If you and your colleagues come to class in costume, this class meeting will be one of the most memorable sessions of the year!

Internet Site: http://www.cwu.edu/~warren/today.html. *Today in the History of Psychology*, an APA searchable site devoted to the history of psychology.

3.   Students are often surprised at the prevalence of mental disorders. They often underestimate rates of disorder, although some go to the other extreme and claim that "everyone is crazy." This demonstration gets students to think more carefully about the proportion of adults in the United States with various disorders and supplies statistics from a nationwide epidemiological survey to bring home the point.

Very briefly describe the symptoms of substance use disorders, anxiety disorders, affective (mood) disorders, schizophrenia, antisocial personality disorder, and cognitive disorders. You may want to use the following descriptions:

Substance use disorders: excessive use of chemicals (for example, alcohol, marijuana, heroin) that jeopardizes health, social, or occupational functioning or that involves tolerance (need for larger doses) or withdrawal (physical symptoms after stopping intake).

Anxiety disorders: persistent problems of anxiety and worry either in response to a specific object (a phobia), a specific situation (social phobia or agoraphobia), sudden bouts of intense anxiety (panic attacks), or posttraumatic stress syndrome.

Affective disorders: uncontrolled and persistent intense emotions—either depression (including eating and sleeping problems, apathy, fatigue, and thoughts of suicide or hopelessness) or swings of mood from extreme elation to depression.

Schizophrenia: inability to function due to incoherent thought; withdrawal from social relationships; hallucinations; and delusions.

Antisocial personality disorder: exploitative interactions with others; disdain for following social rules often leading to impulsive criminal acts, lack of empathy or remorse, and thrill seeking.

Cognitive disorders: severe problems in memory or judgment caused by brain damage in such conditions as Alzheimer's disease, stroke, and traumatic brain injury.

Tell students to think of all the people in the United States over age eighteen. Ask students to estimate the percentage of people who, over a one-month period, could be diagnosed with any of the disorders named above. (This figure is the one-month prevalence for mental disorders in the United States.) Ask which disorder they think is most common and which is least common. Ask if they think certain disorders are more common in men than women or more common in women than in men. Ask if they think age groups differ in their likelihood of suffering these disorders. Put their verbal responses on the blackboard. See if there is a consensus in estimated magnitude of the problem of mental disorder. Then distribute the handout based on the Epidemiological Catchment Area survey (Robins et al., 1984). Point out the high level of anxiety problems in women in early and middle age; the big jump in cognitive disorders among the elderly; and the sex differences in substance disorders, affective disorders, and antisocial personality disorders. Ask students why discrepancies between their estimates and these nationwide data might exist.

Copyright © Houghton Mifflin Company. All rights reserved.

As a final point, tell students that for every one percent indicated on the table, roughly two million Americans are suffering with the disorder. Alternatively, use your town's or city's population to estimate the number of people who, in the month you give this lecture, suffer from the disorders.

Source: Robins, L. N., Helzer, J. E., Weissman, M. M., Orvaschel, H., Gruenberg, E., Burke, J. D., & Regier, D. A. (1984). Lifetime prevalence of specific psychiatric disorders in three sites. *Archives of General Psychiatry, 41,* 949–958.

Internet Site: http://www.apa.org/science/lib.html. An APA site that defines and describes all behaviors that the American Psychiatric Association considers abnormal.

4.   The following quotations give students an idea of how mental patients were treated before the advent of moral therapy. The information comes from Glover, M. R. (1984). *The retreat York: An early Quaker experiment in the treatment of mental illness.* York, England: Williams Sessions.

> At the time The Retreat was founded (1796), when William Tuke and his physician, Timothy Maud, were reading books and visiting hospitals in order to learn as much as they could about the treatment of the insane, they discovered a dominant orthodoxy, which based medical treatment on what was roughly dehydration, the draining away of fluid out of the body. For this purpose a number of methods were used: bleeding, vomits, purges, and blisters. In many hospitals these treatments were a matter of routine. Dr. Monro, the physician at Bethlem, described the practice there: "They are ordered to be bled about the latter end of May, or the beginning of May, according to the weather; and after they have been bled they take vomits once a week for a certain number of weeks, after that we purge the patients; that has been the practice invariably for years, long before my time. It was handed down to me by my father, and I do not know any better practice." A naval hospital for the insane was criticised for not using these treatments.

> A letter from William Tuke dated February 1798 speaks of treatment procedures in use at The Retreat:

> "James Fawcett has bn v bad. Frequently high and noisy. He made gt efforts for mastery, and if in his power would have done a mischief to those about him, but for some days past has bn pretty quie...he was bled in the arm; had a pretty strong Emetic and Cathartic, also a blister, and since that was bled with leaches."

> Patients were then as now sometimes treated by shock, but the 18th century shocks were cruder. One of them was the "bath of surprise"; the patient fell without warning through a trap door into cold deep water. Another in common use was the revolving chair; the patient was strapped into the chair which was then whirled around until he lost consciousness.   (pp. 8–9)

Internet Site: http://www.nextas.com:8080/people/aca3/LPM.HTM.   The Lifschitz Psychology Museum, which is the world's first Virtual Museum of Psychology.

5.   This exercise will get students thinking about the criteria they use to define abnormality. Before you lecture on the practical definitions of abnormality (deviance, discomfort, and dysfunction), write up a hypothetical case study in four versions. An example is given in the Handout for Demonstration 5, which varies gender and duration of symptoms. Distribute the write-ups randomly throughout the class. Each student reads and rates only one. Ask students to rate on a ten-point scale the degree or severity of abnormality they feel the case deserves. After they have made their ratings, tell them that they are involved in a little experiment to see if gender and duration of symptoms are influential factors in their definitions of *abnormal.* Explain how the independent variables were manipulated. On the board, draw the cells for a two-by-two study and, for each cell (group) ask what their rating was. Compute the averages for each of the four groups and record in the appropriate cell on the board. Although it is too

Copyright © Houghton Mifflin Company. All rights reserved

unwieldy to compute standard deviations and actually do the statistics to see if a significant difference occurred (this possibility could be alluded to in the class when you discuss research methods), you can eyeball the data to see if trends exist.

If gender appears to be influential in ratings, link this trend to the multicultural perspective discussed in the text. Your data would support the proposal that some of the gender differences in epidemiological findings are a result of diagnostic bias. Differences in ratings due to duration of symptoms seem more benign and are "legitimate" criteria used in the DSM. However, students can notice that the term *too long* is culturally defined. Depressive symptoms that last ten weeks may be seen as normal (after parental divorce) or abnormal (after the death of a pet turtle).

Ask students what other factors might influence ratings of disorder severity. Likely candidates are age of the individual, proximity of symptoms to stressful events (the ease with which symptom onset can be explained), race or ethnic status, and income. All these factors support the multicultural perspective's case that disorder is in the eye of the culture and is affected by cultural majority standards.

Internet Site: http://www.apa.org/science/lib.html. An APA site that defines and describes all behaviors that the American Psychiatric Association considers abnormal in the DSM series.

6. Try introducing your students to the idea that not only individuals can be dysfunctional but that families, workplaces, neighborhoods, cities, and universities can be, too. Have the students form small groups of 4-7 individuals, depending on your class size and space limitations. Each group is to develop a listing of dysfunctional workplaces or jobs they have had. Have each group describe the features that were dysfunctional: mean co-workers, random management style, rules of conduct that changed. Ask each group to develop this list with the most salient examples first. Each group could then have a spokesperson deliver a short talk about the best examples. You could provide a blank overhead transparency to each group at the beginning of this demonstration.

7.   Using the same group format as in number 6 above, assign students to work in small groups. Have each group develop a list of words they use in everyday life to label normal persons and then develop a second list of words used to label abnormal persons. Each group could then have a spokesperson deliver a short talk about the best examples. You could provide a blank overhead transparency to each group at the beginning of this demonstration. As an alternative, collate the lists into two master lists and make a brief overhead transparency of the best examples. Often you will find that more words are listed for abnormal persons than for normal ones. Ask for suggestions about why these lists are of different length. Finally, ask students to evaluate the positive and negative connotations of the list. Lead a discussion of the negative effects of labeling.

Internet Site: http://www.mentalhealth.com/p.html. Internet Mental Health, an encyclopedia of mental health information.

8.   To make the students aware of services that are available to them on campus, invite the director of the campus mental health/counseling services to discuss the range of services offered. The main purpose of this guest speaker is to reduce the fear and stigma of seeking any type of personal counseling services on campus. The second purpose of this activity is to let the students know where to seek help should any personal issues arise during the semester. Be sure to allow your students time for questions and answers. Ask them to write down a list, without identifying themselves, of services or information sessions they would like to see offered by the campus mental health/counseling center. Let the students know you will compile the recommendations into one list. The results will later be shared with both the class and the director of the campus mental health/counseling center.

Copyright © Houghton Mifflin Company. All rights reserved.

HANDOUT FOR DEMONSTRATION 1:
STUDENT SURVEY OF PSYCHOLOGICAL PROBLEMS

This is a survey to assess the prevalence of psychological problems in students' lives. Please do *not* identify yourself. You can be assured that the data will be kept confidential. Only group data will be shared with the class.

If a close family member currently has or once had a particular psychological problem, check the space under "close family member." Do the same under "close friend." The problem could have been diagnosed as such by a professional or be one you feel the individual has or had. If more than one family member or friend has had the problem, you should indicate with as many check marks as individuals involved.

Psychological Problem	*Close Family Member*	*Close Friend*
1. Drinking problem (alcohol abuse or alcoholism)	_____	_____
2. Frequent periods of anxiety or seriously limiting fears	_____	_____
3. Stress-related physical disorder such as migraine or ulcer	_____	_____
4. Schizophrenia	_____	_____
5. Dependency on illicit drug such as marijuana or cocaine	_____	_____
6. Alzheimer's disease	_____	_____
7. Depression lasting at least two weeks	_____	_____
8. Eating disorders such as anorexia or bulimia	_____	_____
9. Mental retardation	_____	_____

Copyright © Houghton Mifflin Company. All rights reserved

HANDOUT FOR DEMONSTRATION 3:
ONE-MONTH PREVALENCE RATES FOR MENTAL DISORDERS, UNITED STATES, OVER EIGHTEEN YEARS OLD

Disorder

Group	Any	Sub	Anxiety	Aff	Schiz	ASP	Cogn
Both sexes, all ages	15.4	3.8	7.3	5.1	0.6	0.5	1.3
Men, all ages	14.0	6.3	4.7	3.5	0.6	0.8	1.4
18–24	16.5	4.9	4.9	3.4	0.7	1.5	0.7
25–44	15.4	7.9	4.7	4.5	0.8	1.2	0.5
45–64	11.9	4.1	5.1	3.1	0.6	0.2	1.4
65 and older	10.5	1.8	3.6	1.4	0.1	0.1	5.1
Women, all ages	16.6	1.6	9.7	6.6	0.6	0.2	1.3
18–24	17.3	4.5	10.4	5.3	0.7	0.4	0.5
25–44	19.2	1.9	11.7	8.2	1.1	0.3	0.4
45–64	14.6	0.4	8.0	7.2	0.3	0.0	1.0
65 and older	13.6	0.3	6.8	3.3	0.1	0.0	4.7

Sub = Substance use disorder
Anxiety = Anxiety disorders
Aff = Affective (mood) disorders
Schiz = Schizophrenias
ASP = Antisocial Personality Disorder
Cogn = Cognitive disorders

Copyright © Houghton Mifflin Company. All rights reserved.

HANDOUT FOR DEMONSTRATION 5:
RATING THE SEVERITY OF ABNORMAL BEHAVIOR

Hypothetical case 1

Tiffany is a junior college student whose parents have divorced after 25 years of marriage. The divorce came as a complete surprise to her and shook her confidence in both parents. She has become quite depressed—sleeping poorly, eating little, and showing little interest in school work. These symptoms have now gone on for two weeks.

Rate the severity of Tiffany's abnormality on a scale from 1 to 10 where 10 is "very severe." _____

Hypothetical case 2

Timothy is a junior college student whose parents have divorced after 25 years of marriage. The divorce came as a complete surprise to him and shook his confidence in both parents. He has become quite depressed—sleeping poorly, eating little, and showing little interest in school work. These symptoms have now gone on for two weeks.

Rate the severity of Timothy's abnormality on a scale from 1 to 10 where 10 is "very severe." _____

Hypothetical case 3

Tiffany is a junior college student whose parents have divorced after 25 years of marriage. The divorce came as a complete surprise to her and shook her confidence in both parents. She has become quite depressed—sleeping poorly, eating little, and showing little interest in school work. These symptoms have now gone on for ten weeks.

Rate the severity of Tiffany's abnormality on a scale from 1 to 10 where 10 is "very severe." _____

Hypothetical case 4

Timothy is a junior college student whose parents have divorced after 25 years of marriage. The divorce came as a complete surprise to him and shook his confidence in both parents. He has become quite depressed—sleeping poorly, eating little, and showing little interest in school work. These symptoms have now gone on for ten weeks.

Rate the severity of Timothy's abnormality on a scale from 1 to 10 where 10 is "very severe." _____

Copyright © Houghton Mifflin Company. All rights reserved

SELECTED READINGS

Freedheim, D. K., Freudenberger, J. J., Kessler, J. W., Messer, S. B., Peterson, D. R., Strupp, H. H., & Wachtel, P. L. (Eds.) (1992). *History of psychotherapy: A century of change.* Washington, DC: American Psychological Association.

Humphreys, K. (1996). Clinical psychologists as psychotherapists: History, future, and alternatives. *American Psychologist, 51,* 190–197.

Rosen, G. (1975). *Madness in society: Chapters in the historical sociology of mental illness.* New York: Anchor Books.

Rosenhan, D. (1973). On being sane in insane places. *Science, 179,* 250-258. p. 253.

Spanos, N. P. (1978). Witchcraft in the histories of psychiatry: A critical appraisal and an alternative conceptualization. *Psychological Bulletin, 35,* 417–439.

Szasz, T. S. (1960). The myth of mental illness. *American Psychologist, 15,* 113–118. This is a must read classic article.

VIDEO RESOURCES

Abnormal Psychology (video, color, 29 min.). Emphasizes the problems of distinguishing between normal and abnormal behavior within the context of the DSM system of classification. Coast District Telecourses, 11460 Warner Avenue, Fountain Valley, CA 92708.

Dr. Pinel Unchains the Insane (16 mm, 25 min.). An enactment of Pinel's plea to bring moral treatment to the mentally ill. McGraw-Hill Text films, 1221 Avenue of the Americas, New York, NY 10020.

Emotional Illness (16 mm, 30 min.). Introductory movie discusses abnormal behavior and distinguishes neurotic, psychotic, and psychosomatic illnesses. Audio Visual Center, Indiana University, Bloomington, IN 47405.

Sigmund Freud: The View from Within (16 mm, color, 29 min.). Describes the influences that moved Freud in the direction of psychoanalytic theory. Department of Cinema, University of Southern California, University Park, Los Angeles, CA 90007.

Brainwaves (VHS, color, 60 min.). From the PBS *Madness* series. Explores the physical explanations and treatments for mental illness from late eighteenth-century Europe to the present. PBS Video Catalog. 1-800-344-3337.

The Dark Side of the Moon (VUS, color, 25 min.). Chronicles the lives of three men with mental disorders, from living on the streets to becoming useful members of society. They now work to help other people in similar situations. Fanlight Productions. 1-800-937-4113.

Out of Sight (VHS, color, 60 min.). From the PBS *Madness* series. Discusses the development of institutions for the mentally ill and traces custodial care practices of the mentally disturbed. PBS Video Catalog. 1-800-344-3337.

Copyright © Houghton Mifflin Company. All rights reserved.

To Define True Madness (VHS, color, 60 min.). From the PBS *Madness* series. Examines mental illness through history and considers the progress of understanding these disorders. PBS Video Catalog. 1-800-344-3337.

ON THE INTERNET

http://krantzj.hanover.edu/APS details the American Psychological Society, which emphasizes the experimental areas of psychology.

http://www.apa.org is the American Psychological Association, the first and largest association devoted to psychology in the United States (also has many members from Canada and other countries).

http://www.cmhc.com is the web site for a company that develops and provides technology and management information systems for mental health centers.

http://www.mentalhealth.com is the web site for Internet Mental Health, which provides resources and some full length articles of psychological disorders, medications, an other important research.

http://www.mhsource.com is a general resource provided by Mental Health InfoSource.

http://www.nami.org is the web site for the National Alliance for the Mentally Ill, an advocacy organization for people with mental illness and their families.

http://www.nimh.nih.gov is the web site for the National Institute of Mental Health (a division of the National Institutes of Health), which offers information about diagnosis and treatment of numerous mental health disorders and other useful references.

Copyright © Houghton Mifflin Company. All rights reserved

CHAPTER 2
Models of Abnormal Behavior

CHAPTER OUTLINE

I. Models in the study of psychopathology

    1.   The case of Steven V.

   A. The biological models

    1.   The human brain (composed of neurons)

      a.   The forebrain

      b.   The midbrain and hindbrain

    2.   Biochemical theories

    3.   Genetic explanations

    4.   Criticisms of the biological model

   B. Psychodynamic models

    1.   Personality structure

    2.   Psychosexual stages

    3.   Anxiety and psychopathology: realistic, moralistic, and neurotic anxiety

    4.   Defense mechanisms

    5.   Psychoanalytic therapy

    6.   Neo-Freudian's perspective

    7.   Criticisms of psychodynamic models

   C. Genetic explanations

    1.   The Human Genome Project

   D. Criticisms of the biological model

II.   Humanistic and existential approaches: agree on importance of subjective reality, freedom of choice, and wholeness of person

   A. The humanistic perspective

    1.   Actualizing tendency

      a.   Self-actualization: motive to enhance self

      b.   Self-concept: view of self and values attached to self

    2.   Development of abnormal behavior

      a.   Conditions of worth distort self-concept

      b.   Incongruence leads to symptoms

      c.   Need for unconditional positive regard

Copyright © Houghton Mifflin Company. All rights reserved

        3. Person-centered therapy: nondirective; use of reflection of feelings

    B. The existential perspective

        1. Differences from humanistic approach

           a. Less optimistic

           b. Individual seen in larger context

           c. Greater stress on responsibility to others

    C. Criticisms of the humanistic and existential approaches

        1. Emphasis on subjective makes empirical investigation difficult

        2. Limited usefulness with severely disturbed clients

III. Psychodynamic models

    A. Personality structure

    B. Psychosexual stages

    C. Anxiety and psychopathology: realistic, moralistic, and neurotic anxiety

    D. Defense mechanisms

    E. Psychoanalytic therapy

    F. Post-Freudian perspectives

    G. Criticisms of psychodynamic models

IV. Behavioral models

    A. The classical conditioning model

    B. Classical conditioning in psychopathology

    C. The operant conditioning model

    D. Operant conditioning in psychopathology

    E. The observational learning model

    F. Observational learning model in psychopathology

    G. Criticisms of the behavioral models

 V. Cognitive models

    A. Irrational and maladaptive assumptions and thoughts

    B. Distortions of thought processes

    C. Cognitive approaches to therapy

    D. Criticisms of the cognitive models.

VI. Humanistic and existential approaches: agree on importance of subjective reality, freedom of choice, and wholeness of person

VII. The family systems model: personality ruled by family attributes; abnormality reflects unhealthy family dynamics; treat whole system

    A. Family treatment approaches

        1. Communications

        2. Strategic (power issues)

        3. Structural (relationship involvement)

    B. Criticisms of the family systems model

        1. Definition of family is culture bound

        2. Excessively blames parents

VIII. Models of diversity and psychopathology

Copyright © Houghton Mifflin Company. All rights reserved

A. Multicultural models of psychopathology

B. Criticisms of the multicultural model

    1. Universality of some disorder symptoms

    2. Lack of empirical validation

IX. An integrative approach to models of psychopathology

A. A tripartite framework for understanding abnormal psychology

    1. Individual level

    2. Group level

    3. Universal level

LEARNING OBJECTIVES

1. Define *psychopathology* and describe what a model is. Discuss how models are used in describing psychopathology and how a clinician's choice of a model influences thought and action toward abnormal behavior. (pp. 35–37)

2. Describe the biological models, including the major structures of the human brain, neurons, and the role of neurotransmitters, and how knowledge of biochemistry can be used in the treatment of mental disorders. (pp. 37–41; Table 2.1)

3. Discuss the relationship between genetics and psychopathology, including the differences between genotype and phenotype, and explain how the Human Genome Project is revolutionizing our understanding of the impact that genes have on human life. (pp. 40–43)

4. List the criticisms of the biological model and describe how the diathesis-stress approach has tried to address some of these criticisms. (p. 43)

5. Describe the basic concepts of psychodynamic theory, including the components of personality structure, the concepts of psychosexual stages and defense mechanisms, and the role anxiety plays in the development of psychopathology. (pp. 43–46)

6. Briefly describe psychoanalytic therapy and how the psychoanalysis of the neo-Freudians differed from traditional Freudian psychoanalysts. (pp. 46–48; Tables 2.2 & 2.3))

7. Discuss the criticisms of the psychodynamic model. (pp. 46–47)

8. Discuss the concerns of the behavioral models of psychopathology. Describe the components of the classical conditioning model and relate those components to psychopathology. (pp. 48–50)

9. Discuss how operant conditioning can be applied to understanding psychopathology. Specify the assumptions of the operant conditioning model and compare them with classical conditioning. (pp. 50–52)

10. Describe the observational learning model and its relevance to psychopathology. Evaluate the behavioral models. (pp. 52–53)

11. Describe the assumptions of the cognitive models and how unproductive schemas, irrational and maladaptive thoughts, and distortions of thought processes contribute to psychopathology. Describe the elements of cognitive therapy. (pp. 53–54; Table 2.4)

12. Evaluate the cognitive models. (pp. 54–56)

13. Describe the contributions of the humanistic and existential approaches including the notions of the concept of the self and the actualizing tendency. Discuss the development of abnormal behavior and its treatment according to Carl Rogers. (pp. 56–58)

14. Discuss the criticisms of the humanistic and existential approaches. (pp. 58-59)

Copyright © Houghton Mifflin Company. All rights reserved

15. Identify the three distinct assumptions of the family systems approach, including the development of personality and identity within the family, the relationship between family dynamics and psychopathology, and treatment approaches. (pp. 59–60)

16. Evaluate the strengths and limitations of the family systems model. (p. 60)

17. Discuss the assumptions of the multicultural models of psychopathology, including the inferiority and deprivations/deficit models, and relate these ideas to psychopathology. Evaluate the strengths and limitations of the multicultural model. (pp. 60–64; Mental Health & Society)

18. Using Table 2.5, compare and contrast the biological, psychodynamic, humanistic/existential, behavioral, cognitive, family systems, and multicultural models of psychopathology. Discuss the utility of integrating models into an eclectic approach such as that found in the "tripartite framework." (pp. 64–69; Table 2.5)

19. Discuss the case of Steven V. from various etiological models and how each model would treat Steven V. (pp. 36-37; 65–67)

CLASSROOM TOPICS FOR LECTURE AND DISCUSSION

1.   Two important issues that all models should address are (1) whether people with disorders are responsible for their problems, and (2) whether they are responsible for solutions to their problems. These ideas are wonderfully summarized in an *American Psychologist* article by Philip Brickman et al. (1982). The medical model assumes that people are responsible for neither their problems nor the solutions to them. The model implies that professionals must provide help and that disturbed people are relatively passive during recovery. In the extreme form, humanistic-existential thinkers suggest that people are responsible for both creating and solving their difficulties. Some might consider this a moral model: Only the sinner can help himself or herself. Two other quadrants exist as well. One asserts that although people may create their own troubles, they must rely on to solve them. Finally, a "compensatory" model argues that people may not be responsible for the cause of their problems, but they must be responsible for solving them.

You can use the handout for this lecture topic and ask students where the biogenic model and the humanistic-existential perspective should be placed and why. This should lead to a discussion of what helpers can do, the disturbed person's adoption of a "sick role," the phenomenon of blaming the victim, and other consequences of adopting a particular model. Another related topic is the disease model of addiction. If alcoholics are the cause of their own problem and should be responsible for the solution, they would be seen in the "moral" cell. In many people's minds, alcoholism is a disease (the alcoholic is responsible for neither the problem nor its solution). Do students agree with this model? Do they see people addicted to cigarettes in the same way? What about compulsive gamblers? Another point implicit in the grid is that responsibility for the cause of a problem does not necessitate responsibility for its solution (and vice versa). Ask students if they can think of disorders or other life problems in which a person who is not responsible for the cause is held responsible for its solution. Does this model seem "fair"? The discussion could conclude with the idea that adopting a model is anything but a neutral act.

Source: Brickman, P., Rabinowitz, V. C, Karuza, J., Coates, D., Cohn, E., & Kidder, L. (1982). Models of helping and coping. *American Psychologist*, 37, 368–384.

Internet Site: http://www.neuropsychologycentral.com/index.html. Massive site with links to all topics in the neurosciences.

2.   You can ask students to assess their own preferred theoretical perspective and its implications. Present the following short hypothetical case as the focus for this discussion:

Copyright © Houghton Mifflin Company. All rights reserved

John is 17 and has been drinking heavily since he was 12. He drinks almost every day, but when he is particularly anxious, he drinks until he passes out. His father and his grandfather were diagnosed alcoholics; the father drank himself to death when John was 14. His mother and older brother do not drink at all, and they have always told John that he is the family's black sheep, the rebellious who is destined to be like his father.

Ask students what they think causes John's behavior—genetics? early childhood experiences? problems with feelings and thoughts? current circumstances? wider society? Ask them to defend their choice. The ensuing discussion may lead to an examination of the methods by which we could discover the causes of alcoholism. It should also show how multiple perspectives can shed light on a single case.

From the biogenic perspective, you could list genetic vulnerability and briefly explain the concept of concordance. If John had an identical twin, would he, too, drink heavily and at the same times? Also under the biogenic heading, neurochemical differences can be discussed. If we found that John metabolized alcohol differently from his older brother, would that support a biogenic explanation? Point out the need for a preexisting biological difference. Finally, this example can give students an appreciation of diathesis-stress theory. If John has a preexisting, inherited vulnerability, is he doomed to become an alcoholic? (Most likely, a combination of genetic factors and family and social stressors produced this pattern of use.)

From the psychodynamic perspective, you could discuss oral fixation. Is dependency a result or a cause of drinking? What information would suggest that early deprivation caused John's adolescent behavior? John probably engages in the defenses of rationalization, denial, and projection.

Humanistic theorists might focus on John's lack of self-esteem or the conditions of worth that his family might have placed on loving him. Alienated from society, he may find comfort in intoxication and escape from responsibility. Does he freely choose to drink heavily? Is he being honest with his feelings?

Behaviorists would look at how John's father and grandfather modeled how to drink heavily. At the same time, they probably introduced a good deal of stress in the boy's life, and he probably learned that drinking reduced that stress. If his mother and brother criticized him a great deal, perhaps drinking became an operant behavior that alleviated the criticism temporarily, illustrating operant conditioning's concept of negative reinforcement. Finally, if the sight and smell of alcohol now produce an automatic response in John, we could see his use as having a classically conditioned quality, too.

If students mention that John probably thinks that he can function only when he is drunk, they appreciate the cognitive viewpoint. He may catastrophize discomforting circumstances in his life and thereby give himself a rationale for drinking heavily. Irrational beliefs such as "unless I am perfect no one will love me, so I might as well get drunk" are part of Ellis's A-B-C theory of personality. Beck would emphasize illogical thought processes John might have, such as a tendency to maximize any perceived hurt and minimize the effects drinking has on his life.

If students focus on the family's definition of John as black sheep and the brother as perfect, they are in tune with systems thinking. His mother and father most likely were in frequent conflict; perhaps John resented that or was ignored. How did the family deal with the father's death? John's symptoms may only reflect a wider family pathology; in fact, the family may need to have a black sheep so other members maintain their roles. Therefore, mother and brother may unconsciously assist John in staying drunk. You can discuss "enabling" here.

Finally, John may be acting out sex- and age-role stereotypes. The multicultural perspective would look at the cultural norms for John and adolescents like him. What is the peer culture like? Are others labeling him "alcoholic" prematurely or using a cultural standard that is inappropriate?

Copyright © Houghton Mifflin Company. All rights reserved

The discussion should show that the same information about a person can be interpreted quite differently and that each perspective has something valuable to offer. An eclectic approach is attractive, but note that complete eclecticism is untenable. For example, isn't it logically impossible for John to be both free in his actions and the product of determinism?

3.   A pair of articles points out the tendency for researchers who support a particular orientation to selectively report evidence. The issue in this case is the explanation for the phenomenon of violent men fostering the development of violent sons. Widom (1989) presented what she considered a comprehensive examination of evidence on the question of violence begetting violence. She concluded that violence in adolescence and adulthood stems from being abused as a child. She marshaled considerable support for her environmental/familial explanation.

Not long afterwards, DiLalla and Gottesman (1991) argued that Widom left out part of the story. With equal vigor and credibility, DiLalla and Gottesman show that evidence from twin and adoption studies, plus physiological research (on testosterone and 5-HIAA levels, for example), suggests a biological contribution to violence. They do not deny the importance of the environment but suggest that "cultural influence is just one of the paths that make children similar to their parents" (p. 128).

Discuss with your students whether scientists are more or less likely than nonscientists to look in an unbiased fashion at the evidence for and against their position. Ask them what, as consumers of information, they must do to protect themselves from researchers who present a biased interpretation of information while claiming to be thorough in their analysis.

Sources: DiLalla, L. F., & Gottesman, I. I. (1991). Biological and genetic contributions to violence—Widom's untold tale. *Psychological Bulletin, 109*, 125–129; Widom, C. S. (1989). Does violence beget violence? A critical examination of the literature. *Psychological Bulletin, 106*, 3–28.

4.   The diathesis-stress model has become paradigmatic for much of the field. A good way to show the diathesis-stress idea is by drawing on the board a graph with low and high vulnerability along the x-axis and low and high stress along the y-axis. A diagonal line would separate those who develop the disorder from those who do not: At very high levels of vulnerability, almost any stress exceeds threshold values; at very low levels of vulnerability, even very high stress levels fail to generate the disorder. However, even a simple two-factor model (genetic vulnerability plus environmental stress) becomes quite complicated, given greater sophistication in our understanding of life stress. Monroe and Simons (1991) note that we have trouble determining a threshold level of vulnerability (who is vulnerable?) or gradations of vulnerability (who is highly vulnerable?). Furthermore, we cannot yet determine what type of life stress is important, in what context, with what frequency, and for what disorder. Monroe and Simon's work focuses on depression. A more complete review of the concept is provided for schizophrenia (Fowled, 1992).

Sources: Fowled, D. C. (1992). Schizophrenia: Diathesis-stress revisited. *Annual Review of Psychology, 43*, 303–336; Monroe, S. M., & Simon, A. D. (1991). Diathesis-stress theories in the context of life stress research: Implications for depressive disorders. *Psychological Bulletin, 110*, 406–425.

5.   Information that supplements the text's coverage of operant conditioning will prove important in explaining disorders later in the book. Students will need to understand positive and negative reinforcement, punishment, extinction, and shaping. A handout using a four-cell diagram can communicate this clearly and quickly.

The diagram shows four operant processes by which we can alter the strength of a response, all related to the consequences that immediately follow the response. Consequences can either be positive or

Copyright © Houghton Mifflin Company. All rights reserved

negative and can either be presented or removed. This should simplify the underlying mechanisms of operant conditioning.

It is always difficult for students to differentiate negative reinforcement from punishment. Use the example of behavior in a rainstorm. If you walk out into the rain and get soaked and cold, you are unlikely to do the same thing again. If you walk out into the rain and then put up an umbrella, it removes a negative stimulus and you are more likely to use an umbrella in the next storm. The former is punishment; the latter is negative reinforcement or avoidance learning.

Shaping is crucial for understanding abnormal behavior. Explain to students that complex behaviors are made up of component tasks. If we are required to master the complex behavior before receiving any reinforcement, we are unlikely to ever learn it. Parents and coaches know this; they expect and reinforce only the crudest approximations of the "finished" behavior at first. The standard for reinforcement increases incrementally as more and more components of the behavior are added. Ask student athletes how they first learned a complex motor behavior such as a tennis serve or golf swing. Did their coach shape them at an appropriate rate? What happened when they had an off day and dropped back in performance?

Next discuss how shaping naturally occurs in families—without the conscious effort involved in teaching a motor skill. How do parents shape their children for keeping their rooms clean, for table manners, for the expression of feelings? Further, don't children also shape their parents for a variety of behaviors? A good way to end this portion of your lecture is to discuss how you shape your students (smiling when they take notes or ask good questions) and how they shape you (laughing at your jokes, making eye contact). Everyday life is a shaping dance: a pattern of reinforcing interactions in which we often unconsciously attempt to alter others' behavior even as they attempt to alter ours.

Internet Site: http://www.indiana.edu/~iuepsyc/topics/cognitive.htm. Contains examples and demonstrations of classical and operant conditioning.

6.   Many professionals and nonprofessionals make liberal use of the term *dysfunctional family*. Unfortunately, the term has stretched to the point of describing everything, and, therefore, nothing. You can start a discussion by asking students to list the behaviors or factors they think define dysfunctional. You can compare these with the following concepts presented by Epstein and Bishop (1981) in what they call the McMaster model of family systems:

Problem-solving difficulties. Most-effective families are able to identify problems, communicate their existence to other family members or relevant outsiders, develop alternative solutions to the problem, decide on a solution, take action to implement the solution, and evaluate its impact. Families are less and less effective if they are incapable of performing these problem-solving tasks. The most dysfunctional cannot do the first step of identifying the problem.

Communication problems. Most-effective families communicate directly (to the person to whom the message is intended) and in a clear manner. Least-effective families communicate indirectly (to someone other than the message's target) and in a masked manner. This sets up a four-cell model: clear and direct, clear and indirect, masked and direct, masked and indirect. Examples help teach these concepts.

> Tom's wife is angry at him for not listening to her. Here are examples of communications for each of the four cells.
> Clear and direct: Tom, when you don't listen to me, I get really angry.
> Clear and indirect: Boy, men can really make you angry when they don't listen.
> Masked and direct: Tom, you look like hell today!
> Masked and indirect: Men! What are you gonna do about them.

Copyright © Houghton Mifflin Company. All rights reserved

Roles in the family. Most-effective families have specific roles for family members (provide nurturance, make decisions, provide financial resources), although the roles are flexible when circumstances change. The least-effective families are chaotic; no one knows or maintains a role so no one can depend on another family member.

Difficulties in expressing emotions. Most-effective families are able to get emotional needs taken care of. Family members can be sad, happy, angry, guilty, or relaxed as they need to be, although there are limitations on the intensity of such expression. Least-effective families allow no emotional expression or are out of control.

Difficulties in being emotionally involved with one another. Most-effective families show interest in the welfare and activities of other family members. Least-effective families, in accordance with Minuchin's structural approach, are either enmeshed (overinvolved) or disengaged (completely uninvolved) from one another.

Behavior control difficulties. Most-effective families can control family members' actions so there are clear expectations for specific situations. However, these families use a flexible and rational system of control so that the reasons for controls and opportunities for change are clear. Least-effective families are inconsistent, where one parent operates on a laissez faire basis while the other is rigidly controlling, or worse, both parents shift suddenly from one extreme to the other.

Source: From "Problem-Centered Systems Therapy of the Family," by N. B. Epstein & D. S. Bishop, in *Handbook of Family Therapy,* edited by A. Gurman & D. Kniskern, copyright © 1981. Reprinted with permission from Brunner/Mazel, Inc., and the author.

Copyright © Houghton Mifflin Company. All rights reserved

HANDOUT FOR CLASSROOM TOPIC 1:
THE BRICKMAN GRID

Attribution to Self of Responsibility for Problem   *Attribution to Self of Responsibility for Solution*

	High	Low
High	*Moral*	*Enlightenment*
Perception of self	Lazy	Guilty
Actions expected of self	Striving	Submission
Actions expected of others	Exhortation	Discipline
View of human nature	Strong	Bad
Low	*Compensatory*	*Medical*
Perception of self	Deprived	Ill
Actions expected of self	Assertion	Acceptance
Actions expected of others	Mobilization	Treatment
View of human nature	Good	Weak

Copyright © Houghton Mifflin Company. All rights reserved

HANDOUT FOR CLASSROOM TOPIC 5:
FOUR PROCESSES IN OPERANT CONDITIONING

Type of Consequence

	Positive	*Negative*
Present	**Positive reinforcement** (increased response strength)	**Punishment** (decreased response strength)
Remove	**Extinction** (negative punishment) (decreased response strength)	**Negative reinforcement** (increased response strength)

Copyright © Houghton Mifflin Company. All rights reserved

CLASSROOM DEMONSTRATIONS

1.   It is important for students to think about the implications of genetically transmitted mental disorders. A role-play exercise may bring this home. Divide the class into groups of seven or so and distribute the handout for Demonstration 1, which provides information about the revolutionary (and hypothetical) discovery of a genetic marker for depression. Tell the students that the U.S. government wants them to brainstorm on how this new discovery can or should be used to prevent depression. Ask them to analyze each idea group members suggest in terms of its cost and the benefits it would provide. Each group should come to a consensus on what should be done nationally. Allow ten to fifteen minutes for this discussion. Circulate to answer any questions. Then ask each group to report to the full class. Write their recommendations on the board. Ask about ideas that were rejected. Ethical concerns over invasion of privacy, self-fulfilling prophecies, and overprediction should arise. You may want to note that an American geneticist was motivated to identify the gene for Huntington's disease because her family has a history of this tragic disorder. After years of work she was successful and helped develop a test that can identify a carrier of the gene. However, she herself would not submit to testing—she would rather not know.

Internet Site: http://www.med.jhu.edu/Greenberg.Center/tutorial.htm#basics. An in-depth discussion of genetics and inheritance.

2.   An in-class exercise that reveals unconscious processes is a helpful teaching demonstration. Find several ambiguous pictures from magazines that show men and women in some form of interaction. Advertisements are a good source of pictures. Hold up the pictures or, if they reproduce well, photocopy them and hand them out to the class. Ask students to write out TAT-type stories for each picture: "Make up a creative story about what is going on in this picture. What led up to this scene? How will it turn out? What are the people feeling?"

Do not ask for public readings of student stories, but explain how their stories about the protagonists might reveal aspects of their own needs and concerns. Discuss how males and females might be described differently and how recurring themes might reveal unconscious feelings toward men (father) and women (mother) in general. Student skepticism should be accepted. Responses to skepticism can range from how a psychoanalyst would identify disbelief as a form of repression to how critics of psychoanalytic assessment would question the reliability and validity of such interpretations.

3.   In the class period before you lecture on psychoanalytic concepts, ask for eight volunteers. Tell them that you want them to pair up and write skits that illustrate the major defense mechanisms. The students will be more accurate in their depictions if you supply a handout that lists four defenses— repression, reaction formation, projection, and displacement—and gives a brief description of each. The volunteers can pick the defense they want to illustrate. Encourage them to be creative in their role play; the more dramatic, the better the point is driven home to the other students.

When the class period for discussing defense mechanisms arrives, have the students come to the front of the room and give their skits. Do not announce to the class which defense each pair is supposed to be illustrating. Ask the class to identify the defense they think is being depicted. Provide any corrections that are needed.

Ask the participants in the skits how they felt while performing. Help the class discuss how the exaggeration of each defense could lead to interpersonal conflicts and disorders. You may want to link certain disorders with defenses (projection with delusions, repression with dissociative disorders). Also,

Copyright © Houghton Mifflin Company. All rights reserved

you could point out the need for defenses. Students often think that defenses are either good or bad; you should emphasize the balance that is required for good mental health.

4.   The humanistic-existential perspective stresses personal freedom and responsibility. The biogenic and psychodynamic perspectives place much greater emphasis on determinism based on past biological or psychological events. Present students with this short story:

Bill suffers from auditory hallucinations (he hears voices telling him to kill). If he tries very hard, he can keep the voices from being loud enough to influence him, but it is tiring to do so. One day, Bill was too worn out to stop the voices. He listened to them, picked up a gun, and shot a complete stranger on the sidewalk.

Ask students if they think Bill's actions were done out of free will. Should he be held personally responsible for his actions? Is Bill a product of biological or psychological forces outside his control? Urge students to take a position. Use two corners of the classroom to segregate students into those that take a free will position and those that take a determinism position. Ask students from each group to explain their thinking and describe which of the theoretical perspectives (biogenic, psychoanalytic, humanistic-existential) they agree with most. Ask several students what additional facts could get them to move from one corner to the other corner or more toward the middle.

5.   Classical and operant conditioning lend themselves to in-class demonstrations. Classical conditioning demonstrations using loud noises and some conditioned stimulus (for example, picking up an eraser) can be very effective. The demonstration also allows examination of generalization (Will students cringe if another professor picks up an eraser?) and discrimination (Will students cringe only when they walk into your classroom?). Habituation can also be pointed out.

For operant conditioning, shaping can be demonstrated with a clicker or even finger snaps. A volunteer from the class is asked to leave the room for a moment while the rest of the class is informed that shaping will be demonstrated. Tell the other students that you will use the sounds of a clicker or finger snaps to tell the volunteer that he or she is "getting warmer" or "getting colder" to a target behavior such as walking in a circle or scratching his or her nose. The volunteer is invited back and is asked to move about the front of the room and to consider the clicks he or she hears as reinforcers. The greater the frequency of clicks, the greater the reinforcement. This demonstration will show students the small increments of change that some behavior therapists must come to expect when teaching complex skills.

Internet Site: http://www.indiana.edu/~iuepsyc/topics/cognitive.htm. Examples and demonstrations of classical and operant conditioning.

6.   This demonstration (Hughes, 1990) is appropriate for students with moderate anxiety in the presence of certain animals. Earthworms, snakes, and spiders are often the object of squeamishness if not outright phobic responses. You or some expert you know should come to class with the animal you choose, hold it with confidence, and discuss some facts about the animal, stressing its essential harmlessness. Students who fear the animal should be encouraged, but not coerced, to come forward and take gradual steps toward it. Deep breathing and encouragement should be used to help the student or students take an additional step: standing next to the animal, examining it carefully, touching it for an instant, touching it for longer, and finally holding it.

The demonstration shows the power of modeling and, perhaps more subtly, the power of positive peer pressure. Both are important in understanding the development and treatment of psychopathology. The demonstration can also be expanded to ask the students who come forward to verbalize their thoughts. This will increase their awareness (and that of the other students in the class) of cognitive mediating properties. As students take steps closer to making contact with the animal, suggest that they talk to

Copyright © Houghton Mifflin Company. All rights reserved

themselves to remain calm and to give themselves reinforcing self-statements ("I'm pretty brave to be doing this. Good for me!").

Source: Adapted from "Participant Modeling as a Classroom Activity," by D. Hughes, *Teaching of Psychology, 17,* 1990, pp. 238–240. Copyright © 1990. Used by permission of Lawrence Erlbaum Associates, Inc. and the author.

7.   Put the students into discussion groups. Ask the groups to develop an explanation for alcohol abuse and dependence using the concepts of modeling and social learning theory. Ask one person from each group to share a summary of the group discussion with the entire class. This topic usually provokes a lively discussion, with students relating examples about their family and friends.

Copyright © Houghton Mifflin Company. All rights reserved

HANDOUT FOR DEMONSTRATION 1: IMPLICATIONS OF GENETICALLY TRANSMITTED MENTAL DISORDERS

You have been selected by the U.S. government to participate in a task force to decide how the nation should use some startling information. Pretend that researchers have discovered that severe depression, one of the most common and lethal forms of mental disorder, can be genetically predicted to a degree. A simple blood test is all that is needed to detect this genetic vulnerability. Further, imagine that scientists know that if this genetic marker shows up in the blood, in 75 percent of cases the person will become severely depressed within five years unless he or she takes a certain medication. In the other 25 percent of cases, there will either be mild or no depression at all without medication and no chance of depression if the medication is taken.

The government wants to know what to do with this information. Can or should it be used to prevent a terrible mental disorder? What are the dangers, if any, of making this news public? What are the costs and benefits of massive blood screenings? What should be done about making the medication available?

Your group must come to a consensus about what, if anything, the nation should do with the information the task force has. You can assume that no one else knows about this hypothetical scientific breakthrough except your group and the scientists.

Be prepared to report the results of your deliberations to the full class.

Copyright © Houghton Mifflin Company. All rights reserved

HANDOUT FOR DEMONSTRATION 3:
DEPICTIONS OF DEFENSE MECHANISMS

You and your partner will be assigned to do a short skit depicting one of the following defense mechanisms. First, decide on an interpersonal situation in which the defense mechanism is likely to be used. Provide the audience with some background to the scene you will play: what led up to the situation, where it takes place, and the relationship between the two people. Then develop a script for the interaction so that you can accurately illustrate the defense. Your skit will be especially effective if you add the voice quality and gestures that might accompany the defense.

1. **Repression:** the defense mechanism that prevents unacceptable impulses from reaching consciousness. Repression always involves some form of motivated forgetting. Sometimes emotionally charged life events, such as being assaulted by another person, are pushed out of consciousness. In other cases, unacceptable impulses or thoughts (sexual or violent) are banished from consciousness so that people who may have lustful or rageful impulses are unaware that they have them. Be clear that repression is *not* intentional; people who consciously decide not to think about or remember certain events are not engaged in defense mechanisms.

2. **Reaction formation:** the defense mechanism in which a repressed desire is expressed by taking on an opposite attitude or pattern of behavior. One illustration of this defense mechanism is when people threatened by their strong sexual feelings express a strict, puritanical attitude. They might vehemently campaign against anything that is even slightly sexual in nature. Another example is the daredevil individual who seems to laugh at death but, according to psychoanalysts, is defending against an unacceptable fear of death. The phrase Shakespeare used, "Me thinks the lady doth protest too much" is a good summary of reaction formation.

3. **Projection:** the defense mechanism by which a person attributes to others the objectionable characteristics that are actually in him or herself. A person who feels violent impulses toward others will not accept these feelings but rather see others as intending to harm him or her. Projection often takes the form of inaccurate mind reading: believing that others are motivated by or thinking about certain emotionally charged ideas that are actually within the observer's mind. In its extreme form, projection becomes paranoia—believing that others are in a conspiracy to harm one despite a lack of plausible evidence for this belief.

4. **Displacement:** the defense mechanism that redirects an unacceptable emotional response from an object that is seen as threatening or unacceptable toward one that is less so. Misplaced anger is a classic example of displacement: kicking the cat when you are really angry with a friend. However, other emotional responses can be displaced, such as when a child who is fearful of a bully at school unconsciously develops a phobia of going to school.

Copyright © Houghton Mifflin Company. All rights reserved

SELECTED READINGS

Bandura, A. (1977). *Social learning theory.* Englewood Cliffs, NJ: Prentice-Hall. This book is a must read.

Beck, A. T., & Clark, D. A. (1988). Anxiety and depression: An information processing perspective. *Anxiety Research, 1,* 23–36.

Blatt, S. J., & Lerner, H. (1991). Psychodynamic perspectives on personality theory. In M. Hersen, A. E. Kazdin, & A. S. Bellack (Eds.) *The clinical psychology handbook* (2nd ed.). New York: Pergamon, pp. 147–169.

Mahoney, M. J. (1988). Recent developments in cognitive approaches to counseling and psychotherapy. *Counseling Psychologist, 16,* 190–234.

Rosenhan, D. (1973). On being sane in insane places. *Science, 179,* 250-258. p. 253

Urban, H. (1991). Humanistic, phenomenological, and existential approaches. In M. Hersen, A. E. Kazdin, & A. S. Bellack (Eds.) *The clinical psychology handbook* (2nd ed.). New York: Pergamon, pp. 200–219.

VIDEO RESOURCES

Albert Bandura, Parts 1 and 2 (video, color, 57 min.). Bandura reviews his theoretical and research contributions, including modeling, cognitive behavior modification, the classic Bobo doll experiment, media effects on violence, self-efficacy, and his plans for the future. University Film & Video, University of Minnesota, Suite 108, 1313 Fifth Street, S.E., Minneapolis, MN 55414-1524.

B. F. Skinner and Behavior Change: Research, Practice, and Promise (16 mm, color, 45 min.). Skinner and other psychologists discuss the philosophical, ethical, and scientific questions generated by behavioral psychology. Research Press, Box 317740, Champaign, IL 61820.

Behavior Therapy: An Introduction (VHS, color, 29 min.). Shows three models of learning (classical, operant, and observational) applied to treatment. Penn State University Film Library, University Park, PA 16802.

Charting the Unconscious Mind (2 parts, 13 min. each). Teaches the basics of psychoanalytic theory. Human Relations Media, 175 Tompkins Avenue, Pleasantville, NY 10570.

Childhood Aggression: A Social Learning Approach to Family Therapy (16 mm, color, 35 min.). Dr. Gerald Patterson's behavioral family intervention in treating a coercive child. Shows changes in family as treatment progresses; based on an actual case. Psychological Cinema Register, Pennsylvania State University, University Park, PA 16802.

Freud: The Hidden Nature of Man (16 mm, 29 min.). Actors play Freud and his patients to show the development and power of unconscious motivations and repression. Audio Visual Center, Indiana University, Bloomington, IN 47405

Hillcrest Family Series (16 mm, color, times range from 12 to 32 min.). Eight films—four family interviews, all with the same family, and four brief talks with the therapists who conducted the interviews. Family is seen by Nathan Ackerman, Murray Bowen, Don Jackson, and Carl Whitaker. Psychological Cinema Register, Pennsylvania State University, University Park, PA 16802.

Hugs 'n' Kids: Parenting Your Preschooler (video, color, 36 min.). This type of video, combined with a manual, is used in behaviorally oriented parenting classes. It presents common parent-child impasses

Copyright © Houghton Mifflin Company. All rights reserved

and ways to solve them. Available in Spanish and English. Guilford Publications, 72 Spring Street, New York, NY 10012-9941.

Maslow: Self-Actualization (16 mm, 60 min.). Abraham Maslow discusses his theory of self-actualization by assessing case material. Psychological Films, Inc., 189 N. Wheeler Street, Orange, CA 92669.

Neurotic Behavior: A Psychodynamic View (16 mm, color, 19 min.). Shows operation of various defense mechanisms in reducing anxiety. CRM Educational Films, 1011 Camino Del Mar, Del Mar, CA 92014.

"Neurotransmitter Animation" from *The Psychology Show* videodisc series (55 min.). Houghton Mifflin Company.

Otto Series (video, color, 25–30 min. each). A series of five films. The first presents a dramatized case study of a middle-aged man. The four others present an analysis of the case from a psychoanalytic, behavioral, phenomenological, and sociocultural perspective, followed by a panel discussion of the merits of each perspective's view of Otto. Audio Visual Center, Indiana University, Bloomington, IN 47405.

Psychological Birth of the Human Infant (16 mm or video, 48 min.). Margaret S. Mahler narrates her psychoanalytic concept of separation-individuation. The film covers the four subphases of the process (differentiation, practicing, rapprochement, and object constancy) over the first three years of life. Mahler Foundation Film Library, P.O. Box 315, Franklin Lakes, NJ 07417.

"Psychotherapy" from *Discovering Psychology* series (#22) (VHS, color, 30 mins.). The relationships among theory, research, and practice and how treatment of psychological disorders has been influenced by historical, cultural, and social forces. The Annenberg/CPB Collection, Dept. CA94, P.O. Box 2345, S. Burlington, VT 05407-2345; to order, call 1-800-532-7637.

Rollo May on Existential Psychology (16 mm, color, 28 min.). May discusses what existential psychology is and how we give meaning to experience. Concepts covered include will, freedom, being, and anxiety. American Association for Counseling and Development, 5999 Stevenson Avenue, Alexandria, VA 22304.

"The Enlightened Machine" from *The Brain* series (#1) (VHS, color). Covers material from nineteenth century phrenology to current use of microphotography to show how neurotransmitters cross the synaptic gap. The Annenberg/CPB Collection, Dept. CA94, P.O. Box 2345, S. Burlington, VT 05407-2345; to order, call 1-800-532-7637.

Three Approaches to Psychotherapy, Part III: Dr. Albert Ellis (16 mm, 37 min.). Dr. Ellis describes rational-emotive psychotherapy and illustrates by interviewing a patient. Film Rental Library, University of Kansas, Division of Continuing Education, Lawrence, KS 66045.

B. F. Skinner on Behaviorism (VHS, color, 28 mm.). Skinner discusses behavior modification and shaping of human behavior using positive reinforcement. Insight Media. 1-800-233-9910.

Carl Rogers: Part I (VHS, color, 50 mm.). Dr. Rogers discusses his humanistic theories, comparing them to other established theories of the time. Insight Media. 1-800-233-9910.

Conversations with Albert Ellis: Introduction (VHS, color, 30 mm.). Dr. Ellis discusses his theory of rational-emotive therapy (RET). Insight Media. 1-800-233-9910.

Sigmund Freud (VHS, color, 50 mm.). This video covers Freud's life from childhood through most of his adult years. It discusses many of Freud's theories of psychoanalysis and personality development. Insight Media. 1-800-233-9910.

Copyright © Houghton Mifflin Company. All rights reserved

ON THE INTERNET

http://www.apa.org is the site for The American Psychological Association

http://gablab.stanford.edu/brainiac The site is designed to help you learn about fMRI scanning and SPM statistical analysis.

http://www.iret.org is the site for Rational Emotive Therapy, where you can find additional information on Ellis's rational-emotive therapy.

http://www.apsa.org is the American Psychoanalytic Association's Web page

http://www.coedu.usf.edu/behavior/bares.htm is the web site for Behavior Analysis Resources, and provides excellent resources on behaviorism and learning.

Copyright © Houghton Mifflin Company. All rights reserved

CHAPTER 3
Assessment and Classification of Abnormal Behavior

CHAPTER OUTLINE

I. Reliability and validity

1. Reliability: consistent results under same circumstances
2. Validity: test performs function it was intended to
3. Standard administration and standardization sample aid reliability and validity

II. The assessment of abnormal behavior

A. Observations

1. Controlled and naturalistic
2. Problems: check validity of observations when patient is from another culture; reactivity

B. Interviews: affected by professional discipline and theoretical orientation

1. Standardization: degree of structure
2. Errors: information exchange blocked, anxiety in interviewee, interviewer orientation

C. Psychological tests and inventories

1. Projective personality tests
   a. Rorschach technique (inkblots)
   b. Thematic Apperception Test (pictures)
   c. Sentence-completion test
   d. Draw-a-person test
2. Self-report inventories
   a. Minnesota Multiphasic Personality Inventory (MMPI, recently revised into MMPI-2): 567 true-false items; yields scores on ten clinical and three validity scales; pattern analysis)
   b. Beck Depression Inventory (BDI): example of inventory for specific trait or problem
3. Intelligence tests
   a. Wechsler Adult Intelligence Scale (WAIS-III) for adults; WISC-III (for children ages six and older); and WPPSI-R (for ages four to six)
   b. Stanford-Binet Scale: more complicated; gives one IQ score
   c. Controversies: debate re innate intelligence versus cultural/social factors; disagreement re predictive validity; disagreement re criterion variables; inadequacy of current conceptions of IQ tests and intelligence
4. Kaufman Assessment Battery for Children (K-ABC): for wide range of children

Copyright © Houghton Mifflin Company. All rights reserved

     5. Tests for cognitive impairment

       a. Large discrepancy between WAIS verbal and performance IQ

       b. Bender-Gestalt Visual-Motor Test: designs copied

       c. Halstead-Reitan Neuropsychological Test Battery: eleven tests (six or more hours)

       d. Luria-Nebraska Neuropsychological Battery: twelve scales ($2\frac{1}{2}$ hours)

D. Neurological tests

    1. Computerized axial tomography (CAT scan)

    2. Positron emission tomography (PET scan)

    3. Electroencephalogram (EEG)

    4. Magnetic resonance imaging (MRI)

    5. Functional magnetic resonance imaging: high resolution, noninvasive views of neural activity

E. Ethics of assessment: questions of privacy and long-range benefits

    1. Use of computers in assessment

    2. Cultural differences lead to biased assessments

III. The classification of abnormal behavior

A. Problems with early diagnostic classification systems

    1. Reliability

       a. Poor interrater reliability in early DSM editions

       b. Improvements in DSM-III, DSM-IV, and DSM-IV-TR

    2. Validity

       a. Critics question validity of psychiatric classification

B. The current system: DSM-IV-TR

    1. Uses five factors (axes)

       a. Axis I—clinical syndrome and other conditions that may be a focus of clinical attention

       b. Axis II—personality disorders and mental retardation

       c. Axis III—general medical conditions

       d. Axis IV—psychosocial and environmental problems

       e. Axis V—global assessment of function (GAF)

C. DSM-IV mental disorders

    1. Disorders usually first diagnosed in infancy, childhood, or adolescence

    2. Delirium, dementia, amnestic, and other cognitive disorders

    3. Mental disorders due to a general medical condition

    4. Substance-related disorders

    5. Schizophrenia and other psychotic disorders

    6. Mood disorders

    7. Anxiety disorders

    8. Somatoform disorders

    9. Factitious disorders

    10. Dissociative disorders

    11. Sexual and gender identity disorders

Copyright © Houghton Mifflin Company. All rights reserved.

12. Eating disorders

13. Sleep disorders

14. Impulse control disorders

15. Adjustment disorders

16. Personality disorders

D. Evaluation of the DSM classification system

1. Problems: medical emphasis; usefulness; sexist (controversy over premenstrual dysphoric disorder); symptoms more valuable than placement in categories

2. Alternative: behavioral classification scheme (superior to DSM in reliability and validity) but DSM is dominant system

E. Objections to classification and labeling

1. A label can predispose people to interpret all activities of the affected individual as pathological

2. A label may lead others to treat a person differently

3. A label may lead those who are labeled to believe that they do indeed possess such characteristics

4. A label may not provide the precise, functional information that is needed

LEARNING OBJECTIVES

1. Define the term *psychodiagnosis* and describe its functions. (p. 73)

2. Identify the characteristics of good tests, including reliability and validity. Define *reliability*, and differentiate among test-retest, internal, and interrater reliability. Define *validity*, and differentiate among predictive, criterion-related, construct, and content validity. (pp. 73–74)

3. Define *assessment* and discuss its role in clinical psychology. Describe and discuss various psychological assessment techniques and their strengths and limitations, including observation of behavior, clinical interviews, and tests and inventories. (pp. 74–87; Table 3.1)

4. Describe the nature and purposes of projective personality tests, including the Rorschach, Thematic Apperception Test (TAT), sentence-completion test, and draw-a-person test. Discuss the strengths and weaknesses of projective tests. (pp. 77–80)

5. Describe the nature and purposes of self-report inventories, including the Minnesota Multiphasic Personality Inventory (MMPI-2). Discuss the strengths and weaknesses of personality inventories. (pp. 80–82; Figure 3.1)

6. Describe the purposes and characteristics of the Wechsler and Stanford-Binet intelligence tests and the Kaufman Assessment Battery for Children (K-ABC). Discuss the strengths and limitations of these tests. (pp. 82-85)

7. Describe methods for assessing cognitive impairments due to brain damage (*organicity*), including the WAIS-III, Bender-Gestalt Visual-Motor Test, Halstead-Reitan Neuropsychological Test Battery, and Luria-Nebraska Neuropsychological Battery. (pp. 85-86)

8. Describe neurological procedures for detecting brain damage, including CAT and PET scans, EEGs, MRIs, and functional MRIs. (pp. 86–87)

9. Discuss ethical issues involved in assessment, particularly how cultural differences may influence clinical judgments. (pp. 87–89; Critical Thinking)

10. Explain the goals of classifying abnormal behaviors and review the history of classification systems. Discuss how validity problems have been raised and dealt with. (pp. 90-91)

Copyright © Houghton Mifflin Company. All rights reserved.

11. Describe the characteristics of the DSM-IV-TR, including its five axes, the broad categories of mental disorders, and how the DSM-IV-TR places diagnosis in a cultural context. (pp. 91–9; Mental Health and Society)

12. Discuss the objections to the DSM classification system and the arguments supporting its use. (pp. 94–98)

13. Describe four problems associated with classification and labeling and the research related to these problems. Discuss how the findings of Rosenhan (1973) relate to the impact of labeling. (pp. 98–100; Mental Health and Society)

CLASSROOM TOPICS FOR LECTURE AND DISCUSSION

1. Students need to understand that a diagnosis has many long-lasting implications. Incorrectly labeling someone with a psychiatric diagnosis has a greater stigmatizing effect than mislabeling a person with a medical diagnosis. The instructor can illustrate this with a simplified version of signal detection theory. Put the following diagram on the board:

Actual State of Affairs

Clinician's Diagnosis	Person Is Sick	Person Is Not Sick
Person is sick	Hit	False alarm
Person is not sick	Miss	Correct rejection (another kind of hit)

First, explain the terms *hits*, *misses*, and *false alarms* and then ask the class to consider this scenario: An adult comes to a general-practice physician (GP) complaining of headaches, blurred vision, and nausea. The GP is not sure whether these symptoms are signs of a peculiar flu or, at worst, a brain tumor. Assuming that the patient is sick with something serious (and hoping that he or she isn't), the GP sends the patient to the hospital for tests. When the tests show nothing and the symptoms go away, we have a false alarm; everyone is happy and relieved, and no harm has been done. Physicians are trained to be on the safe side and consider people sick even if they aren't.

Now ask the class to consider this scenario: An adult comes to a psychologist complaining of voices that say "thud" and "empty" (the same symptoms Rosenhan's pseudopatients used). The psychologist isn't sure what's wrong. What are the effects of assuming that the person may have schizophrenia and sending the person to a mental hospital for a psychological evaluation (the equivalent of medical tests)? What happens if there is a false alarm? This exercise will help students see that what is "conservative" diagnostic practice in medicine can be dangerous in psychology.

2. Instructors may want to expand on the text's treatment of reliability and validity and the relationship between the two by subdividing reliability into internal consistency, test-retest, and interrater. You can explain the first two categories in terms of the evaluation method an instructor uses for teaching abnormal psychology. Ask students how they would feel if questions unrelated to course material (What is the capital of New Jersey? What is the shape of benzene?) appeared on their first exam. All items should contribute to the test's total score; otherwise error is introduced. Suggest to students that it is a good idea for exams to evaluate them repeatedly at about the same level. For example, how much faith could they put in exams if on the first one they got an A, on the second they got a D, and on the third they got a B? This discussion should lead them to think about changes in study habits, motivation, and test content. Point out that psychologists have the difficult task of measuring something

Copyright © Houghton Mifflin Company. All rights reserved.

that is in flux. Then ask them what would happen if they could take precisely the same test over again. This question should start discussion on invalidation of psychological tests. Finally, interrater reliability should be discussed in relation to some physical attribute such as attractiveness or neatness. Ask the class to rate you (or some celebrity) on a scale from 1 to 10 on the attribute. If there is disagreement on ratings, how useful are any of them? Conclude with a discussion of training people to rate consistently; perhaps this is a goal of graduate training.

You can also explain validity in terms of classroom evaluations. To what extent do consistent scores on in-class tests reflect actual knowledge? Ask students why they think the assumption that "consistent data equal useful data" is fallacious. By what criteria do we judge that an A in a course really measures what we want to measure? Finally, a helpful way to show the relationship between reliability and validity is to use Venn diagrams. A large circle labeled *Reliability* should have a smaller circle labeled *Validity* within its borders.

3.   Students are often interested in the methods of administering and interpreting psychological tests. Objective and projective tests should be highlighted and demystified (without invalidating them). A short self-report inventory such as the Crowne-Marlowe Social Desirability Scale can provide insight into objective tests. Students can begin to see the difficulties of developing tests that cannot be faked, but that measure what they are supposed to. In this regard the Crowne-Marlowe is particularly useful, as is discussion of the validity scales on the MMPI. An abbreviated version of the Crowne-Marlowe scale is provided in a handout. Faking is also important when you discuss projectives. You could draw several symmetrical blobs on the board and ask students to write down what they see in each. Ask them how they could fake their responses and whether their responses would be different if they knew the responses would be made public.

Given the doubts about testing that this discussion and the text's information might suggest, you should balance this picture with information about test batteries. The student needs to know that single tests are never the sole determinant of a diagnosis and that hypotheses are continually supported, modified, and rejected by test, interview, and observational data.

4.   The new version of the Minnesota Multiphasic Personality Inventory (MMPI-2) represents the first overhaul in over 50 years of the most used objective personality test. The MMPI-2 has been normed on a much larger and more representative sample than the original MMPI, which used as its normative sample 600 visitors to the University of Minnesota hospitals in 1940. Another improvement is that separate adolescent norms were used in creating the MMPI-2. The new version also generates, in addition to the 10 clinical scales, 15 content scales that assess self-esteem, cynicism, family problems, and anxiety, among other issues.

Although the new edition uses improved norms and may measure new clinically important concepts, some of the problems with the old test have gone unsolved and some new problems may have been added (Helmes & Reddon, 1993). The MMPI and MMPI-2 are very long tests, using 567 items. However, they are inefficient because only 383 items are actually scored on the clinical and validity scales, whereas those items making up these scales are scored on an average of 2.07 times. Considerable overlap occurs in the clinical scales, and the tests still remain to be cross-validated. The complexity of using pattern analysis on the old version is retained in the MMPI-2. Finally, the developers of the MMPI-2 curiously used a 704-item experimental version of the new test on the normative sample, not the actual 567-item final version. As Helmes and Reddon (1993) mention, old users of the test will not be dissuaded by the MMPI-2, but this celebrated test missed an opportunity to address old problems.

Source: Helmes, E., & Reddon, J. R. (1993). A perspective on developments in assessing psychopathology: A critical review of the MMPI and MMPI-2. *Psychological Bulletin, 113,* 453–471.

Copyright © Houghton Mifflin Company. All rights reserved.

Internet Site: http://assessments.ncs.com/assessments/tests/mmpi_2.htm. Contains information on the MMPI-2.

5.   Accurately reading nonverbal communication is a vital part of assessment, especially in interviewing. Cultural and gender differences in nonverbal communication styles are potential reasons for weak reliability and validity in assessment. One form of nonverbal communication is the degree of personal space people require when communicating. The study of personal space is called *proxemics*. Each culture has norms for the "personal bubble," the comfortable space between us and others. In all cultures, the personal bubble is much smaller for people with whom we have intimate relationships and much larger for strangers. However, Americans have a larger bubble than people from Middle Eastern or Latin American cultures. In the United States, 4 to 12 feet separate us from most of our coworkers, acquaintances, and friends in face-to-face meetings. This "social distance zone" can be violated at crowded parties, in elevators, and in waiting lines. We make great efforts not to touch or to excuse touching in these situations. In elevators, we take pains not to make eye contact. In Middle Eastern or Latin American cultures, the social distance zone is often several feet less. Since this issue is rarely talked about, the European or American diagnostician may find the Arab or Latin client to be aggressive or disrespectful if he or she stands too close while the client may see the American as being aloof and disinterested.

You can illustrate the personal bubble idea by walking up to a student in the first row while you make these comments. You will probably get nonverbal messages of discomfort as you break the 4-foot barrier: giggles, angling of the torso away from you, and so on.

In spite of gender differences, the ways women and men send and receive nonverbal messages overlap considerably. Small differences exist, however, and may contribute to the misreading of clients' communication. For example, women are more likely than men to display messages that convey warmth and submission and less likely to engage in touching. Women are also more likely to adopt "closed" body postures—sitting up straight, having both feet on the floor, and keeping their arms close to the body. Men are more likely to have "open" postures—their backs angled back in a chair and one ankle crossed over the thigh of the other leg. This posture looks more relaxed. Gender differences probably relate to status differences. High-status individuals tend to communicate nonverbally that they are dominant (touching is a means of showing higher status) and relaxed in the situation. Women are less likely than men to have experienced high status. Women are more likely to make eye contact while speaking and listening. This difference, too, is probably connected to status issues since low-status individuals gaze longer at a high-status individual than the other way around. However, when eye gaze goes on too long, it is perceived as staring, a dominant cue. Women stare less than men. It is also interesting that cultures vary on the meaning of eye contact. Native Americans are taught that making eye contact is a sign of disrespect.

Copyright © Houghton Mifflin Company. All rights reserved.

Finally, children have much smaller personal bubbles than adults and are largely unaware of how they may invade others' space. Girls have greater interest in and awareness of nonverbal messages than boys have. Girls are consistently more accurate than boys are in interpreting others' nonverbal signals, that is, in reading emotional states and intentions. The diagnostician who is unaware of cultural, gender, and age differences in nonverbal communications is likely to make many unfounded judgments about the personality of interviewees.

Copyright © Houghton Mifflin Company. All rights reserved.

HANDOUT FOR CLASSROOM TOPIC 3: EXAMPLE OF SOCIAL DESIRABILITY ITEMS

The following items come from the Crowne-Marlowe Social Desirability Scale, a research instrument that has been used to identify an individual's tendency to present himself or herself in a socially approved light. Answering True to the first five items and False to the next five indicates a person who is high in social desirability. Consider how the validity of psychological assessment based on self-report inventories would be jeopardized in such a person. How would self-report inventories need to compensate for such a tendency?

1. I never hesitate to go out of my way to help someone in trouble.

2. I have never intensely disliked anyone.

3. I am always careful about my manner of dress.

4. No matter who I am talking to, I am always a good listener.

5. I don't find it particularly difficult to get along with loud-mouthed, obnoxious people.

6. It is sometimes hard for me to go on with my work if I am not encouraged.

7. I sometimes feel resentful when I don't get my way.

8. Sometimes I feel like rebelling against people in authority even though I know they are right.

9. I sometimes try to get even, rather than forgive and forget.

10. Sometimes I feel like smashing things.

Copyright © Houghton Mifflin Company. All rights reserved.

CLASSROOM DEMONSTRATIONS

1.   This in-class exercise can illustrate the behavioral approach to assessment and, at the same time, may assist students in evaluating their study habits. Ask students to individually assess their study habits on the basis of the components of the behavioral classification system. By using the Handout for Demonstration 1, students will have a better understanding of the frequency and quality of their study behavior (behavioral repertoire), the antecedent conditions (stimulus controls) that facilitate or impede studying, and the consequences that increase or decrease studying frequency (incentive systems). In addition, they can examine the self-reinforcement or self-punishment components in their behavior pattern (aversive self-reinforcing systems).

After you have allowed time for their individual assessments, ask the students what they think is the most common impediment to more frequent or higher quality studying. List some of these impediments on the board and categorize them in terms of the behavioral classification system. Ask students for suggested "treatments." This demonstration should illustrate how behaviorists use monitoring and functional analysis to direct therapy.

2.   Conducting an interview before the class can illustrate the various types of interviews that exist and the sources of assessment error in interviewing that Kleinmuntz delineates (the interviewee, the interviewer, and the relationship). A classroom volunteer or a colleague should be contacted before class. In the first interview, use a structured format, as in Spitzer's evaluation form (for example, What kind of moods have you been in recently? What kind of things do you worry about? How often do you feel tense or nervous? When you are nervous, do you react physically [nausea, diarrhea, etc.]?). Read the questions from a clipboard and record responses with a pencil while making little eye contact with the interviewee. Then ask the interviewee to discuss how this interview felt. Ask the class how they would have reacted to such an interviewer.

In a second interview with the same person, ask more Rogerian questions and ask for reflections of feeling (for example, Can you tell me what concerns you today? You seem to feel _____ about that.) while making appropriate eye contact and leaning forward in the chair. Allow the interview to be guided by the responses of the interviewee. Then ask the interviewee to comment on how this interview felt. Ask the students for their feelings. What are the pros and cons of doing unstructured interviews? To what extent are reactions based on the nonverbal behavior of the interviewer and not the structure?

3.   If drawing a person (Machover's Draw-a-Person test) is a method for assessing personality, what about doodling? Pass out sheets of unlined paper and ask your students to doodle on the page. Ask them not to draw a figure and reassure them that drawing ability is not important. Give them five minutes or so, and then collect the pages and shuffle them. Hand back the shuffled pages.

Copyright © Houghton Mifflin Company. All rights reserved.

Use the following scoring scheme or make up your own. Students should give one point for each occurrence of the following in their doodles:

Squares	masculine
Circles	feminine
Arrows or points	aggression
Eyes	paranoid
Houses	security needs
Small doodles	depression
Dark shading	confidence
Light shading	tentativeness
Highly symmetrical and detailed	obsessive
Half completed	easily distracted

Ask students for additional scoring ideas. Discuss their difficulties in scoring the doodles. You will probably find that many doodles are "unscorable" because their features do not overlap with the scoring classifications. This should spark discussion on the reliability of projective tests, since scoring them tends to be subjective and somewhat inconsistent. Mention that the scoring system above reflects a psychoanalytic viewpoint and tends to find pathology in personality. Ask students how much validity they feel this kind of test would have. Do they believe in handwriting analysis?

Finally, discuss with them the methods by which doodle testing could become more reliable and valid. The following points should be made: (1) the need to form a large normative sample; (2) the development of a standardized way of administering the test; (3) a classification and scoring scheme that includes the most common types of doodles; (4) correlational statistics to determine the interrater reliability of classifying and scoring doodles; (5) the statistical identification of scoring patterns that discriminate one personality from another; (6) the use of an existing, reliable indicator of personality with which to correlate doodling scores; and (7) the cross-validation of findings with another sample. There are still other phases in the development of a psychometrically strong test, but this activity will give students an appreciation for what goes into valid assessments.

Source: Adapted from *Annotated Instructor's Manual* for Morris, *Psychology*, 6/e by T. F. Pettijohn. Copyright © 1986. Used by permission of Prentice-Hall.

4.   As the cognitive approach becomes stronger in abnormal psychology, so will cognitive assessment. This out-of-class assignment will help students appreciate the prospects and problems concerning cognitive assessment. One or two class periods before you discuss assessment, distribute the handout for this demonstration. Instruct students to complete each section at the end of each day. Encourage them to be honest and thorough. Assure them that you will not collect these pages but that they will be used in a classroom discussion.

On the day you discuss assessment, ask students to consult their monitoring sheet(s). Ask for a show of hands from those who recorded at least one interaction that was negative (embarrassing, anger- or anxiety-provoking). Ask for a show of hands if at least one interaction was positive (joyful, reassuring, relaxed). If there is bias in the conversations we choose to recall, it will affect any such monitoring project. According to Beck, anxious individuals are likely to monitor and have automatic thoughts about anxiety-provoking incidents, whereas depressed individuals are more likely to monitor thoughts about failure (Beck & Clark, 1988). The bias in recollections may thus assist diagnosis. In fact, automatic thoughts questionnaires have been developed for adults (Hollon & Kendall, 1980) and children (Stark et al., 1986).

Copyright © Houghton Mifflin Company. All rights reserved.

Discuss with students the types of thoughts they had during and after conversations. Some students will "speak" positively about themselves ("You were very clever in that conversation." "That was really neat!"); many others will be more negative ("Why can't you think of anything to say?" "I need to keep my mouth shut.").

Ask students if the types of thoughts (positive versus negative) were different during the study period. Studying, which is less interpersonal, may provoke more thoughts involving ability or intellectual challenge than ones having to do with embarrassment or other emotions. This topic could spark a discussion of the types of thoughts we have about ourselves in different situations.

Finally, the representativeness and accuracy of thought monitoring is important. In cardiology, monitoring of heart rhythms has been improved by giving patients portable electrocardiograms so that continuous monitoring or monitoring in specific situations (such as when the heart skips a beat) is possible. In psychological research, teenagers have been asked to write down their emotions when signaled by a beeper they wore. Results showed large and frequent mood swings, sometimes within the space of minutes (Csikszentmihalyi & Larson, 1984). A similar use of technology could help psychotherapy clients monitor their thoughts and the situations in which they occur.

Sources: Beck, A. T., & Clark, D. A. (1988). Anxiety and depression: An information processing perspective. *Anxiety Research, 1,* 23–36.

Csikszentmihalyi, M., & Larson, R. (1984). Being adolescent: Conflict and growth in the teenage years. New York: Basic Books.

Hollom S. D., & Kendall, P. C. (1980). Cognitive self-statements in depression: Development of an automatic thoughts questionnaire. *Cognitive Therapy and Research, 4,* 383–395.

Stark, K. D., Best, L., & Adam, T. (1986). The automatic thoughts questionnaire for children: The development and validation of a measure of depressive cognitions in children. Unpublished manuscript, University of Texas, Austin.

5.   This demonstration will get students thinking about matching assessment tools with specific referral questions. First, provide a handout listing the assessment tools available to the clinician, including

Controlled observations in clinic or laboratory
Naturalistic observations in office, home, school
Logs kept by parents, friends, the client
Interviews (structured and unstructured)
Projective personality tests (Rorschach, TAT, sentence-completion, draw-a-person)
Self-report inventories (MMPI-2, Beck Depression Inventory)
Intelligence tests (WAIS-R, WISC-R, WPPSI; Stanford-Binet; K-ABC)
Tests for organicity (Bender-Gestalt, Halstead-Reitan, Luria-Nebraska)
Neurological tests (CAT and PET scans, EEG, MRI)

Divide the class into small groups. Each group will be presented with several hypothetical cases. The task is to decide how to best assess the individual. Instruct group members to use any of the list of assessment tools and be able to explain how that tool helps in the assessment. Caution them against "throwing in the kitchen sink," since it is unethical to subject individuals to invalid test procedures. Excessive testing is also costly in time and money.

Allow 15 minutes for groups to discuss the cases. One person in each group should record the assessment tools agreed upon and the reasons for using each. What, exactly, will the assessment devices

Copyright © Houghton Mifflin Company. All rights reserved.

discover that is relevant to the referral question? The recorder should tell the rest of the class what the group decided.

Here are satisfactory responses for hypothetical case #1: Observe the child in school and at home as well as in the diagnostician's office. Try to simulate school situations (following instructions, repetitive tasks). Note his responses when there are noises or other distractions and when there is silence. Give intelligence test (WISC-R or Stanford-Binet) to determine intellectual ability. Have parents and teachers keep logs of his behavior over time. Ask the boy what he thinks is going on (unstructured interview).

Satisfactory responses for hypothetical case #2 are the following: observation and logs in work environment to assess level of impairment at work; MMPI-2 and projective tests (Rorschach and TAT) to assess man's personality; Beck Depression Inventory to assess level of depression; interview man and his wife (separately and together) in unstructured interview to get their understanding of the problems and to observe their behavior; WAIS-R or Luria-Nebraska test battery to assess degree of cognitive impairment; neurological tests such as PET scan and MRI to assess any brain damage.

6.   Bring a copy of the DSM-IV-TR to class and point out the axes approach it uses. If you have access to other editions bring them to class and read the descriptions of disorders that the students would like to understand from different versions. You could use an overhead transparency to keep a list of the differences among editions. Are the criteria similar to what students thought they would be? Discuss how the DSM-IV-TR arrived at these specific criteria and acknowledge the many controversial classifications that still exist.

Internet Site: http://behavenet.com/capsules/disorders/dsm4Trclassification.htm. A site that consists of terms and definitions of DSM criteria.

7.   Assign your students to collect questionnaires from popular magazines or self-help books. Many students will have taken these "pop" psychology items in their favorite magazines. On an overhead transparency, compare items from different sources. Then compare these items with standardized personality inventories such as the MMPI. Lead a discussion on the differences and why they are important.

Internet Site: http://www.apa.org/books/431615A.htm. An APA site that reviews Butcher's guide to the MMPI-2.

Copyright © Houghton Mifflin Company. All rights reserved.

HANDOUT FOR DEMONSTRATION 1:
STUDY BEHAVIOR ASSESSMENT EXERCISE

This exercise is designed to help you assess your own studying behavior. Please be as honest as possible.

For each of the last five days, remember and record the following information about your studying behavior: how long you studied, the quality of the studying time (on a scale from 1 to 10), where you studied, how you felt before and after studying, and the activity in which you engaged immediately after studying.

Day	Length of Time You Studied	Quality Rating (1–10)	Place	Feelings Before (+ or –)	Feelings After (+ or –)

Copyright © Houghton Mifflin Company. All rights reserved.

1. Do any particular situations typically precede high-quality studying?

    Describe.

2. Do any particular situations typically precede poor-quality studying?

    Describe.

3. How are your feelings, before and after, related to studying?

    Describe.

4. What kind of immediate rewards might you use to increase the quantity and quality of studying?

    Describe.

5. While you are studying do thoughts go through your head that reduce your ability to concentrate?

    Describe.

Copyright © Houghton Mifflin Company. All rights reserved.

HANDOUT FOR DEMONSTRATION 4: MONITORING YOUR THOUGHTS

Over the next two days, monitor your thoughts during interpersonal interactions and while studying. At the end of each day, think of a specific conversation—with a close friend, an acquaintance, or even a stranger. As accurately as possible, record the topic of the conversation, what you were thinking while it was occurring, and what you said to yourself immediately after it was over. Also, at the end of each day, think about a particular study period and, as accurately as possible, record what you were studying, and what you were thinking during and after studying.

Day 1	Topic of the Conversation	What You Thought During	What You Thought After

	Subject You Were Studying	What You Thought During	What You Thought After

Copyright © Houghton Mifflin Company. All rights reserved.

	Topic of the Conversation	What You Thought During	What You Thought After
Day 2			

	Subject You Were Studying	What You Thought During	What You Thought After

Copyright © Houghton Mifflin Company. All rights reserved.

HANDOUT *A* FOR DEMONSTRATION 5:
LISTING OF PSYCHOLOGICAL ASSESSMENT TOOLS

1. Controlled observations in clinic or laboratory

2. Naturalistic observations in office, home, school

3. Logs kept by parents, friends, the client

4. Structured interview

5. Unstructured interview

6. Projective personality tests (Rorschach, TAT, sentence-completion, draw-a-person)

7. Self-report inventories (MMPI-2, Beck Depression Inventory)

8. Wechsler's tests (WAIS-III, WISC-III, WPPSI-III)

9. Neuropsychological tests for organicity (Bender-Gestalt, Halstead-Reitan, Luria-Nebraska)

10. Neurological tests (CAT and PET-scans, EEG, MRI, fMRI)

Copyright © Houghton Mifflin Company. All rights reserved.

HANDOUT *B* FOR DEMONSTRATION 5: HYPOTHETICAL CASES NEEDING ASSESSMENT

Hypothetical case 1

A ten-year-old boy who seems very intelligent to his parents and teacher is getting very low grades. He is frequently inattentive to the teacher and seems "spaced out." There is no history of trauma to the head and no indications of serious mental disorder. It is not clear whether his problems occur solely in the classroom or elsewhere, too. The boy and his parents come to you for an assessment.

Discuss and list relevant assessment tools.

Hypothetical case 2

A 57-year-old man with a history of heavy drinking is frequently sad, angry, and anxious. His work performance has suffered—he is forgetful, disorganized, and low in energy. The man's doctor wonders if the drinking has impaired his cognitive abilities; his wife wonders if he is simply very depressed. The man himself feels that he has lived his life for everyone but himself. Your assessment should respond to the concerns of the client, his doctor, and wife.

Discuss and list relevant assessment tools.

Copyright © Houghton Mifflin Company. All rights reserved.

SELECTED READINGS

Burke, M. J., & Normand, J. (1987). Computerized psychological testing: Overview and critique. *Professional Psychology: Research and Practice, 18*, 42–51.

Dana, R. H. (1993). *Multicultural assessment perspectives for professional psychology.* Boston: Allyn & Bacon.

Matarazzo, J. D. (1992). Psychological testing and assessment in the 21st century. *American Psychologist, 47*, 1007–1018.

Pope, B. (1979). *The mental health interview: Research and application.* New York: Pergamon Press.

Rosenhan, D. (1973). On being sane in insane places. *Science, 179*, 250-258. p.253.

Widiger, T. A., & Trull, T. J. (1991). Diagnosis and clinical assessment. *Annual Review of Psychology, 42*, 109–133.

VIDEO RESOURCES

Administration of Projective Tests (16 mm, 19 min.). The film demonstrates TAT and sentence-completion tests. Psychological Cinema Register, Pennsylvania State University, University Park, PA 16802.

Assessment (VHS or Beta video, color, 30 min.). This film uses the case of *Larry P. v. Riles* to illustrate cultural bias in IQ testing and recent research on reducing bias in testing. Indiana University Radio and Television Services, Indiana University, Bloomington, IN 47401.

Behavioral Interviewing with Couples (16 mm, color, 14 min.). Interviewing techniques from a behavioral perspective during initial counseling sessions. Research Press, Box 317740, Champaign, IL 61820.

Context Analysis of Family Interviews, Part I (16 mm, color, 28 min.). Analysis of an interview between professionals and a family. Concerned with visible and audible behaviors as they relate to one another in a pattern. Psychological Cinema Register, Pennsylvania State University, University Park, PA 16802.

"Looking at Abnormal Behavior" from *The World of Abnormal Psychology* (video, color, 60 min.). This segment explores the definitions of abnormal behavior and explains how psychologists employ interviews and testing to assess individuals. The Annenberg/CPB Collection, Dept. CA94, P.O. Box 2345, S. Burlington, VT 05407-2345; to order, call 1-800-532-7637.

"Measuring Intelligence" from *The Psychology Show* videodisc series (3:11). Houghton Mifflin Company.

Personality (16 mm, color, 30 min.). A college student undergoes an assessment by clinical psychologists, including a number of traditional tests (MMPI, WAIS, TAT). The student's way of viewing himself and the perceptions of his parents, roommate, and girlfriend are included, too. The student is impressed with the accuracy of the assessment. CRM McGraw-Hill Films, 110 Fifteenth Street, Del Mar, CA 92014.

"Testing and Intelligence" from *Discovering Psychology* series (#16) (video, color, 30 min.). Psychological testing reveals how values are assigned to different abilities, behaviors, and personalities. The Annenberg/CPB Collection, Dept. CA94, P.O. Box 2345, S. Burlington, VT 05407-2345; to order, call 1-800-532-7637.

Basic Interviewing Skills (VHS, color, 51 mm.). Focuses on the five basic skills needed to interview a client. Insight Media.

Copyright © Houghton Mifflin Company. All rights reserved.

The Clinical Psychologist (VHS, color, 24 mm.). Shows an initial assessment using both formal and informal methods of assessment. Insight Media.

ON THE INTERNET

http://www.apa.org is The American Psychological Association home page.

http://www.behavenet.com/capsules/disorders/dsm4TRclassification.htm   This site contains terms and definitions of DSM criteria.

http://www.ericae.net is the Web site for the ERIC Clearinghouse on Assessment and Evaluation, which gives you information about assessment of all types.

http://www.apa.org/science/lib.html is an APA site that consists of terms and definitions included in the DSM series This site defines and describes all behaviors that are considered to be abnormal by the American Psychiatric Association.

Copyright © Houghton Mifflin Company. All rights reserved.

CHAPTER 4

The Scientific Method
in Abnormal Psychology

CHAPTER OUTLINE

I. Reasons for skepticism when reading research

    A. Nonreplicated results, many examples offered

II. The scientific method in clinical research (tests hypotheses and uses theory)

    A. Characteristics of clinical research

        1. Potential for self-correction

        2. Hypothesizing relationships

        3. Operational definitions

        4. Reliability and validity of measures and observations

        5. Base rates

            a. If high, investigator may mistakenly assume phenomenon causes disorder

        6. Statistical versus clinical significance

III. Experiments

    A. The experimental group: exposed to independent variable

    B. The control group: similar in every way to experimental, but no independent variable

    C. The placebo group: controls for expectations

    D. Additional concerns in clinical research

        1. Blind design: clinicians do not know purpose of research study

        2. Double-blind design: neither subjects nor the individual researchers know experimental conditions

IV. Correlations: measure extent to which variables co-vary

    A. Correlational coefficient

    B. Does not imply causation

    C. Problems with Sanders and Giolas (1991) correlational study

V. Analogue studies

    A. Simulate real situation under controlled conditions

    B. Give insight into behavior but only an approximation of real life

VI. Field studies—events recorded in natural environment

    A. Primary technique is observation

    B. Requires training and self-discipline

VII. Single-subject studies

Copyright © Houghton Mifflin Company. All rights reserved

A.   Idiographic approach: in-depth study of one person; valuable for clinical work

B.   The case study: clinical data on one person

C.   Single-participant experiment: person's own behavior acts as control condition

VIII.   Biological research strategies

A.   Human Genome Project

B.   Genetic linkage studies

C.   Biological markers: biological indicators that may or may not cause disorder

D.   Other concepts in biological research

1.   Iatrogenic effects: unintended changes in behavior due to treatment; hypnosis by therapist may create memories

2.   Penetrance: degree to which genetic characteristic is seen in people carrying a gene associated with it

3.   Pathognomonic: degree to which symptom is specific to a disorder

4.   Biological challenge tests: monitor behavior change after presentation of a specific chemical

IX.   Epidemiological and other forms of research

A.   Survey

B.   Longitudinal

C.   Historical

D.   Twin studies

E.   Treatment outcome studies

F.   Treatment process studies

G.   Program evaluation

H.   Epidemiological research

1.   Prevalence: number of cases of disorder in population

2.   Incidence: number of new cases in a specific period

X.   Ethical issues in research: balancing harm to participants versus benefit to humanity

A.   Withholding treatment from controls

B.   Deceiving subjects

C.   Creating discomfort or embarrassment

D.   Using detrimental treatment with participants

E.   Inducing pain in animal subjects

F.   Bias in diagnosis

LEARNING OBJECTIVES

1.   Explain the roles of skepticism and replication in science. Discuss the current status of scientific "facts" in abnormal psychology that have received subsequent investigation, including facilitated communication and the identification of an alcoholism gene. (pp. 103–104; Critical Thinking)

2.   Discuss the characteristics of the scientific method in clinical research, including the proper stating of hypotheses, operational definitions, and the need for reliable and valid measures and observations. (pp. 105–106; Mental Health & Society)

Copyright © Houghton Mifflin Company. All rights reserved.

3. Describe the concepts of base rates, statistical significance, and clinical significance. (pp. 106-109)

4. Identify the components of a basic experiment, and describe the need for placebos, blind and double-blind research designs. (pp. 109–112)

5. Discuss the characteristics of correlational studies and their strengths and limitations, specifically their ambiguous conclusions with respect to causality. Use the Sanders and Giolas (1991) study to discuss how correlational research can be improved. (pp. 112–115)

6. Describe analogue and field studies, and discuss their strengths and limitations. (pp. 115–116)

7. Define the nomothetic and idiographic orientations toward research. Discuss the characteristics and limitations of case studies and single-participant experiment designs. (pp. 116–118)

8. Discuss the biological research strategies, including genetic linkage studies, biological markers, iatrogenic effects, genetic penetrance, pathognomonic symptoms, and biological challenge tests. (pp. 118–120; Critical Thinking)

9. Describe various research strategies used in the study of abnormal behavior, including epidemiological research. Differentiate between prevalence and incidence. (pp. 120–122)

10. Discuss the ethical issues in conducting research and the American Psychological Association's guiding principles on ethics, including the use of animals, and research with culturally diverse populations. (pp. 122–123)

CLASSROOM TOPICS FOR LECTURE AND DISCUSSION

1.   The word *Experiment* is frequently misused. It is important to clarify the term's use so that students will understand that *experiment* is not a synonym for "research." The concepts of independent and dependent variables are often difficult for students to master. A good way to teach these concepts is to state that every experimental hypothesis is an "if, then" statement. The independent variable fills in the blank after the "if," and the dependent variable fills in the blank after the "then." In other words, experiments tend to be titled "The effects of (independent variable) on (dependent variable)."

Correlations, on the other hand, involve hypotheses that read, "As X goes up, Y goes up/down." Two factors are presumed to be related to each other in a particular way, but the assumption of causality is missing. Correlational studies tend to be titled "The relationship between X and Y" (when neither factor is an independent variable) or at least fail to include language that indicates an independent variable.

To test students on this concept, read the titles of several recent articles from the *Journal of Abnormal Psychology* or *Journal of Consulting and Clinical Psychology*. A handout of appropriate titles is included. Ask students whether or not they think there was an independent variable. Have them identify the dependent variables. After they have speculated on the nature of these studies, distribute a summary (the abstract) from the article, provided below.

Source: Jeffrey, R. W., & Wing, R. R. (1995). Long-term effects of interventions for weight loss using food provision and monetary incentives. *Journal of Consulting and Clinical Psychology, 63,* 793–796.

> One hundred and seventy-seven men and women who had participated in an eighteen-month trial of behavioral interventions involving food provision and financial incentives were examined twelve months later. Food provision, but not financial incentives, led to better weight loss than standard behavior treatment during the eighteen-month trial, but over twelve additional months of no-treatment follow-up, all treated groups gained weight, maintained only slightly better weight losses than a no-treatment control group, and did not differ from each other. [The study illustrates an experiment in which food provision and monetary incentives were independent variables and weight loss was the dependent variable. It also illustrates a therapy outcome study.]

Copyright © Houghton Mifflin Company. All rights reserved.

Source: King, C. A., Radpour, L., Naylor, M. W., Segal, H. G., et al. (1995). Parents' marital functioning and adolescent psychotherapy. *Journal of Clinical and Consulting Psychology, 63,* 749–753.

Parents' marital functioning and adolescent psychotherapy were investigated in two studies. The first study compared parents' marital satisfaction, conflict over child rearing, affective communication, and traditional role orientation in matched samples of psychiatric inpatient and control-group adolescents. The second study examined associations between specific dimensions of marital functioning and adolescent depression severity, suicidal ideation, and social adjustment in a larger sample of adolescent inpatients. In Study 1, parents of inpatients reported less marital satisfaction and more conflicts over child rearing than parents of control-group adolescents reported. In Study 2, marital conflicts over child rearing were associated with a less active or involved farther-adolescent relationship and more severe school behavior and spare time problems. Marital functioning was not associated with depression severity or suicidal ideation. [Although there are two groups in Study 1, both studies are correlational because subjects were not randomly assigned to conditions—people were not placed in inpatient care randomly. The second study is more clearly an illustration of a correlational study relating marital functioning to childrens' problems.]

Source: Seguin, J. R., Pihl, R. O., Harden, P. W., Tremblay, R. E., et al. (1995). Cognitive and neuropsychological characteristics of physically aggressive boys. *Journal of Abnormal Psychology, 104,* 614–624.

Cognitive-neuropsychological tests were given to adolescent boys (N = 177) to investigate processes associated with physical aggression. Factor analysis yielded four factors representing verbal learning, incidental spatial learning, tactile-lateral ability, and executive functions. Physical aggression was assessed at ages 6, 10, 11, 12, and 13, and three groups were created: stable aggressive, unstable aggressive, and nonaggressive. The authors found main effects for only the executive functions factor—nonaggressive boys performed better than stable or unstable aggressive boys performed. [This study is a longitudinal, correlational study because no variable under the control of the experimenter was introduced. Executive functions, those dealing with planning and self-control, were associated with aggression.]

Source: Sutker, P. B., Davis, J. M., Uddo, M., & Ditta, S. R. (1995). War zone stress, personal resources, and posttraumatic stress disorder in Persian Gulf War returnees. *Journal of Abnormal Psychology, 104,* 444–452.

Posttraumatic stress disorder (PTSD) can occur subsequent to war stress, but not all troops are negatively affected. A discriminant function model was used to study associations between personal and environmental resources and psychological outcomes subsequent to war zone stress. Among 775 Persian Gulf War exposed troops, two subsets were identified: 97 returnees with PTSD diagnoses and 484 who had no psychological distress. Personality hardiness commitment, avoidance coping, and perceived family cohesion emerged as consistent predictors of PTSD diagnosis. [This study is a correlational study because neither war zone experiences nor personal resources could be manipulated by the researcher. The two groups that formed (those with PTSD and those with no distress) can be compared. This research design is frequently used in abnormal psychology, but it still does not fit the formula for a true experiment.]

Source: Telch, M. J., Schmidt, N. B., Jaimez, T. L, Jacquin, K. M., et al. (1995). Impact of cognitive-behavioral treatment on quality of life in panic disorder patients. *Journal of Consulting and Clinical Psychology, 63,* 823–830.

Panic disorder (PD) is associated with significant social and health consequences. This study examined the impact of treatment on PD patients' quality of life. Patients (N = 156) meeting DSM-III-R criteria for PD with agoraphobia were randomly assigned to group cognitive behavioral

Copyright © Houghton Mifflin Company. All rights reserved.

treatment (CBT) or a delayed-treatment control. An assessment battery measuring the major clinical features of PD as well as quality of life was administered at baseline, posttreatment (week 9), and six-month follow-up. Compared with delayed-treatment control participants, CBT participants showed significant reductions in impairment that were maintained at follow-up. [This study is a true experiment because subjects were randomly assigned to treatment and control conditions; it is also an illustration of an outcome study.]

Internet Site: http://www.ats.ucla.edu/stat/spss is UCLA's Academic Technology Services, which provides resources to help learn and use SPSS.

2.   Operational definitions get some space in the text, but sampling does not. To a considerable degree, the usefulness of psychological research depends on the quality of sampling. Note that research is always an endeavor that balances the practical against the ideal. In abnormal psychology, the difficulty of obtaining large and representative samples is, by definition, much harder than in most other fields of psychology, since the topic ensures rarity and some level of stigmatization.

Easily obtained samples are often not representative ones. Describe for students some characteristics of antisocial personalities—such as impulsive, risk-taking, law-breaking, and callous behaviors. Now ask them how a researcher would get a sample of such people for research. One often-suggested source is prison, and, in fact, the prison system is where many subjects for research come from. However, ask how a prison population is likely to be a biased sample. Point out that factors such as socioeconomic status, intelligence, and prison life itself may make these subjects nonrepresentative. Prisoners, after all, are the ones who got caught, convicted, and not yet paroled or released. One researcher had an ingenious method of attracting nonincarcerated antisocial personalities: she put classified personal ads in the newspaper offering a research stipend to people "who like to take risks and live on the edge." Explore with students other populations that are difficult to recruit: drug addicts, people with sexual problems, introverts, and agoraphobes (those fearful of being in public alone). Further, note how much easier it is to obtain *treated* samples but how their very status of being in treatment affects their thinking, behavior, and feeling.

As consumers of research, students need to see that conclusions from research can only go as far as the representativeness of the sample involved. We know a great deal more about college students than we know about other age groups and we know more about treated mental patients than we know about the majority of mental patients who receive no care. You can make this point by bringing in several research articles and describing in depth the means by which sampling was done. Ask students to describe the limitations that the sample places on generalization to other groups.

Epidemiological research is an excellent topic for discussing sampling as well. Ask students how we could know the incidence or prevalence of lung cancer in the United States. They will probably suggest the use of medical records. We assume that most people with lung cancer will see a family doctor or visit an emergency room sometime after developing symptoms. Now ask students how we could learn the incidence and prevalence of childhood depression. Mental health facilities might supply some statistics, but they might not be useful. First, the child is dependent on parents or teachers to identify such problems. Second, the symptoms of childhood depression are far less clear than the symptoms of lung cancer. Third, there is greater social stigma in the label "childhood depression" than in lung cancer, so parents and even professionals may be less likely to acknowledge the condition. In short, individuals with mental disorders are more difficult to locate and count (the essence of epidemiology) compared with individuals with most physical disorders. The most reasonable way to do the work is extremely labor intensive: ring doorbells and interview thousands of people. Here again, sampling the doorbells (census tracts) is a highly complex task as is deciding whom to interview and how to substitute for those who refuse participation or are not home. Given this information, students should be impressed with the fact that the National Institute of Mental Health's Epidemiological Catchment Assessment survey (used in many places in the text) interviewed approximately 20,000 people in five different locations.

Copyright © Houghton Mifflin Company. All rights reserved.

Internet Site: http://www.ats.ucla.edu/stat/spss is UCLA's Academic Technology Services, which provides resources to help learn and use SPSS.

3.   Students are usually unaware of the process by which research is conducted, written up, judged worthy, and published. In fact, frequently asked questions are, Who does this research, anyway? and Why do they do it? (The second question is much harder to answer than the first.) If you plan to assign a research term paper in the course, this is a good time to explain how research comes to be done, the journal and peer review system, and the library strategies for finding published research articles.

As a kind of show-and-tell, bring to class copies of the *American Journal of Psychiatry*, the *Journal of Abnormal Psychology*, *Psychological Bulletin*, and *Psychological Abstracts*. Showing students the subject index of *Psychological Abstracts* will impress upon them the enormous amount of research in the field of psychology, and paging to one topic, such as schizophrenia, will document how much is written in abnormal psychology. If your library or department subscribes to PsychLit (the CD-ROM search resource), you can do a demonstration search on a specific topic prior to class, or ask your students for several topics about which they would like more information and produce the search results in the next class period. The advertisements in the *American Journal of Psychiatry* can spark a good discussion of the medical model and possible political/economic involvements of pharmaceutical companies in the business of science. *Psychological Bulletin* will show students the difference between a research article and a review article and highlight the treasure trove that is a reference section in a *Psychological Bulletin* article. Finally, the *Journal of Abnormal Psychology* can show the range of research articles in abnormal behavior.

If you conduct research, it is useful to describe your personal research interests, how particular research studies came into being, funding issues, how manuscripts are submitted and to whom, and the peer review experiences you have had. It is eye opening for students to find out that, in many journals, the rejection rate for manuscripts is 80 percent or higher. This topic might lead to a discussion of the "tyranny" of the 0.05 level and the temptations of fudging data.

Internet Site: http://www.apa.org/journals. Home page for the American Psychological Association; contains listings on many journals.

4.   Three conditions must be met to answer the most important question in abnormal psychology: What causes a disorder? The three conditions correspond to different forms of research: correlational, longitudinal, and experimental. Condition 1 is the covariation of events. It is necessary to demonstrate a reliable association between the presence or change of two events or characteristics. If we are to say that child abuse causes eating disorders, we must first show that when child abuse is present so are the symptoms of eating disorders. Moreover, we would assume that as child abuse varies (in severity or frequency, for instance) eating disorders vary, too. Students can be asked what type of research can fulfill condition 1. They should be able to see the value of correlational and epidemiological research here. However, these research methods cannot easily fulfill condition 2: the time-order relationship of the variables. To have a causal relationship, one event or factor must precede the other. Child abuse must reliably predate the onset of eating disorders in order for it to be a cause. Longitudinal research is crucial to establish this piece of information.

It is tempting to see causal relationships in cross-sectional information, but such an inference should be resisted. For example, if child abuse is reported in a group of nine year olds, abuse and early signs of eating disorders in a group of twelve year olds, and full-blown eating disorders in fifteen year olds, we might imagine that six years later, the nine year olds (now experiencing abuse) will become the eating-disordered fifteen year olds. However, we cannot distinguish cohort effects (the nine year olds are living in a different social situation than the fifteen year olds) from longitudinal ones unless we follow the nine year olds through time to see if they have a disproportionate rate of developing eating disorders. In abnormal psychology, longitudinal research is extremely valuable and just as difficult. It is difficult

Copyright © Houghton Mifflin Company. All rights reserved.

because we are looking for rarely occurring conditions (requiring large samples at the outset of the study) and because these conditions usually take many years to develop (leading to high attrition rates among subjects and burnout rates among researchers).

What clinches a causal relationship is condition 3: the elimination of plausible alternatives. Actually, this condition is never met completely because another plausible explanation must always be ruled out. However, only the experiment can shed bright light on this condition, and experimentation in abnormal psychology is exceedingly difficult. In the research above, even if we found that child abuse reliably predated the onset of the eating disorder, we could not know whether child abuse was the sole explanation. Perhaps parents who abuse their children also advocate unreasonable body images in their teenage daughters. If such were the case, we could hardly say that the abuse was causal. But how could we do an experiment to tell? Ethics, of course, would preclude such an investigation; how could we allow some children (chosen at random) to be abused (in a prescribed way) and followed without intervention while waiting for eating disorders to arise? Perhaps an analogue study on nonhuman animals might be ethical, but hardly anyone thinks that rats or mice starve themselves out of fear of becoming fat. What we gain in internal validity in controlled experiments, we may lose in external validity because the subjects or conditions of the experiment bear little resemblance to real life. In short, research on the causes of psychological disorders is just as difficult to do as it is important to do.

Internet Site: http://www.behavenet.com/capsules/disorders/dsm4Trclassification.htm. A glossary of terms and definitions of DSM criteria.

Copyright © Houghton Mifflin Company. All rights reserved.

HANDOUT FOR CLASSROOM TOPIC 1: TITLES OF RECENT JOURNAL ARTICLES

The following journal article titles are taken from the *Journal of Abnormal Psychology* and the *Journal of Consulting and Clinical Psychology,* two of the major professional publications in the field. From the titles, try to guess whether the research study was an experiment in which there is an independent variable (one manipulated by the experimenter) or a correlational study in which variables are not manipulated by the experimenter. The nature of some of the factors described in the title will probably help you decide.

"Long-term effects of interventions for weight loss using food provision and monetary incentives"

Experiment or correlation?   Identify independent (if any) and dependent variables.

"Parents' marital functioning and adolescent psychotherapy"

Experiment or correlation?   Identify independent (if any) and dependent variables.

"Cognitive and neuropsychological characteristics of physically aggressive boys"

Experiment or correlation?   Identify independent (if any) and dependent variables.

"War zone stress, personal resources, and posttraumatic stress disorder in Persian Gulf War returnees"

Experiment or correlation?   Identify independent (if any) and dependent variables.

"Impact of cognitive-behavioral treatment on quality of life in panic disorder patients"

Experiment or correlation?   Identify independent (if any) and dependent variables.

Copyright © Houghton Mifflin Company. All rights reserved.

CLASSROOM DEMONSTRATIONS

1.   Students often imagine that there is one perfect way to study a particular problem. This exercise may help students learn that there are many paths to understanding.

Before students break up into groups of four or five, describe this problem in abnormal behavior: Laypeople (and some mental health professionals) often make two assumptions about alcohol use and anxiety. First, they assume that the two are positively correlated (as anxiety increases, so does consumption). Second, they assume that anxiety causes alcohol consumption. Because these assumptions are often based on armchair speculation, there is no way to determine whether they are correct. Your group's job is to propose three different types of research studies (experimental, longitudinal, and field) that might shed light on the accuracy of these assumptions.

Guided by the Handout for Demonstration 1, each group should brainstorm and discuss the specific features of three original studies. Each group needs to reach a consensus about the best way to study the problem given the constraints of the research method. Tell students that money and logistics are of no concern.

After the groups have completed their discussions, they should present their proposals to the rest of the class. Draw a grid on the board; write the words *Experiment, Longitudinal*, and *Field* at the top of the grid and *Group 1, Group 2, Group 3*, and so on, down the left side. Write a brief summary of each group's ideas in each of the cells and comment on similarities or differences as they arise. A fitting conclusion to the class period is to say that researchers can have honest differences of opinion about how to "skin the cat" and that no one way is perfect.

2.   American Psychological Association ethical guidelines suggest that the value of research must outweigh the risks of performance. This guideline is not as straightforward as it sounds. A demonstration can help students understand how complicated the issues are and can clarify their own ethical principles.

Present the students with this hypothetical research study: Anxiety is a key component of many forms of psychological disorder. A researcher wants to study the biochemical aspects of anxiety, specifically which changes in brain chemistry contribute to anxiety and which eliminate it. To conduct this study, chemicals that induce extremely uncomfortable anxiety are injected into subjects, followed by other chemicals that are intended to reduce the anxiety. There is no doubt that subjects in these experiments will be uncomfortable for several hours, but the researcher sees little risk of discomfort after that. The question for students is: At what point do the potential benefits of this research outweigh its risks or discomforts?

Copyright © Houghton Mifflin Company. All rights reserved.

Put the following grid on the board:

Useful Application of Research Results

Probability of Complete Success	*Within 1 to 2 Years*	*Within 8 to 10 Years*
25 percent		
50 percent		
75 percent		
95 percent		

The grid is intended to indicate that the value of the research can be seen in two ways. First, every chemical that is used has some probability of becoming an anxiety eliminator (a complete success). As the likelihood of success increases, does the willingness to take risks increase, too? Second, the value of some research is delayed, either because it is basic research or because a long chain of discoveries must be made before it can be applied. Other studies may have almost immediate applicability. As the likelihood of immediate benefits increases, does the willingness to take risks increase, too?

Now ask students to imagine they are on a research review board. They need to vote (by raising their hands) on whether this proposed research on anxiety (with the extreme discomfort described above) should be allowed under the circumstances of potential value described in each cell of the grid. Larger numbers of students are likely to say yes in the "southwest" corner of the grid. Ask those who say no to explain their answer. As a final question, ask students whether they would have a different opinion about the study if they were participants rather than review board members.

Internet Site: http://www.apa.org/ethics/code.html. The American Psychological Association site that deals with ethical principles of psychologists and defines the code of conduct.

3.   This short demonstration gives students feedback on how well they understand various types of research designs and their value. You can describe these hypothetical studies orally or use the handout provided. Students then critique each and identify the strengths and weaknesses of that type of design.

1. A teenager with severe obsessions (unwanted thoughts) and compulsions (uncontrolled, ritualistic behaviors) tried to commit suicide by shooting himself in the head. He survived the shooting and discovered that all his obsessions and compulsions were gone. A psychologist did in-depth interviews with this person and linked the area of brain damage from the shooting with obsessions and compulsions.

(Case study. Strengths: rich information, naturalistic setting, promising leads for future research, rare event can be studied. Weaknesses: low generalizability, no control over variables, cannot determine cause-effect relationship.)

2. Ninety adults with chronic abdominal pain keep records on the frequency and intensity of their pains. Family members are interviewed concerning their experiences of illness, family conflict, and behaviors that encourage expression of pain. It is discovered that subjects with highest frequency and intensity of pain reports have families in which illness is common and family members engage in behaviors that encourage pain expression.

Copyright © Houghton Mifflin Company. All rights reserved.

(Correlational study. Strengths: studies a problem that cannot be experimentally induced, allows statistical measurement of covariation in two or more factors, is generalizable to other populations. Weaknesses: cannot assert causal relationship.)

3. Thirty phobic and thirty nonphobic individuals are shown slides of either fear-inducing scenes or non-fear-inducing scenes. Measures of brain functioning (PET scan and electroencephalogram) show higher levels of arousal in phobics, but only when they observe the fear-inducing slides.

(Biological marker and experimental designs combined. Strengths: controls for factors other than the slides and implies that fear-inducing scenes alter the brain functioning of phobics. Weaknesses: without controlling for expectations (it needs a placebo condition) cannot determine if effects are due to slide watching, may not be realistic (does not use actual fear-inducing situation.)

4.   This activity has two goals: increasing class participation and illustrating basic research concepts. It also shows you have a sense of humor. It is a modification by Fein and Spencer (1996) of Bernardo Carducci's (1990) icebreaker activity that tests the irrational belief of some students that participating in class will kill them.

Random selection and assignment. The first step is to select at random a sample of students from the class. The sample is then divided into two conditions. The size of the sample depends on your class size and the time you want to devote to the activity. Half of the sample will be asked to say a few brief things to the rest of the class, so budget your time accordingly. Twenty students, ten in each condition, is a reasonable sample.

How you do random selection will illustrate an important point. One way is to select students in advance using a random number table, but it is better to show students the use of such a table in class. Have the students take a small piece of paper as they enter the classroom. Each piece of paper has a number on it ranging from one to the number enrolled in the class. Use a random number table to select the sample. Call out the number and ask the students whose numbers were called to stand. After the sample is selected, flip a coin to assign each student to either a Treatment or Control condition. You could ask students sitting next to the sampled students to do the coin flip as a way to increase audience participation. Have the selected students write down whether they have been assigned to the Treatment or Control condition and have them return to their seats. Also, explain the purposes of random selection and random assignment and how they differ from convenience sampling or self-selection.

State the hypotheses as follows: "Class participation benefits all students by increasing involvement and providing ideas from students as well as the instructor. I know that some students are afraid to speak out in class. They fear that something awful will happen if they make a mistake. I sympathize with your concerns. This experiment will demonstrate scientifically that you should not be afraid." Now write on the board the following statement: Hypothesis 1: Class participation will kill you. Further down write the following: Hypothesis 2: Class participation will not kill you. Announce that you are going to test these rival hypotheses and that you are so sure of Hypothesis 2 that you are willing to bet their lives on it. (To add more humor, you may want to say something like, "Of course, I could be wrong, so people in the Treatment condition may want to hug their neighbors goodbye, if it's OK with them.")

Copyright © Houghton Mifflin Company. All rights reserved.

Hand out the pretreatment questionnaire.

The treatment: class participation. Have students who are not in either condition come up with three questions that students in the Treatment condition should answer in front of the class. Explain that these questions should be innocuous, ones they would be willing to answer themselves. Examples might be hometown, favorite movie, name, or reason for taking the course. Explain that, for the purpose of testing the hypotheses, this will signify "class participation." Note here that this is but one operational definition of the term. Once the three questions are decided, have everyone in the Treatment condition come forward and answer the questions in front of the class. You may want to ask each student a lighthearted follow-up question to establish a norm that give-and-take (conversation) is likely in the class. Students in the Control condition should walk to the front of the room but not be asked anything. Point out that you have attempted to control for all factors except participation.

Now hand out the posttreatment questionnaire (on the same page as the pretreatment questionnaire). Explain that the dependent measure is whether or not subjects were killed during the experiment. Point out the need for reliable pre- and posttreatment measures and that you are using a self-report instrument. Indicate the limitations of self-report measures, particularly in abnormal psychology. Ask students to help you design an observational measure of whether students were killed in the experiment. Now conduct your observation of subjects and record the number alive in each condition.

Data collection, analysis, and conclusions. Collect the questionnaires and report to the class the number of subjects in each condition, the number of subjects in each condition reporting themselves alive in the pretreatment questionnaire, the number of subjects in each condition reporting themselves alive in the posttreatment questionnaire, and the number observed to be alive. Results should show that class participation did *not* kill more participants than nonparticipants. If some students, trying to be funny, indicated they were dead, you can emphasize the point about the reliability of self-reports and the value of multiple measures. Ask students why a control was necessary in the experiment. Be sure to explain the importance of random selection if you have not already done so.

If you are at all concerned with using the words *kill* or *dead* as part of the activity, you could substitute other hypotheses, such as class participation will not cause students to spontaneously combust or be laughed out of the class room.

Sources: Fein, S., & Spencer, S. (1996). *Instructor's resource manual for social psychology* (3rd ed.). Boston: Houghton Mifflin

Carducci, B. J. (1990). Will class participation "kill" you? Refuting a common irrational belief by teaching research methods. In V. P. Makosky, C. C. Sileo, L. G. Whittemore, C. P. Landry, & M. L. Skutley (Eds.) *Activity handbook for the teaching of psychology* (Vol. 3, pp. 203–205). Copyright © 1990 by the American Psychological Association. Reprinted with permission.

5.   This activity shows students how to think scientifically about common psychological concepts that are the focus of abnormal psychology research. Distribute the handout and have students record individually how they think each concept can be defined operationally. That is, require them to define each term that could be tested in a research study. Emphasize that there are multiple ways of defining each of the terms and that after they are finished working alone, they will be able to see the range and originality of definitions.

If you wish, you can review the material from Chapter 2 on different perspectives and assign certain groups in the class to define terms from a particular perspective. For example, one group of students might be assigned the biological perspective and they would be expected to define *anxiety* in terms of heart rate, perspiration, or muscle tension. Those assigned to a cognitive perspective would be expected to define the same term as, for example, "frequency of thoughts about threatening events."

Copyright © Houghton Mifflin Company. All rights reserved.

6.   This demonstration can introduce your students to the concept of validity in testing. Have the students form small groups of between 4-7 individuals depending on your class size and space limitations. Most of your students have taken the SATs or ACTs. Ask your students to discuss whether the tests were valid for college admission. Do they believe that the SATs or ACTs were a good predictor of their college GPA? If these tests were not used for college admission, what method or methods should be used instead? Ask each group to develop this list with the most salient examples first. Each group could then have a spokesperson deliver a short talk about the best examples. You could provide a blank overhead transparency to each group at the beginning of this demonstration.

Internet Site: http://www.ets.org. The Educational Testing Service Web site. This organization is the copyright holder on many standardized tests.

7.   How would it feel to be labeled schizophrenic or bipolar? Ask the students to imagine that they have been diagnosed with one of these disorders—or any other, for that matter—and think about the implications such a diagnosis might have for other areas of their lives, such as finding jobs, insurance coverage, and relationships. Now have students develop a method to tell their best friend that they have a diagnosable mental disorder. Ask for student volunteers to share how they would tell their best friend. Ask each volunteer what they expect the reaction to be from their friends. Would they be treated the same or differently by their friends after this revelation?

Copyright © Houghton Mifflin Company. All rights reserved.

HANDOUT FOR DEMONSTRATION 1: PROPOSALS FOR RESEARCH STUDIES

Your group's assignment is to develop proposals for three different research studies. All the research is aimed at answering some aspect of this problem: Does stress cause alcohol consumption? Please recognize that *stress* can be defined in many ways and that alcohol consumption can range from light, social drinking to heavy, daily use. Be sure to give operational definitions for all the variables you use when describing your proposed studies.

1.   The first proposal should be in the form of an experiment that could be performed within the walls of the psychology department at your college or university. Remember that in all experiments the researcher manipulates the existence or absence of an independent variable and randomly assigns subjects to experimental and control groups.

2.   The second proposal should be a longitudinal study. In longitudinal studies, you collect data on the same group of people several times over a span of time. Please consider the type of people and the amount of time necessary so that stress and drinking are likely to occur.

3.   The third proposal should be a field study. In field studies you must leave the laboratory and collect data about behaviors and events as they are happening "in the wild." Please consider settings in which both stress (as you define it) and alcohol consumption are likely to happen. Also consider a way of collecting data that will not disturb the behavior you want to study.

Copyright © Houghton Mifflin Company. All rights reserved.

HANDOUT FOR DEMONSTRATION 3: STRENGTHS AND WEAKNESSES OF RESEARCH DESIGNS

1. A teenager with severe obsessions (unwanted thoughts) and compulsions (uncontrolled, ritualistic behaviors) tried to commit suicide by shooting himself in the head. He survived the shooting and discovered that all his obsessions and compulsions were gone. A psychologist did in-depth interviews with this person and linked the area of brain damage from the shooting with obsessions and compulsions.

    What type of research is illustrated here? _____

    What are the strengths of this type of research? _____

    _____

    What are the weaknesses of this type of research? _____

    _____

2. Ninety adults with chronic abdominal pain keep records on the frequency and intensity of their pains. Family members are interviewed concerning their experiences of illness, family conflict, and behaviors that encourage expression of pain. It is discovered that subjects with highest frequency and intensity of pain reports have families in which illness is common and family members engage in behaviors that encourage pain expression.

    What type of research is illustrated here? _____

    What are the strengths of this type of research? _____

    _____

    What are the weaknesses of this type of research? _____

    _____

3. Thirty phobic and thirty nonphobic individuals are shown slides of either fear-inducing scenes or non-fear-inducing scenes. Measures of brain functioning (PET scan and electroencephalogram) show higher levels of arousal in phobics, but only when they observe the fear-inducing slides.

    What type of research is illustrated here? _____

    What are the strengths of this type of research? _____

    _____

    What are the weaknesses of this type of research? _____

    _____

Copyright © Houghton Mifflin Company. All rights reserved.

HANDOUT FOR DEMONSTRATION 4:
PRETREATMENT QUESTIONNAIRE

Please respond to each of the following questions by circling the appropriate answer.

Pretreatment Questionnaire

To which condition were you assigned?   **Control Treatment**

Are you currently alive or dead?   **Alive   Dead**

Posttreatment Questionnaire

To which condition were you assigned?   **Control Treatment**

Are you currently alive or dead?   **Alive   Dead**

Copyright © Houghton Mifflin Company. All rights reserved.

HANDOUT FOR DEMONSTRATION 5: MAKING OPERATIONAL DEFINITIONS

For each of the following concepts, develop a definition that could be used in a research study. The concept should be defined so that anyone would recognize it. Furthermore, it should be defined so that it can be observed by someone other than the subject experiencing it. For instance, *anger* might be defined as a state during which a person's voice is louder than usual, facial expression includes baring of teeth and narrowing of eyebrows, and objects are thrown.

Anger:

_____

_____

Sociability:

_____

_____

Anxiety:

_____

_____

Addiction:

_____

_____

Depression:

_____

_____

Copyright © Houghton Mifflin Company. All rights reserved.

SELECTED READINGS

Critelli, J. W., & Neumann, K. F. (1984). The placebo: Conceptual analysis of a construct in transition. *American Psychologist, 39,* 32–39.

Garber, J., & Hollon, S. D. (1991). What can specificity designs say about causality in psychopathology research? *Psychological Bulletin, 110,* 129–136.

Hock, R. R. (1992). *Forty studies that changed psychology: Explorations into the history of psychological research.* Englewood Cliffs, NJ: Prentice-Hall.

Keith-Speigel, P., & Koocher, G. P. (1985). *Ethics in psychology: Professional standards and cases.* New York: Random House.

Monroe, S. M., & Roberts, J. E. (1991). Psychopathology research. In M. Hersen, A. E. Kazdin, & A. S. Bellack (Eds.) *The clinical psychology handbook* (2nd ed.). New York: Pergamon.

VIDEO RESOURCES

Inferential Statistics: Hypothesis-Testing—Rats, Robots, and Roller Skates (16 mm, 28 min.). Uses humorous sketches to illustrate hypothesis testing, random assignment, control and experimental conditions, and statistical inference. John Wiley & Sons, Inc., 605 Third Avenue, New York, NY 10016.

Methodology: The Psychologist and The Experiment (film, color, 31 min.). This is a fast-paced and enjoyable introduction to the experiment; using as examples the work of Stanley Schachter's fear-and-affiliation study and Austin Riesen's work on kitten visual-motor behavior. Terms such as independent variable and dependent variable and concepts such as control, replication, and random assignment are nicely illustrated. McGraw-Hill Films, 1221 Avenue of the Americas, New York, NY 10020.

Research Methods for the Social Sciences (video, 1995). This program describes different types of experimental designs and when they would be appropriate. It shows the seven steps of the scientific method and conveys both the practice and ethical issues in experimentation. Insight Media, 2162 Broadway, New York, NY 10024; to order, call 212-721-6316.

Statistics: For All Practical Purposes (video, 30 min. each program). This five-part series covers sampling, data collection, descriptive statistics, sampling distributions and the normal curve, standard deviation, central limit theorem, and inferential statistics. Insight Media, 2162 Broadway, New York, NY 10024; to order, call 212-721-6316.

"Understanding Research" from Discovering Psychology Series (#2) (video, 30 min.). The Annenberg/CPB Collection, Dept. CA94, P.O. Box 2345, S. Burlington, VT 05407-2345; to order, call 1-800-532-7637.

Writing for the Social Sciences (video, 30 min.). Very useful if you are assigning a term paper or research report, this video illustrates the key points in writing for the social sciences. Insight Media, 2162 Broadway, New York, NY 10024; to order, call 212-721-6316.

How We Study Children (VHS, color, 24 mm.). Looks at research techniques used with children. Focuses on different types of observational techniques. Insight Media, 2162 Broadway, New York, NY 10024; to order, call 212-721-6316.

Copyright © Houghton Mifflin Company. All rights reserved.

ON THE INTERNET

http://www.apa.org is the American Psychological Association's home page

Good sites for discussions of casual relationships and experimental research, including on-line demonstrations (as well as experiments your students may wish to participate in) are:

http://www-psych.stanford.edu/~psiexp

http://psychexps.olemiss.edu/Exps/labexperiments.htm_(this site has many lab experiments for use in the classroom, but you'll need to download Macromedia's WebPlayer, which is free)

http://writing.colostate.edu/references/research/experiment/pop2b.cfm These sites may be useful in designing your lectures for this chapter

Copyright © Houghton Mifflin Company. All rights reserved.

CHAPTER 5
Anxiety Disorders

CHAPTER OUTLINE

I. Manifestations of anxiety

    A. Anxiety disorders meet one of these criteria

        1. Anxiety itself is a major disturbance

        2. Anxiety is manifested only in particular situations

        3. Anxiety results from attempt to master other symptoms

    B. Cognitive manifestation: thoughts ranging from worry to panic

    C. Behavioral manifestation: avoidance of fear-inducing situations

    D. Somatic manifestation: changes in muscular tension, indigestion, and so on

    E. Five groups of anxiety disorders: panic disorder, generalized anxiety disorder, phobias, obsessive-compulsive disorder, acute and posttraumatic stress disorders

    F. Panic attacks: intense fear with somatic symptoms; can occur in all anxiety disorders

        1. Situationally bound: attacks in response to specific stimulus

        2. Situationally predisposed: tendency to have attacks in response to stimulus

        3. Unexpected: attacks occur without warning

II. Panic disorder and generalized anxiety disorder (GAD)

    A. Panic disorder: severe apprehension and feelings of impending doom lasting minutes to hours; recurrent unexpected attacks and at least one month worry about another attack

        1. Sometimes develops into agoraphobia

        2. Risk factors: disturbed childhood environment, stressors

        3. Lifetime prevalence: 3.5 percent; two times more likely in women

        4. Panic attacks common (45 percent of college coeds within past year)

    B. Generalized anxiety disorder: persistent anxiety and worry, hypervigilance, physiological symptoms (but less reactive than panic disorder) lasting six months or more

        1. Lifetime prevalence 5 percent of adult population; two times as likely for women

        2. Risk factors: lower threshold for uncertainty; erroneous beliefs

    C. Etiology of panic disorder and generalized anxiety disorder

        1. Psychodynamic perspective: stresses internal conflict originating in sexual and aggressive impulses

        2. Cognitive behavioral: negative thoughts or overattention to bodily sensations serve as internal triggers for panic attacks; sets up feedback loop

        3. Biological perspective

Copyright © Houghton Mifflin Company. All rights reserved

a. Focus on neural structures/neurochemical responses to stressful stimuli preliminary and conflicting

b. Panic disorder associated with oxygen misregulation resulting from dysfunction in locus ceruleus in brain

c. Biological challenge tests: sodium lactate or carbon dioxide produces panic attack in those with the disorder

d. Genetic studies: higher concordance rates for MZ than for DZ twins for panic disorder; less support for genetics in GAD

D. Treatment of panic disorder and generalized anxiety disorder

1. Biochemical treatment

a. Antidepressant and antianxiety medications; relapse after stopping drug therapy quite common

b. Benzodiazepines (Valium and Librium) useful in GAD but cause tolerance and dependence

2. Behavioral treatment: higher success rates than medication; 80 percent getting cognitive behavioral treatments for panic disorder were panic free

III. Phobias

A. Agoraphobia: fear of being in public places where escape or help may not be readily available; fear of panic symptoms

1. More common in females than in males

2. Panic attacks typically precede agoraphobia, but relationship is unclear

3. 81 percent report catastrophic cognitions; they may misinterpret events and bodily sensations

B. Social phobia: fear of being scrutinized

1. Three subcategories: performance (such as public speaking), limited interactional (such as going out on a date), and generalized (extreme anxiety in most social situations)

2. Prevalence: 3.7 percent of adults; twice as common in females than males

C. Specific phobias: irrational fear to object or situation

1. In DSM-IV-TR, five types: animals, natural environmental (such as thunder), blood/injection, situational (such as elevators), and other (such as choking)

2. Most common are small animals, heights, the dark, and lightning

3. Two times more prevalent in women than in men; men may lie about fears more than women

4. Most children with phobias lose fear without treatment

D. Etiology of phobias

1. Psychodynamic perspective: displaced sexual or aggressive conflict; little Hans's fear that a horse would bite him

2. Behavioral perspective

a. Classical conditioning perspective: conditioned emotional responses; some research and clinical support

b. Observational learning perspective: negative information and modeling are major factors accounting for childhood fears

c. Negative information perspective: negative information acquired largely from television

d. Cognitive behavioral: negative thoughts and overestimates of unpleasant future events in those with phobias

Copyright © Houghton Mifflin Company. All rights reserved

   3. Biological perspective: genetic predisposition for fear reactions

  E. Treatment of phobias

   1. Biochemical treatments

       a. Drugs used typically affect neurotransmitters and/or reduce depression

       b. Methodological flaws hamper evaluation research on effectiveness

   2. Behavioral treatments

       a. Exposure therapy: gradually introduce contact with feared situation

       b. Cognitive strategies: alter unrealistic thoughts

       c. Systematic desensitization: relaxation while imagining increasingly anxiety-provoking situations

       d. Modeling therapy

IV. Obsessive-compulsive disorder: intrusive repetitive thoughts and need to perform ritual acts

  A. Symptoms are ego-dystonic (seem alien and beyond voluntary control)

  B. Lifetime prevalence: 2.5 percent; equal in men and women

  C. Obsessions: most common are bodily wastes, germs, and environmental contamination

   1. 80 percent of normal samples report unpleasant intrusive thoughts

   2. Obsessive-compulsive obsessions are more intense, longer lasting, and harder to dismiss than "normal" obsessions

  D. Compulsions: need to perform an act to reduce anxiety; if severe must be performed perfectly

  E. Etiology of obsessive-compulsive disorder

   1. Psychoanalytic perspective: obsessive-compulsive behaviors are attempts to fend off sexual urges

   2. Behavioral and cognitive perspectives

       a. Obsessive-compulsive behaviors reduce anxiety

       b. Obsessions are the result of a "catastrophic misinterpretation" of intrusive thoughts or images

   3. Biological perspective: relate to brain structure, genes, and biochemical abnormalities

  F. Treatment of obsessive-compulsive disorder

   1. Biological treatments:

       a. SSRIs are more helpful than minor tranquilizers, but 60-80 percent of people with OCD do not respond to the medications

       b. relapse after medication is discontinued

   2. Behavioral treatments:

       a. Exposure (continued actual or imagined exposure to fear-arousing stimuli)

       b. Response prevention (prevented from performing rituals)

       c. Cognitive component (identify and modify irrational thoughts)

V. Acute and posttraumatic stress disorder

  A. Acute stress disorder (ASD): from exposure to traumatic stress results in dissociation, reliving experience, and avoiding reminders of traumatic event lasting more than two and less than thirty days occurring within four weeks of event

  B. Posttraumatic stress disorder (PTSD): lasts more than thirty days; develops in response to specific stressor; intrusive memories of the traumatic event, emotional withdrawal, heightened autonomic arousal

  C. Diagnosis of acute and posttraumatic stress disorder

Copyright © Houghton Mifflin Company. All rights reserved.

1. Most people with ASD develop PTSD
2. DSM-IV-TR criteria:
   a. Reexperiencing the event in disturbing dreams of intrusive memories
   b. Emotional numbing, or avoiding stimuli associated with trauma
   c. Heightened autonomic arousal

3. Prevalence for Americans between ages fifteen and fifty-four is 8 percent; twice as many women as men

D. The individual's perception of the event: strong correlation between level of danger perceived from a trauma and likelihood of developing PTSD

E. Etiology and treatment of acute and posttraumatic stress disorder
   1. Behavioral perspective:
      a. Classical conditioning: lack of extinction, low support, thoughts about events: treatment with exposure, modeling, virtual reality
      b. Cognitive factors: treat with crisis intervention, cognitive coping strategies
      c. EMDR (eye movement desensitization and reprocessing): visualizing disturbing imagery, describing it using all sensory modalities, then track lateral movements of clinician's finger or pencil
   2. Biological perspective and treatment
      a. Hypersensitivity to stimuli similar to traumatic event
      b. Neurochemical and neuroanatomical circuitry in amygdala
      c. Use of tricyclic antidepressants and SSRIs, which alter serotonin levels at the level of the amygdala and its connections, desensitizing the fear network; unfortunately, the side effects lead to twice the discontinuation rate as behavioral treatments

LEARNING OBJECTIVES

1. Describe the nature and cognitive, behavioral, and somatic manifestations of anxiety in anxiety disorders and list the five major groups of anxiety disorders. (pp. 127-130; Figure 5.1)

2. Describe the symptoms and discuss the prevalence of panic disorder. (pp. 130-132)

3. Describe the symptoms and frequency of generalized anxiety disorder. (p. 132)

4. Discuss the psychodynamic, cognitive-behavioral, and biological theories of cause for panic disorder and generalized anxiety disorder. (pp. 132-136)

5. Compare the biochemical and behavioral treatment approaches for panic disorder and generalized anxiety disorder and discuss their relative efficacy in treating these disorders. (pp. 136-137)

6. Discuss the symptoms and prevalence of phobias, including agoraphobia, specific phobia, and social phobia. (pp. 137-142; Tables 5.1 & 5.2)

7. Discuss the psychodynamic, behavioral, cognitive, and biological theories for the cause of phobias. (pp. 142-146)

8. Discuss the biochemical and behavioral treatment of phobias, including systematic desensitization, exposure, and modeling therapy. (pp. 146-149; Mental Health & Society)

9. Distinguish between obsessions and compulsions and describe the symptoms and prevalence of obsessive-compulsive disorder. (pp. 149-152; Table 5.3)

10. Discuss the psychodynamic, behavioral, and biological theories of the cause of obsessive-compulsive disorder. (pp. 152-155)

Copyright © Houghton Mifflin Company. All rights reserved

11. Describe and discuss the biological, behavioral, and cognitive treatment of obsessive-compulsive disorder. (pp. 155-156)

12. Differentiate between acute stress disorders (ASD) and posttraumatic stress disorders (PTSD) and the DSM-IV's criteria for their diagnoses. (pp. 155-156; Table 5.4)

13. Discuss the causes and treatment of PTSD, including prolonged exposure and eye movement desensitization and reprocessing. (pp. 160-163)

CLASSROOM TOPICS FOR LECTURE AND DISCUSSION

1.   Panic attacks appear to be rather common, but it is possible that some "panic attacks" are not psychologically induced at all. It is increasingly clear that another common problem having to do with the heart may be the cause of some panic attacks. This heart defect, which is rarely life endangering or severe, is called *mitral valve prolapse*. The mitral valve of the heart usually closes flush with the wall that separates the atrium from the ventricle. In mitral valve prolapse, for reasons that are not well understood, the valve folds in on itself when it closes. The effect is to produce a racing heart, fainting, profuse sweating, and dizziness—many of the signs of a panic attack. These episodes occur randomly, and not all attacks are a result of psychological panic. The wise clinician would encourage a client to have a physical examination to rule out such physical causes as mitral valve prolapse.

Internet Site: http://www.apa.org/pubinfo/panic.html. An APA site that covers the basics on panic attacks and treatments.

2.   The world seems to be a more and more dangerous place. The problem of posttraumatic stress disorder and its prevention should be mentioned in this section of the course. Whether natural or caused by human agency, the disasters people suffer need not lead to long-lasting and disabling conditions. One description of such a prevention effort was a response to the 1981 Hyatt Regency Hotel disaster in Kansas City, Missouri. Two skywalks in the hotel collapsed, killing 113 people and injuring 200 others. The survivors had significant psychological aftereffects, as did the rescue workers. Grist and Stolz (1982) describe what mental health professionals in the region did to prevent posttraumatic stress disorder.

A good discussion question is, "Should local or state governments provide funds and facilities so that citizens who are victims of such disasters are assured of psychological services?" A follow-up question is, "How much should we provide if, as research indicates, about 15 percent of those involved in disasters need professional treatment within a year of the event?"

Sources: Gist & Stolz (1982) Community response to the Kansas City hotel disaster. *American Psychologist*, 37, 1136–1139.

3.   The textbook does not give a clear indication of the scenes that are used in flooding therapy. A good discussion topic is the need for truly graphic imagery and the ethical considerations for both client and therapist. For a person with a spider phobia, the following script might be used.

> Close your eyes and see a hairy spider at your feet. See it crawl around your feet and ankles. Make yourself pick it up and put it in your lap. You don't want to do it, but you make yourself pick it up. Look at the spider in your lap. Feel it moving around. Keep your hand on the spider and prevent it from walking away. Feel the texture of its hairy surface as it moves around in your hand. Bring the spider up closer to your face. Force yourself to look at it.

The intense anxiety that the client with spider phobia will feel is exactly what must occur, but explain to students that this therapy is done only after the client is informed of what will happen and the reasons for it. Also note that the therapist, who probably does not enjoy the thought of creating terror in a client,

Copyright © Houghton Mifflin Company. All rights reserved.

must believe in the therapy and "stick it out" despite the client's anxiety. If the therapist starts to use flooding, there is no turning back. Stopping the presentation of fear-inducing scenes before there has been an extinction of anxious responses will reinforce avoidance. Students may want to discuss whether the slower, more comfortable (but often less effective) process of systematic desensitization is preferable to the distressing (but effective) method of flooding.

4.   A new theory of anxiety and depression (Higgins, 1987) proposes that people define themselves in terms of an *actual* self (the attributes that describe how they actually are), an *ideal* self (the way they aspire to be), and an *ought* self (the way they are morally obligated to be). The latter two are considered "self guides" and may be based on a personal standpoint or the standpoints of important others such as parents or teachers. The degree of inconsistency between actual and ideal or ought selves is a person's self-discrepancy. Higgins argues that depressive emotions are related to discrepancy between the actual and the ideal self. Anxiety is related to discrepancy between the actual and the ought self, particularly the ought self as defined by others.

Scott and O'Hara (1993) identified small samples (Ns were less than 10) of university students who met the criteria for depression or generalized anxiety disorder and had them complete the Selves Questionnaire (Higgins et al., 1985). As predicted, depressed students showed greater actual-ideal self-discrepancy than anxious or normal students showed. Anxious students showed greater actual-ought self (other-defined) than depressed or normal students showed. These findings largely replicate those of Strauman (1992), extend Strauman's work by including students with anxiety problems other than social phobias, and, given the small samples, indicate that a real effect is present.

Sources: Higgins, E. T. (1987). Self-discrepancy: A theory relating self and affect. *Psychological Review, 94,* 319–340.

Higgins, E. T., Klein, R., & Strauman, T. J. (1985). Self-concept discrepancy theory: A psychological model for distinguishing among different aspects of depression and anxiety. *Social Cognition, 3,* 51–76.

Scott, L., & O'Hara, M. W. (1993). Self-discrepancies in clinically anxious and depressed university students. *Journal of Abnormal Psychology, 102,* 282–287.

Strauman, T. J. (1992). Self-guides, autobiographical memory, and anxiety and dysphoria: Toward a cognitive model of vulnerability to emotional distress. *Journal of Abnormal Psychology, 101,* 87–95.

CLASSROOM DEMONSTRATIONS

1.   The Velten method of inducing mood (Velten, 1968) has been successfully applied to a range of emotional states including anxiety. The method uses a stack of cards that contain statements associated with a particular emotion. Subjects first read the cards silently, then aloud, and finally spend five or so minutes concentrating on a time in their life when they experienced the same emotional state. Borkovec and colleagues (Borkovec et al., 1983; York et al., 1987) have developed mood inductions for both worry and somatic anxiety. In the first case, statements focus on cognitive concerns: "I am plagued by my racing mind" or "I am so worried that I cannot concentrate on anything." The somatic anxiety statements highlight bodily sensations brought on by anxiety: "My stomach is starting to feel queasy" or "I can feel my muscles tensing up." Borkovec has shown that both worry-induced and somatic-anxiety-induced subjects had more intrusive negative thoughts in a subsequent testing session than those in a neutral emotional condition. Cardiovascular activity was also significantly increased in both induced states.

You could either make a set of such cards or present the statements to the class via overhead transparencies or verbally. Statements should take the following form: "I am very tense and nervous." "My heart is beating very fast now." "My muscles are tense and twitching." "I am worried." "I can't deal

Copyright © Houghton Mifflin Company. All rights reserved

with the uncertainties in my life." "I have many fears." "I must avoid upsetting places at all costs." "My stomach feels queasy because of my nervousness." "I worry that I will not be able to keep my mind from racing." You must make a lengthy presentation of such statements (at least 20–30) to alter the mood state of the reader/listener. Further, the public nature of the classroom may work against the "suspension of disbelief" necessary for such statements to induce mood. However, the fact that such statements are often made by clients with anxiety disorders can be a point of departure for discussion of the cognitive cause or maintenance of such problems as panic disorder, generalized anxiety disorder, phobias, and obsessive-compulsive disorder.

Sources: Borkovec, T. D., Robinson, E., Pruzinsky, T., & Depree, J. A. (1983). Preliminary exploration of worry: some characteristics and processes. *Behaviour Research & Therapy, 21*, 9–16.

Velten, E. (1968). A laboratory task for the induction of mood states, *Behavior Research and Therapy, 6*, 473–482.

York, D., Borkovec, T. D., Vasey, M., & Stern, R. (1987). Effects of worry and somatic anxiety induction on thoughts, emotion, and physiological activity. *Behaviour Research & Therapy, 25*, 523–526.

2.   The treatment of all anxiety disorders involves the elimination of anxiety. Systematic desensitization accomplishes this in a gradual and comforting way. You can demonstrate the basic elements of systematic desensitization by giving a quick, deep muscle-relaxation demonstration and suggesting how an anxiety hierarchy would be constructed and used. You can make this exercise even more relevant and useful by applying it to test anxiety, a problem in any class. A script for the relaxation training is provided in a handout. Completion of the relaxation demonstration takes about five minutes. You can either read it to the class or distribute the handout and instruct students to practice on their own time. An *example* of an individual's hierarchy of fears dealing with classroom examinations is given below. The intensity of anxiety in each situation is averaged and rated in terms of what Joseph Wolpe called *Standard Units of Distress* (SUDS). Make it clear to students that each person has his or her own anxiety hierarchy; those in the class who suffer from test anxiety will relate to the listing on the next page but will undoubtedly apply different numbers to the test-related situations in their own lives.

Copyright © Houghton Mifflin Company. All rights reserved.

SUDS	Situation
10	Reading the syllabus and finding out that there will be three exams in a course
20	Reading course material and thinking that there will be an exam on it
50	Hearing the instructor ask whether anyone has questions about the exam next class period
70	Studying for the exam the night before
80	Walking toward the classroom on the day of the exam
90	Taking the exam paper from the instructor and looking at the first item
100	Reading three items and not knowing the answer to any of them

After a client (student) learns to relax quickly and completely, relaxation is paired with imagined scenes of the least anxiety-provoking situations. When anxiety is felt, the client "turns off" the scene, becomes relaxed again, and imagines the scene again. People are rarely able to imagine highly stressful scenes while completely relaxed, but reducing anxiety to manageable levels usually improves performance.

Internet Site: http://www.kuvaszinformation.com/kuvaszfear.htm. An in-depth discussion of systematic desensitization.

3.   The cognitive component in anxiety disorders is receiving considerable research attention. In 1986, Reiss et al. developed a research instrument to measure people's beliefs that anxiety experiences (cognitive, behavioral, and somatic) have negative consequences such as illness, humiliation, and further anxiety. Ever alert to even small body changes, people with this anxiety sensitivity interpret a skipped heart beat to be a sign of a heart attack. Fearful of the consequences of anxiety symptoms, they even worry about becoming anxious. In a series of studies, Reiss et al. (1986) reported that their Anxiety Sensitivity Index (ASI) had good psychometric properties (test-retest reliability was .75; internal consistency was shown by 13 of the 16 items having a factor analytic loading of .4 or more).

The demonstration will show students a research instrument and allow class members to compare their scores with those of other college students and two samples of patients with anxiety disorders. Reiss et al. reported that scores on the ASI for female college students were significantly higher (mean = 20.5) than scores for male college students (mean = 15.4). Scores were significantly higher among agoraphobic outpatients (mean = 38.3) than among outpatients with other anxiety disorders (mean = 23.9) who scored higher than the college students. The findings give support to the idea that agoraphobia is associated with a fear of fear.

Preface this demonstration with some cautionary statements. Make it clear that scores on the index diagnose **no** condition and that the completion of the index is for educational purposes—to see how researchers in the field measure concern about anxiety symptoms. Insist that students not identify themselves on the scale and assure them that you are interested in group data only—comparing the class's means with those that Reiss et al. (1986) reported. Scoring is straightforward: "Very little" scores 0 points; "a little" scores 1 point; "some" scores 2 points; "much" scores 3 points; and "very much" scores 4 points. An individual's ASI score is the sum of the scores on all 16 items.

Source: Reprinted from *Behavior Research and Therapy*, Vol. 24, Reiss, S., Peterson, R. A., Gursky, D. M., and McNally, R. J., "Anxiety Sensitivity, Anxiety Frequency, and the Prediction of Fearfulness," pp. 1–8. Copyright 1986, with permission from Elsevier Science Ltd., The Boulevard, Langford Lane, Kidlington OX5 1GB, UK.

Copyright © Houghton Mifflin Company. All rights reserved

Internet Site: http://www.med.nyu.edu/Psych/screens/anx.html The New York University Department of Psychiatry online screening for anxiety disorders.

4.   Wolpe (1973) suggests that the Willoughby Personality Schedule can be used prior to beginning systematic desensitization. This questionnaire identifies interpersonal situations that elicit anxiety, presumably more important for those with social phobias. Have your students fill it out, but caution them that the purpose of the exercise is to better appreciate what goes on in behavioral assessment and treatment; it is *not* designed for self-diagnosis. Norms are not available.

Another useful questionnaire is the Wolpe-Lang Inventory (Wolpe & Lang, 1969), which assesses sources of more specific fears than the Willoughby Personality Schedule. The full questionnaire has 108 items, but five samples from it are listed below. Ask your students to generate a longer list on their own or have them make suggestions in class to gain a more complete understanding of the exercise.

Items in the Wolpe-Lang Inventory questionnaire refer to things and experiences that may cause fear or other unpleasant feelings. Students should indicate how much each item disturbs them, using the following categories: Not at All, A Little, A Fair Amount, Much, and Very Much.

1.   Speaking in public
2.   Thunder
3.   Receiving injections
4.   Cats
5.   Being in an elevator

Source: From J. Wolpe & P.J. Lang. *Fear Survey Schedule.* Copyright © 1969. Reprinted with permission from Wolpe, J. (1973). *The practice of behavior therapy* (2nd ed.). New York: Pergamon.

5.   People who are high in trait anxiety (generalized anxiety disorder) seem to interpret life as more threatening than it needs to be. Presented with alternative interpretations of situations, anxious people disproportionately endorse dangerous ones (Butler & Mathews, 1983). Anxious individuals tend to write down more threatening meanings to words that sound alike but have different meanings (homophones) (Mathews et al.,1989).

Sources: Butler, G., & Mathews, A. (1983). Cognitive processes in anxiety. *Advances in Behaviour Research and Therapy, 5,* 51–62.

Mathews, A., Richards, A., & Eysenck, M. (1989). Interpretation of homophones related to threat in anxiety states. *Journal of Abnormal Psychology, 98,* 31–34.

6.   Since panic attacks are so common, students will want to know the symptoms that accompany them. The corresponding handout lists the DSM-IV-TR diagnostic criteria for panic attack. Remind students of "medical students' syndrome" at this junction. This chapter represents the first of the chapters devoted to clinical disorders, and you need to remind students to "take with a grain of salt" any concern they may have that they have a disorder.

Internet Site: http://www.apa.org/pubinfo/panic.html. An APA site that answers your questions about panic disorder. It covers the basics on panic attacks and treatments.

7.   Use the following to demonstrate what a mild panic attack might be like. This demonstration is best done with a class with which you have developed a positive rapport. Assign some outside reading,

Copyright © Houghton Mifflin Company. All rights reserved.

and the publications put on reserve in the library several weeks prior to this demonstration. Ask the students to complete these readings by the date of this demonstration for discussion in class.

On the day of this demonstration, come to class late and act very angry. Explain that you have learned that a student from the class was in your office the last hour complaining about cheating on the last test. Indicate that you have decided to invalidate the last test and give everyone a zero on it since you cannot identify the specific students who cheated. You have decided to give a pop quiz on the assigned reading to replace the test.

Be very formal if any students question your authority. Hand out a real pop quiz. Tell the students that they have until the end of the class to finish. Sit at the front of the classroom for about five minutes; this will allow most of the students to experience a mild panic attack. Stop the demonstration and tell the students that they will not be graded on this pop quiz. I have even given extra credit for the students that started the pop quiz. Begin to brief the students and lead a discussion of the mild anxiety they felt. The level of panic they experienced is relatively low; use this time to summarize the symptoms of panic attack.

Internet Site: http://www.apa.org/pubinfo/panic.html. An APA site that answers your questions about panic disorder. It covers the basics on panic attacks and treatments.

8.   Invite a clinical professional to be a guest lecturer for your class on the topic of anxiety disorders. A person who deals with individuals who have these disorders can give a short introduction with some examples and then invite discussion. Real examples will help the students understand the types of problems these individuals experience and how they are treated by the professional community.

Internet Site: http://www.apa.org/pubinfo/panic.html. An APA site that answers your questions about panic disorder. It covers the basics on panic attacks and treatments.

9.   Bring the DSM-IV-TR to class, and prepare an overhead transparency or PowerPoint slide ahead of time for your lecture on anxiety disorders. Describe the in-depth material from the DSM-IV-TR while using the transparency or PowerPoint slide as an outline. Lead a discussion on the differences between different anxiety disorders. Encourage student input about individuals they have known with these symptoms.

Copyright © Houghton Mifflin Company. All rights reserved

HANDOUT FOR DEMONSTRATION 2:
SCRIPT FOR RELAXATION TRAINING

The following script can be used to make a tape recording that will help the listener learn to relax. It incorporates three of the major techniques in relaxation training: progressive muscle relaxation, breathing control, and visualization. Students should practice relaxation training for 15 to 20 minutes twice per day for five days or so. After that amount of practice they should be able to determine which component—muscle tightening, breathing, or visualization—is most relaxing. They can modify the script to increase the amount of time they spend on the relaxation that works best for them.

Relaxation practice should be done in a place and at a time when few interruptions are likely. It is advisable to keep the lighting low, to sit or lie comfortably, and to keep one's eyes closed. Practicing in bed late at night may interfere with acquiring the relaxation response, because rather than practicing, the person will simply go to sleep. This result is valuable for people with insomnia, but not for those with test anxiety.

Sit in a comfortable position with your legs uncrossed and your arms at your sides. Now make your hands into fists. Notice the tension in your hands, wrists, and forearms. Hold it. Now open your hands and let the muscles completely relax. Note the contrast between the tension that was there and the relaxation that you now feel. Try to let the relaxation go even further than usual. (Pause) Now tighten your hands into fists again and try to touch your shoulders with your fists. Feel the tension throughout your arms. Hold it. (Pause) Now drop your arms and open your hands. Let the tension flow down your arms and out through your fingertips. If you haven't already, close your eyes to help imagine the tension flowing out. Let your arms become completely relaxed.

To tighten the muscles in your shoulders, try to touch your shoulders to your ears. Hunch up and hold it. Now relax. Let the muscles loosen up and get quiet. (Pause). [Instructions are discontinued here, but, in full relaxation training, they would include the face, back, chest, stomach, buttocks, legs, toes, and so on.]

Now concentrate on your breathing. Try to make your breathing perfectly smooth and regular. Breathe slowly, smoothly, and very regularly. Concentrate only on your breathing. Each time you breathe out, think the word *relax* and let your body grow just a bit more limp. Every breath is a chance to relax a bit more. If your mind wanders, just bring it back to your breathing. Make your breathing perfectly regular and relax a bit more each time you exhale. Let your body become completely quiet and calm. Enjoy the relaxed feeling. (Pause.)

While you are breathing smoothly and becoming more and more relaxed, I want you to imagine that you are at the top of a hill overlooking the ocean. The sky is blue with small puffy clouds; the ocean is a sparkling blue with small white waves. Try to be there now. Feel the warm, salty breeze in your hair. See the ocean as the waves come in regularly. You are alone and quiet in this place. You have no worries; you can be completely relaxed and at peace. Notice that the waves come in perfectly timed with your breathing. And every time you breathe out, you get a little more relaxed.

Enjoy this peaceful place. Allow yourself to enjoy the wonderful feeling of being relaxed and peaceful. (Thirty-second pause)

Soon we will have to come back to the classroom. When I count to three, you will be back in the class but feeling relaxed and alert. One: You can begin to move your arms and legs. Two: Slowly open your eyes. Three: You are fully back and feeling fine.

Copyright © Houghton Mifflin Company. All rights reserved.

HANDOUT FOR DEMONSTRATION 3: ANXIETY SENSITIVITY INDEX

Please do *not* identify yourself in any way. Your instructor is interested in group data and will compute only the average scores for males and females in your class. Consider this an educational exercise. It cannot and should not be used to diagnose an anxiety disorder.

For each item, respond by circling a phrase (very little, a little, some, much, or very much). Please be sure to answer all 16 items with one phrase each.

1. It is important to me not to appear nervous.

    very little   a little   some   much   very much

2. When I cannot keep my mind on a task, I worry that I might be going crazy.

    very little   a little   some   much   very much

3. It scares me when I feel "shaky" (trembling).

    very little   a little   some   much   very much

4. It scares me when I feel faint.

    very little   a little   some   much   very much

5. It is important to me to stay in control of my emotions.

    very little   a little   some   much   very much

6. It scares me when my heart beats rapidly.

    very little   a little   some   much   very much

7. It embarrasses me when my stomach growls.

    very little   a little   some   much   very much

8. It scares me when I am nauseous.

    very little   a little   some   much   very much

9. When I notice that my heart is beating rapidly, I worry that I might have a heart attack.

    very little   a little   some   much   very much

10. It scares me when I become short of breath.

    very little   a little   some   much   very much

Copyright © Houghton Mifflin Company. All rights reserved

11. When my stomach is upset, I worry that I might be seriously ill.

| very little | a little | some | much | very much |

12. It scares me when I am unable to keep my mind on a task.

| very little | a little | some | much | very much |

13. Other people notice when I feel shaky.

| very little | a little | some | much | very much |

14. Unusual body sensations scare me.

| very little | a little | some | much | very much |

15. When I am nervous, I worry that I might be mentally ill.

| very little | a little | some | much | very much |

16. It scares me when I am nervous.

| very little | a little | some | much | very much |

Reprinted from *Behavior Research and Therapy*, Vol. 24, Reiss, S., Peterson, R. A., Gursky, D. M., and McNally, R. J., "Anxiety Sensitivity, Anxiety Frequency, and the Prediction of Fearfulness," pp. 1–8. Copyright 1986, with permission from Elsevier Science Ltd., The Boulevard, Langford Lane, Kidlington OX5 1GB, UK.

Copyright © Houghton Mifflin Company. All rights reserved.

HANDOUT FOR DEMONSTRATION 4: WILLOUGHBY PERSONALITY SCHEDULE, REVISED

Instructions: The questions in this schedule are intended to indicate various emotional personality traits. It is not a test in any sense because the questions do not have right or wrong answers.

After each question, you will find a row of numbers whose meaning is given below. All you have to do is to circle the number that describes you best.

0 means *no, never, not at all,* or similar terms.
1 means *somewhat, sometimes, a little,* or similar terms.
2 means *about as often as not, an average amount,* or similar terms.
3 means *usually, a good deal, rather often,* or similar terms.
4 means *practically always, entirely,* or similar terms.

1. Do you get anxious if you have to speak or perform in any way in front of a group of strangers?   0 1 2 3 4

2. Do you worry if you make a fool of yourself or feel you have been made to look foolish?   0 1 2 3 4

3. Are you afraid of falling when you are on a high place from which there is no real danger of falling—for example, looking down from a balcony on the tenth floor?   0 1 2 3 4

4. Are you easily hurt by what other people do or say to you?   0 1 2 3 4

5. Do you keep in the background on social occasions?   0 1 2 3 4

6. Do you have changes of mood that you cannot explain?   0 1 2 3 4

7. Do you feel uncomfortable when you meet new people?   0 1 2 3 4

8. Do you daydream frequently, that is, indulge in fantasies not involving concrete situations?   0 1 2 3 4

9. Do you get discouraged easily by failure or criticism?   0 1 2 3 4

10. Do you say things in haste and then regret them?   0 1 2 3 4

11. Are you ever disturbed by the mere presence of other people?   0 1 2 3 4

12. Do you cry easily?   0 1 2 3 4

13. Does it bother you to have people watch you work even when you do it well?   0 1 2 3 4

14. Does criticism hurt you badly?   0 1 2 3 4

15. Do you cross the street to avoid meeting someone?   0 1 2 3 4

16. At a reception or tea, do you go out of your way to avoid meeting the important person present?   0 1 2 3 4

17. Do you often feel just miserable?   0 1 2 3 4

18. Do you hesitate to volunteer in a discussion or debate with a group of people whom you know more or less?   0 1 2 3 4

19. Do you have a sense of isolation, either when alone or among people?   0 1 2 3 4

Copyright © Houghton Mifflin Company. All rights reserved

20. Are you self-conscious before "superiors" (teachers, employers, authorities)?   0 1 2 3 4

21. Do you lack confidence in your general ability to do things and to cope with situations?   0 1 2 3 4

22. Are you self-conscious about your appearance even when you are well-dressed and groomed?   0 1 2 3 4

23. Are you scared at the sight of blood, injuries, and destruction even though there is no danger to you?   0 1 2 3 4

24. Do you feel that other people are better than you?   0 1 2 3 4

25. Is it hard for you to make up your mind?   0 1 2 3 4

From Joseph Wolpe, *The Practice of Behavior Therapy.* Copyright © 1973 by Allyn and Bacon. Reprinted with permission.

Copyright © Houghton Mifflin Company. All rights reserved.

HANDOUT FOR DEMONSTRATION 6: DIAGNOSTIC CRITERIA FOR PANIC ATTACK

The main feature of a panic attack is a period of intense fear or discomfort that develops abruptly and reaches a peak within ten minutes. To be considered a panic attack, the episode must be accompanied by four or more of the following symptoms:

1. Palpitations, pounding heart, or accelerated heart rate

2. Sweating

3. Trembling or shaking

4. Sensations of shortness of breath or of smothering

5. Feeling of choking

6. Chest pain or discomfort

7. Nausea or abdominal distress

8. Feeling dizzy, unsteady, lightheaded, or faint

9. Derealization (feelings of unreality) or depersonalization (being detached from oneself)

10. Fear of losing control or going crazy

11. Fear of dying

12. Paresthesias (numbness or tingling sensations)

13. Chills or hot flushes

Copyright © Houghton Mifflin Company. All rights reserved

SELECTED READINGS

Clark, D. M (1988). A cognitive model of panic attacks. In S. Rachman & J. D. Maser (Eds.), *Panic: Psychological perspectives*. Hillsdale, NJ: Lawrence Erlbaum, 71–89.

McNally, R. J. (1987). Preparedness and phobias: A review. *Psychological Bulletin, 100*, 283–303.

Neal, A., & Turner, S. M. (1991). Anxiety disorder research with African-Americans: Current status. *Psychological Bulletin, 109*, 400–410.

Pynoos, R. S., Frederick, C., Nader, K., Arroyo, W., Steinberg, A., Eth, S., Nunez, F., & Fairbanks, L. (1987). Life threat and posttraumatic stress in school age children. *Archives of General Psychiatry, 44*, 1057–1063.

Turner, S. M., Beidel, D. C., & Nathan, R. S. (1985). Biological factors in obsessive-compulsive disorders. *Psychological Bulletin, 97*, 430–450.

Sattler, D., Shabatay, V., & Kramer, G. (1998). *Abnormal psychology in context: Voices and perspectives*. Boston, MA: Houghton Mifflin Company. Chapter 1, Anxiety Disorder.

Clipson, C. & Steer, J. (1998). *Case studies in abnormal psychology*. Boston, MA: Houghton Mifflin Company. Chapter 2, Panic Disorder. Chapter 3, Obsessive-Compulsive Disorder. Chapter 4, Posttraumatic Stress Disorder.

VIDEO RESOURCES

Anxiety: The Endless Crisis (16 mm, color, 60 min). Describes the causes and types of anxiety as well as physiological and psychological reactions. Differentiates between state and trait anxiety. Indiana University, Audiovisual Center, Bloomington, IN 47405.

Behavioral Therapy Demonstration (16 mm, color, 32 min). Dr. Joseph Wolpe demonstrates his therapy with a woman showing social phobia. Deep muscle-relaxation training and pairing of relaxation and imagined scenes are depicted. PCR, Pennsylvania State University, University Park, PA 16802.

The Concept of Anxiety (16 mm, 44 min). Anxiety as a universal experience. Video Nursing, Inc., 2645 Girard Avenue, Evanston, IL 60201.

Interview with an Obsessive-Compulsive (VHS or Beta video, color, 50 min). Part of a series of case histories, this video explores the symptoms and experience of being obsessive-compulsive. Media Guild, 118 South Acacia, Box 881, Solana Beach, CA 92075.

Neurotic Behavior: A Psychodynamic View (16 mm, color, 19 min). The film uses compulsive behavior to illustrate how irrational thinking leads to self-defeating behavior and exaggerated fears. Defense mechanisms are shown, as well as means for exploring and facing them so as to reduce neurotic symptoms. PCR, Pennsylvania State University, University Park, PA 16802.

Obsessive-Compulsive Neurosis (16 mm, 28 min). The case of a middle-aged man with obsessive-compulsive behaviors. Modern Talking Picture Services, 1212 Avenue of the Americas, New York, NY 10036.

Copyright © Houghton Mifflin Company. All rights reserved.

Pathological Anxiety (16mm, 30 min). A disturbed office worker experiences panic and terror when he is unable to suppress his hostilities. PCR, Pennsylvania State University, University Park, PA 16802.

Cognitive Therapy for Panic Disorder (VHS, color, 45 mm.). From the APA Psychotherapy Videotape Series II: Specific Treatments for Specific Populations. American Psychological Association. 1-800-374-2721.

Obsessive-Compulsive Disorder (VHS, color, 75 mm.). Covers diagnosis and treatment of obsessive-compulsive disorder. Insight Media. 1-800-233-9910.

Obsessive-Compulsive Disorder: The Boy Who Couldn't Stop Washing (VHS, color, 28 mm.). Specially adapted Phil Donahue show with Dr. Judith Rapport, author of the book by the same title considers symptoms, diagnosis, and possible cures. Films for the Humanities and Science. 1-800-257-5126.

Panic Attacks (VHS, color, 15 mm.). Covers the diagnosis and treatment of panic attacks and related disorders. Films for the Humanities and Science. 1-800-257-5126.

ON THE INTERNET

http://www.algy.com/anxiety/ is the Anxiety Panic internet resource.

http://www.apa.org is the American Psychological Association's home page. This site contains information on anxiety disorders.

http://www.lexington-on-line.co./naf.html is the west site for the National Anxiety Foundation.

http://www2.health-center.com (then link to mental health) to find several types of phobias and information on how individuals deal with anxiety, fears, and stress throughout their life.

http://www.nimh.nih.gov is the National Institute of Mental Health home page, which offers information about diagnosis, treatment, and research into anxiety disorders, obsessive-compulsive disorder, and phobias.

An e-mail discussion group called ANXIETY-L has a great deal of activity on the whole range of anxiety-related subjects. To subscribe, address the message SUBSCRIBE ANXIETY-L YOURNAME to listproc@frank.mtsu.edu (or through the algy.com/anxiety web site listed above)

Copyright © Houghton Mifflin Company. All rights reserved

CHAPTER 6
Dissociative Disorders and Somatoform Disorders

CHAPTER OUTLINE

I. Dissociative disorders dissociative amnesia, dissociative fugue, dissociative identity disorder (multiple personality), and depersonalization disorder

    A. Most are rare, but reports of dissociative identity disorder in United States have increased

    B. Dissociative amnesia: partial or total loss of personal information (due to traumatic event)

        1. Types

            a. Localized amnesia—loss of all memory for a short time (most common type)

            b. Selective amnesia—loss of details about an incident

            c. Generalized amnesia—total loss of memory for past

            d. Systemized—loss of memory for selected types of information

            e. Continuous amnesia—inability to recall any events from a specific time until present (least common type)

        2. May be analogous to posthypnotic amnesia, but difficult to tell

    C. Dissociative fugue: dissociative amnesia plus travel; usually incomplete change of identity; recovery usually abrupt and complete

    D. Depersonalization disorder: feelings of unreality and perceptual distortion

        1. Most common form of dissociative disorder

        2. May create great anxiety

        3. Precipitated by physical or psychological stress

    E. Dissociative identity disorder (formerly multiple personality disorder)

        1. Characteristics

            a. Two or more independent personalities exist in one person

            b. One personality evident at a time; usually amnesia in personality that is not present, although personalities may have awareness of other personalities

            c. Often opposite personalities

            d. More prevalent in women in United States, but no gender differences found in Switzerland

            e. Conversion symptoms, depression, and anxiety are common

        2. Diagnostic controversy

            a. Fewer than 200 cases reported worldwide prior to 1970s, now about 6,000 new cases per year

Copyright © Houghton Mifflin Company. All rights reserved.

b.   Some clinicians believe it is underreported, others believe it is iatrogenic

c.   Core symptoms (amnesia, lack of autobiographical memory for childhood, chronic depersonalization, alteration of identity) are distinct with DID

d.   Rare outside United States and Canada

F.   Etiology of dissociative disorders

1.   Hard to separate faking from real; reliable diagnostic methods do not currently exist

2.   Psychodynamic perspective

a.   If repression to block traumatic events doesn't work, dissociation may occur

b.   Four factors necessary for DID: capacity to dissociate, exposure to severe stress, walling off experience, and developing different memory systems

3.   Behavioral perspective

a.   Avoidance of stress by indirect means

b.   Iatrogenic or therapist-produced

G.   Treatment of dissociative disorders

1.   No specific medications for DID; medications prescribed for associated problems of anxiety or depression

2.   Three-part group format

a.   Psychoeducation

b.   Use of group resources

c.   Develop cognitive and social skills

3.   Dissociative amnesia and fugue and spontaneously

4.   Depersonalization disorder has slower rate of spontaneous remission, so treatment focuses on relieving anxiety, depression, or fear of going insane

5.   Dissociative identity disorder

a.   Treatment more likely successful with those who can integrate their personalities

b.   Combination of psychotherapy and hypnosis

c.   Develop coping skills, even if personalities not integrated

d.   Problem-focused therapy holds patients responsible for their behavior as a whole person

II.   Somatoform disorders: physical symptoms without physiological basis

A.   Cross-cultural differences in somatic complaints

B.   Somatization disorder

1.   DSM-IV-TR criteria: physical complaints involving four or more sites on body (at least two gastrointestinal, one sexual, one pseudoneurological), doctor-shopping, unnecessary operations, anxiety, and depression

2.   Undifferentiated somatoform disorder: not fully meeting criteria, but at least one physical complaint for six months

3.   Overall prevalence rate of 2 percent; more prevalent among females and African Americans

C.   Conversion disorder

1.   Characteristics: physical impairment without physical cause

2.   Differentiate from physical by lack of atrophy in paralyzed extremity, neurological impossibility (glove anesthesia), relation to stress

3.   Discriminating those who fake is difficult

Copyright © Houghton Mifflin Company. All rights reserved.

D. Pain disorder

1. Characteristics: severe or excessive pain with no physiological basis or long after injury has healed

2. Pain is complex phenomenon with both physiological and psychological bases, but descriptions of the pain and its location are vague.

E. Hypochondriasis

1. Characteristics: preoccupation with health, anxiety and depression; reassurance has no impact

2. Prevalence: 4 to 9 percent of general medical patients

3. Predisposing factors: history of physical illness, parental attention to somatic symptoms, low pain threshold, greater sensitivity to somatic cues

F. Body dysmorphic disorder

1. Characteristics: preoccupation with imagined defect in appearance in a normal-appearing person/excessive concern over slight physical defect producing marked clinical distress; mirror checking; frequent surgery

2. Diagnostic problems

a. Normal dissatisfaction with appearance high (46 percent of college students have some preoccupation with appearance)

b. Overlap with delusional disorder or obsessive-compulsive disorder

G. Etiology of somatoform disorders

1. Diathesis-stress: hypervigilance and sensitivity to body sensations followed by stressor

2. Psychodynamic perspective

a. Repression of conflict converted to physical

b. Primary gain: protected from anxiety

c. Secondary gain: attention and dependency needs met

3. Behavioral perspective

a. Assume sick role for reinforcement/avoidance

b. Modeling important

c. Fordyce (1988) reports physicians unwittingly reinforce; male patients with supportive wives experience more pain when wife is present

4. Sociocultural perspective

a. Term *hysteria* (now conversion disorder) comes from Greek for uterus

b. Freud's case of Anna O. was actually unsuccessful treatment

c. Social restrictions on women lead to symptoms

5. Biological perspective

a. High arousal levels, higher sensitivity to bodily sensations

H. Treatments of somatoform disorders

1. Psychodynamic treatment

a. Psychoanalysis to relive feelings associated with repressed event

b. Hypnotherapy

2. Behavioral treatment

a. Exposure and response prevention to extinction and prevent reinforcement of complaints

Copyright © Houghton Mifflin Company. All rights reserved.

      b.   Operant-behavioral: change social and environmental reinforcers to reinforce appropriate behavior, ignore complaints

      c.   Cognitive approach: modify patient's cognitions about pain by identifying negative thoughts and replacing with more adaptive ones

   3. Biological treatment

      a.   Antidepressant medications and SSRIs

      b.   Increasing physical activity

   4. Family systems treatment

      a.   Explore function of the problem

      b.   Teach the family adaptive ways to support each other and to deal with problems

LEARNING OBJECTIVES

1. Discuss the fundamental characteristics involved in dissociative disorders, and list the four types of dissociative disorders. (pp. 167-168; Figure 6.1)

2. Discuss the characteristics of the four types of dissociative amnesia and the process by which they occur. (pp. 169–170)

3. Describe the characteristics of dissociative fugue and depersonalization disorder. (pp. 170–173)

4. Discuss the controversy over the validity of "repressed memories" and research that indicates the possibility of false memories. (pp. 170–171; Critical Thinking; First Person)

5. Describe the characteristics of dissociative identity (multiple personality) disorder and its prevalence. (pp. 173–175)

6. Discuss the diagnostic controversies concerning dissociative identity disorder. (pp. 175–176)

7. Discuss and distinguish the psychodynamic, behavioral, and iatrogenic (therapist-produced) explanations for dissociative disorders. (pp. 176–179)

8. Discuss the treatment of dissociative amnesia and fugue, depersonalization disorder, and dissociative identity disorder. (pp. 179–183; Mental Health & Society)

9. Describe the basic characteristics of somatoform disorders and distinguish them from malingering and factitious disorders. (pp. 173, 183-185; Mental Health & Society; Figures 6.4 & 6.4B)

10. List and describe the five subtypes of somatoform disorder, including somatization disorder, conversion disorder, pain disorder, hypochondriasis, and body dysmorphic disorder. (pp. 184–191; Table 6.1; Mental Health & Society)

11. Describe and discuss the causes of somatoform disorders from the psychodynamic, behavioral, sociocultural, and biological perspectives, and the diathesis-stress model. (pp. 192–195)

12. Describe and discuss the treatment of somatoform disorders with psychoanalytic, behavioral, and family systems therapies. (pp. 195–196)

CLASSROOM TOPICS FOR LECTURE AND DISCUSSION

1.   Dissociative identity disorder (multiple personality) is a favorite topic for discussion and evaluation because it is so bizarre and dramatic. A good way to start a discussion is to contrast this disorder with schizophrenia, even if the psychoses have not yet been presented, since there are many misconceptions about what "split personality" means. One way of clarifying the difference is to draw a set of partially interconnected circles on the board to show the relatively distinct components that make

Copyright © Houghton Mifflin Company. All rights reserved.

up multiple personality and a dotted circle next to these to indicate the fractured nature of schizophrenia, where not even one intact personality is found.

Once these differences are established, it is useful to examine the functions of separate personalities for a person who has endured prolonged physical or sexual abuse. The cases of Billy Milligan (Keyes, 1981), Sybil (Schreiber, 1973), and Jonah (Ludwig et al., 1972) all show a timid (superego) core personality with opposite personalities that are sexually promiscuous, aggressive, or both (id). Ask the class to imagine the events that might produce such dissociated personalities. In addition, a competent, rational personality often "bails out" the other two. This can be seen as pure ego. Students who are skeptics of psychoanalysis are often impressed with this tripartite split among personalities. It even seems that Eve (who had some 21 faces before she was successfully treated) had personalities that came out in groups of three (Sizemore & Pittillo, 1977).

Sources: Keyes, D. (1981). *The minds of Billy Milligan*. New York: Bantam.

Ludwig, A. M., Brandsma, J. M., Wilbur, C. B., Bendfeldt, F., & Jameson, D. H. (1972). The objective study of multiple personality. *Archives of General Psychiatry, 26,* 298–310

Schreiber, F. R. (1973). *Sybil*. Chicago: Regnery.

Sizemore, C., & Pittillo, E. (1977). *I'm Eve*. New York: Doubleday.

Internet Site: http://www.issd.org/indexpage/isdguide.htm. Contains guidelines for treating dissociative identity disorder (DID).

2.   What are the advantages of being sick? Students can better understand the behavioral and family systems view on somatoform disorder by looking at the positive consequences of making somatic complaints. Ask students how many of them when they were younger faked or exaggerated illnesses to get out of difficult academic or interpersonal situations. How did their parents react to these complaints, and what effect did the reactions have? If parents helped these children avoid responsibilities, we can expect that illness complaints increased in frequency. On the other hand, if parents routinely ignored such complaints, children probably learned to face responsibility.

This discussion should raise questions about soft- and hard-heartedness and the danger of parents wrongly suspecting fakery. This mirrors the dilemma of the physician or psychologist with a client who repeatedly complains of pain or other problems in the absence of a physiological explanation. Instructors can suggest a reasonable middle ground: that complaints need to be thoroughly checked out for possible physical causes before one assumes that there are other reasons. Even so, it is dangerous to assume that medical assessment has reached the zenith of accuracy.

3.   The idea of iatrogenic disorders deserves expanded attention. The instructor can help students to appreciate how therapists react to "interesting" cases. Therapists tend to spend more time thinking about these clients, consulting books and colleagues to better understand them, and paying attention to their subtle verbal and nonverbal messages. Like other people, clinicians become enthused by puzzles they have trouble solving. If nothing else, multiple personalities are puzzles that are hard to solve. In some ways, it may be a disappointment to find an interesting case becoming an ordinary case so, some clinicians may inadvertently influence clients to exaggerate the symptoms of multiple personality.

The opposite of this effect may also occur with clients whose problems seem more pesky than interesting. Conversations with hypochondriacal clients are continuous battles to steer the topic away from their health concerns. (The worst thing a clinician can do is ask a hypochondriacal client, "How are you doing?") Again, despite their training, clinicians are like other people and have a point at which they want to hear no more about somatic complaints. The therapist then works at reducing or discounting

Copyright © Houghton Mifflin Company. All rights reserved.

complaints—the opposite of what goes on in the iatrogenic process of fostering dissociative identity disorder.

4.   Dissociative identity disorder (DID) has largely been reported and researched in North America. Modestin's (1992) research from Switzerland, cited in the text, suggests that DID is quite rare in Europe. The first large sample study of DID in Europe indicates that DID patients in the Netherlands are strikingly similar to those in North America (Boon & Draijer, 1993). Boon and Draijer (1993) gave the Structured Clinical Interview for Dissociative Disorders, the Structured Trauma Interview, and the Dissociative Experiences Scale to 71 patients being treated for dissociative identity disorder. The comparison with the Ross et al. (1990) sample of 102 cases from North America is noteworthy. The following table points out the similarities. For each item, the percentage of the sample reporting or qualifying for that item is given.

Item	Boon & Draijer (1993)	Ross et al. (1990)
Childhood physical or sexual abuse	94.4	95.1
Sexual abuse	77.5	90.2
Physical abuse	80.3	82.4
Suicide attempts	62.9	72.5
Drinking problem	32.4	33.3
Street drugs	22.5	28.4
Some form of amnesia	100.0	100.0

Sources: Boon, S., & Draijer, N. (1993). Multiple personality disorder in The Netherlands: A clinical investigation of 71 patients. *American Journal of Psychiatry, 150,* 489–494.

Ross, C.A., Miller, S. D., Reagor, P., Bjornson, L., Fraser, G. A., & Anderson, G. (1990). Structured interview data on 102 cases of multiple personality disorder from four centers. *American Journal of Psychiatry, 147,* 596–601.

Internet Site: http://www.sidran.org A non-profit education and advisory organization for traumatic life events.

5.   Rabinowicz (1989) describes a way of demonstrating dissociative identity disorder in the classroom. Students take the Imagination Potential Scale, and the top three scorers are given the task of playing a serial killer interviewed by a court-appointed clinician. The role play is based on the Hillside Strangler murder case and highlights the issues of differentiating multiple personality from faking, as discussed in the text.

Source: Rabinowicz, F. E. (1989). Creating the multiple personality: An experiential demonstration for an undergraduate abnormal psychology class. *Teaching of Psychology, 16,* 69–71.

Internet Site: http://www.sidran.org A non-profit education and advisory organization for traumatic life events.

6.   The first controlled therapy outcome study on body dysmorphic disorder was published in 1995. Rosen, Reiter, and Orosan (1995) randomly assigned 54 body dysmorphic disorder subjects with to cognitive behavioral therapy or to a no-treatment control group. Patients met for eight two-hour sessions in small groups. Their beliefs concerning the importance of physical appearance were challenged, they monitored and modified their thoughts about body dissatisfaction, and they practiced techniques for eliminating body checking. An exposure/response prevention component of treatment put subjects in situations they normally avoided because of concern over their appearance. Checking and intrusive

Copyright © Houghton Mifflin Company. All rights reserved.

thoughts were significantly reduced in treated subjects, and in 82 percent of cases the disorder was eliminated at posttreatment. In only one case was there relapse at follow-up.

Clearly this study indicates that cognitive-behavioral therapy can be useful in the treatment of body dysmorphic disorder. However, further studies comparing different approaches to treatment are needed to see if more effective and efficient methods can be found.

Source: Rosen, J. C., Reiter, J, & Orosan, P. (1995). Cognitive-behavioral body image therapy for body dysmorphic disorder. *Journal of Consulting and Clinical Psychology, 63*, 263–269.

Internet Site:
http://www.brown.edu/Administration/George_Street_Journal/v22/v22n5/dysmorph.html.   Defines and discusses treating body dysmorphic disorder.

7.   When clinicians assume that somatic complaints are the result of somatoform disorders, they must be quite certain of their diagnosis. A false negative (failing to see an existing physiological condition) is a much more serious mistake than a false positive (claiming that a physiological condition exists when there is none). The wise psychologist makes sure that every conceivable medical test and specialist has been used prior to concluding that conversion disorder is the correct diagnosis. Consider this case presented by Fishbain and Goldberg (1991):

A young man was in a fight when he was hit over the head with a bottle. He was arrested for assault and taken to the hospital. He never lost consciousness and x-rays of his skull showed no fracture. Neurological examinations were normal. However, the patient complained that he was unable to move his left arm and leg. He was reassured by hospital personnel and when given the direct suggestion that he was able to move the arm and leg, he moved them. Over a period of time, the patient continued to complain of an inability to move his left limbs, was reassured that he could, and showed movement. He was diagnosed with conversion disorder. Only later, using CAT scans, which can detect damage better than x-rays, did doctors discover that he had a hemotoma (bloody swelling) in the right frontoparietal area of the cortex, which accounted for his incomplete loss of movement on the left side.

In a study of 30 patients diagnosed with conversion disorder, 80 percent were eventually found to have a medical disorder that was the cause or contributing factor of symptoms that were originally believed have a psychological origin (Gould et al., 1986). In many cases, current technology cannot detect physiological causes of neurological disorders in their earliest stages. To immediately assume that disorders are conversion disorders, with the social stigma attached, is to be reckless in diagnosis.

Two key factors in separating conversion from physiological disorders are selective symptoms and la belle indifference. Selective symptoms are evident when, for instance, a paralyzed leg moves when the person is asleep or when blind individuals can see well enough to catch an object thrown unexpectedly. La belle indifference is a traditional sign of conversion: the individual's way of discussing symptoms and their impact in a dispassionate, even unconcerned, manner. Patients with organic disorders, especially those whose impairment has been sudden and traumatic, are likely to be quite upset about their symptoms. However, this "beautiful indifference" is reported in only about one-third of individuals with conversion disorder so this is not a very strong means of differentiating psychological and physiological disorders either.

Sources: Fishbain, D. A., & Goldberg, M. (1991). The misdiagnosis of conversion disorder in a psychiatric emergency service. *General Hospital Psychiatry, 13*, 177–181.

Gould, R., Miller, B. L., Goldberg, M., & Benson, D. F. (1986). The validity of hysterical signs and symptoms. *Journal of Nervous and Mental Disease, 174*, 593–597.

Copyright © Houghton Mifflin Company. All rights reserved.

Internet Site: http://www.mc.vanderbilt.edu/peds/pidl/adolesc/convreac.htm. This site consists of material on somatoform disorders, including statistics on the prevalence of theses disorders.

CLASSROOM DEMONSTRATIONS

1.   A behavioral perspective on multiple personality stresses role playing and selective attention. To relate this concept to students' everyday lives, ask them to report their behavior in widely different social situations. This kind of exercise underscores the extreme situationist viewpoint of some personality theorists—that traits are illusions. It is also possible to connect this exercise to research on self-monitoring. High self-monitors tend to change their behavior to meet the needs of social situations. They are "tuned in" to the reactions they create in others and shape their behavior to get the reactions that are socially valued. They are also more adept at playing roles and enjoying the theatrical aspects of interactions. It is not such a long step from this style to the development of dissociative identity disorder, especially if the disorder is seen as a response to the expectations of the therapist (iatrogenic). The 18-item Self-Monitoring Scale is provided as a handout. The following items answered True are scored in the direction of high self-monitoring: 4, 5, 6, 8, 10, 12, 17, and 18. The following items answered False are also scored in the direction of high self-monitoring: 1, 2, 3, 7, 9, 11, 13, 14, 15, and 16.

Have students report their scores anonymously. Compute the class mean. Gangestad and Snyder (1985) found that among college students, the median split for self-monitoring was between scores of 10 and 11. For greater purity of high- and low-self-monitoring groups, they suggest scores of 13 and over and 7 and under.

As a further exploration of the topic of changing "personalities" in response to different social expectations, ask students to write down how they act in the following situations:

1.   In the middle of a crowd at an exciting football game
2.   With their parents during Thanksgiving dinner
3.   After watching a sad movie by themselves
4.   When they walk into a party where they know no one
5.   When someone almost crashes into their car on the highway
6.   When they are in a silly mood and talk to a close friend
7.   When they are in a class taught by a boring professor (certainly not you!)

Are they the same person in every situation? To what extent do they act the part that is expected of them? To what degree do they ignore aspects of themselves that do not fit the situation's demands?

At the extreme, this adaptive behavior does not represent much of a difference from the way multiple personalities react. However, it bears repeating that multiple personalities do not just ignore certain aspects of themselves. They have no information about certain aspects of themselves.

Source: Gangestad, S., & Snyder, M. (1985). To carve nature at its joints?: On the existence of discrete classes in personality. *Psychological Review*, 92, 317–349.

Internet Site: http://www.sidran.org A non-profit education and advisory organization for traumatic life events.

2.   The diagnosis of conversion disorder is something like a detective game. The following group exercise can give students some appreciation of the difficulties. Divide the class into groups of four or five and assign the groups the task of developing strategies for detecting conversion disorder as opposed to malingering or physiologically based disorders. Use the case study on the Handout for Demonstration 2 to get a discussion rolling. Then ask a reporter in each group to describe to the class the strategies group members thought of. List these on the board and then comment on or ask for ideas about the pros and cons of each.

Copyright © Houghton Mifflin Company. All rights reserved.

The detective issue is sometimes played out on a larger scale Kiesler & Finholt, (1988). An epidemic of painful arm, hand, and wrist conditions called repetitive strain injury or repetitive motion syndrome has overwhelmed Australian workers' compensation funds. The article explores the explanations, including the possibility that the epidemic is related to job dissatisfaction.

Sources: Kiesler & Finholt, (1988). The mystery of RSI. *American Psychologist, 43,* 1004–1015.

Internet Site: http://www.mc.Vanderbilt.Edu/peds/pidl/adolesc/convreac.htm. This site describes conversion disorder as a loss or change in bodily functioning that results from a psychological conflict or need.

3.   Cardena and Spiegel (1993) report that in a sample of graduate students the incidence of dissociative reactions immediately after the San Francisco Bay Area earthquake of October 1989 was surprisingly high. Symptoms such as hypervigilance, difficulty concentrating, exaggerated startle response, and confusion were reported by more than half of the respondents one week after the quake. Four months after the event, fewer than one-third reported having these symptoms.

Survey students for their experience of dissociative symptoms during "baseline" conditions and compare the percentages with those from Cardena and Spiegel (1993). A handout is provided. Another possibility is to ask students if they have experienced an extraordinary life event (for example, life-threatening car accident, violent crime, or natural disaster). The event should be stressful enough to have had an intense impact for a week or more. If a large enough sample exists, ask these students to fill out the questionnaire using the week after their particular stressful event as the period for reporting their reactions. This exercise can spark discussion of several topics: how to decide the base rate of dissociative reactions, the reliability of retrospective symptom reporting, and why dissociative reactions occur in the wake of trauma.

Here are the findings of Cardena and Spiegel showing the percentage of 100 graduate students reporting each dissociative symptom at one week and at four months after the Loma Prieta earthquake. In every case the symptom was less likely to be reported at four months, most with $p < .001$.

		1 Week	*4 Months*
1.	Difficulty taking in new information	55	26
2.	An exaggerated startle response	67	29
3.	Periods of confusion	55	16
4.	Hypervigilance (extreme alertness and being "on guard")	76	39
5.	Having your attention automatically drawn toward thoughts of an unpleasant event	56	33
6.	Intrusive recollections of an unpleasant event	39	17
7.	Difficulties with everyday memory	29	14
8.	Recurrent dreams about an unpleasant event	22	11
9.	Distressful associations about an unpleasant event	39	18
10.	Detailed memories about an unpleasant event	55	23
11.	The reliving of an unpleasant event	29	14
12.	The sensation that time was expanding	51	19
13.	The sensation that your surroundings were unreal or dreamlike	40	12
14.	A lack of interest in usually interesting activities	40	12
15.	A tendency to avoid certain activities	26	10
16.	Withdrawal from other people	28	13
17.	A tendency to avoid thoughts about an unpleasant event	30	15

Copyright © Houghton Mifflin Company. All rights reserved.

18. A sensation that your self is detached from your body	25	6
19. A feeling that events are occurring at a distance	40	13
20. A feeling that sensations (hearing and seeing) are occurring at a distance	17	3
21. Numbing or slowness	23	7
22. Unusual body sensations	27	10
23. A feeling that your thoughts are occurring at a distance	22	7
24. A restricted range of emotions	23	9

Note: The wording of the questionnaire items differs from that of the Cardena and Spiegel instrument and makes direct comparison impossible. The 24-item list above is a truncated version of the 98-item Standard Acute Stress Reaction Questionnaire (SASRQ) and focuses on dissociative reactions.

Source: Cardena, E., & Spiegel, D., "Dissociative reactions to the San Francisco Bay Area earthquake." *American Journal of Psychiatry, 150,* 474–478, 1993. Copyright 1993, the American Psychiatric Association. Reprinted by permission.

4.   Introduce your students to the idea that common conceptions of dissociative disorders are often incorrect. Have the students form small groups of 4-7 individuals depending on your class size and space limitations. Ask group members to recall incidents of amnesia from movies, prime time television, or daytime television. The other group members are then asked to determine if the amnesia or fugue state meet DSM-IV criteria. They will find that most of these incidents are designed for the storyline but do not meet the definition of amnesia. Ask each group to develop this list with the most salient examples first. Each group could then have a spokesperson deliver a short talk about the best examples. You could provide a blank overhead transparency to each group at the beginning of this demonstration.

Internet Site: http://human-nature.comodmh/dissocation.html. A listing of information on dissociation disorders (some links don't work)

5.   Invite a guest speaker who is a psychologist or psychiatrist specializing in the treatment of dissociative disorders. Have the students develop questions during the class period before the guest lecturer is scheduled. These professionals are usually very busy, but if you schedule early enough they will usually be happy to lecture to your class.

6.   Bring the DSM-IV-TR to class, and prepare an overhead transparency or PowerPoint slide ahead of time for your lecture on somatoform disorders. Describe the in-depth material from the DSM-IV –TR while using the transparency or PowerPoint slide as an outline. Lead a discussion on the differences between different anxiety disorders. Encourage student input about individuals they have known with these symptoms.

Copyright © Houghton Mifflin Company. All rights reserved.

HANDOUT FOR DEMONSTRATION 1: SELF-MONITORING SCALE

This 18-item measure of self-monitoring can give you a general idea of whether you are a high or low self-monitor. Your instructor will explain the concept of self-monitoring and its relevance to such dissociative disorders as dissociative identity disorder. Please read each item carefully, consider how you typically act, and answer *true* or *false*. Your instructor will show you how to score and interpret your score on this scale.

1. I find it hard to imitate the behavior of other people.   true   false

2. At parties and social gatherings, I do not attempt to do or say things that others   true   false
   will like.

3. I can only argue for ideas in which I already believe.   true   false

4. I can make impromptu speeches even on topics about which I have almost no   true   false
   information.

5. I guess I put on a show to impress or entertain others.   true   false

6. I would probably make a good actor.   true   false

7. In a group of people I am rarely the center of attention.   true   false

8. In different situations and with different people, I often act like very different   true   false
   people.

9. I am not particularly good at making other people like me.   true   false

10. I'm not always the person I appear to be.   true   false

11. I would not change my opinions (or the way I do things) in order to please   true   false
    someone or win their favor.

12. I have considered being an entertainer.   true   false

13. I have never been good at games like charades or improvisational acting.   true   false

14. I have trouble changing my behavior to suit different people and different   true   false
    situations.

15. At a party I let others keep the jokes and stories going.   true   false

16. I feel a bit awkward in company and do not show up quite as well as I should.   true   false

17. I can look anyone in the eye and tell a lie with a straight face (if for a right end).   true   false

18. I may deceive people by being friendly when I really dislike them.   true   false

Source: From *Public appearance, private realities* by Snyder. © 1987 by W. H. Freeman and Company. Used by permission.

Copyright © Houghton Mifflin Company. All rights reserved.

HANDOUT FOR DEMONSTRATION 2: DIAGNOSING CONVERSION DISORDER

1. Each group should choose a member who will be the reporter. The reporter keeps track of the ideas the group develops and reports those ideas to the rest of the class when everyone reconvenes.

2. Everyone in the group should read the case below:

> Jane works as a word processor for a large insurance company. Her job, which she detests, involves inputting hundreds of numbers into a computer. She has gone to her family physician because she feels a constant tingling in her fingers and a sharp pain in her fingers, wrist, and forearm but only at certain times. Her doctor is not a neurological specialist but can see nothing obviously wrong with Jane's hands or wrists. Jane is depressed and anxious about this condition. She says, "Here I am only 29 and already I have pains that are worse than my 76-year-old grandmother has. What will I be like in 20 years? Already it is agony for me to do my work."

3. Group members should list ways in which Jane's condition could be evaluated. You cannot be expected to be experts in neurology, but you should think through ways of detecting malingering, voluntary inducement of symptoms, physical causes, and psychological causes. What information would you need to decide whether Jane

   - is malingering?
   - has a factitious disorder (is consciously inducing the symptoms)?
   - has a "real" physiological disorder?
   - has a somatoform disorder such as conversion disorder?

4. After developing a list of assessment strategies, the group should think about the order in which these tests and evaluation strategies should be conducted. What makes sense to rule out first?

Copyright © Houghton Mifflin Company. All rights reserved.

HANDOUT FOR DEMONSTRATION 3: INCIDENCE OF DISSOCIATIVE REACTIONS

Please indicate whether any of the following reactions have occurred to you. Do not indicate your name. All information will be grouped, and individual data will not be used. Please answer as honestly as possible.

During the past four months have you experienced

		Yes	No
1.	difficulty taking in new information?		
2.	an exaggerated startle response?		
3.	periods of confusion?		
4.	hypervigilance (extreme alertness and being "on guard")?		
5.	having your attention automatically drawn toward thoughts of an unpleasant event?		
6.	intrusive recollections of an unpleasant event?		
7.	difficulties with everyday memory?		
8.	recurrent dreams about an unpleasant event?		
9.	distressful associations about an unpleasant event?		
10.	detailed memories about an unpleasant event?		
11.	the reliving of an unpleasant event?		
12.	the sensation that time was expanding?		
13.	the sensation that your surroundings were unreal or dreamlike?		
14.	a lack of interest in usually interesting activities?		
15.	a tendency to avoid certain activities?		
16.	withdrawal from other people?		
17.	a tendency to avoid thoughts about an unpleasant event?		
18.	a sensation that your self is detached from your body?		
19.	a feeling that events are occurring at a distance?		
20.	a feeling that sensations (hearing and seeing) are occurring at a distance?		
21.	numbing or slowness?		
22.	unusual body sensations?		
23.	a feeling that your thoughts are occurring at a distance?		
24.	a restricted range of emotions?		

Source: Cardena, E., & Spiegel, D. "Dissociative reactions to the San Francisco Bay Area earthquake." *American Journal of Psychiatry*, 150, 474–478, 1993. Copyright 1993, the American Psychiatric Association. Reprinted by permission.

Copyright © Houghton Mifflin Company. All rights reserved.

SELECTED READINGS

Ford, C. V. (1995). Dimensions of somatization and hypochondriasis. Special issue: Malingering and conversion reactions. *Neurological Clinics, 13*, 241–253.

Kellner, R. (1986). *Somatization and hypochondriasis.* New York: Praeger-Greenwood.

Loewenstein, R. J. (1991). Psychogenic amnesia and psychogenic fugue: A comprehensive review. In A. Tasman & S. M. Goldfinger (Eds.) *Annual review of psychiatry.* Washington, DC: American Psychiatric Press, pp. 223–247.

Phillips, K. A. (1991). Body dysmorphic disorder: The distress of imagined ugliness. *American Journal of Psychiatry, 148*, 1138–1149.

Putnam, Frank W. et al. (1986). The clinical phenomenology of multiple personality disorder: A review of 100 recent cases. *Journal of Clinical Psychiatry, 47*, 285–293.

VIDEO RESOURCES

Case Study of Multiple Personality (16 mm, 30 min). The actual Eve (Chris Sizemore) interviewed by a psychiatrist during and after treatment. Background information also presented; poor sound quality. Psychological Cinema Register, Pennsylvania State University, University Park, PA 16802.

Conversion Reaction—A Demonstration (16 mm, 20 min). A re-creation of an interview demonstrating conversion symptoms. U.S. National Audiovisual Center National Archives and Record Service, Washington, DC 20014.

Hypnosis and healing (VHS, 54 min). Patients and physicians tell of success in using hypnosis: a rash developed 30 years prior during a wartime brush with death is eliminated; a mute individual is able to speak again while in a trance; a previously asthmatic youngster is cured with hypnosis. This 1982 video was produced by the BBC. Psychological Cinema Register, Pennsylvania State University, University Park, PA 16802.

Mind of a Murderer (VHS, 120 min). Interviews with psychologists and psychiatrists of Kenneth Bianchi, the "Hillside Strangler." Bianchi attempts to feign MPD in order to enter an insanity plea. Graphically demonstrates the ability of a clever psychopath to dupe experts into believing that he was a multiple personality. The Pennsylvania State Library.

Multiple Personality Disorder: In the Shadows (VHS, color, 28 min.). Discusses the causes of and treatment for multiple personality disorder. Films for the Humanities. 1-800-257-5126.

Copyright © Houghton Mifflin Company. All rights reserved.

ON THE INTERNET

http://www.sidran.org/ is the Web site for The Sidran Foundation, which focuses on trauma and trauma-related disorders. It provides a glossary of dissociative disorder terms, a brochure on dissociative identity disorder, as well as tips for survivors and an article on the effects of dissociative identity disorder on children of trauma survivors.

http://mental-health-matters.com is the Mental Health Matters home page, which offers information and links for mental health, self-help, and psychology information and resources.

http://www.mc.vanderbilt.edu/peds/pidl/adolesc/convreac.html includes material on somatoform disorders, including statistics on the prevalence of theses disorders, and references.

http://www.merck.com/pubs/mmanual/section15/chapter186/186a.htm   This is chapter 186 of the Merck Manual of Diagnosis and Treatment that deals with somatoform disorders.

http://www.brown.edu/Administration/George_Street_Journal/v22/v22n5/dysmorph.html is a text only site that defines and discusses treating body dysmorphic disorder..

Copyright © Houghton Mifflin Company. All rights reserved.

CHAPTER 7
Psychological Factors Affecting Medical Conditions

CHAPTER OUTLINE

I. Introduction

    A. Sudden death syndrome

        1. Most common cause of death in industrial societies (often coronary heart disease)

        2. Physiological changes include blood clotting more easily, increased blood pressure, and changes in heart rhythm (ventricular fibrillation, bradycardia, tachycardia, and arrhythmia)

        3. Among immigrants may result from severe culture shock

    B. Change from traditional separation of psychosomatic disorders from other illnesses

        1. In DSM-IV-TR, "psychological factors affecting medical condition" and listed on Axis III

        2. The term "psychosomatic disorder" has been replaced with psychophysiological disorder-any physical disorder with a strong psychological basis

        3. Separate from conversion: actual tissue damage in psychophysiological disorders

        4. DSM-IV-TR diagnosis requires presence of a medical condition plus one of the following: time relationship between psychological factors and onset of or recovery from medical condition, psychological factor interferes with treatment, and psychological factors are added health-risk factor

II. Models for understanding stress

    A. Definitions

        1. Stressor: an external event that places physical or psychological demand on a person

        2. Stress: an internal response to stressor

    B. General adaptation model (Selye): Biological, psychological, and social stressors all produce three-stage response

        1. Alarm stage: immediate, short-term vulnerability to infection

        2. Resistance stage: mobilization to defend against threat

        3. Exhaustion stage: symptoms reappear, may lead to death

        4. Stress is known to affect immune system, heart function, hormone levels, nervous system, metabolic rates and leads to diseases (hypertension, chronic pain, heart attacks, cancer, and the common cold)

    C. Life change model (Holmes & Holmes): All changes affect person

        1. Greater life change units produce greater chance of illness, more severe form of illness

            a. Measured with Social Readjustment Rating Scale

        b.   Stress potential values are called life change units (LCUs)

    2. Different cultures vary in the way they rank stressors

    3. Negative life changes are more detrimental than positive life changes

    4. Personal interpretations and characteristics matter

  D. Transaction model (Lazarus)

    1. Both stressor and person

    2. Complex interaction of psychosocial, physiological, and cognitive factors

    3. How situation is interpreted affects its impact

III.   Stress and the immune system

  A. Mechanisms by which cognitive/emotional state can influence the course or severity of disease:

    1. Biological: direct physiological reaction or changes in immune functioning

    2. Behavioral: response to stress by engaging in poor health practices

    3. Cognitive: feelings of hopelessness or optimism impact health decisions positively or negatively

    4. Social: stressor or emotional state may cause deterioration or increase in social support

    5. Conflicting evidence on the course of AIDS

  B. The immune system

    1. Components

        a.   Lymphocytes (B-cells, T-cells, and NK cells)

        b.   Phagocytes

    2. Stress-induced release of neurohormones may impair immune functioning

        a.   Corticoseteroids: strong immunosuppressive actions

        b.   Endorphins: decrease natural killer cells' tumor-fighting ability

  C. Decreased immunological functioning as a function of stress

    1. Direct effects: spouses of dementia victims, divorced or bereaving individuals show weaker immune systems

    2. Indirect effects: stressed person eats poorly, gets less sleep

  D. Mediating the effects of stressors

    1. Helplessness or control

        a.   Control increases lifespan of nursing home residents

        b.   Control decreases epinephrine levels and feelings of tension and depression; aids rejection of cancer cells

    2. Hardiness: personality characteristics and mood state

        a.   Openness to change, commitment, control

        b.   Psychological factors are modest at best

    3. Self-efficacy and optimism (positive sense of self, of personal control, and optimism may help people cope with stress)

  E. Personality, mood states, and cancer (connection remains to be shown)

IV. Psychological involvement in specific physical disorders

  A. Coronary heart disease

    1. Associated with cigarette smoking, obesity, high cholesterol, and other lifestyle issues

Copyright © Houghton Mifflin Company. All rights reserved.

2. Job stress and poor relations with boss increase blood clotting factor in women

3. Anxiety symptoms predict death due to cardiac arrest

4. Type A personality

5. Questioning the Type A hypothesis (irritability and hostility are the risk factors)

B. Stress and essential hypertension (high blood pressure with no known cause)

1. Stressors related to hypertension

2. Blood pressure higher when angry

3. Gender differences in effect of anger suppression

   a. High job status and belief that success requires great effort increases blood pressure in women and African-American men

4. Ethnic factors in hypertension: most prevalent in African Americans

C. Migraine, tension, and cluster headaches

1. Migraine: constriction and then dilation of cerebral blood vessels

   a. Classic: intense pain, neurological signs before throbbing pain

   b. Common: less pain and few neurological signs

   c. More hereditary than stress or personality based

2. Tension: not necessarily related to muscular tension; less severe than migraine

3. Cluster: excruciating pain around the eye

D. Asthma: chronic inflammatory disease of the airways in the lungs

1. Characteristics: often worst at night and early morning; mostly in youngsters

2. Psychological factors important in producing attacks (e.g., negative family environment)

3. In most cases physical and psychological causes interact

E. Perspectives on etiology

1. Psychodynamic perspective: each physical ailment produced by specific unconscious conflict, related to aggression and dependency (Alexander)

2. Biological perspective

   a. Evidence for genetic base

   b. Somatic weakness hypothesis and autonomic response specificity hypothesis

   c. General adaptation syndrome

3. Behavioral perspective

   a. Classical conditioning explains generalization after physiological reaction first occurs

   b. Operant conditioning: autonomic responses can be influenced by reinforcement (attention)

4. Sociocultural perspective

   a. Higher rates of cardiovascular disease in countries stressing individualism versus collectivism; the latter had higher rates of cerebrovascular disease

   a. Acculturated Japanese in California have higher heart disease rates than traditional Japanese

V. Treatment of psychophysiological disorders

A. Behavioral medicine merges a range of disciplines that study the social and psychological influences on health and provides approaches to medical conditions

B. Relaxation training: tense and relax each muscle group

Copyright © Houghton Mifflin Company. All rights reserved.

C. Biofeedback: information (feedback) on internal changes gives patient a means of altering visceral response

1. An operant technique

2. Used for blood pressure, headache, muscle tensions, blood flow control

D. Cognitive-behavioral interventions

1. Self-instruction and cognitive restructuring

2. When biological processes have primary influence and when psychological processes primary influence is not clear yet

LEARNING OBJECTIVES

1. Describe the sudden death syndrome and the factors related to it. Discuss how culture shock can lead to sudden death among Hmong immigrants. (pp. 199-200; Mental Health & Society)

2. List the DSM-IV-TR criteria for diagnosis of psychological factors affecting medical conditions. Explain the rationale for changes in terminology from "psychosomatic" to "psychophysiological." (pp. 200-201)

3. Discuss the three models for understanding stress, including Selye's general adaptation syndrome, the life change model, and Lazarus's transaction model. (pp. 201-205)

4. Discuss the research linking emotional states to vulnerability to infection. Discuss the evidence for and against the claim that stress influences the development of Acquired Immune Deficiency Syndrome (AIDS). (pp. 206-208)

5. Describe the components of the immune system and evidence that stress decreases its functioning. (pp. 208-209)

6. Describe the mediating effects of control and hardiness on stress. (pp.209-211)

7. Discuss the evidence linking personality, mood, and cancer. (pp. 211-213; Mental Health & Society)

8. Describe the relationship between stress and coronary heart disease and the influence of the Type A personality on CHD. (pp. 213-216; Critical Thinking)

9. Describe the relationship between stress and essential hypertension, and the ethnic and social factors associated with it. (pp. 216-219)

10. Describe the nature of migraine, tension, and cluster headaches. (pp. 219-221)

11. Describe asthma and the psychological factors related to it. (pp. 221-223)

12. Discuss the psychodynamic and biological perspectives on psychophysiological disorders, including the somatic weakness, autonomic response specificity, and the general adaptation hypotheses. (pp. 223-224)

13. Discuss the behavioral perspective on psychophysiological disorders, including the influence of classical conditioning and operant conditioning. Describe how sociocultural factors influence coronary heart disease. (pp. 225-226)

14. Define behavioral medicine and describe various interventions for psychophysiological disorders, including medical, relaxation training, biofeedback, and cognitive-behavior therapy. (pp. 226-228)

CLASSROOM TOPICS FOR LECTURE AND DISCUSSION

1. The effects of stressors on physical and psychological health are influenced by the availability of social support. A good deal of research indicates that support has a main effect on health; people with support are healthier, and some findings also indicate an interaction (stress-buffering) effect. For more

Copyright © Houghton Mifflin Company. All rights reserved.

information on this topic, see Cohen, S., and Wills, T. A. (1985). Stress, social support, and the buffering hypothesis. *Psychological Bulletin, 98,* 310–357.

Social support takes a variety of forms. Some support activities involve emotional validation and ventilation. Having someone to talk to about emotional experiences and problems appears to reduce stress reactions and lengthen life expectancy. Instrumental support includes helping that involves money, tools, babysitting, and other tangible resources. Another type of social support is providing information. Informational support can be especially beneficial in work settings and when a person is a newcomer to a situation.

An important distinction in social support is between that which is received and that which is perceived. Many studies have shown that the expectation that support is available or its rating of utility is protective of our mental and physical health. It may be that the support we see is as important as the support we actually obtain. It is possible that perceived support develops out of an individual's sense of optimism or pessimism, in which case support perception is more an individual personality variable than an environmental one. There is also the distinction between effective and ineffective supports. In some cases, people have such abrasive or dependent styles that interactions that might otherwise be mutually supportive become aversive. Excessive support can be seen as meddling or paternalism. On the other side of the coin, providing help can be such a draining and frustrating experience that the support provider may be extinguished by helping. Clearly, long-term support given by family members for those with Alzheimer's disease has negative health and emotional effects on the support provider (Basic Behavioral Science Task Force, 1996).

In many ways, the topic of social support emphasizes that stress reactions are not merely the result of environmental demands or personality patterns. The availability of psychosocial resources surrounding a stressful situation and the individual's capacity to make use of these resources influence the process as well.

A handout is provided to get students thinking about the structure and quality of the support network around them. It can lead to some emotional moments, particularly for students who feel isolated or insufficiently supported. Be sure to provide individual time for those students who might want to discuss the problems they see in their own support system.

Source: Basic Behavioral Science Task Force of the National Advisory Mental Health Council (1996). Basic behavioral science research for mental health: Family processes and social networks. *American Psychologist, 51,* 622–630.

Internet Site: http://www2.health-center.com/mentalhealth This site defines stress in several different ways.

2.   The Type A personality pattern may be reinforced and modeled in work and school situations. Where Type A leaves off and "workaholism" begins is not clear. A good topic for discussion is the tendency for some managers, professors, and others to encourage time-pressured and highly competitive modes of behavior. You should point out to students that Type A personalities do not usually rise to the top of corporations for any of several plausible reasons: (1) Some hard-driving Type A's may die prematurely and never reach the top; (2) Type A's tend to irritate others, making it difficult for them to maintain friendships and win the support of the backers they need to achieve the highest levels of management; and (3) Type A's tend to perform best at tasks that require little compromise and contemplation—not exactly the kinds of tasks that confront top-level managers.

Internet Site: http://www.2h.com/Tests/personality.phtml. This site contain a large selection of personality tests that you can take on the Internet including type A personality.

Copyright © Houghton Mifflin Company. All rights reserved.

116   *Chapter 7*

3.   Many of the physiological changes that occur during stress involve the hypothalamus-pituitary-adrenal axis and are influenced by the hormone cortisol. Therefore, changes in cortisol levels reflect changes in stress responses. A well-documented sex difference in corticosterone levels exists in lab rats: females are higher at baseline and respond to stressors like restraint or shock with increased secretion. Kirschbaum et al. (1992) report the first studies of laboratory-induced psychological stress in humans during which repeated cortisol levels were assessed. In four experiments the researchers show a dramatic sex difference in stress (cortisol) response.

Subjects experienced stress in a number of ways. Some were told to take the role of a job applicant and speak for five minutes before three strangers who acted as a selection committee. Some were asked to subtract, as quickly as possible, the number 13 from 1022 and start over if they made a mistake. Some pedaled stationary bicycles with the tension increased every two minutes until they were exhausted. Finally, others were given injections of corticotropin-releasing hormone. Cortisol levels were assessed by a recently developed saliva test every ten minutes during the fifty- to one hundred-minute test sessions.

Men and women showed nearly identical baseline cortisol levels and very similar curves as cortisol levels increased and decreased in response to the biological stressor of muscle fatigue and the physiologically induced changes caused by the corticotropin-releasing hormone injection. This result indicates that men and women are similar in their biological reactivity. However, in the public speaking and arithmetic situations, both of which increased cortisol levels two to four times baseline levels, men showed much higher peaks than women. In fact, men averaged from 1.5 to 2 times higher in cortisol than women did. Kirschbaum et al. (1993) argue that, although not conclusive, these sex differences stem from different interpretations of distressing psychosocial situations which, in turn, alter cortisol levels and perceived stress.

Source: Kirschbaum, C., Wust, S., & Hellhammer, D. (1992). Consistent sex differences in cortisol responses to psychological stress. *Psychosomatic Medicine, 54*, 648–657.

4.   The text describes cluster headaches as excruciating. Indeed, sufferers often contemplate suicide. Fortunately, some European physicians have found some promising prevention and treatment techniques. A group of Spanish physicians (Pascual, Peralta, & Sanchez, 1995) report that of four patients with chronic cluster headache, two were dramatically helped with a two-week course of hyperbaric oxygen. However, the other two patients remained either unimproved or had the frequency of headaches reduced. Given the lack of a control group and the extremely small sample, this technique's effectiveness is still in doubt. Another approach on larger samples has shown greater cause for optimism. A team in Italy reports that applying Caspian, the active ingredient in chile peppers, to the nasal passages can prevent the onset of cluster headaches (Fusco, Fiore, et al., 1994; Fusco, Marabini, et al., 1994). Cluster headaches occur on one side of the head (usually behind one eye) and cause the nose to become blocked. This team gave Caspian to either the same-side nostril as the headache or to the opposite side in fifty-one patients with episodic cluster headaches and nineteen with chronic cluster headaches. Same-side Caspian was significantly more effective and, among the episodic headache patients, 70 percent reported marked improvement. Although chronic patients obtained relief for no more than forty days, finding any preventative is a hopeful sign. Research with rats and humans has found that Caspian stimulates pain fibers in the nose and perhaps triggers changes in blood flow to the brain, which may explain the therapeutic effect. Internet Site: http://www.clusterheadaches.com/ is devoted to the understanding of cluster headaches.

Sources: Fusco, B. M., Fiore, G., Gallo, F., Martelletti, P., et al. (1994). "Capsaicin-senstivity" sensory neurons in cluster headache. *Headache, 34*, 132–137.

Fusco, B. M., Marabini, S., Maggi, C. A., Fiore, G., et al. (1994). Preventative effect of repeated nasal applications of Capsaicin in cluster headache. *Pain, 59*, 321–325.

Pascual, J., Peralta, G., & Sanchez, U. (1995). Preventive effect of hyperbaric oxygen in cluster headache. *Headache, 35*, 260–261.

Copyright © Houghton Mifflin Company. All rights reserved.

HANDOUT FOR CLASSROOM TOPIC 1:
MAPPING YOUR SOCIAL SUPPORT NETWORK

All of us, to one degree or another, rely on others to cope with life stresses. This activity will help you see the structure and quality of the social support system that is around you. One way to do this experience is to focus on a specific, recent stressful event and the people who supported you. Another way is to think more generally about the helpful people in your life.

Step 1

On a separate sheet of paper (preferably unlined), draw three equally spaced concentric circles so that they take up the entire page. The inside ring will show the people in your support system to whom you feel closest, those who know you most intimately and provide the most crucial support. Those in the second ring have a somewhat less intimate relationship with you; those in the outer ring are still supportive but not as critically important to you. Now consider the major categories of people in your life: family, friends from high school, current friends, people you know from work, and so on. There may be three, four, or more such categories. By drawing lines from the middle of the inner most circle, divide the concentric circles into as many pie-shaped pieces as you have categories of support people.

Step 2

On the next page, list by initials the people you consider to be the major supportive individuals in your life. Some could be "specialists," people to whom you go for help on specific problems; some will be "generalists." Some people you may see virtually every day; some you may see only periodically. Some might provide emotional support (listening to your problems or letting you know you are important to them); some might provide informational support (how to do something); some might provide instrumental support (loaning you money when you are broke); and, of course, some will provide combinations of these types of support. Don't worry if you don't have twenty-six names; just stop when you run out of names. Finally, decide whether your relationship with each person is in the inner (most intimate and supportive), the second, or third ring. You may also want to rate the quality of the support each person provides.

Step 3

Now write the initials of each person on the diagram in the location that identifies his or her closeness to you and the category or sphere of your life where you interact (family, work, school, and so on). Draw a small circle around each of the initials (people). At this point you can do many things to depict the nature of your support system. One is to draw lines between all the people in the network who know or are friends with one another. This activity will reveal the density of the network (the number of connections out of the total possible). It can also reveal how integrated or isolated the various spheres of your life might be. For instance, if you draw many lines across boundaries of your life, you have a highly integrated network—people at school know your family, and people at work know friends you made in high school. You can use colors or other designations to indicate the kinds of support that people provide (one for emotional, one for information, one for instrumental). You could indicate whether the direction of support is usually from that individual toward you or is mutual—you provide as much support as he or she does. One more issue you could examine is the direction of the relationship: Is the person moving toward the inner ring, toward the outer ring, or staying at the same level of intimacy/support? You can also examine other aspects of the network, but this exercise should have made it messy enough!

Copyright © Houghton Mifflin Company. All rights reserved.

Supportive Individuals

Initials	*Closeness (Ring)*
1.	
2.	
3.	
4.	
5.	
6.	
7.	
8.	
9.	
10.	
11.	
12.	
13.	

Supportive Individuals

Initials	*Closeness (Ring)*
14.	
15.	
16.	
17.	
18.	
19.	
20.	
21.	
22.	
23.	
24.	
25.	
26.	

Copyright © Houghton Mifflin Company. All rights reserved.

CLASSROOM DEMONSTRATIONS

1.   If biofeedback equipment is available, an in-class demonstration is the best way to show how information about internal changes can make involuntary responses come under conscious control. Finger temperature indicators are relatively inexpensive and require no training to use. In addition, finger temperature feedback is a method of treating migraine headaches.

Internet Site: http://www.aapb.org/. This site is the Association of Applied Psychophysiology and Biofeedback.

2.   Most stress models now accept the idea that individual differences in the perception of events and means of coping with them alter stress reactions. Furthermore, some stress and coping behaviors act as stressors themselves, keeping the person in distress, whereas others relieve stress. The following exercise can help students develop a cyclic model of stress that includes stressors, perceptions, physical and psychological reactions, and coping responses (some of which may produce new stressors).

Divide the class into four groups. Handouts are provided for four groups of students. Rather than segregating students by topic, all students could complete the four sections of the handout. Group 1 is assigned the task of brainstorming examples of stressors that are common among students they know (such as arguments with a roommate). After the group has developed a long list of such items, the group must decide on the half-dozen or so that occur most frequently. Group 2 is assigned the task of coming up with a list of perceptual statements or self-statements that they feel students commonly use when dealing with stressors (such as, "I can't deal with this any more."). They, too, must cull their list to the most commonly occurring statements in student populations. Group 3 is assigned the task of deciding, in similar fashion, what kinds of physical and psychological stress reactions they think are most common (such as headaches or restless walking). Group 4 should come up with a list of frequently used coping methods (such as shopping or talking with friends).

On the board draw four large boxes in a diamond shape. Label the boxes Stressors, Perceptions, Physical and Psychological Reactions, and Coping Responses. Put an arrow to connect each box. Ask students to report the results of their deliberations and write the ideas in the appropriate boxes on the board. Explain to them that, at each step in the process, individuals exercise some control (even in the area of stressors). Changes at any point in the cycle can reduce stress. Also suggest that each coping response can have short-term positive consequences (which is why it is considered a coping response), but that some coping responses may have long-term negative consequences that produce more stressors, not fewer. The key to stress management is finding methods of coping that produce positive consequences in both the short and long term.

Internet Site: http://www2.health-center.com/mentalhealth. This site defines stress in several different ways.

3.   The cognitive perspective has had a major impact on our understanding of the stress-illness relationship. Where once psychologists viewed the sheer number of life events as the best way of measuring stress, current researchers emphasize the way those events are perceived. The first semester of college, for instance, can be a deeply threatening dislocation for one person and a delightful opportunity for another. The Perceived Stress Scale (PSS), developed by Cohen et al. (1983), is a fourteen-item tool that measures the stressfulness of recent experience. It asks about the degree to which recent situations have seemed overwhelming, uncontrollable, and unpredictable.

Students can complete the questionnaire (see handout section) and score it themselves in class. Here is the scoring key: Items that are scored positively are 1, 2, 3, 8, 11, 12, and 14; items that are reverse-scored are 4, 5, 6, 7, 9, 10, and 13. For reverse-scored items, 0 = 4, 1 = 3, 2 = 2, 3 = 1, and 4 = 0. Mean scores for males, females, and overall, reported by Cohen et al. (1983), are as follows: males 22.1; females 24.7; overall 23.5. The difference between males and females is not statistically significant.

Copyright © Houghton Mifflin Company. All rights reserved.

The PSS is a good discussion starter. Students can be asked about the combinations of environmental and cognitive factors that account for their stresses, the impact on health-related behaviors such as eating and sleeping, and illness consequences. It is good to ask if any student has a high level of perceived stress but relatively good health. Ask him or her for explanations for what seems like a health-protective phenomenon. Mention such factors as low biological reactivity, strong social supports, and good health practices.

Source: From "A Global Measure of Perceived Stress," by S. Cohen, T. Kamarck, & R. Mermelstein, *Journal of Health and Social Behavior*, 24, pp. 385–396. Copyright © 1983. Used by permission.

4.   Stressful life events are key psychological factors in physical disorders, but there is controversy over how to measure life events. The original, and still widely used, instrument is the Social Readjustment Rating Scale (SRRS) (Holmes & Rahe, 1967). An alternative is the Life Experiences Survey (LES) (Sarason et al., 1978). It would take too long for students to fill out both surveys, but you can present shortened versions of them to illustrate their strengths and weaknesses.

Holmes, Rahe, and their colleagues surveyed thousands of people in a variety of cultures and had them rate the impact of the SRRS items. By averaging these ratings, they give life change unit scores for each. The problem is that what is average for thousands of people may not be appropriate for an individual. Further, the SRRS implies that positive as well as negative events are stressful and linked to illness. However, a review of the literature finds that changes for the better are not correlated with distress (Thoits, 1983). See if your students note a glaring problem with the SRRS: personal illness is scored as both a stressor and the thing stressors are supposed to predict—illness!

The LES gives the respondent control over rating the event's impact, opening the door to denial, exaggeration, or other forms of bias. It, too, lists what are presumed to be common stressful events. It does have the advantage of leaving blanks for unlisted events that the respondent experienced. However, it, like the SRRS, leaves some events undefined (for example, "trouble with in-laws"). Ask students what life events they would add to such surveys and whether different populations require different lists of events. Finally, suggest that daily hassles may have as much or more relationship to physical and mental distress as the major, discrete events listed in these measures (Zarski, 1984). This partially explains the relatively weak correlations between stressful life event scores and near-term illness.

Copyright © Houghton Mifflin Company. All rights reserved.

Items from the Social Readjustment Rating Scale

In the past six months, have you experienced any of the following?

	Event	Life Change Units (LCUs)
1.	Death of a spouse	100
2.	Divorce	73
3.	Jail term	63
4.	Personal injury or illness	53
5.	Marriage	50
6.	Gain of new family member	39
7.	Change in responsibilities at work	29
8.	Begin or end school	26
9.	Change in recreation	19
10.	Christmas	12

Items from the Life Experience Survey

Please check the events you have experienced in the recent past and indicate the period during which you have experienced each event. Also, for each item checked, please indicate the extent to which you viewed the event as having either a positive or negative impact on your life at the time it occurred.

Event	0–6 mo	7–12 mo	Extreme (Negative)	Moderate	Some	None	Some (Positive)	Moderate	Extreme
1. Marriage			−3	−2	−1	0	+1	+2	+3
2. Major change in eating habits (much more or much less)			−3	−2	−1	0	+1	+2	+3
3. New job			−3	−2	−1	0	+1	+2	+3
4. Death of close friend			−3	−2	−1	0	+1	+2	+3
5. Trouble with in-laws			−3	−2	−1	0	+1	+2	+3
6. Breaking up with boyfriend/girlfriend			−3	−2	−1	0	+1	+2	+3
7. Failing a course in school			−3	−2	−1	0	+1	+2	+3
8. Borrowing for a major purchase (e.g., home)			−3	−2	−1	0	+1	+2	+3

Copyright © Houghton Mifflin Company. All rights reserved.

Other recent experiences that have had an impact on your life

Event	0–6 mo	7–12 mo	Negative				Positive		
			Extreme	*Moderate*	*Some*	*None*	*Some*	*Moderate*	*Extreme*
_____			–3	–2	–1	0	+1	+2	+3
_____			–3	–2	–1	0	+1	+2	+3

Sources: Reprinted by permission of the publisher from "Items from the Social Readjustment Rating Scale," by T. Holmes and R. Rahe, *Journal of Psychosomatic Research, 11,* 1967, pp. 213–218. Copyright © 1967 by Elsevier Science Inc.

Life Experience Survey from "Assessing the Impact of Life Changes: Development of the Life Experiences Survey," by I. G. Sarason, J. H. Johnson, & J. M. Siegel, *Journal of Consulting and Clinical Psychology, 46,* pp. 932–946. Copyright 1978 by the American Psychological Association. Reprinted by permission of the American Psychological Association and the author;

Thoits, P. A. (1983). Dimensions of life events as influences upon the genesis of psychological distress and associated conditions: An evaluation and synthesis of the literature. In H. B. Kaplan (Ed.), *Psychosocial stress: Trends in theory and research.* New York: Academic Press; Zarski, J. J. (1984). Hassles and health: A replication. *Health Psychology, 3,* 243–251.

5.   A major stressor for students is finals week. The general adaptation and life-events models of stress-related illnesses suggest that large numbers of students should become sick during finals or just after they are over. On the other hand, the transaction model would emphasize the importance of thoughts and coping methods as mediators of a stressor-illness relationship. You can informally put these models to the test by asking students to recall the finals period in the semester or quarter prior to the one you are teaching. Ask them to recall the situation and give an overall rating of its stressfulness. Then have them list the physical symptoms they might have experienced during and after finals. A handout is provided. Compile their responses and cluster their responses into categories of high, medium, and low stressfulness. During class time, examine whether, on average, students in the high-stressful group were more likely than those in the low-stressful group to fall ill during or after finals. If the high-stressful group lists more symptoms than the low-stressful group, there is support for the general-adaptation and life-events approaches. If not, there may be mediating factors such as coping methods, beliefs, and health behaviors that might account for the results. These would support Lazarus's transaction model. Ask students to describe what their lives were like during and after finals. What explanations do they offer for the results?

Another element in this demonstration is to ask students to predict the stressfulness of finals week for the present semester or quarter and their estimated likelihood of becoming ill during it. When finals week arrives, you can survey students about their current health to see how well they predicted their own future. You can keep these predictions on file and share them with the next class you teach.

Copyright © Houghton Mifflin Company. All rights reserved.

Remind your students that the first activity's retrospective research opens itself to several kinds of bias. Students may inaccurately recall the degree or number of stressors they faced in the previous finals period, they may fail to recall or inflate the recollection of illnesses, and they may inaccurately date their occurrence. The prospective design of the second activity avoids these problems but is vulnerable to a different bias: having made a personal prediction, students may alter their reporting of current circumstances to prove those predictions accurate.

Copyright © Houghton Mifflin Company. All rights reserved.

HANDOUT FOR DEMONSTRATION 1: STRESSORS, THOUGHTS, STRESS REACTIONS, AND COPING BY STUDENTS

This activity is designed to get you thinking about the range of events, thoughts, stress reactions, and coping mechanisms you might see in college students. The activity requires you to brainstorm first and then reduce your list of ideas to the best three or four. *Brainstorming* means that each person in the group should come up with as many ideas as he or she can. Criticism is forbidden although requests for clarification are permitted. For each of the four topics in this exercise, the group should generate a *minimum* of ten ideas. When no more ideas are coming, the group should think about the three or four *most commonly occurring* examples from the original list. In other words, if group members came up with thirteen different coping methods that students use to deal with stress, they will need to decide on the three or four most commonly used methods they have seen in themselves, their friends, and others.

Depending on how your instructor set up the activity, your group will either complete all four parts below or just the part that was assigned to you.

I.   STRESSORS

List ten or more stressful situations that are common in the life of college students. These can include discrete life events such as taking final exams or breaking up with boyfriend/girlfriend or more prolonged situations such as not having enough money or driving an unreliable car.

1. _____   6. _____
2. _____   7. _____
3. _____   8. _____
4. _____   9. _____
5. _____   10. _____

The most common stressors facing students

1. _____
2. _____
3. _____

II.   STRESS-RELATED THOUGHTS

List at least ten thoughts that you or others commonly think tend to inflate stress reactions. Sometimes called "catastrophic thoughts," they can be about the event (This is the worst thing that ever happened.); about the expected consequences of the event (If I have to face her again, I'll die of embarrassment.); or about the individual's perceived capacity to deal with the event (I know I cannot deal with these situations.).

1. _____   6. _____
2. _____   7. _____
3. _____   8. _____
4. _____   9. _____
5. _____   10. _____

Copyright © Houghton Mifflin Company. All rights reserved.

The most common stress-inflating thoughts

1. _____
2. _____
3. _____

III.   STRESS REACTIONS

List ten or more stress reactions that are common in the life of college students. These can include behaviors such as irritability or crying or medical conditions such as headache or nausea. Ask if the psychophysiological conditions listed in the book (asthma, ulcer, hypertension, migraine, and tension headaches) are commonplace.

1. _____   6. _____
2. _____   7. _____
3. _____   8. _____
4. _____   9. _____
5. _____   10. _____

The most common stress reactions

1. _____
2. _____
3. _____

IV.   COPING METHODS

List ten or more coping methods that college students use to respond to stress. These can include outward behaviors such as talking with friends and shopping or more internal reactions such as meditating or praying. Some coping mechanisms are focused on reducing bad feelings while others directly attack the problem at hand. Include both types in your first list.

1. _____   6. _____
2. _____   7. _____
3. _____   8. _____
4. _____   9. _____
5. _____   10. _____

The most common coping methods

1. _____
2. _____
3. _____

Copyright © Houghton Mifflin Company. All rights reserved.

HANDOUT FOR DEMONSTRATION 3:
PERCEIVED LEVEL OF STRESS

Instructions: The questions in this inventory ask you about your feelings and thoughts during the last month. In each case, you will be asked to indicate how often you felt or thought a certain way. Although some of the questions are similar, there are differences between them, and you should treat each one as a separate question. The best approach is to answer each question fairly quickly. That is, don't try to count the number of times you felt a particular way, but rather indicate what seems like a reasonable estimate. For each question, choose from the following alternatives:

0 = never   1 = almost never   2 = sometimes   3 = fairly often   4 = very often

1. In the last month, how often have you been upset because of something that happened unexpectedly? _____

2. In the last month, how often have you felt that you were unable to control the important things in your life? _____

3. In the last month, how often have you felt nervous and stressed? _____

4. In the last month, how often have you dealt with irritating life hassles? _____

5. In the last month, how often have you felt that things were going your way? _____

6. In the last month, how often have you felt confident about your ability to handle your personal problems? _____

7. In the last month, how often have you felt that things were going the way you expected they would? _____

8. In the last month, how often have you found that you could not cope with all the things that you had to do? _____

9. In the last month, how often have you been able to control irritations in your life? _____

10. In the last month, how often have you felt that you were on top of things? _____

11. In the last month, how often have you been angered because of things that happened that were outside of your control? _____

12. In the last month, how often have you found yourself thinking about things that you have to accomplish? _____

13. In the last month, how often have you been able to control the way you spend your time? _____

14. In the last month, how often have you felt difficulties were piling up so high that you could not overcome them? _____

Source: From "A Global Measure of Perceived Stress," by S. Cohen, T. Kamarck, & R. Mermelstein, *Journal of Health and Social Behavior, 24,* pp. 385–396. Copyright © 1983. Used by permission.

Copyright © Houghton Mifflin Company. All rights reserved.

HANDOUT FOR DEMONSTRATION 5: STRESS AND HEALTH DURING FINALS WEEK

The following questions are designed to help you remember the last finals period you experienced so that you can give it an overall rating in terms of stressfulness.

How many courses were you taking? _____

In how many courses did you take a final exam? _____

In how many courses did you have papers or other assignments due at the end of the semester or quarter? _____

On a scale from 1 to 10 (with 10 = extremely difficult) rate the difficulty level of each course you took.

course 1 _____   course 2 _____   course 3 _____   course 4 _____

course 5 _____   course 6 _____   course 7 _____   course 8 _____

What other events were occurring during the finals period that might have added to its stressfulness?

On a scale from 1 to 10 (10 = extremely stressful) give an overall rating to the stressfulness of the last finals period you experienced. _____

During the last finals period you experienced, did you have any of the following symptoms?

(Circle all that apply)

sore throat	runny nose	fever	fatigue
skin rash	headaches	nausea	diarrhea
insomnia	stomach pain	weight loss	cough
sweating	dizziness	other (specify)	

In the week **after** the last finals period you have experienced did you have any of the following symptoms?

(Circle all that apply)

sore throat	runny nose	fever	fatigue
skin rash	headaches	nausea	diarrhea
insomnia	stomach pain	weight loss	cough
sweating	dizziness	other (specify)	

Copyright © Houghton Mifflin Company. All rights reserved.

SELECTED READINGS

Booth-Kewley, S., & Friedman, H. S. (1987). Psychological predictors of heart disease: A quantitative review. *Psychological Bulletin, 101,* 342–362.

Cohen, S., & Williamson, G. M. (1991). Stress and infectious disease in humans. P*sychological Bulletin, 109,* 5–24.

Friedman, H. S. (Ed.) (1991). *Hostility, coping, and health.* Washington, DC: American Psychological Association.

O'Leary, A. (1990). Stress, emotion, and human immune function. *Psychological Bulletin, 108,* 363–382.

Rodin, J., & Salovey, P. (1989). Health psychology. *Annual Review of Psychology, 40,* 533–579.

Sattler, D., Shabatay, V., and Kramer, G. (1998). *Abnormal psychology in context: voices and perspectives.* Boston, MA: Houghton Mifflin Company. Chapter 6, Psychological Factors and Medical Conditions.

Clipson, C., & Steer, J. (1998) *Case studies in abnormal psychology.* Boston, MA: Houghton Mifflin Company. Chapter 8, Stress-Related Disorders.

VIDEO RESOURCES

Biofeedback: Listening to Your Head (16 mm, color, 22 min). Brain-wave biofeedback as a technique to control diseases and emotional problems and to open new avenues of communication. Ideal School Supply Company, 1100 S. Lavergne Avenue, Oak Lawn, IL 60453.

Biofeedback and Self-Regulation (16 mm, color, 22 min). Interviews with Neal Miller and others illustrate how people can directly control a variety of physiological processes. Harper & Row Media, 10 E. 53rd Street, New York, NY 10022.

Headaches (16 mm, 15 min). This film differentiates the various forms of headache and their causes and describes symptoms that require medical attention. Journal Film, Inc., 930 Pitner Street, Evanston, IL 60202.

Health, Mind, and Behavior (#23) from the *Discovering Psychology* series (video, color, 30 min). This segment reviews recent research on the relationship between mind and body, including psychoneuroimmunology and biofeedback. The Annenberg/CPB Collection, Dept. CA94, P.O. Box 2345, S. Burlington, VT 05407-2345; to order, call 1-800-532-7637.

Management of Asthmatic Children (16 mm, 30 min). The contribution of psychological factors to asthma in young children is illustrated by a lecturer who works with a child's parents. Time-Life Multi-Media, 100 Eisenhower Drive, Paramus, NJ 07652.

Stress (16 mm, 11 min). A very brief description of Selye's work on the general adaptation syndrome and how that syndrome is related to psychophysiological disorders. Contemporary Films, McGraw-Hill, 1221 Avenue of the Americas, New York, NY 10020.

Stress: A Disease of Our Time (16 mm, color, 35 min). This film shows several experiments with disorders such as migraine headache, peptic ulcer, and asthma to relate the experience of stress to illness. Time-Life Multi-Media, 100 Eisenhower Drive, Paramus, NJ 07652.

Copyright © Houghton Mifflin Company. All rights reserved.

Emotion and Illness (VHS, color, 30 mm.). Looks at the immunology research that shows a link between emotional and physical health. Films for the Humanities and Science. 1-800-257-5126.

Hypertension: The Relaxation Response (VHS, color, 50 mm.). Teaches the viewer to use relaxation techniques to manage stress and hypertension. Insight Media. 1-800-233-9910.

Managing Stress, Anxiety, and Frustration (VHS, color, 60 min.). Looks at how stress is linked to many physiological disorders. Insight Media. 1-800-233-9910.

The Nature of Stress (VHS, color, 60 mm.). Part of The World of Abnormal Psychology series.
The Annenberg/CPB Collection, Dept. CA94, P.O. Box 2345, S. Burlington, VT 05407-2345; to order, call 1-800-532-7637.

The Relaxation Response (VHS, color, 30 mm.). Looks at the relaxation response and shows exercises to elicit that response. Films for the Humanities and Science. 1-800-257-5126.

ON THE INTERNET

http://www.pslgroup.com/ is an organization based in Australia that has developed the "Doctor's Guide to the Internet."

http://www.americanheart.org the home page for The American Heart Association, which has an extensive listing of materials on heart disease and stroke.

http://www.takeheart.co.uk at this site individuals can check their own risk for developing coronary heart disease, and learn more about symptoms, course, risk factors, prevention, etc.

Copyright © Houghton Mifflin Company. All rights reserved.

CHAPTER 8
Personality Disorders and Impulse Control Disorders

CHAPTER OUTLINE

I. Personality disorders
   A. Characteristics
      1. Inflexible and maladaptive behaviors
      2. Social difficulties, subjective distress, or problems in functioning
      3. Account for 5 to 15 percent of admissions to hospitals and outpatient clinics; overall lifetime prevalence between 10 and 13 percent
      4. Gender distribution: more men have paranoid, obsessive-compulsive, and antisocial; more women have borderline, dependent, and histrionic
      5. Problems in diagnosis
         a. Recorded on Axis II of DSM
         b. Extreme versions of normal personality traits; DSM requires either-or decision about disorder
         c. Overlap of symptoms with other disorders
         d. Clinicians do not adhere to diagnostic criteria
         e. Criteria: current and long-term personality pattern, either notably impairs functioning or causes distress
   B. Etiological and treatment considerations for personality disorders
      1. Use five-factor model (FFM) of personality and see disorders as extremes
         a. Neuroticism (emotional instability)
         b. Extraversion (prefer interaction)
         c. Openness to experience (curious and willing to entertain new ideas)
         d. Agreeableness (helpful and forgiving)
         e. Conscientiousness (organized)
      2. Causes
         a. Genetics
         b. Family environment
      3. Treatment
         a. Approaches vary
         b. Frequently not sought
         c. Research needed to verify efficacy of different approaches for different personality disorders
      4. Ten personality disorders in three clusters

Copyright © Houghton Mifflin Company. All rights reserved

a. Odd or eccentric behaviors: paranoid, schizoid, schizotypal

b. Dramatic, emotional, or erratic behaviors: histrionic, narcissistic, antisocial, borderline

c. Anxious or fearful behaviors: avoidant, dependent, obsessive-compulsive

C. Disorders characterized by odd or eccentric behaviors

1. Paranoid personality disorder: unwarranted suspiciousness, lack of emotion, hypersensitivity

    a. DSM-IV-TR prevalence estimate is 0.5 to 2.5 percent; somewhat higher among males

    b. Psychoanalytic thinking emphasizes projection

2. Schizoid personality disorder: desired social isolation; relationship to schizophrenia unclear

3. Schizotypal personality disorder: oddities of thinking and behavior without loss of reality contact; social isolation secondary

    a. Occurs in approximately 3 percent of population

    b. Higher risk of schizotypal disorder among relatives of schizophrenics

D. Disorders characterized by dramatic, emotional, or erratic behavior

1. Histrionic personality disorder: self-dramatizing, attention seeking, and exaggerated emotions

    a. Prevalence between 1 and 3 percent

    b. Diagnosed more frequently among women

2. Narcissistic personality disorder: exaggerated self-importance

    a. Denial and devaluation of others to prop up self-concept

    b. Prevalence about 1 percent; more prevalent in males

3. Antisocial personality disorder: guiltless, little loyalty (more on this later)

4. Borderline personality disorder: fluctuations in mood including angry outbursts; identity problems; feelings of emptiness; capricious behaviors

    a. Most commonly diagnosed personality disorder (DSM-IV-TR prevalence estimates prevalence at 2 percent; three times more common in females)

    b. Lack of purposefulness

    c. Etiological theories: psychodynamic (split objects into all good or all bad, including self); social learning (poor coping skills); cognitive (mistaken assumptions and attributions)

E. Disorders characterized by anxious or fearful behaviors

1. Avoidant personality disorder: desires attention from others but hypersensitive to disapproval; fantasies of intimacy; depression and inadequacy

2. Dependent personality disorder: unwilling to assume responsibility; low self-confidence; lets others decide

    a. Prevalence about 2.5 percent

    b. Cognitions: think they are inherently inadequate and need someone to take care of them

3. Obsessive-compulsive personality disorder: perfectionistic; no expression of warmth; demanding of others; indecisive

    a. Prevalence about 1 percent; twice as common in males

II. Antisocial personality disorder

A. Views of ASP:

1. Historically called moral insanity, moral imbecility, moral defect, and psychopathic inferiority

Copyright © Houghton Mifflin Company. All rights reserved.

2. Diagnosis of APD (also called sociopathic or psychopathic personality) has now lost some of the moralistic overtones despite disregard for society rules and morals.

B. Cleckley's checklist of characteristics

1. Superficial charm and good intelligence
2. Shallow emotions, lack of empathy
3. Little life plan or order
4. Failure to learn from experience, lack of anxiety
5. Unreliability and dishonesty

C. DSM-IV-TR symptoms

1. Do not include lack of anxiety, shallow emotions, failure to learn from punishment, or superficial charm
2. Does include history of truancy/delinquency before age 15 (but diagnosis at or after 18 years old)
3. Revised psychopathy checklist has two factors: egocentricity and impulsivity/antisocial behavior; only second factor fades with age

D. Incidence about 3 percent of American males; less than 1 percent females

E. Two types: primary psychopath (lacks guilt) and secondary psychopath

F. Explanations of antisocial personality disorder

1. Psychodynamic perspective

   a. Faulty superego development
   b. Lack of parental identification

2. Family and socialization perspectives

   a. Divorce and socioeconomic indicators weak predictors of disorder
   b. Poor parental involvement and prenatal hostility good predictors of disorder
   c. Antisocial father as model; use social skills to manipulate others

3. Genetic influences

   a. Five times more common among first-degree biologic relatives of males
   b. MZ twins' concordance rate higher than that of DZ twins
   c. Greater likelihood among adoptees whose biologic parents have APD, but does not preclude environmental factors

4. Central nervous system abnormality

5. Autonomic nervous system abnormalities: inability to learn from experiences, absence of anxiety, tendency to engage in thrill-seeking behaviors

6. Fearlessness or lack of anxiety (Lykken, 1982): failure to learn avoidance because of underarousal; research supports hypothesis

7. Arousal, sensation seeking, and behavioral perspectives

   a. Big T's (thrill seekers): either constructive (test pilots) or destructive (antisocial personality)
   b. Type and certainty of punishment are important: physical, social, material punishment ineffective for APD, but loss of memory is effective and when punishment is highly certain

G. Treatment of antisocial personality disorder

1. Antisocial are poorly motivated to change themselves
2. Successful treatment may require behavior controls
3. Behavioral and cognitive approaches are not very effective

Copyright © Houghton Mifflin Company. All rights reserved.

4. Treatment strategies should focus on antisocial youth who seem amenable to treatment and should involve family and peers

III. Disorders of impulse control

A. Characteristics

1. Failure to resist temptations resulting in harm
2. Tension before committing act
3. Release after committing act
4. Guilt may or may not be felt

B. Intermittent explosive disorder: discrete episodes of uncontrolled aggression

C. Kleptomania: recurrent failure to resist impulses to steal; more common in women

D. Pathological gambling: inability to resist gambling

1. About 2 to 3 percent of adults; more common in males
2. Manic while winning; depression follows
3. Cognitive-behavioral approaches focus on erroneous beliefs about ability to influence outcomes governed by chance

E. Pyromania: deliberate fire setting driven by fascination, not revenge

1. Pleasure in observing fires
2. Children are hostile and impulsive
3. More common in males

F. Trichotillomania: irresistible urge to pull out one's own hair

1. More common in women
2. About 1 percent of college students report current or past history

G. Etiology and treatment of impulse control disorders

1. Little information on causes

a. In some ways like obsessive-compulsive disorders, in other ways like substance abuse, in others like sexual deviance

2. Psychoanalytic theory stresses sexual symbolism
3. Behaviorists stress variable reinforcement schedule
4. Lesieur (1989) notes two explanatory camps

a. Impulse control problems on a continuum (behavioral, cognitive, and sociological perspectives)
b. Impulse control disease (psychodynamic and physiological perspectives)

5. Treatments often include behavioral and cognitive methods; can include family and self-help groups (such as Gamblers Anonymous)

LEARNING OBJECTIVES

1. Discuss the general characteristics of personality disorders, the factors involved in considering a personality pattern a disorder, how they are diagnosed in the DSM-IV-TR, and why they are difficult to diagnose. (pp. 231–233)

2. Discuss the prevalence and gender distribution of personality disorders and possible reasons for gender differences. (pp. 231–232; Critical Thinking)

3. Discuss the causal considerations for personality disorders, including the five-factor model and its relevance. Explain why we know little about treating personality disorders. (pp. 232–235; Mental Health & Society)

4. Describe the three clusters of personality disorders. (p. 235; Figure 8.1)

Copyright © Houghton Mifflin Company. All rights reserved.

5. Describe and differentiate among the characteristics of paranoid, schizoid, and schizotypal personality disorders. Discuss how schizoid and schizotypal personality disorders are differentiated from schizophrenia. (pp. 235-239)

6. Describe and differentiate among the characteristics of histrionic, narcissistic, antisocial, and borderline personality disorders. (pp. 239-243)

7. Describe and differentiate among the characteristics of avoidant, dependent, and obsessive-compulsive personality disorders. (pp. 243-245)

8. Describe the characteristics and incidence of antisocial personality disorder and how it is differentiated from criminal behavior. Explain why it is a difficult population to study. (pp. 245-248)

9. Describe and discuss the etiological theories of antisocial personality disorders, including psychodynamic, family and socialization, and genetic theories. (pp. 248-251)

10. Discuss the relationship between central nervous system and autonomic nervous system abnormalities and antisocial personality disorder. Discuss the role of fearlessness, lack of anxiety, underarousal, learning deficits, and thrill-seeking in the disorder. (pp. 251-255; Mental Health & Soceity)

11. Describe treatments for antisocial personality and their success. (pp. 255-256)

12. Define impulse control disorders. Describe and differentiate among the following impulse control disorders: intermittent explosive disorder, kleptomania, pathological gambling, pyromania, and trichotillomania. (pp. 256-261)

13. Discuss how impulse control disorders overlap with other conditions. Describe the two explanatory "camps" for these disorders. Review the treatments for impulse control disorders and their success. (pp. 261-262)

CLASSROOM TOPICS FOR LECTURE AND DISCUSSION

1. It should be easy to impress upon students the huge impact that a small number of antisocial personalities can have on our lives. Charles Manson and, perhaps, Jim Jones stand out as examples. Further, it is alarming that the number of antisocial personalities appears to be growing. Ask students whether the enormous increase in drug-related teenage murder can be considered a symptom of antisocial behavior. (News reporters claim that most of the 366 murders committed in Washington, D.C., in 1988 were by teenagers who, when their drug customers did not pay, simply killed them.) What makes the picture even more grim is the fact that prison does not change antisocial personalities, and psychological treatment has hardly done much better.

Prevention is the critical third option when treatment and punishment prove ineffective. Ask students what aspects of family and social life must change to prevent new cases of antisocial personality. Prod them to think about training for parenthood, the impact of television and movies, drug culture, and unemployment. If antisocial personality is actually genetically based, what should be done with high-risk groups such as the children of antisocial fathers? What hurdles do they see in the way of preventing new cases of the disorder?

http://www2.health-center.com/mentalhealth Search for the main characteristics of antisocial personality disorder.

2. More than in many other chapters, students can come down with "medical student syndrome" while reading about personality and impulse control disorders. It is a good idea to acknowledge this. It is also valuable to point out how resisting forbidden behaviors is a part of everyone's struggle to cope. Ask students to list (privately) behaviors that they have trouble resisting. These might include fingernail

Copyright © Houghton Mifflin Company. All rights reserved.

biting (if hair pulling is a disorder, can nail biting be far behind?), ice cream eating, television watching, shopping, and computer game playing or Internet surfing. Ask them what they are feeling before they engage in the "forbidden" behavior. What do they feel and think during and after? What separates their inability to resist from that of people with impulse control disorders? Point out the degree to which their behavior dominates their lives, the intensity of their feelings, and whether the behavior harms anyone else.

In the end, it is impaired functioning and subjective distress that define disorders, one of the definitions used in Chapter 1.

3.   The Five-Factor Model (FFM) (Digman, 1990) has emerged as the dominant approach to personality patterns in the past ten years. A natural link occurs between this model and the personality disorders, but the use of the model's assessment instrument, the NEO Personality Inventory (Costa & McCrae, 1985), as a diagnostic device has drawn both praise and criticism. Costa and McCrae (1990) report comparisons of their NEO Personality Inventory with the Millon Clinical Multiaxial Inventory-II (a highly regarded assessment instrument for diagnosing personality disorders). The correlation matrix for the two instruments over six personality disorders is as follows:

Five-Factor Dimensions

Personality Disorder	Neuroticism	Extraversion	Openness to Experience	Agreeableness	Conscientious- ness
Borderline	.46***	–.09	–.16	–.22	–.22
Compulsive	–.05	–.03	–.11	.15	.52***
Narcissistic	–.22*	.42**	.17	–.31*	–.24
Paranoid	.04	.24	.12	–.07	.02
Schizotypal	.39**	–.34**	–.07	.06	.01
Antisocial	.15	.21	.08	–.42***	–.40***

The most striking findings are that, with the exception of paranoid personality disorder, each disorder has at least one NEO-PI scale that strongly correlates with it. Most of the results are to be expected. Borderline personality disorder's chief characteristic is fluctuation in moods, which is nearly identical to the meaning of the term *neuroticism*. Obsessive-compulsive personalities are highly organized and detail-oriented, so "conscientiousness" is likely to be high on their list of values. Narcissistic individuals distrust others and deride their abilities, so a negative correlation with "agreeableness" is understandable. Explaining the strong correlation between narcissistic personality disorder and extraversion is somewhat more difficult, although narcissistic individuals want others to notice them and their achievements. Schizotypal individuals, with their bizarre thoughts and interpersonal difficulties, are likely to be both emotionally intense (neuroticism) and withdrawn from others (introverted). One could also predict that people with antisocial personality disorder, who are impulsive and interpersonally predatory, would score low on both conscientiousness and agreeableness.

Widiger and Trull (1992) conclude that while the FFM is a compelling model of personality disorders, it has serious methodological and conceptual limitations. In particular there has been little research on the less known factors (agreeableness, openness to experience, and conscientiousness) and it is difficult to sort out how depression can contribute to personality disorders. Coolidge et al. (1994) identify four reservations about using the FFM as a model for personality disorders. First, in their research comparing the NEO-PI and Millon scales, they found that neuroticism was involved in all of the personality disorders so that it did not help discriminate among them. Second, Coolidge et al. argue that the model implies that all five factors have equal weight when, in fact, neuroticism and extraversion do most of the

Copyright © Houghton Mifflin Company. All rights reserved.

predicting. Third, there is confusion on whether openness to experience is an intellect factor or not. Costa and McCrae themselves suggest that intelligence may be a needed sixth factor in explaining personality disorders. Finally, it is premature to use the NEO Personality Inventory as the only measure of the five factors; other, older measures have tapped many of the same personality factors.

Sources: Coolidge, F. L., Becker, L. E., DiRito, D. C., Durham, R. L., Kinlaw, M. M., & Philbrick, P. B. (1994). On the relationship of the five-factor personality model to personality disorders: Four reservations. *Psychological Reports, 75,* 11–21.

Costa, P., & McCrae, R. R. (1985). *The NEO Personality Inventory Manual.* Odessa, FL: Psychological Assessment Resources.

Costa, P. & McCrae, R. R. (1990). Personality disorders and the five-factor model of personality. *Journal of Personality Disorders, 4,* 362–371.

Digman, J. M. (1990). Personality structure: Emergence of the five-factor model. *Annual Review of Psychology, 41,* 417–440.

Widiger, T. A., & Trull, T. J. (1992). Personality and psychopathology: An application of the five-factor model. *Journal of Personality, 60,* 363–393.

Internet Site: http://www.psych.nwu.edu/~pizzurro/mcadams.html. Site on the five factor model.

4.   The overlap between the impulse control disorders and obsessive-compulsive disorder is interesting. Trichotillomania is a difficult disorder to treat successfully and has many of the characteristics of obsessive-compulsive disorder. Individuals pull their hair out when they feel anxious, and they experience relief after they do so. Despite disfiguring effects, they continue to pull out their hair in a chronic, ritualistic way (Christenson et al., 1991). Interestingly, clomipramine, a drug that is increasingly used to treat obsessive-compulsive disorder, has, in several case studies, helped patients with trichotillomania (Black & Blum, 1992; Gupta & Freimer, 1993; Swedo et al., 1989). It also seems that itchy scalp is a problem for many patients, so the combined use of clomipramine and topical steroid medication may be more effective than either medication alone.

Gupta and Freimer (1993) report on a 13-year-old girl with a 14-month history of hair pulling who had no hair longer than an inch in length and so many bald spots that she wore a wig. After taking 150 mg of clomipramine for two weeks and using a topical steroid medication for itching, she had a complete remission in hair pulling.

Sources: Black, B. W., & Blum, N. (1992). Trichotillomania treated with clomipramine and a topic steroid (letter). *American Journal of Psychiatry, 149,* 842–843.

Christenson, G. A., Mackenzie, T. B., & Mitchell, J. E. (1991). Characteristics of 60 adult chronic hair pullers. *American Journal of Psychiatry, 148,* 365-370.

Gupta, S., & Freimer, M. (1993). Trichotillomania, clomipramine, and topic steroids (letter). *American Journal of Psychiatry, 150,* 524.

Swedo, S. E., Leonard, H. L., Rapoport, J. L., Lenane, M. C., Goldberger, E. L., & Cheslow, D. L. (1989). A double-blind comparison of clomipramine and desipramine in the treatment of trichotillomania (hair pulling). *New England Journal of Medicine, 321,* 497-501.

Internet site: http://www.health-center.com/english/pharmacy/meds/anxiety.htm. Discusses antianxiety medications, which are often used to treat anxiety disorders such as obsessive-compulsive disorders.

Copyright © Houghton Mifflin Company. All rights reserved.

CLASSROOM DEMONSTRATIONS

1.   This exercise emphasizes speculation more than fact, which reflects our current state of knowledge about personality disorders. Have students pair off or form small groups. Present each group of students with two descriptions of hypothetical married couples with personality disorders (see the Handout for Demonstration 1). In their groups, students should first check to be sure they understand the features of each of these personality disorders. Then they should answer the questions on the handout sheet. These questions should help them understand the adaptive nature of personality disorders, the interpersonal conflicts they can engender, and the impact such marriages have on children. Some or all of the student groups should report their answers and speculations to the rest of the class. Examine how universal the impressions are.

There is a danger that this exercise will spawn stereotypes, so you should point out that people are far more complex than mere labels might suggest.

Internet Site: http://www2.health-center.com/mentalhealth Search this site for discussions of all the personality disorders currently defined in the DSM-IV-TR.

2.   Parenting style is often assumed to be a cause of personality disorders. At the extremes, parenting styles can be exceptionally tolerant or authoritarian. At one end of the continuum, we might expect spoiled children, and at the other, brutalized children. In this demonstration, students are asked to consider whether particular personality disorders are the result of spoiling or brutalizing children. The possibility should also be raised that neither or both are true.

After you introduce this exercise, write on the board the words *Spoiled* and *Brutalized*. List on the left side the following: Paranoid, Dependent, Histrionic, Narcissistic, Obsessive-Compulsive, and Schizoid. Have students describe the basic characteristics of each personality disorder as an in-class review. Ask students to speculate on whether each personality disorder is likely to develop in one of these extreme parenting conditions, in neither, or in both. It is likely that they will see low-self-confidence disorders, such as dependent personality disorder, as coming from authoritarian parents, and grandiose disorders, such as narcissistic personality disorder, coming from overly tolerant parents. You may agree or disagree with this, but you should point out the possibility that overt behavior may belie one's underlying self-image (for example, narcissists who try to compensate for low self-confidence). Finally, it is well to note that empirical research on these questions is sorely lacking.

3.   There are so many personality disorders, it will be helpful to give students a handout (provided) that lists them and provides a brief description. The text also indicates current prevalence estimates and whether a gender difference occurs in the diagnosis of the disorder. Use the handout to have students discuss the reasons for gender differences (stereotyping, biased sampling, socialization, and so forth) and the reasons when no such differences occur.

4.   Many characters in television and cinema have extreme personalities, bordering on personality disorders. Ask students to nominate characters from situation comedies, dramas, and the like who they think illustrate the personality disorders. If they are stumped, consider Chrissy (Suzanne Somers's character) on *Three's Company* reruns as an example of the histrionic personality disorder. If students can recall Felix Unger (Tony Randall's character) in *The Odd Couple,* you can use him as an example of the obsessive-compulsive personality disorder.

5.   A number of biographies about famous people with antisocial personality disorder are available. Reading excerpts can give students a nontextbook, nonclinical description of the remorseless,

Copyright © Houghton Mifflin Company. All rights reserved.

exploitative, thrill-seeking manner of these individuals. Examples of biographies are *The Executioner's Song* (about murderer Gary Gilmore) by Norman Mailer, *Helter Skelter* (about Charles Manson) by Vincent Bugliosi, and more recent accounts of Ted Bundy, Jim Jones, and David Koresh.

6.   Antisocial personality disorder is associated with high levels of thrill seeking. Individuals with this disorder feel bored if not stimulated by risky situations, frequent change, and adventure. Perhaps because they are biologically programmed to have low arousal levels, antisocial personalities need to seek out additional sensations to reach an optimal level of arousal. Marvin Zuckerman (1978, 1979) has developed a measure to assess a general sensation-seeking trait. More than 10,000 people have taken this test. You can give a short version to your students and quickly score the results.

Please caution students against making sweeping generalizations about their personalities and, especially, about whether they have antisocial personality tendencies. First, one test cannot be considered a reliable measure of anything about an individual. Second, college-age people tend to take a great many more risks than the general population. Third, antisocial personality disorder involves a good deal more than high sensation seeking. And finally, as Farley (1986) points out, a need for variety and arousal can take both a constructive and a destructive form. Here are the scoring key and norms. Count one point for each of the following items:

1. A	4. B	7. A	10. B
2. A	5. A	8. A	11. A
3. A	6. B	9. B	12. A
			13. B

1–3 points: very low on sensation seeking
4–5 points: low
6–9 points: average
10–11 points: high
12–13 points: very high

Sources: Farley, F. (1986). World of the Type T personality. *Psychology Today, 20,* 45–52.

Zuckerman, M. (1979). *Sensation seeking: Beyond the optimal level of arousal.* Hillsdale, NJ: Lawrence Erlbaum; test reprinted with permission from *Psychology Today Magazine.* Copyright © 1978 (Sussex Publishers, Inc.).

Copyright © Houghton Mifflin Company. All rights reserved.

7.   The Internet Web site http://www.bpdcentral.com (Borderline Personality Disorder Central) has assembled first-person accounts of this disorder—what it is like for people, how their behaviors affect others and themselves—from posts to a newsgroup, from interviews, and from other sources. By reading these comments aloud you can help students become aware of the thinking and emotions that characterize borderline personality disorder. This demonstration should increase students' empathy for people who often get contempt from even well-meaning therapists.

Person A. I think that borderliners are concerned of only one thing: losing love. When cornered, I get very scared and I show that by getting angry: anger is easier than fear and less vulnerable. I strike before being stricken. Real anger, the anger normal persons feel, by getting unjust treatment or being disappointed, I don't feel at all, I don't have that capability. It would require a self, a complete being, self conscience [sic] and self-confidence to get angry because people are treating you badly. Since I don't have a self (or better said: since I put away my own self so deep that I can't reach it myself anymore) I don't have all those things and I can't get angry.

I think this goes for all borderliners; that no BP will admit they are really scared when they are angry. When I'm angry, I can't be reasonable too. When I'm angry, I'm angry and telling myself doesn't help. The only thing that helps is when my husband says to me, "I know you are scared and not angry." At that moment, my anger melts away and I can feel my fear again. But that's the only thing that works.

Person B. It feels terribly lonely to be borderline. I am living in a castle, with very thick defensive walls and a very tightly closed draw-bridge and door. Outside is a crowd and they are having a party. But I can't hear what it's about and I can't join them, although part of me wants to. So I stand at the window and look outside and I don't understand what they are doing. Also I feel like they look at me all the time and laugh at me for not understanding and not belonging. I don't know what I have to do to belong or to understand. The castle is empty. I am the only thing in it. Not only the only living thing, but really the only thing: the castle is completely empty. There is no furniture, no wallpaper, no carpets. The wooden floors are bare, the closets are empty, and the doors are standing ajar. The castle is huge, with many floors, and every floor has many rooms and everything is empty. Try imagining living like this and you can, just for a little bit, understand how we feel.

Person C. We borderlines occasionally cut ourselves because we are hurting so bad, and no one knows how bad we hurt, that we cut ourselves just to somehow externalize how we feel. Like we could never communicate the pain we have (because it is too big and people don't understand) and also because how could we feel so much without it somehow being visible from the outside. There are times when we have cut ourselves because we were really hurting and it comforted us, but then there were those times when we wanted to say, "See how bad I hurt!" like it is a way of communicating and expressing the extent of our pain. Words just are not powerful enough.

Internet Site: http://www.bpdcentral.com. This site is Borderline Personality Disorder Central.

8.   Two films that depict excellent examples of personality disorders are *Fatal Attraction* and *Misery*. Ask for volunteers from the class to view the movies, then make a diagnosis of the lead characters in each. Many students will have seen these films. Alternately, you could rent the films and select short portions to show to the class. Glenn Close's character is identified by many as a classic borderline personality disorder, while the character portrayed by Kathy Bates in *Misery* could be paranoid or schizoid rather than psychotic.

9.   Have the student form small groups of between 4-7 individuals depending on your class size and space limitations. Assign students to collect pictures from magazines of people who seem to have the physical characteristics of some of the personality disorders described in the chapters, such as histrionic, narcissistic, and others. Ask each group to develop this list with the most salient examples first. Each

Copyright © Houghton Mifflin Company. All rights reserved.

group could then have a spokesperson deliver a short talk about the best examples. You could provide a blank overhead transparency to each group at the beginning of this demonstration.

10.   Bring the DSM-IV-TR to class, and prepare an overhead transparency or PowerPoint slide ahead of time for your lecture on personality disorders. Describe the in-depth material from the DSM-IV while using the transparency or PowerPoint slide as an outline. Lead a discussion on the differences between different personality disorders. Encourage student input about individuals they have known with these symptoms.

Copyright © Houghton Mifflin Company. All rights reserved.

HANDOUT FOR DEMONSTRATION 1: EFFECTS OF PARENTING STYLE

For each couple described below, imagine that she is 31 and he is 33. They have been married for ten years, and they have two children—a boy (age nine) and a girl (age five).

The Case of Tom and Mindy

Tom is a classic obsessive-compulsive. He is an engineer who must have everything perfectly orderly and clean at work and at home. Unable to express his emotions, he deals only in facts. In Tom's mind, every action must be rational; all decisions must fit some master formula. Mindy is a classic histrionic personality. She is attractive and tends to be flirtatious and attention seeking. To her, life is a series of crises, but her feelings never seem to be more than superficial. She forgets facts quickly and uses only impressions to describe her world.

Speculate on the answers to these questions:

1. What did Tom see in Mindy that made him want to marry her?

2. What did Mindy see in Tom that made her want to marry him?

3. What are their major points of conflict concerning the house and the children?

4. Who disciplines the children and how?

5. Why do they stay married?

The Case of John and Sarah

John is a classic dependent personality. He tolerates everything his boss, mother, or wife demands. He considers himself a weak and generally incompetent man. Frightened of offending anyone, he keeps any opinions he might have to himself. Sarah is a classic narcissistic personality. She sees herself as the hottest real estate agent in the business and complains bitterly about the poor performance of others. Secretly, she worries that others will not value her, so she puts herself in a good light as much as she can.

Speculate on the answers to these questions:

1. What did John see in Sarah that made him want to marry her?

2. What did Sarah see in John that made her want to marry him?

3. What are their major points of conflict concerning the house and the children?

4. Who disciplines the children and how?

5. Why do they stay married?

Copyright © Houghton Mifflin Company. All rights reserved.

HANDOUT FOR DEMONSTRATION 3:
PERSONALITY AND IMPULSE CONTROL DISORDERS: DESCRIPTIONS, PREVALENCE, AND GENDER DISTRIBUTIONS

Disorder Category	*Estimated Prevalence (percent)*	*Gender Difference*
Odd or eccentric behaviors		
Paranoid: unwarranted suspiciousness, hypersensitivity, controlled	0.5 to 2.5	males somewhat more
Schizoid: social isolation, indifference toward others	uncommon	males slightly more
Schizotypal: peculiar thoughts and behaviors	3.0	unclear
Dramatic, emotional, or erratic behaviors	2.0 to 3.0	females more in some studies
Histrionic: attention seeking, exaggerated emotional expression, dramatic		
Narcissistic: exaggerated self-importance, lack of empathy	1.0	males more
Antisocial: break rules without remorse, impulsive, lack of anxiety	2.0	males 3 times more
Borderline: intense changes in mood, feelings of emptiness, stormy relationships	2.0	females 3 times more
Anxious or fearful behaviors		
Avoidant: fear of rejection and humiliation, hesitant interpersonal relations	< 1.0	no differences
Dependent: unwarranted reliance on others, unwillingness to take responsibility	2.5	unclear
Obsessive-compulsive: perfectionism, rigidity, attention to details	1.0	males more
Impulse control disorders		
Intermittent explosive: loss of control over aggressive impulses	rare	males more
Kleptomania: failure to resist impulses to steal	rare	females more
Pathological gambling: failure to resist impulses to gamble	1.0 to 3.0	males more
Pyromania: recurrent purposeful fire-setting	probably rare	males more
Trichotillomania: failure to resist impulses to pull out one's hair	1.0 to 2.0 (of college students)	females more

Copyright © Houghton Mifflin Company. All rights reserved.

HANDOUT FOR DEMONSTRATION 6: SENSATION-SEEKING SCALE

For each item, circle the letter corresponding to the statement that best describes your preference or opinion. There are no right or wrong answers. Be as honest as possible.

1. A. I would like a job that requires a lot of traveling.
   B. I would prefer a job in one location.

2. A. I am invigorated by a brisk, cold day.
   B. I can't wait to get indoors on a cold day.

3. A. I get bored seeing the same old faces.
   B. I like the comfortable familiarity of everyday friends.

4. A. I would prefer living in an ideal society in which everyone is safe, secure, and happy.
   B. I would have preferred living in the unsettled days of our history.

5. A. I sometimes like to do things that are a little frightening.
   B. A sensible person avoids activities that are dangerous.

6. A. I would not like to be hypnotized.
   B. I would like to have the experience of being hypnotized.

7. A. The most important goal of life is to live it to the fullest and experience as much as possible.
   B. The most important goal of life is to find peace and happiness.

8. A. I would like to try parachute jumping.
   B. I would never want to try jumping out of a plane, with or without a parachute.

9. A. I enter cold water gradually, giving myself time to get used to it.
   B. I like to dive or jump right into the ocean or a cold pool.

10. A. When I go on vacation, I prefer the comfort of a good room and bed.
    B. When I go on vacation, I prefer the change of camping out.

11. A. I prefer people who are emotionally expressive even if they are a bit unstable.
    B. I prefer people who are calm and even-tempered.

12. A. A good painting should shock or jolt the senses.
    B. A good painting should give one a feeling of peace and security.

13. A. People who ride motorcycles must have some kind of unconscious need to hurt themselves.
    B. I would like to drive or ride a motorcycle.

Reprinted with permission from *Psychology Today Magazine*. Copyright © 1978 (Sussex Publishers, Inc.).

Copyright © Houghton Mifflin Company. All rights reserved.

SELECTED READINGS

Adler, G. (1981). The borderline-narcissistic personality disorder continuum. *American Journal of Psychiatry*, 138, 46–50.

Cowdry, R. W., & Gardner, D. L. (1988). Pharmacotherapy of borderline personality disorder: Alprazolam, canbumazepine, trifluoperazine, and tranylcypromine. *Archives of General Psychiatry*, 45, 111–119.

Eron, L. D., Gentry, J. H., & Schlegel, P. (Eds.) (1994). *Reason to hope: A psychosocial perspective on violence and youth*. Washington, DC: American Psychological Association.

Hare, R. D. (1985). Comparison of procedures for the assessment of psychopathy. *Journal of Consulting and Clinical Psychology*, 53, 7–16.

Lesieur, H. R., & Rosenthal, R. J. (1991). Pathological gambling: A review of the literature. *Journal of Gambling Studies*, 7, 5–39.

Sattler, D., Shabatay, V., & Kramer, G. (1998). *Abnormal psychology in context: Voices and perspectives*. Boston, MA: Houghton Mifflin Company. Chapter 8, Personality Disorders and Impulse Control Disorders.

Clipson, C., & Steer, J. (1998). *Case studies in abnormal psychology*. Boston, MA: Houghton Mifflin Company. Chapter 12, Borderline Personality Disorder: One Side Wins, The Other Side Loses. Chapter 13, Antisocial Personality Disorder: Bad to the Bone.

VIDEO RESOURCES

A Psychopath (16 mm, 30 min). This case study examines the childhood and adolescent experiences of a psychopath through recollections and interviews with police and mental health professionals. McGraw-Hill Text-films, 1221 Avenue of the Americas, New York, NY 10020.

Achievement Place (16 mm, 30 min). Illustrates the use of a token economy treatment at a residential setting for predelinquent boys. Achievement Place has been a model for residential treatment of antisocial personality. University of Kansas Audio Visual Center, 746 Massachusetts Avenue, Lawrence, KS 66044.

Criminal Personality (VHS, 28 min). A psychiatrist explains how adult criminality can be traced to childhood experiences. The Center for Cassette Studies, 8110 Webb Avenue, North Hollywood, CA 91605.

"Personality Disorders" (#5) from *The World of Abnormal Psychology* series (video, color, 60 min). The hour is divided into four segments covering antisocial, narcissistic, borderline, and obsessive-compulsive personality disorders. The Annenberg/CPB Collection, Dept. CA94, P.O. Box 2345, S. Burlington, VT 05407-2345; to order, call 1-800-532-7637.

Shotgun Joe (16 mm, 25 min). Illustrates the characteristics of the antisocial personality, including the absence of remorse for socially unacceptable actions. Examines the antisocial personality's relationships with parents and peers. Jason Films, 2621 Palisade Avenue, Riverdale, NY 10463.

Copyright © Houghton Mifflin Company. All rights reserved.

Violent Youth: The Unmet Challenge (16 mm, color, 26 min). Three incarcerated juveniles, a chief of police, a family court judge, and the head of a juvenile detention center are interviewed. Harper & Row Media, 10 East 53rd Street, New York, NY 10022.

Personality Disorders (VHS, color, 60 mm.). The video looks at the different types of personality disorders. The Annenberg/CPB Collection, Dept. CA94, P.O. Box 2345, S. Burlington, VT 05407-2345; to order, call 1-800-532-7637.

ON THE INTERNET

www.nlm.nih.gov/ is the Web site of The National Library of Medicine

http://huizen.dds.nl/~laura_d/ is the home page of a Dutch woman diagnosed with borderline personality disorder. She describes herself, her theory of the disorder.

http://www.bpdcentral.com/ is Borderline Personality Disorder Central.

http://mental-health-matters.com is the Mental Health Matters home page, which offers information and links for mental health, self-help, and psychology information and resources.

http://www.mentalhealth.com/fr00.html has an index feature to explore all the personality disorders.

Copyright © Houghton Mifflin Company. All rights reserved.

CHAPTER 9
Substance-Related Disorders

CHAPTER OUTLINE

I. Introduction

    A. Substance-related disorders: when use of psychoactive drugs causes social, occupational, or physical problems

        1. Substance use: involving dependence and abuse

        2. Substance-induced disorders: intoxication, delirium, and withdrawal (discussed with cognitive disorders in Chapter 15)

        3. Substance abuse: recurrent use over 12 months leading to impairment or distress; continues despite social, physical, occupational, psychological, or safety problems

        4. Substance dependence: several symptoms over 12 months including tolerance or withdrawal

        5. Intoxication: a substance affecting the CNS has been ingested and maladaptive behaviors or psychological changes are evident

        6. Typical pattern from experimentation to abuse or dependence:

            a. Experimentation (usually with tobacco, alcohol, marijuana)

            b. Early regular use-actively seek substance & drug-induced state

            c. Plan daily activities around drug use; unpleasant states worsen and lead to more drug use and self-destructiveness

            d. Drugs (more potent) need to avoid constant dysphoria

II. Substance-use disorders

    A. Most prevalent among youths and young adults

        1. Adult lifetime prevalence for controlled substances is 6.2 percent; greatest for marijuana

        2. Drug of choice varies for different ethnic groups abuse of OTC drugs anticipated to increase for elderly age "baby boomers" age

        1. Recent studies show alcohol use stable but high; cocaine, hallucinogens, and heroin increased in past several years

        2. Adult lifetime prevalence for drug abuse/dependence (excluding alcohol) is 6.2 percent

    B. Gender and ethnic differences

        1. Women less likely to take drugs than men

        2. White Americans have higher lifetime prevalence rates for drug problems than Hispanic Americans or African Americans

    C. Depressants or sedatives: depress central nervous system and slow responses, increase relaxation, lower inhibitions

        1. Alcohol-use disorders

a. Need to use alcohol daily to function

b. Person can abstain but binges when he or she drinks

2. Alcohol consumption in the United States

a. 11 percent of adults consume one ounce or more per day; 35 percent abstain

b. 50 percent of alcohol consumed by 10 percent of drinkers; males drink two to five times more than females

c. Cultural variations: in some cultures with meals; in most cultures, females usually consume less; at older ages, blacks and Hispanics have higher rate of dependence than whites

3. The effects of alcohol

a. Short-term physiological effects

b. Specific effect related to dose, time, weight

c. Short-term psychological effects

d. Long-term psychological effects

e. Long-term physiological effects

4. Narcotics (opiates): opium and derivatives—morphine, heroin, codeine-depress CNS; provide relief from pain, anxiety, tension; are addictive: tolerance builds quickly, withdrawal symptoms are severe euphoria and sometimes nausea; tolerance builds quickly, withdrawal is serious

a. Administered intravenously, causes spread of HIV when needles shared

b. Lifetime prevalence is 0.7 percent; four times more common in men

5. Barbiturates: "downers" induce sleep and relaxation

a. Addicting, common in middle-aged and older people

b. Accidental overdose leads to death; dangerous in combination with alcohol

c. Polysubstance dependence (DSM-IV-TR diagnosis): at least three substances used (not including nicotine and caffeine) for twelve months and meets criteria for any drug

6. Benzodiazepines (for example, Valium): used to relieve tension, but people can develop tolerance and become dependent

D. Stimulants: CNS energizer producing elation, grandiosity, activity, appetite suppression

1. Amphetamines: speed up CNS activity, reduce need for sleep, suppress appetite, increase confidence

a. Increase dopamine concentrations

b. Taken orally, intravenously, snorted, and recently smoked ("ice")

c. Overdose fatal; heavy users can become homicidal, suicidal

d. Lifetime prevalence 2 percent; more men common in men and the poor

2. Caffeine

a. Effects: restlessness, usually transitory

3. Nicotine

a. Smoking is single most preventable cause of death in United States

b. Signs of dependence: attempts to stop are unsuccessful, attempts to stop lead to withdrawal, use continues despite physical disorder such as emphysema

4. Cocaine and crack

a. Growing use: from one to three million cocaine abusers need treatment

Copyright © Houghton Mifflin Company. All rights reserved.

b. Effects: when snorted, increases heart rate, reduces fatigue, produces euphoria; when smoked (crack), produces quicker effects; physical as well as psychological dependence

c. Addiction can develop, sometimes after short period of use; depression when high wears off

d. Crack is a purified and potent form

e. Concern to society for many reasons

5. Hallucinogens—not considered physiologically addictive

a. Marijuana: mildest, most common; 33 percent of United States population has used it; effects include passivity, tranquility, lung damage, memory problems; other risks seen as unsubstantiated

b. LSD: reality distortions and hallucinations; "bad trips"; flashbacks; psychoto-mimetic

c. Phencyclidine (PCP): very dangerous delusions, violence, perceptual distortions

6. Other substance-use disorders include anabolic steroids and nitrous oxide

III. Etiology of substance-use disorders

A. Most integrate biological and psychological factors

B. Biogenic explanations

1. Genetic impact shown through adoption research and twin studies; incidence of alcoholism four times higher for male biological offspring of alcoholic fathers than for offspring of nonalcoholic fathers

a. Familial and nonfamilial alcoholism

b. Specific genes: quantitative trait loci (QTL) analysis used in breeding animals for alcohol preference

c. Risk factors: neurotransmitters, sensitivity to alcohol, central nervous system differences, racial differences in response to drugs

C. Psychodynamic explanations

D. Explanations based on personality characteristics

1. High activity level, emotionality, goal impersistence, and sociability (but not causal)

2. Low frustration tolerance, high tolerance for deviance, antisocial behavior, depression

3. Reviews conclude there is no single alcoholic personality

4. Antisocial behavior and depression associated with drinking problems

E. Sociocultural explanations

1. Different patterns around the world (France and Italy high, Israel and China low)

2. Cultural values concerning tolerance of alcohol abuse

3. Ethnic variations in United States: drug abuse and dependence higher in whites than African Americans and Hispanic Americans; whites have lower alcoholism rates and heroin use

4. Peer identification: good predictor of adolescent smoking is the group a young person identifies with

F. Behavioral explanations

1. Anxiety reduction

a. Believed alcohol reduced anxiety of approach-avoidance conflict

b. Anxiety reduction is reinforcing

2. Learned expectations

Copyright © Houghton Mifflin Company. All rights reserved.

a. Marlatt, Deming, & Reid (1973): "told and given" alcohol or tonic water challenges disease concept of loss of control; expectation important

b. Longitudinal study of adolescent drinking: those who expect social benefits drink more and endorse more positive social benefits to alcohol

3. Cognitive influences

a. Conflicting findings that alcohol is tension reducing

b. Steele and Josephs find alcohol increases or decreases anxiety depending on how alcohol affects thought

c. Different types of stress produce different results

d. Coping styles

4. Relapse: a source of evidence

a. Risk factors: age at onset of drug use; more extensive involvement with substances; antisocial behavior; comorbid psychiatric disorder; less involvement in school or work; less support from drug-free family and peers; type of stressor is also important

b. Risk greatest in first three months following treatment

c. Negative emotional (not physical) states predict relapse

d. Marlatt and Gordon: negative emotional feelings, social pressure to drink/temptation are high-risk situations; coping skills important

e. Biological factors

f. Most heroin-addicted Vietnam vets discontinued use after return to United States

G. Overall theories of the addiction process

1. Solomon (1980): opponent-process theory (acquired motivation to avoid aversiveness of craving)

2. Wise (1988): two-factor model involves positive reinforcement and negative reinforcement

3. Tiffany (1990): theory of automatic processes (rather than conscious) and change-resistant processes

IV. Intervention and treatment of substance-use disorders

A. Detoxification: removal of substance produces withdrawal; followed by intervention programs to prevent return to use

B. Self-help groups

1. Alcoholics Anonymous: based on disease concept; fellowship and self-revelations encouraged in group; many drop out

2. Spinoffs include Al-Anon (for those who live with alcoholic) and Narcotics Anonymous

C. Pharmacological approach

1. Antabuse: to produce aversion to alcohol and stay abstinent

2. Methadone: to ease heroin withdrawal but is addicting itself

3. Nicotine replacement programs for cigarette smoking

D. Cognitive and behavioral approaches

1. Aversion therapy (shock and emetics)

2. Covert sensitization (imagery of nausea paired with drug use)

3. Skills training

4. Reinforcing abstinence

5. Behavioral treatment for cigarette smoking

Copyright © Houghton Mifflin Company. All rights reserved.

      a.   Rapid smoking and nicotine fading

      b.   Nicotine fading

   6.   Other cognitive-behavioral treatments: relaxation, systematic desensitization, extinction of relapse cues, thoughts restructured

   7.   Controlled-drinking controversy

 E. Multimodal treatment: detoxification, inpatient, outpatient, family therapy

 F. Prevention programs

   1.   Education campaigns

   2.   Smoking prevention in junior high

      a.   Resistance to social influence

      b.   Information on social image of smokers

      c.   Information on physical consequences of smoking

      d.   Smoking less likely in those getting intervention than in controls

 G. Effectiveness of treatment

   1.   Most heroin addicts and treated smokers are using within one year

   2.   Some recover on their own

   3.   Same factors predict outcome regardless of substance used

LEARNING OBJECTIVES

1. Distinguish substance-related disorders from substance-use cognitive disorders, substance abuse from substance dependence, and define the terms *tolerance, withdrawal,* and *intoxication.* Discuss the overlap in criteria for dependence and abuse. (pp. 265-68; Figures 9.1-9.3)

2. Describe the nature and scope of substance use and describe the types and prevalence of substance-use disorders in the United States. (p. 268)

3. Categorize the psychoactive drugs according to their properties (sedative, stimulant, or hallucinogenic). (pp. 268-291; Table 9.1)

4. Discuss the nature and magnitude of drinking problems in the United States and the short- and long-term physiological and psychological effects of alcohol. (pp. 270-273; Mental Health & Society)

5. Describe the effects of narcotics, barbiturates, and benzodiazepines. Define polysubstance use and explain why it causes special problems. (pp. 273-276; Mental Health & Society)

6. Describe and discuss the problems of stimulant-use disorders, including amphetamines, caffeine, nicotine, cocaine, and crack. Evaluate the controversy concerning nicotine addiction and its treatment. (pp. 276-278)

7. Describe and discuss the problems of hallucinogen-use disorders, including marijuana, LSD, phencyclidine (PCP), and "other substance-use disorders." Evaluate evidence concerning marijuana's harmful effects. (pp. 278-281)

8. Describe the two general types of etiological theories of substance-related disorders. Describe and evaluate the evidence for specific genes and risk factors related to alcoholism and other forms of substance dependence. (pp. 281-283)

9. Describe and discuss the various explanations for alcoholism and other substance-related disorders, including psychodynamic, personality, and sociocultural explanations. Evaluate research evidence on the relation between drug use and maladjustment. (pp. 283-285; Critical Thinking)

Copyright © Houghton Mifflin Company. All rights reserved.

10. Describe and discuss behavioral explanations for alcohol abuse and dependence, including the anxiety-reduction hypothesis, learned expectations, and cognitive influences. (pp. 285-287)

11. Discuss explanations for relapse among alcoholics and people who are dependent on other substances. Describe and distinguish opponent process, two-factor, and automatic processing theories of the addiction process. (pp. 287-290)

12. Describe the nature and effectiveness of alcohol and drug treatment programs, including self-help groups, pharmacological approaches to substance-use treatment, and controlled-drinking. (pp. 290-292)

13. Describe and compare the cognitive and behavioral approaches to treating substance-related disorders, including aversion therapy, covert sensitization, rapid smoking, nicotine fading, relaxation and social learning methods, and cognitive-change treatments. (pp. 292-296; Mental Health & Society)

14. Discuss what is meant by multimodal treatment. Describe and evaluate the evidence concerning treatment effectiveness for alcohol, smoking cessation, and other substance-related disorders. (pp. 296-298)

CLASSROOM TOPICS FOR LECTURE AND DISCUSSION

1. One of the mysteries of alcohol and drug abuse is that continued use occurs even when all the apparent consequences are negative. This seems to fly in the face of basic behavioral principles. It is useful to separate the short-term positive consequences of drug use from the more distant negative consequences. Develop a list on the blackboard of the short-term positive and negative consequences of drug use. Make another list of long-term positive and negative consequences. As abuse becomes physical addiction, the short-term consequences become positive indeed. The addict has a choice each day to either feel much better after one or two doses of the drug or wait through several very uncomfortable days (detoxification and withdrawal) before feeling human again. Some withdrawal syndromes, especially in poorly nourished individuals, can create medical emergencies.

This discussion of the power of immediate consequences should lead into a discussion of treatment. Behavior therapy stresses the need to disentangle the drug from its positive effects and to find alternative, drug-free ways of deriving pleasure. Cognitive approaches also must restructure the expectations of the user, from seeing the benefits of continued use to understanding the benefits of cutting down or quitting.

Internet Site: http://www.apa.org/divisions/div28. The Division of Psychopharmacology and Substance Abuse of the American Psychological Association.

2. The text notes that there are cultural differences in alcohol use. These are also reflected in the guidelines that health care professionals give their patients concerning drinking. In Great Britain for the past five or six years, general practitioner physicians and other health care professionals have been educating the public about sensible alcohol consumption. They have taught the public how to count alcoholic drinks in "units": one unit is equal to one-half pint of ordinary strength beer, a 125-ml glass of wine, or a single measure of 80-proof spirits. The Health Education Authority in conjunction with the British Medical Association has developed recommended separate "sensible" limits for men and women. For men it is 21 drinks per week with one or two drink-free days, for women 14 drinks per week with one or two drink-free days. A second range of drinking, described as "increasing risk," is 22 to 50 units for men and 15 to 35 units for women. "Harmful" drinking for men is given as more than 50 units per week and more than 35 for women. The gender differences are due to the greater mass and water content in men, which dilutes the alcohol and reduces blood alcohol concentrations even if the same dose is taken. Surveys show that 27 percent of men and 11 percent of women in Britain drink beyond this sensible zone (Edwards, 1996).

Copyright © Houghton Mifflin Company. All rights reserved.

Ask students if they think these numbers of drinks would be considered "sensible" in the United States. They may be amazed to find out that in 1996, a British government agency (not the British Medical Association) decided to revise the guidelines *upward!* The revised sensible zone was up to 28 drinks for men and 21 for women. Some have doubted the motivations for making the change because it is not based on scientific evidence; in addition, two of the 13 members of the deciding group were employees of the British ministry that works closely with the distilling industry. Most physicians have refused to go along with the new guidelines (Edwards, 1996).

Sources: British Health Education Authority (1994). *That's the limit: A guide to sensible drinking.*

Edwards, G. (1996). Sensible drinking: Doctors should stick with the independent medical advice. *British Medical Journal, 312,* 1.

3.   Although the text does not discuss the need for family treatment in most substance-abuse disorders, consider with students the following case:

An alcoholic and Valium-abusing mother has been unable to meet her family responsibilities for several years. Her eldest daughter has taken over many of these but has missed out on her own adolescence. The woman's husband no longer relies on her to meet intimacy needs. Mother goes off for inpatient treatment that does not include the rest of the family. She returns home sober and wanting her "rightful" place in the family.

Ask students how the family adapted to the woman's drug problem. Describe how the husband and daughter might react when the woman returns. Explain, in family system terms, the ways in which families can unconsciously promote relapse. Finally, discuss why family-oriented therapy should be more effective in the long run than traditional individual treatment.

4.   Miller and Rollnick (1991) provide a wealth of information on how professionals can help addicted individuals overcome their ambivalence about changing and consent to treatment. They use Prochaska and DiClemente's (1986) model of the change process, which states that change is usually cyclic and involves the following stages: precontemplation, contemplation, determination, action, and maintenance. At each stage the professional must present appropriate information in a nonthreatening manner in order to help motivate clients. For example, during contemplation, the client is highly ambivalent. The professional should be empathic and voice the client's reservations, help him or her to assess the costs and benefits of change, and subtly tip the balance in favor of change.

Because the six stages of change occur in a cycle, draw a circle on the board and divide it into five sections (contemplation through maintenance), leaving precontemplation outside the circle of change. Draw arrows from contemplation to determination, from determination to action, from action to maintenance. Draw two arrows from maintenance—one to permanent exit and another to relapse. This points out the possibility of establishing a new habit on the first trip around the cycle, but the greater likelihood of relapse. Relapse often leads to precontemplation but also can return to contemplation (a part of the change process). Successfully conquering an addiction typically takes several journeys around the cycle.

According to Miller and Rollnick (1991), five general principles for motivational interviewing (interacting with addicted individuals to foster change) are as follows:

1. *Express empathy:* Your acceptance of the client facilitates change. Be a skillful reflective listener. Appreciate that ambivalence and fear about change is normal.

Copyright © Houghton Mifflin Company. All rights reserved.

2. *Develop discrepancy:* Provide information about the consequences of continued drug use. A discrepancy between present behavior and important personal goals motivates change. Orchestrate the interview so that the client presents the arguments for change.

3. *Avoid argumentation:* Arguments are unproductive and breed defensiveness. Do not engage in labeling (for example, alcoholic or in denial).

4. *Roll with resistance:* Use psychological judo to take the client's momentum and shift perceptions. Turn problems back to the client so he or she can find solutions and avoid "yes, but..." games.

5. *Support self-efficacy:* Foster a belief that change is possible. Help the client see that he or she is responsible for choosing and carrying out personal change. Give a range of ways to change; a series of failures is not cause to give up.

Sources: Miller, W. R., & Rollnick, S. (1991). *Motivational interviewing: Preparing people to change addictive behavior.* New York: Guilford Press.

Prochaska, J. O., & DiClemente, C. C. (1986). Toward a comprehensive model of change. In W. R. Miller & N. Heather (Eds.) *Treating addictive behaviors: Processes of change.* New York: Plenum Press, pp. 3–27.

5.   The text notes that treatment outcomes for heroin users are often disheartening, with more than half of addicts readdicted within a year of treatment. One reason for this depressing statistic is the fascinating phenomenon called "needle habit." Before heroin addicts inject themselves, there are many preliminary behaviors. Injection equipment and drugs must be acquired and a suitable place found for injecting—often a bathroom. The drug is cooked, mixed with water, loaded into the syringe; a vein is found, tied off, and so on. All of these behaviors and the stimuli that are associated with them become conditioned stimuli paired with the unconditioned stimulus of the heroin itself. After many pairings, the ritual of injection takes on reinforcing properties by itself.

A heroin user (Powell, 1973) is quoted as saying, "Once you decide to get off, it's very exciting. It really is. Getting some friends together and some money, copping, deciding where you're going to do it, getting the needles out and sterilizing them, cooking up the stuff, tying off, then the whole thing with the needle, booting, and the rush, that's all part of it... *Sometimes I think that if I just shot water I'd enjoy it as much.*" (Italics added.)

O'Brien (1974) reports a study in which heroin addicts were given Naloxone, a narcotic antagonist (a drug that stops the pharmacological effect of a drug). This drug ensured that none of the subjects were actually experiencing any physiological "high." Addicts were then allowed to shoot up with their own equipment and use their own rituals in a special bathroom that simulated the usual setting for injection. Subjects either injected themselves with saline solution, a low dose of heroin, or a high dose. Since it was a double-blind study, no one but the experimenter (who was not present) knew what was being injected. Regardless of what they injected, the subjects reported experiencing pleasure after shooting up. Only after three to five injections did ratings come down to neutral, but one subject continued saying he felt a rush after 26 injections that could not have had a pharmacological effect! It turns out he was giving himself saline solution. So part of the relapse process in heroin addiction may be that the ritual of injection and its conditioned euphoria are missed—not just the physiological effects of the heroin.

Sources: O'Brien, C. P. (1974). "Needle freaks": Psychological dependence on shooting up. In *Medical World News, Psychiatry Annual.* New York: McGraw-Hill.

Powell, D. H. (1973). A pilot study of occasional heroin users. *Archives of General Psychiatry, 28,* 586–594.

Copyright © Houghton Mifflin Company. All rights reserved.

CLASSROOM DEMONSTRATIONS

1.   The following role-play can illuminate several issues in drug and alcohol treatment. First, it explores the role of denial in both the user and others in keeping people from getting help. Second, it points out the difficulties of confronting someone who denies that drugs are a problem. Third, it raises the issue of whether treatment can or should be forced on someone who does not want it. Finally, since the names in the main roles are sex-ambiguous, it examines whether identical behaviors are perceived as different depending on whether a male or a female is the drug abuser. Instructors can note many other issues as well.

A good topic to touch on after the groups report is how to motivate people for treatment. One approach, called *intervention* by the Johnson Institute, uses pressure and the creation of a personal crisis to break down defenses. Family members and friends are instructed to monitor incidents in which the substance abuser has affected them and, after some coaching from a counselor, confront the abuser as a group. In the meeting, the target person cannot speak until all of the family members and friends have their say. They should convey the message that while they care about the abuser, they must let him/her know how they feel and how they have been affected by drug-related behavior. The object is to cause such discomfort in the abuser that he or she becomes open to help. The group then provides support and, having already arranged it, rapid transition into treatment. A second approach emphasizes empathy and a kind of mental judo in which motivation comes not from direct confrontation but from subtle persuasion. The method, called *motivational interviewing*, is growing in popularity. It is founded on the transtheoretical model of change (Prochaska & DiClemente, 1986) that sees change as occurring in stages. If the user is ambivalent about changing, motivation comes by helping the person do a cost-benefit analysis of use and voicing the user's own doubts about maintaining the status quo. More information on these ideas are presented in item 4 in "Topics for Classroom Lecture and Discussion" in this chapter.

Divide the class into groups of six. (If class size is not a multiple of six, the character of Tracy can be dropped in enough groups to use all students.) Set the stage for the role play: Pat (the protagonist) has been called into a meeting convened by a psychologist (Dr. Dwight) because Kim and Terry have "had it" with Pat's poor behavior. Pat is adamant about not having a drug problem. Karen is sure Pat is unhappy but does not see drugs or alcohol as the source. Kim and Terry are certain that drugs and alcohol are the basis of Pat's problems, but they see different solutions to the problem. Tracy is ambivalent. Dr. Dwight plays the role of convener and facilitator.

Each group is given a copy of the Handout for Demonstration 1, and members select the roles they wish to play. Emphasize that the demonstration works well only when students stay "in role" (although you can expect some giggling and laughter). Each group is to play out the meeting/confrontation and resolve what will happen to Pat (forced into treatment? convinced that treatment will help? successful in thwarting attempts at treatment?). Once the groups are formed and you have answered any questions, you should plan to leave the room for five minutes or so to allow acting to go on without the students feeling that you are looking over their shoulders.

Let discussion go on until half of the groups seem to have come to some resolution (perhaps 15 minutes). Reconvene the class and write on the board abbreviated descriptions of each group's process and resolution. Be sure to ask about the ethics of confronting (and not confronting) drug abusers. Ask whether the students would have seen Pat and Kim differently if they were of the opposite sex.

Source: Prochaska, J. O., & DiClemente, C. C. (1986). Toward a comprehensive model of change. In W. R. Miller & N. Heather (Eds.) *Treating addictive behaviors: Processes of change.* New York: Plenum Press, pp. 3–27.

2.   A thought-provoking topic for discussion is whether drug and alcohol use is perceived as pathological or "normal." Present the following descriptions of drug use to students and ask them to rate each on a four-point scale (1 = no sign of abuse; 4 = a sure sign of abuse).

Copyright © Houghton Mifflin Company. All rights reserved.

A man who has been diagnosed with terminal cancer takes enough morphine to keep himself in a permanently drugged state.

A college student with sleep problems drinks by himself or herself in the dormitory room until drunk enough to fall asleep.

A fashion model uses amphetamines each day so that she can burn off enough calories and suppress her appetite to the point where she can stay as slim as the modeling agency requires.

A middle-aged man with a history of heart disease continues to smoke cigarettes because after six attempts at stopping in the past, he feels he will die a smoker.

A writer feels she cannot create significant poetry without being high on alcohol or marijuana.

A college student uses up all her month's spending money on cocaine within the first few days of the month.

Using a show of hands, tally the number of people rating each behavior as 1, 2, 3, or 4. Ask those who rate the behaviors as "normal" what would have to change for them to see a problem. Ask those who give a rating of 4 to explain their perceptions.

Some research (Leavy & Dunlosky, 1989) on undergraduate student and faculty perceptions of problem drinking indicates that heavier drinkers are less likely than light drinkers to perceive drinking problems and that students are less likely than faculty to perceive problems, even when differences in drinking habits are controlled.

Source: Leavy, R. L., & Dunlosky, J. T. (1989). Undergraduate student and faculty perceptions of problem drinking. *Journal of Studies on Alcohol, 50,* 101–107.

3. Legal restrictions have been placed on nearly all of the substances discussed in the current chapter. Ray and Ksir (1996) point out that, in many cases, crackdowns on drugs make some drugs less available but other, sometimes more dangerous drugs, more available. In 1644 the Emperor of China forbade tobacco smoking, an edict that was largely responsible for a surge in opium smoking. Opiate use in the United States was widespread in the late nineteenth and early twentieth century until the Harrison Act (1914), designed to tax the manufacture and sale of these drugs, became a way to make them illegal. The result was that opiate addicts switched to intravenous heroin.

Another point of view is to accept the inevitability of drug use and encapsulate it or reduce its harm on users and others. One example is the idea of providing clean needles to intravenous drug users so that the incidence of HIV is reduced. The needle exchange program in Liverpool, England, succeeded in slowing the spread of HIV. However, many would suggest that such programs make drug abuse easier and more attractive (Ray & Ksir, 1996).

The dilemma is this: Do we try to reduce the overall amount of drugs in society or to reduce the harm that drug use may inflict? Ask your students to examine their position on this critical issue. What do they think the goal of drug policy should be? Is drug policy a moral issue: Is it simply wrong to allow the spread of drug use?

Source: Ray, O., & Ksir, C. (1996). *Drugs, society, & human behavior* (7th ed.). St. Louis: Mosby.

4. Most students are interested in substance-abuse disorders, particularly as they affect adolescents. This demonstration conveys the most important risk factors for adolescent substance abuse and asks

Copyright © Houghton Mifflin Company. All rights reserved.

students to consider how much they feel these factors can be modified to reduce the incidence of abuse problems. The handout gives a consolidated list of factors taken from an exhaustive review by Hawkins et al. (1992). exhaustive review. For each risk factor, students should consider possible interventions to prevent adolescent substance abuse. You can also engage them in discussion of the costs to society for such interventions versus the costs of doing nothing. The full fifteen-page table of risk factors and research findings on successful and unsuccessful interventions in Hawkins et al. (1992) is well worth reading.

Source: Hawkins, J. D., Catalano, R. F., & Miller, J. Y. (1992). Risk and protective factors for alcohol and other drug problems in adolescence and early adulthood: Implications for substance abuse prevention. *Psychological Bulletin, 112,* 64–105.

5.　　The early identification of a problem makes its solution easier than if the problem progresses to full flower. Several screening devices can help nip alcohol abuse and dependence in the bud. One such instrument, the Alcohol Use Disorder Identification Test (AUDIT) is provided (see handout) but should be given to students with caution. No screening instrument can provide a diagnosis of a condition, and this caveat is especially true of alcohol abuse. There is no "gold standard" by which alcoholism can be defined, because many of the criteria offered by DSM-IV are subjective. For instance, the degree to which alcohol use impairs social or occupational functioning—for how long and how intensely—is a personal judgment. Nevertheless, you should discuss with students these screening devices so they can see what physicians, counselors, and others use to identify drinkers who may require further assessment for problems. The screening devices can generate discussion about potential errors in the detection of substance-related disorders. Those who are concerned with their own drinking might speak with you privately and be referred to your college or university counseling service for a more extensive evaluation.

The CAGE (Ewing, 1984) is a set of four questions that is widely used in clinical practice in the United States. Each question focuses on a lifetime problem that contributes to the acronym CAGE: Have you ever felt the need to Cut down on your drinking? Have you ever felt Annoyed by someone criticizing your drinking? Have you ever felt Guilty about your drinking? Have you ever felt the need for an Eye-opener (a drink first thing in the morning)? Two positive responses are considered the cutoff for making a fuller evaluation of the individual's drinking and its consequences. The sensitivity (ability to identify all potential cases) and specificity (ability to disregard noncases) for the CAGE ranges from 60 to 95 percent and 40 to 95 percent, respectively. The large range probably results from using different cutoff scores, asking in different ways, and sampling different populations. The advantages of the CAGE are its brevity and the ease with which a clinician can remember the questions. The disadvantage is that it asks about lifetime problems and omits current consumption or concerns. As with all self-report instruments, it relies heavily on the respondent's honesty.

The Alcohol Use Disorder Identification Test (AUDIT) developed for the World Health Organization is somewhat longer, focuses on consumption and problems in the past year, and has been tested internationally (Babor & Grant, 1989). It is a two-part device including ten items that can be done in a structured interview or as paper-and-pencil measure and a series of laboratory tests and alcohol-related physical measures. The ten-item survey is given on the handout. The maximum score is 41, the minimum 0. Using a cutoff score of 8, its sensitivity (92 percent) and specificity (93 percent) seem superior to the CAGE. Fleming reports using a cutoff score of 11 with college students.

Sources: Babor, T. F., & Grant, M. (1989). From clinical research to secondary prevention: International collaboration in the development of the Alcohol Use Disorder Identification Test (AUDIT). *Alcohol Health and Research World, 13,* 371–374.

Ewing, J. A. (1984). Detecting alcoholism: The CAGE questionnaire. *Journal of the American Medical Association, 252,* 1905–1907.

Copyright © Houghton Mifflin Company. All rights reserved.

6.   Have the students form small groups of 4-7 individuals depending on your class size and space limitations. Ask them to rewrite either the DUI/DWI laws or the laws pertaining to possession of a controlled substance and the consequences for breaking those laws. Ask each group to develop this list with the most salient examples first. Each group could then have a spokesperson deliver a short talk about the best examples. You could provide a blank overhead transparency to each group at the beginning of this demonstration. The class should discuss whether the laws were written to be tougher or easier on those who break the law.

7.   Have the student form small groups of 4-7 individuals depending on your class size and space limitations. Ask them how parents should talk to their children about drugs and alcohol. What would be effective? Would it change the parents' credibility if the child knows that the parents have used drugs and/or alcohol? Ask each group to develop this list with the most salient examples first. Each group could then have a spokesperson deliver a short talk about the best examples. You could provide a blank overhead transparency to each group at the beginning of this demonstration.

Copyright © Houghton Mifflin Company. All rights reserved.

HANDOUT FOR DEMONSTRATION 1: ROLE-PLAY

Pat: A 26-year-old junior high social studies teacher, Pat has worked at the same school for four years. Pat usually gets to work, but never has a lesson plan and "wings it" using films and rambling conversations with students. Papers and tests are superficially graded. Pat has fallen well behind the planned curriculum. Performance has declined rapidly in the past three months.

Pat smokes marijuana every morning before work and through the evening. On Friday nights, Pat drinks eight to ten drinks, and over the weekend, consumes three six-packs of beer. Pat has not gone more than two days without marijuana in the past two years.

Pat will not talk about drug or alcohol use, but focuses exclusively on the "lousy kids I have to teach" and old hurts and dissatisfactions in love life.

Kim: Pat's roommate of two years and friend from college, Kim is now concerned about Pat's increasing drug and alcohol use. Kim is angry at Pat's lack of responsibility. Kim complains to Pat of Pat's lack of professionalism at school and failure to help with shared costs and apartment clean-up. Pat gets verbally abusive when drunk, which scares and angers Kim. Kim has threatened to throw Pat out of the apartment unless there are changes. Kim called Dr. Dwight for help about Pat.

Terry: Pat's supervisor at the junior high (the social studies department head), Terry, is upset with the decline in Pat's teaching performance. Pat used to be involved with the kids while being fairly disciplined, but now Terry thinks that "Pat has a mental problem or hates teaching or is on drugs." Terry is very shy about confronting Pat, but will have to be honest when teacher evaluations are written in two weeks. Secretly, Terry wishes Pat would get out of the school and out of teaching.

Karen: Pat's 49-year-old divorced mother, Karen, left her alcoholic husband ten years before and has always considered Pat "my problem child." She wants Pat to "grow up and stop leaning on me," but denies that Pat has a drinking or drug problem. When Pat is in deep financial trouble, Karen always bails Pat out, although she feels angry about this afterward. While Karen isn't thinking that Pat has mental problems, she thinks that Pat is the one who ruined the family.

Dr. Dwight: A psychologist in private practice, Dr. Dwight, has convened this meeting and is taking no sides. Dr. Dwight believes that treatment works only when a client voluntarily asks for help. In this meeting, Dr. Dwight moves the conversation along and does not offer professional wisdom.

Tracy: Pat's 19-year-old brother, Tracy, has admired Pat for being the "wild one" in the family. Tracy is a highly responsible student and family helper. He has always been ambivalent about Pat, being sometimes jealous and sometimes furious.

Copyright © Houghton Mifflin Company. All rights reserved.

HANDOUT FOR DEMONSTRATION 4:
RISK FACTORS FOR ADOLESCENT SUBSTANCE ABUSE

Risk Factor	Evidence	What Could Be Done to Reduce Risk?
1. Laws		
a. Taxation	Increase in alcohol tax led to sharp decrease in consumption and cirrhosis mortality.	Raise taxes
b. Legal age	Higher drinking age associated with fewer teen traffic fatalities.	Raise and enforce age restrictions
2. Availability	Increased alcohol availability led to increased alcohol consumption.	Enforce laws; teach peer resistance skills
3. Neighborhood	Drug trafficking associated with high crime, mobility, low attachment in neighborhood.	Early family support for families in poverty
4. Physiological		
a. Biochemical	Low harm-avoidance predicts early-onset alcoholism.	Target interventions with those having markers, especially boys
b. Genetic	Slow-wave EEGs in children of alcoholics.	
5. Family drug use	Use by oldest brother and parents has independent effects on younger brother's use.	Parent-skills training for drug-using parents
6. Family management	Lack of or inconsistent parental discipline predicts initiation into drug use.	Parents skills training; family therapy
7. Family conflict	Marital discord and divorce predictors of drug use.	See 5 and 6
8. Early and persistent problem behavior	Aggressiveness and hyperactivity in boys age 5 to 7 predicts drug problems in adolescence.	Social competence training for child; parent-skills training
9. School failure	Failure in school predicts adolescent drug abuse.	Tutoring; parent involvement; alteration of classroom methods
10. Low school commitment	Students expecting to attend college have lower rates of learning in drug-use classroom.	Cooperative
11. Peer rejection in elementary grades	Low social competency associated with higher drug use.	Social-competence training
12. Association with drug-using peers	Influence of peers on use stronger than that of parents.	Social-influence resistance training
13. Alienation and rebelliousness	Alienation from dominant social values; resistance to authority are related to drug use.	Prosocial activities (for example, sports)
14. Early onset of drug use	Later onset predicts lower drug involvement.	Educate at a young age

Source: Consolidated from "Risk and Protective Factors for Alcohol and Other Drug Problems in Adolescence and Early Adulthood: Implications for Substance Abuse Prevention," by J. D. Hawkins, R. F. Catalano, & J. Y. Miller, *Psychological Bulletin, 112* (1), 1992, pp. 64–105. Copyright © 1992 by the American Psychological Association. Reprinted with permission from the American Psychological Association and the author.

Copyright © Houghton Mifflin Company. All rights reserved.

HANDOUT FOR DEMONSTRATION 5:
ALCOHOL USE DISORDER IDENTIFICATION TEST (AUDIT)

The following are questions about your use of alcoholic beverages (beer, wine, liquor) *during the   past year*.

Record the score for each question in the box on the right side of the question [   ].

1. How often do you have a drink containing alcohol?
[ ] Never	(0)	[ ]
[ ] Monthly or less	(1)	
[ ] 2 to 4 times a month	(2)	
[ ] 2 to 3 times a week	(3)	
[ ] 4 or more times a week	(4)	

2. How many drinks containing alcohol do you have on a typical day when you are drinking?
[ ] None	(0)	[ ]
[ ] 1 or 2	(1)	
[ ] 3 or 4	(2)	
[ ] 5 or 6	(3)	
[ ] 7 or 9	(4)	
[ ] 10 or more	(5)	

3. How often do you have six or more drinks on one occasion?
[ ] Never	(0)	[ ]
[ ] Less than monthly	(1)	
[ ] Monthly	(2)	
[ ] Weekly	(3)	
[ ] Daily or almost daily	(4)	

4. How often during the last year have you found that you were unable to stop drinking once you had started?
[ ] Never	(0)	[ ]
[ ] Less than monthly	(1)	
[ ] Monthly	(2)	
[ ] Weekly	(3)	
[ ] Daily or almost daily	(4)	

5. How often during the last year have you failed to do what was normally expected of you because of drinking?
[ ] Never	(0)	[ ]
[ ] Less than monthly	(1)	
[ ] Monthly	(2)	
[ ] Weekly	(3)	
[ ] Daily or almost daily	(4)	

Copyright © Houghton Mifflin Company. All rights reserved.

6. How often during the last year have you needed a first drink in the morning to get yourself going after a heavy drinking session?
   [ ] Never   (0)   [ ]
   [ ] Less than monthly   (1)
   [ ] Monthly   (2)
   [ ] Weekly   (3)
   [ ] Daily or almost daily   (4)

7. How often during the last year have you had a feeling of guilt or remorse after drinking?
   [ ] Never   (0)   [ ]
   [ ] Less than monthly   (1)
   [ ] Monthly   (2)
   [ ] Weekly   (3)
   [ ] Daily or almost daily   (4)

8. How often during the last year have you been unable to remember what happened the night before because you had been drinking?
   [ ] Never   (0)   [ ]
   [ ] Less than monthly   (1)
   [ ] Monthly   (2)
   [ ] Weekly   (3)
   [ ] Daily or almost daily   (4)

9. Have you or someone else been injured as the result of your drinking?
   [ ] Never   (0)   [ ]
   [ ] Less than monthly   (1)
   [ ] Monthly   (2)
   [ ] Weekly   (3)
   [ ] Daily or almost daily   (4)

10. Has a relative, friend, or doctor or other health worker been concerned about your drinking or suggested that you cut down?
    [ ] Never   (0)   [ ]
    [ ] Less than monthly   (1)
    [ ] Monthly   (2)
    [ ] Weekly   (3)
    [ ] Daily or almost daily   (4)

Record the total of the specific items.   [ ]

Copyright © Houghton Mifflin Company. All rights reserved.

SELECTED READINGS

Ellickson, P. L., & Bell, R. M. (1990). Drug prevention in junior high: A multi-site longitudinal test. *Science, 247*, 1299–1305.

Gallant, D. M. (1987). *Alcoholism: A guide to diagnosis, intervention and treatment.* New York: W. W. Norton.

Glantz, M., & Pickens, R. (Eds.) (1991). *Vulnerability to drug abuse.* Washington, DC: American Psychological Association.

Miller, W. R., & Hester, R. K. (1986). Inpatient alcoholism treatment: Who benefits? *American Psychologist, 41*, 794–805.

Nathan, P. E. (1993). Alcoholism: Psychopathology, etiology, and treatment. In P. B. Sutker & H. E. Adams (Eds.) *Comprehensive handbook of psychopathology.* New York: Plenum Press, pp. 451–476.

Sattler, D., Shabatay, V., & Kramer, G. (1998). *Abnormal psychology in context: Voices and perspectives.* Boston, MA: Houghton Mifflin Company. Chapter 9, Substance-Related Disorders.

Clipson, C. , & Steer, J. (1998) *Case studies in abnormal psychology.* Boston, MA: Houghton Mifflin Company. Chapter 9, Alcohol Dependence: The Web that Denial Weaves.

VIDEO RESOURCES

ACA Recovery: Meeting the Child Within (video, color, 25 min). Vignettes depict the childhood experiences of Adult Children of Alcoholics (ACAs) and the process of getting better by appreciating their unmet childhood needs and the covert messages they learned. University of Minnesota Film and Video Service, Suite 108, 1313 Fifth Street S.E., Minneapolis, MN 55414-1524.

The Addictive Personality (slides and audio cassettes, 45 min). An examination of the addictive personality. Emotional needs that predispose an individual to drug use are described, as well as the effects of addiction and its treatment. IBIS Media, P.O. Box 308, Pleasantville, NY 10570.

Alcohol and Drugs: How They Affect Your Body (16 mm, color, 20 min). A description of how the brain regulates functioning in the rest of the body and how drugs interfere with normal functioning, leading to long-term deterioration. Barr Films, P.O Box 5667, Pasadena, CA 91107.

Alcoholism: Out of the Shadows (16mm, color, 30 min). An ABC-TV documentary giving first-hand accounts of individuals whose alcoholism seriously affected their own lives and those of others. American Broadcasting Corporation TV, 1330 Avenue of the Americas, New York, NY 10019.

Fetal Alcohol Syndrome (16 mm, color, 13 min). Describes the effects of alcohol abuse by mothers during pregnancy. Shows physical abnormalities and retardation at birth and throughout the child's development. Films, Inc., 1144 Wilmette Avenue, Wilmette, IL 60091.

LSD: Insanity or Insight? (16 mm, color, 18 min). The film shows what is known about the psychological and physiological effects of LSD. Adverse effects such as chromosomal damage, brain chemistry changes, and the malformation of fetuses are emphasized. Interviews with users are also presented. Phoenix/BFA Films and Video, Inc., 470 Park Avenue South, New York, NY 10016.

Copyright © Houghton Mifflin Company. All rights reserved.

An Ounce of Prevention (16 mm, color, 26 min). The film assesses the individual and community damage wrought by alcohol abuse. Community treatment and prevention efforts are discussed. Harper & Row Media, 10 East 53rd Street, New York, NY 10022.

Psychoactive (16 mm, 30 min). Through live action and animation, the film shows the physiological effects of barbiturates, opiates, hallucinogens, and stimulants. Emphasis is given to the development of dependence, the effects of prolonged use, and programs to detoxify users. Pyramid Film Productions, P.O. Box 1048, Santa Monica, CA 90406.

"The World of Abnormal Psychology" (#6) from the series *Substance Use Disorders* (VHS, 60 min). The focus is on alcohol, cocaine, and nicotine addiction—their effects on the individual and society. The film also discusses risk factors, AA policy, Native American approaches and has a strong segment on relapse prevention. The Annenberg/CPB Collection, Dept. CA94, P.O. Box 2345, S. Burlington, VT 05407-2345; to order, call 1-800-532-7637.

Substance Abuse Disorders (VHS, color, 60 mm.). From The World of Abnormal Psychology series. The Annenberg/CPB Collection, Dept. CA94, P.O. Box 2345, S. Burlington, VT 05407-2345; to order, call 1-800-532-7637.

ON THE INTERNET

http://www.health.org/ is the Web site for the National Clearinghouse for Alcohol and Drug Information (NCALI) a government agency that provides a wealth of information.

http://www.nida.nih.gov is another government source, the National Institute on Drug Abuse (NIDA).

http://www.jointogether.org/ has information on funding, public policy, community action programs, a national forum on drug abuse prevention and treatment (The Coffee House), and searches for documents on all the above.

http://www.ca.org/ is a site for Cocaine Anonymous (CA) and http://www.alcoholics-anonymous.org/ is for Alcoholics Anonymous.

Copyright © Houghton Mifflin Company. All rights reserved.

CHAPTER 10
Sexual and Gender Identity Disorders

CHAPTER OUTLINE

I.   What is "normal" sexual behavior?

   A.   President Clinton and "normal" sexual behavior

      1.   Is oral sex normal?

      2.   Does oral sex constitute "sex"?

      3.   Does the use of a "cigar" in sex play constitute perversion

      4.   Is the former President a "sex addict"?

      5.   Defining "perversion" is difficult; it is affected by changing perspectives over time and differences in cultural perspective

   B.   The study of human sexuality

      1.   Kinsey; first scientific studies; used self-report and questionnaire-interview methods

      2.   Masters and Johnson observed sexual behavior in laboratory; dispelled myths of less sexuality in women and vaginal orgasm; described "normal" sexual response cycle

      3.   Janus Report (1993): large cross-sectional survey (1,347 women; 1,418 men) including older populations

   C.   The sexual response cycle

      1.   Appetitive (desire for sexual activity)

      2.   Excitement (physiological arousal)

      3.   Orgasm (involuntary muscular contractions and release of sexual tension)

      4.   Resolution (relaxation of body after orgasm)

   D.   Homosexuality: DSM-III-R and DSM-IV-TR do not include homosexuality as a disorder

      1.   Homophobia: the irrational fear of homosexuality "

      2.   Reasons homosexuality is not a disorder

         a.   No physiological differences in arousal between homosexuals and heterosexuals

         b.   No difference in psychological disturbance

         c.   No gender identity confusion in homosexuals

         d.   Because of homophobia, homosexual sexual concerns may differ significantly from heterosexuals' concerns

         e.   not a lifestyle choice, but a naturally occurring biological phenomenon

   E.   Aging and sexual activity

      1.   Sexual frequency in older men reflects frequency at younger age

      2.   Among most active, fewest dysfunctions

      3.   Janus Report (1993)

Copyright © Houghton Mifflin Company. All rights reserved

a. Sexual activity of people 65 and over declined little

b. Ability to reach orgasm diminished little, desire unchanged

4. Physiological changes only slow sexual response; more warmth and intimacy after sex

II. Sexual dysfunctions

A. Prevalence: range from 5 to 60 percent, depending on gender and specific problem

B. DSM-IV-TR requires problem to be recurrent and persistent disruption for a diagnosis of sexual dysfunction; also considers: frequency, chronicity, subjective distress, and effect on other areas of functioning

C. Sexual desire disorders: hypoactive sexual desire disorder and sexual aversion disorder

1. Questions about category when there are marital problems or job stress

2. About 20 percent of adult population believed to suffer hypoactive sexual desire disorder

3. Wide range of "normal" for sexual involvement

D. Sexual arousal disorders

1. Erectile dysfunction: inability of male to attain or maintain erection sufficient for sexual intercourse and/or psychological arousal during sexual activity

a. difficult to distinguish between primarily biological and primarily psychological even nocturnal penile tumescence (NPT) assessment is imprecise

b. primary erectile dysfunction: never able; secondary erectile dysfunction: previous success

c. prevalence difficult to estimate; prior to Viagra, perhaps 10-15 million American men; current estimates: 30 million (one reason may be greater comfort in reporting)

2. Female sexual arousal disorder: inability to attain or maintain physiological response and/or psychological arousal during sexual activity

a. lack signs of excitement (e.g., lubrication)

b. may be primary or secondary; often from learned negative attitudes

c. prevalence estimates: 10 to 50 percent of female population

3. Differentiation between biological and psychological cause is difficult—even assessment by nocturnal penile tumescence (NPT) imprecise

E. Orgasmic disorders (inability to achieve orgasm despite adequate stimulation)

1. Female orgasmic disorder (inhibited female orgasm)

a. Clinician judges whether stimulation is "sufficient"

b. Need to reevaluate "necessity" for coital orgasm

c. Primary and secondary forms

d. Wakefield (1988): diagnosed only if women have had experiences conducive to orgasm (masturbation)

2. Male orgasmic disorder (inhibited male orgasm): inability to ejaculate intravaginally; relatively rare

3. Premature ejaculation:

a. Common varied definitions of "too fast"

b. a common problem (possibly 50 percent for women, 33 percent for men)

F. Sexual pain disorders

1. Dyspareunia: persistent pain in genitals before, during, or after intercourse

2. Vaginismus: involuntary spasms of outer third of vagina restricting penile penetration

Copyright © Houghton Mifflin Company. All rights reserved.

    G. Etiology and treatment of sexual dysfunctions

        1. Biological factors and medical treatment

           a. sex hormones

           b. prescribed medications can affect sex drive

           c. constitutional hypersensitivity

           d. insufficient blood flow into genital area

           e. treatment (for men): vascular surgery (penile implants, injections of papaverine and phentolamine into penis, pumps) or medication (Viagra)

        2. Psychological factors and behavioral therapy

           a. predisposing or historical factors)unconscious hostility, parentalattitudes, early conditioning)

           b. current factors (relationship stress, performance anxiety, self-focus, guilt)

        3. Therapy usually includes education, anxiety reduction, structured behavioral exercises, communication training

           a. Specific techniques for specific disorders: masturbation for female orgasmic disorder, start-stop and squeeze techniques for premature ejaculation, relaxation and successively larger dilators for vaginismus

           b. Evaluation of behavior therapy: questions about high success rate; relapse a concern

III. Gender identity disorders: conflict between anatomical sex and self-identification

    A. Transsexualism: early sex role conflicts; cross-gender identification

        1. Asexual, heterosexual, and homosexual histories

        2. Mostly males; prevalence between 1 in 100,000 and 1 in 30,000 for males; 1 in 400,000 to 1 in 100,000 in females

    B. Gender identity disorders not otherwise specified involve cross-dressing without identity problems or preoccupation with castration without desire for sex characteristics of other sex

    C. Etiology of gender identity disorders

        1. Biological perspective

           a. Animal studies support role of sex hormones

           b. Children in one study adopt gender identity imposed by parents regardless of genetic sex

        2. Some believe gender identity is malleable

        3. Behavioral perspective: parental encouragement of feminine behavior, lack of male playmates, peer ostracism

    D. Treatment of gender identity disorders

        1. Children get sex education and male therapist as role model

        2. Parents trained to reinforce sex-appropriate behavior

        3. Behavior therapy with adults

        4. Sex reassignment surgery

IV. Paraphilias: for at least six months person has acted on or is severely distressed by recurrent urges or fantasies involving nonhuman objects, nonconsenting others, real or simulated suffering or humiliation

    A. Paraphilias involving nonhuman objects

        1. Fetishism: sexual attraction to inanimate objects (panties, shoes); rare among women

        2. Transvestic fetishism: arousal from cross-dressing; if cross-dressing only during course

Copyright © Houghton Mifflin Company. All rights reserved.

of gender identity disorder, rules out transvestic fetishism

    a.   Majority are heterosexuals

    b.   Feel they have alternating male and female personalities

B. Paraphilias involving nonconsenting persons

    1. Exhibitionism: exposing genitals to strangers for shock effect

        a.   relatively common; men show sexual arousal to erotically neutral females

        b.   Tend to be young married men

        c.   Exposing has a compulsive quality

    2. Voyeruism: urges, acts, or fantasies of observing an unsuspecting person disrobing or engaging in sexual activity

        a.   risk of arrest; prefer victim is a stranger (95%)

        b.   because it is repetitive, arrest is predictable

    3. Frotteurism: recurrent fantasies and behavior of rubbing against nonconsenting person

    4. Pedophilia: sexual gratification from fantasies or sexual contact with children

        a.   DSM-IV-TR criteria: at least sixteen years old and five years older than victim; may include own children (incest)

        b.   Child sexual abuse common (20 to 30 percent of women report being victims)

        c.   Pedophile usually family member or friend

        d.   In one study 25 percent of victims were under six, 25 percent six to ten, 50 percent eleven to thirteen years

        e.   Highest recidivism rate among sex offenders

        f.   Pedophile profile: passive, impulsive, alcoholic, low social skills, possible brain dysfunction

        g.   Victims seriously affected: physical symptoms, nightmares, acting out, sexually focused behavior

C. Paraphilias involving pain or humiliation

    1. Sadism and masochism: sexual gratification from pain (sadist inflicts; masochist receives); DSM-IV-TR requires acting on urges or being distressed by them

        a.   Majority enjoy both roles; activity is planned

        b.   Aggressive sex fantasies common in "normals"; sadism/masochism deviant because pain is necessary

        c.   Possible brain dysfunction in right temporal area

D. Etiology and treatment of paraphilias

    1. Biological perspective: too little known about neurohormones to make assertions

    2. Psychodynamic perspective: castration anxiety; actions symbolic of unconscious conflict

    3. Behavioral perspective: early conditioning

        a.   Masturbation fantasies

        b.   Preparedness accounts for normal sexual cues

    4. Treatments

        a.   Extinction or aversive conditioning

        b.   Strengthen appropriate behaviors

        c.   Develop social skills

        d.   Aversive behavior rehearsal (for exhibitionism)

Copyright © Houghton Mifflin Company. All rights reserved.

V. Sexual aggression

    A. Rape: intercourse accomplished through force or threat of force; seen as crime of violence

        1. Statutory rape: sexual intercourse with a girl younger than a certain age

        2. Prevalence: 102,000 cases reported in 1990 (large underestimate)

        3. Rape victims: mostly young; date rape common

            a. Characteristics of men who coerce women: create situation, interpret friendliness as provocation manipulate with drugs or alcohol attribute failures to negative features of woman

        4. Effects of rape

            a. Acute phase: disorganization

            b. Long-term phase: reorganization

        5. Etiology of rape

            a. Power rapists—to compensate for personal inadequacy

            b. Anger rapists—at women in general

            c. Sadism rapists—satisfaction from torture and pain

            d. More common in college men than expected

            e. Media portrayals of violent sex

            f. "Cultural spillover"—rape more common in cultures that encourage violence

            g. socio-cultural and socio-biological perspectives

        5. Etiology: sociobiological reasons

    B. Incest

        1. Wide range of incidence estimates (48,000 to 250,000 cases per year); 75 percent of sibling incest is consensual

        2. Daughter victims seriously affected

        3. Incestuous fathers more likely to have experienced child sexual abuse than nonincestuous, but rare

    C. Treatment for incest offenders and rapists

        1. Conventional

            a. Imprisonment main form (but not treatment)

            b. Behavior therapies: some treatment programs effective with child molesters and exhibitionists, but treatment has not been effective for rapists

        2. Controversial treatments

            a. Surgical castration

            b. Chemical therapy (Depo-Provera)

LEARNING OBJECTIVES

1. Distinguish between sexual dysfunctions, paraphilias, and gender identity disorders. (p. 301)

2. Discuss the problems of defining "normal" sexual behavior. (pp. 302-305; Mental Health & Society)

3. Indicate the contributions of Kinsey, Masters and Johnson, Kaplan, and the Janus Report in the history of studying human sexuality. (p. 305)

4. Describe and discuss the four stages of the human sexual response cycle. (pp. 305-306)

5. Explain why homosexuality is not considered a mental disorder. (pp. 306-309)

Copyright © Houghton Mifflin Company. All rights reserved.

6. Discuss the results of research on sexuality among those over age sixty. (pp. 309-311)

7. Describe and differentiate sexual desire disorders in men and women, sexual arousal disorder in men and women, and male and female orgasmic disorder. Describe and discuss the causes of sexual pain disorders. (pp. 311-318)

8. Discuss the biological causes and treatments for psychosexual dysfunctions. (pp. 318-321)

9. Discuss the psychological factors that cause, and the behavioral therapy techniques used to treat, sexual dysfunctions. (pp. 321-323)

10. Define gender identity disorders and describe their symptoms. Discuss the biological, psychodynamic, and behavioral explanations for these disorders and how gender identity disorders are treated. (pp. 323-327)

11. Define paraphilias and list the three categories of these disorders. Describe and differentiate fetishism, transvestic fetishism, exhibitionism, voyeurism, frotteurism, pedophilia, sadism, and masochism. (pp. 327-334)

12. Discuss the problems of people who were childhood victims of sexual abuse. (pp. 331-332)

13. Discuss the biological, psychodynamic, and behavioral etiological theories of paraphilia and how those theories lead to different forms of treatment. (pp. 334-336)

14. Differentiate the terms *sexual coercion, sexual aggression, rape,* and *incest.* Describe the effects of rape on victims, including the acute and long-term phases of rape trauma syndrome. Discuss what is known about the cause of rape, including the three motivational types of rapists. (pp. 336-343; Mental Health & Society)

15. Discuss the effects of media portrayals of sexual violence and sociocultural variables. (pp. 342-343; Critical Thinking)

16. Describe and evaluate the conventional and controversial treatments provided for incest offenders and rapists. (pp. 343-344)

CLASSROOM TOPICS FOR LECTURE AND DISCUSSION

1. You can augment the information given in the text about the normal sexual response cycle for men and women by using Masters and Johnson's *Human Sexual Response* (1966). On the board, draw the generic curve of sexual arousal for males, showing that the process toward orgasm is typically more rapid for males than it is for females. The refractory period for males should also be described and discussed. In part, the related problems of female orgasmic difficulty and male premature ejaculation are linked to basic differences in the timing of sexual arousal and release. Further, it is useful to point out the need for relaxation plus arousal in order to have a male erection and female orgasm. If either relaxation is absent (and anxiety takes its place) or arousal is insufficient, sexual difficulties are more likely.

2. Ask students to indicate their gender and nothing else at the top of a page. Assure them that, in the exercise to follow, only group data will be of interest. To further lower concern, let students know that they can refrain from participation by simply turning in blank sheets of paper.

Ask students to write a description of a person that comes to mind when the following words are read: (1) impotent man, (2) lesbian, (3) flasher, (4) frigid woman, (5) AIDS victim.

Have students fold their papers in half and pass them in. You can do a quick tally of positive, negative, and neutral adjectives for each hypothetical person. Put on the board some of the more commonly listed adjectives for each sex separately. Do male students show stronger negative reactions than female students? Discuss why this might be so (males are expected to be sexually dominant; women are

Copyright © Houghton Mifflin Company. All rights reserved.

socialized to be more nurturing). Ask students whether their responses might have been different if DSM-IV-TR language had been used, such as *erectile dysfunction* or *exhibitionist*. This should lead to a discussion of whether changes in names would effectively prevent stereotypic attitudes and discriminatory behavior.

3.   The sheer number of separate sexual deviances listed in this chapter may indicate that people in the United States are particularly concerned with what is "right" or "normal" sexual behavior. Challenge students to think of any other naturally occurring behavior that has as many emotionally charged and incorrect ways of being performed (some suggested behaviors are sleeping, eating, drinking, and walking).

A related issue is the fact that the paraphilias are predominantly a male problem. Discuss with students why males are so much more likely to be plagued with these problems. One reason might be that women traditionally deny their sexuality and tend to be passive in their sexual behavior. If, in the future, women come to be as involved and explicit about their sexuality as men, will they develop paraphilias, too? Another reason might be the pressure placed on men to perform within a narrow range of sexually correct behaviors. When they are socially immature and unable to be sexually successful under stressful circumstances, they resort to extraordinary measures to feel competent and dominant. Note that exhibitionists and voyeurs, for example, tend to be socially immature men.

Internet Site: http://www.goaskalice.columbia.edu/index.html. "Go Ask Alice" a sexual health question and answer service by Columbia University.

4.   There has been an explosion in the number of allegations of child sexual abuse stemming from the recovery of memories of such abuse. Clients, usually women, coming to therapy for problems as common and diverse as depression, sexual dysfunction, low self-esteem, or anxiety, recover memories of childhood abuse during treatment. Elizabeth Loftus, a highly-respected researcher on memory, challenges the validity of many of these cases (Loftus, 1993).

First, we are unclear what the base rate for repression may be. In one study of women treated for substance abuse, one-half reported sexual abuse in childhood, but only 18 percent claimed they forgot the abuse for a period of time and later remembered it. In another study, 38 percent of women known to have been abused were amnesic.

Second, some of the memories being recalled seem highly implausible. In some cases, richly detailed recollections of abuse during infancy are given. Research shows that our earliest recollections do not date back before age three; most of our early memories are remembrances of things told to us by others.

Third, therapists tend to be uncritical of recollections reported by clients. In one small study of clinicians who had had at least one repressed memory case, the great majority invariably believed whatever the client said. As one clinician reported, "If a woman says it happened, it happened." (Loftus, 1993, p. 524)

Popular magazine articles and books have flooded the media with reports of childhood abuse, such as revelations by Roseanne Barr Arnold and former Miss America Marilyn Van Derbur. The book *The Courage to Heal* (Bass & Davis, 1988) is very popular and gives victims a great deal of comfort. However, it also counsels readers to "assume that your feelings are valid. So far, no one we've talked to thought she might have been abused, and then later discovered that she hadn't been . . . If you think you were abused, and your life shows the symptoms, then you were" (p. 22). The symptoms, however, are pervasive: depression, self-destructive thoughts, low self-esteem, and sexual dysfunction. In one book (Farmer, 1989) repression is the expected result of abuse: "The more severe the abuse, the more likely you were to repress any conscious recollection of it" (p. 52).

Copyright © Houghton Mifflin Company. All rights reserved.

Research with hypnosis and direct insertion of false information (Loftus & Coan, in press) demonstrates that therapists can take actual events or dreams and suggest that abuse occurred or can generate memories out of whole cloth. For example, children who lived in a neighborhood where a sniper attack occurred on a playground vividly remembered the attack even though they were not present.

Repression probably does occur, but we do not know the base rate. It seems unlikely that recovery of repressed memories for child sexual abuse occurs with the frequency that is currently being reported. It is difficult to square the rate of abuse repression with the fact that, in a study of children who witnessed the murder of a parent, not a single child repressed the memory. To the contrary, they could not get the images and emotions out of their minds (Malmquist, 1986).

Loftus (1993) argues that uncritical acceptance of even the most dubious allegations is a drain on society in interminable therapy, a source of unspeakable anguish for wrongly accused parents, and, perhaps most tragic, the "increased likelihood that society in general will disbelieve the genuine cases of childhood sexual abuse that truly deserve our sustained attention" (p. 534).

Sources: Bass, E., & Davis, L. (1988). *The courage to heal.* New York: Harper & Row.

Farmer, S. (1989). *Adult children of abusive parents.* New York: Ballantine.

Loftus, E. F. (1993). The reality of repressed memories. *American Psychologist, 48,* 518–537.

Loftus, E. F., & Coan, D. (in press). The construction of childhood memories. In D. Peters (Ed.) *The child witness in context: Cognitive, social, and legal perspectives.* New York: Kluwer.

Malmquist, C. P. (1986). Children who witness parental murder: Post-traumatic stress. *Journal of the American Academy of Child Psychiatry, 25,* 320–325.

Internet Site: http://www.qrd.org/QRD/orgs/NAMBLA/. Journal and research reports on pedophilia.

5.   The range of cultural norms about sexuality is extraordinary. Nevid, Rathus, and Greene (1994) offer these glimpses into the cultural anthropology of sex.

- Among the Abkhasian people of the southern part of the former Soviet Union, men are sexually aroused by women's armpits. Only a husband is permitted to see a wife's armpits.

- Some societies believe that men and women eating together is a mild form of sexual behavior. Therefore, in such societies brothers and sisters are forbidden from eating meals together since this behavior approaches incestuous relations.

- Kissing is unknown among the Siriono of Bolivia and the Thonga of Africa. The Thonga, upon learning that Europeans kiss, caused one man to say, "Look at them—they eat each others' saliva and dirt!"

- It is considered polite among the Native American Aleut people of Alaska for a husband to offer his wife to a visitor.

- In Pakistan, where men's testimony is considered more believable than women's, women who accuse men of raping them have sometimes been imprisoned themselves. Some women who have charged men with rape have been prosecuted for adultery, but their assailants, claiming that if sex occurred it was consensual, have been acquitted.

Copyright © Houghton Mifflin Company. All rights reserved.

Internet Site: http://www.goaskalice.columbia.edu/index.html. "Go Ask Alice" a sexual health question and answer service by Columbia University.

6.   Masters and Johnson's book (1970) on treating sexual dysfunctions made the case for fear as the cause of many problems. They suggested that tension caused by fear of failure created a self-fulfilling prophesy in the form of erectile disorder and female orgasmic disorder. Helen Singer Kaplan (1979) claimed that all sexual dysfunctions were caused by anxiety. David Barlow and his colleagues (Barlow, Sackheim, & Beck, 1983; Abrahamson, Barlow, Sackheim, Beck, & Athanasiou, 1985; Barlow, 1986) have tested this hypothesis in the laboratory and found it only partially accurate. Fear, it seems, can lead to *increased* arousal and performance in some men, *decreased* arousal in others. The difference seems to be cognitive. The research went through the following steps.

The initial study sought to simulate in the laboratory the fearfulness some experience in the bedroom. All subjects were sexually functional men, and all were given a harmless but somewhat painful electric shock before being put into one of three conditions. In condition one (control), the subjects were told they were going to watch an erotic movie and they should just enjoy it. In condition two, subjects were told that there was a 60 percent chance of receiving an electric shock while they were watching the erotic movie. Nothing they would do could alter the chances of getting the shock (a noncontingent condition). Condition three was contingent shock: Subjects were told that if they did not achieve an "average" erection, they had a 60 percent chance of receiving a shock. This condition was seen as most closely simulating performance anxiety in the bedroom. In no case did subjects receive a shock. The results were surprising. Subjects in both shock conditions showed *more* arousal than those who simply relaxed and the *contingent* shock group were significantly *more* aroused than the noncontingent group. Clearly, anxiety not only did not impair performance, it enhanced it. Incidentally, research on women (Palace & Garzalka, 1990) produced similar findings.

Later, the Barlow team found that although sexually functional men showed increased performance in the shock-demand condition, sexually dysfunctional men showed reduced sexual arousal. Further, although the functional men were significantly less aroused if distracted by nonsexual stimuli (listening to a nonerotic narrative over earphones), dysfunctional men's arousal was not decreased by nonsexual distractions. Functional men were accurate in estimating their level of arousal, but dysfunctional men underestimated it. Barlow constructed a model that accounts for these puzzling findings and applies to sexual arousal disorders. In essence, functional men have a positive feedback loop that interprets both external and internal sexual stimuli in a way to increase arousal, whereas dysfunctional men have a negative feedback loop that does the opposite. Here are the components of the model:

For functional men: When there are explicit or implicit demands for sexual performance, they think of past positive experiences, perceive themselves to be in control, and maintain a positive mood. They focus their attention on the erotic stimuli, and when they feel increases in arousal, pay further attention to erotic cues. They approach the sexual situation and perform satisfactorily. For dysfunctional men: When there are similar demands for sexual performance, they think of past failures, perceive themselves to have little control, and maintain a negative mood. They focus their attention on the negative consequences of not performing adequately or on other nonerotic stimuli. They underestimate their level of autonomic arousal, focus greater attention on negative consequences and other distractions leading to avoidance of the sexual situation, and perform unsatisfactorily.

Other factors account for sexual-arousal disorders, including physical causes, socialization, and interpersonal difficulties, but this model helps us understand that anxiety alone is not the cause. In fact, the model suggests that channeling performance concerns through certain cognitions leads to increased arousal and presumably enjoyment for some people.

Sources: Abrahamson, D. J., Barlow, D. H., Sakheim, D. K., Beck, J. G., & Athanasiou, R. (1985). Effects of distraction on sexual responding in functional and dysfunctional men. *Behavior Therapy, 16,* 503–515;.

Copyright © Houghton Mifflin Company. All rights reserved.

Barlow, D. H., Sackheim, D. K., & Beck, J. G. (1983). Anxiety increases sexual arousal. *Journal of Abnormal Psychology, 92,* 49–54.

Barlow, D. H. (1986). Causes of sexual dysfunction: The role of anxiety and cognitive interference. *Journal of Consulting and Clinical Psychology, 54,* 140–148.

Kaplan, H. S. (1979). *Disorders of sexual desire.* New York: Brunner/Mazel.

Masters, W. H., & Johnson, V. E. (1970). *Human sexual inadequacy.* Boston: Little, Brown.

Palace, E. M., & Gorzalka, B. B. (1990). The enhancing effects of anxiety on arousal in sexually dysfunctional and functional women. *Journal of Abnormal Psychology, 99,* 403–411.

CLASSROOM DEMONSTRATIONS & HANDOUTS

1.   Presentations by professionals who come in contact with raped or sexually abused individuals can have a powerful and informative impact. Many police forces have special departments for rape and sexual abuse. Officers from these departments can provide information on the legal issues involved and the frustration of prosecuting these offenders. Rape counselors from mental health or freestanding service organizations can describe the psychological crisis of rape and the difficulties involved in sorting out which of several options the woman will take in dealing with the trauma. Hospital emergency room nurses can provide yet another vantage point, the immediate response to rape, whereas mental health professionals can describe the longer term reactions, which parallel posttraumatic stress syndrome. Finally, all these people can be included in a discussion of our society's tendency to blame the victim. Ask them what the implications of this tendency are in terms of reporting rapes, prosecuting rapists, and getting adequate help to overcome the physical and psychological trauma of the event.

2.   Marcia Freer (1992) uses this exercise to give students a way to voice and compare their opinions about sexual behavior without being embarrassed. The exercise also provides data for keeping track of trends in sexual attitudes over the years. It is bound to generate discussion.

Because students need to move around the classroom, this demonstration is probably feasible for classes with no more than 40 or 50 students. It works only if there is a 60/40 or a more even distribution of males and females in the class. Freer estimates that 30 minutes is an average time involved, including discussion.

Copy two versions of the Handout for Demonstration 2—one on pink paper, for females; one on blue paper, for males. Complaints about the colors and sex-role stereotyping will help you during discussions later. Students fill out the questionnaire anonymously. They are instructed to fold it in half and pass it up to you. Shuffle the questionnaires and redistribute. Caution anyone who gets his/her own questionnaire not to reveal this information to the rest of the class.

Designate five locations around the room to correspond with the five possible ratings (strongly agree to strongly disagree) on the questionnaire. Tell students to move to the location corresponding to the answer given for the first question (about premarital sex) on the questionnaire they are holding. For each successive item, students move to the corresponding location.

The exercise has several benefits. Students can register opinions anonymously, since the position they take around the room represents someone else's attitude. The color of the paper the student holds indicates the gender of the respondent, so gender differences in attitudes are easily noted. Third, as the behaviors become more controversial, a physical shift of bodies around the room illustrates conservative and liberal attitudes, as well as points of consensus or controversy. At any point the instructor can ask

Copyright © Houghton Mifflin Company. All rights reserved.

why shifts in opinion are occurring. Finally, if an assistant keeps numerical track of the distribution of "votes" for each item, data can be fed back to the class and maintained for comparison with next year's group.

If time permits and the group is small, have students fill out the values clarification form (see handout) and turn in folded, completed forms. Shuffle them so they can be returned to other students. Have them silently read these comments and pass them to a second student, giving closure and a sense of validation at the end of the exercise.

3.   This chapter is a good one for confronting homophobia. The AIDS epidemic has added a new rationalization for discriminating against gays. The following exercise may become heated but can help identify some of the students' blind spots and the reasons for them.

Have students split up into small groups (four or five per group). Distribute the Handout for Demonstration 3 and ask each group member to answer the questions without consulting others. Then, for each situation, have each group member announce which way he or she "voted." For each question, the individuals should discuss why they took the stand they did. Ask students whether their fears are based on anything even remotely rational or whether they are using unconscious defense mechanisms. What defenses might they be?

Students may paint a more progressive and tolerant picture of themselves than their actual attitudes and behaviors suggest. One way to slice through some of this is to ask what would happen if they were told that, as a requirement of this course, they were to walk through campus hand in hand with a person of the same sex. How many would drop the course rather than do the assignment?

4.   Despite increased discussion of sexuality and more permissive attitudes in our society, many men and women still subscribe to sexual myths. These untrue beliefs seem to affect sexual functioning, and contribute to needless anxiety about sexual behavior. Baker and DeSilva (1988) presented a list of male sexuality myths constructed by Bernie Zilbergeld to groups of sexually dysfunctional and functional men. Those with dysfunctions reported significantly more beliefs in these myths than functional men did. It is not clear what is cause and what is effect, but a relationship seems to exist between beliefs, emotions, and behaviors. The Handout for Demonstration 4 has two lists of sexuality myths: one for women and one for men.

Ask students to think about how strongly they agree or disagree with each item. Do not ask for them to reveal their responses, but ask them to discuss what they think the "average" person would say. They will feel less personally vulnerable in the discussion that ensues while still taking something personal from the activity. Ask them the degree to which they think these beliefs have changed in the recent past. How do they predict their parents or grandparents would respond to them? How do they think their children will respond to them? This could spark a discussion of gender role stereotyping and the value of teaching children to be more psychologically androgenous.

Internet Site: http://www.goaskalice.columbia.edu/index.html. "Go Ask Alice" a sexual health question and answer service by Columbia University.

5.   Sex is one of the ways advertisers get our attention and sell their products. You can use the Handouts for Demonstration 5 in one of two ways to increase student awareness of sexual themes in the media and spark class discussion about our culture's sexual expectations. This subject, in turn, can be linked to sexual dysfunctions and sexual deviances. In the first, assign students to watch two or three hours of evening television before the next class period. Have them use the television handout to record advertisements and program content they believe have sexual content. They should indicate to whom they think these sexual messages are targeted and the degree to which they think such messages have an

Copyright © Houghton Mifflin Company. All rights reserved.

impact on thinking or behavior. In class, have students meet in small groups and compare their recordings, ratings, and comments. Ask them if they themselves have ever been influenced by advertisements or portrayals of reality in television programs. They will probably not say yes. Ask them who they think *are* influenced by television ads and programs. How might the equation of sexual attractiveness, sexual activity, and "the good life" affect heterosexual attitudes? Ask if any mention (direct or indirect) was made of making sex safer. Link this to our fight to prevent HIV infection and AIDS. Finally, ask them to imagine how the large minority of sexually dysfunctional individuals in society must respond to seeing such portrayals of sexual behavior.

To take a second look at the media, buy (or ask students to buy) a range of magazines. Include magazines targeted at teens, middle-aged women, men, and general audiences. Students can page through the magazines in small groups and record advertisements and articles with sexual themes, rate them, and evaluate their impact on target audiences on the media handout. This exercise should also get into issues of being personally influenced, the role of the media in preventing HIV, and how those with dysfunctions might react to the portrayal of the sexual world in magazines.

6.   The main character on the television show, Ellen, revealed that she was gay, (the show was later canceled.) This episode was one of the highest-rated television shows of the year. What has changed in our society that makes now the time to have an openly lesbian lead character on a prime time television show? Do you see the gay lifestyle becoming more acceptable in the future?

Additionally both ABC and NBC have launched top, rated sitcoms with openly gay men as main characters (Will and Grace is the NBC program). Lead the class in a discussion of this trend in the media. Do students think this trend will continue?

7.   Invite a guest speaker who is a psychologist or psychiatrist specializing in treatment of sexual disorders. Have the students develop questions during the class period before the guest lecturer is scheduled. These professionals are usually very busy but if you schedule early enough they will usually be happy to lecture to your class.

8.   Bring the DSM-IV-TR to class, and prepare an overhead transparency or PowerPoint slide ahead of time for your lecture on gender identity disorders. Describe the in-depth material from the DSM-IV while using the transparency or PowerPoint slide as an outline. Lead a discussion on the differences between different sexual disorders. Encourage student input about individuals they have known with these symptoms.

HANDOUT FOR DEMONSTRATION 2:
ASSESSING SEXUAL ATTITUDES AND BEHAVIOR

Instructions: On the line before each item, place the number representing one of these five responses to indicate how you feel about the sexual behavior.

5 Strongly approve
4 Approve somewhat
3 Neutral
2 Disapprove somewhat
1 Strongly disapprove

_____ 1. Premarital sex when the couple is engaged

_____ 2. Premarital sex when the couple is only casually acquainted

_____ 3. Masturbation

_____ 4. Homosexuality

_____ 5. Extramarital sex (a married person having sex with someone other than his/her spouse)

_____ 6. Mouth-genital sex (or oral-genital sex—cunnilingus or fellatio)

_____ 7. Anal intercourse

_____ 8. Cross-dressing to become sexually aroused

_____ 9. Nonviolent pornographic films

_____ 10. Violent pornographic films

Source: Adapted from "A Technique for Assessing Sexual Attitudes and Behavior," by Dr. Marcia M. Freer, Presentation to Midwestern Psychological Association Convention, 1992. Used by permission of Dr. Marcia M. Freer.

Copyright © Houghton Mifflin Company. All rights reserved.

HANDOUT FOR DEMONSTRATION 3:
RESPONSES TO GAY MEN AND LESBIAN WOMEN

For each situation described below, please respond as honestly as you can. Think of the reasons for your reaction.

1. You and your spouse have decided that you want to build a house of your own. You hear that John Smith is an outstanding architect. After several weeks of talking with Mr. Smith, you discover that he has superb ideas for your new home. You also discover that Mr. Smith is gay and that his partner, Mr. Jones, is also his lover.

     In this situation, what is the likelihood that you would cancel any business dealings with Mr. Smith?

Definitely Cancel	Probably Cancel	Not Sure	Probably Not Cancel	Definitely Not Cancel
1	2	3	4	5

2. You are the parent of a 14-year-old boy. One of his favorite teachers is Mr. Thomas, a brilliant English teacher. Your son has developed a flair for writing and a love of reading that stems from Mr. Thomas's excellent teaching. One day, you pick your son up after school and see that Mr. Thomas is in his car with another man. They then hug and kiss each other.

     In this situation, what is the likelihood that you would forbid your son from talking with Mr. Thomas for the rest of the school year?

Definitely Would Forbid	Probably Would Forbid	Not Sure	Probably Would Not Forbid	Definitely Would Not Forbid
1	2	3	4	5

3. [For female students] You have just had your third appointment with a new gynecologist, Dr. Holdon. She is exceptionally understanding and careful in her examinations, unlike the male gynecologists you have used or heard about in the past. Then you find out that Dr. Holdon is a lesbian.

[For male students] You have just had your third appointment with a new general practice physician, Dr. Holdon. He is exceptionally understanding and careful in his examinations, unlike the other doctors you have had in the past. Then you find out that Dr. Holdon is a homosexual.

     In this situation, what is the likelihood that you would stop using Dr. Holdon as your physician?

Definitely Stop Using	Probably Stop Using	Not Sure	Probably Not Stop Using	Definitely Not Stop Using
1	2	3	4	5

Copyright © Houghton Mifflin Company. All rights reserved.

HANDOUT FOR DEMONSTRATION 4: MYTHS OF SEXUALITY

SA = strongly agree   A = agree   SD = strongly disagree   D = disagree

Myths of female sexuality (Heiman & LoPiccolo, 1988)

1. Sex is only for women under thirty.   SA A D SD
2. Normal women have an orgasm every time they have sex.   SA A D SD
3. All women can have multiple orgasms.   SA A D SD
4. Pregnancy and delivery reduce women's sexual responsiveness.   SA A D SD
5. A woman's sex life ends with menopause.   SA A D SD
6. Different kinds of orgasms are related to a woman's personality. Vaginal orgasms are more feminine and mature than clitoral orgasms.   SA A D SD
7. A sexually responsive woman can always be turned on by her partner.   SA A D SD
8. Nice women aren't aroused by erotic books or films.   SA A D SD
9. You are frigid if you don't like the more exotic forms of sex.   SA A D SD
10. If you can't have an orgasm quickly and easily, there is something wrong with you.   SA A D SD
11. Feminine women don't initiate sex or become wild and unrestrained during sex.   SA A D SD
12. You are frigid if you don't have sexual fantasies and wanton if you do.   SA A D SD
13. Contraception is a woman's responsibility, and she's just making excuses if she says contraceptive issues are inhibiting her sexually.   SA A D SD

Myths of male sexuality (Zilbergeld, 1992)

1. We're liberated folks who are very comfortable with sex.   SA A D SD
2. A real man isn't into sissy stuff like feelings and communicating.   SA A D SD
3. All touching is sexual and should lead to sex.   SA A D SD
4. A man is always interested in and always ready for sex.   SA A D SD
5. A real man performs in sex.   SA A D SD
6. Sex is centered on a hard penis and what's done with it.   SA A D SD
7. Sex equals intercourse.   SA A D SD
8. A man should be able to make the earth move for his partner, or at the very least knock her socks off.   SA A D SD
9. Good sex requires orgasm.   SA A D SD
10. Men don't have to listen to women in sex.   SA A D SD
11. Good sex is spontaneous, with no planning and no talking.   SA A D SD
12. Real men don't have sex problems.   SA A D SD

Sources: (lists) Barlow, D. H., & Durand, V. M. (1995). *Abnormal psychology: An integrative approach.* Pacific Grove, CA: Brooks/Cole; Baker, C. D., & DeSilva, P. (1988). The relationship between male sexual dysfunction and belief in Zilbergeld's myths: An empirical investigation. *Sexual and Marital Therapy, 3,* 229–238; Heiman, J. R.,& LoPiccolo, J. (1988). *Becoming orgasmic: A sexual and personal growth program for women* (rev. ed.). New York: Prentice-Hall; Zilbergeld, B. (1992). *The new male sexuality.* New York: Bantam Books.

Copyright © Houghton Mifflin Company. All rights reserved.

HANDOUT FOR DEMONSTRATION 5:
SEXUAL THEMES IN THE MEDIA (TELEVISION)

I am female _____   male _____.

I watched television from _____P.M. until _____ P.M. on _____.

(date and day of the week)

1. List the advertisements you saw that had a sexual theme; for example, in which a man or a woman is posed or dressed provocatively or there is the implication that using the product will lead to sexual success.

    Name of product: _____

    Sex-related   theme: _____

    Name of product: _____

    Sex-related   theme: _____

    Name of product: _____

    Sex-related   theme: _____

2. List sex-related themes or portrayals during television programs.

    Name of show: _____

    Sex-related theme or portrayal: _____

    Name of show: _____

    Sex-related theme or portrayal: _____

    To whom do you think these messages were directed?

    Do you think you are influenced by them? yes no

    Do you think other people are influenced by them? yes no   If yes, who?

Copyright © Houghton Mifflin Company. All rights reserved.

HANDOUT FOR DEMONSTRATION 5:
SEXUAL THEMES IN THE MEDIA (MAGAZINES)

I am female _____   male _____.

List the print advertisements you saw that had a sexual theme; for example, in which a man or a woman is posed or dressed provocatively or where there is the implication that using the product will lead to sexual success.

Name of product: _____

Sex-related theme: _____

Magazine name and its target audience: _____

Name of product: _____

Sex-related theme: _____

Magazine name and its target audience: _____

Name of product: _____

Sex-related theme: _____

Magazine name and its target audience: _____

Sex-related magazine article content: _____

Magazine name and its target audience: _____

Sex-related magazine article content: _____

Magazine name and its target audience: _____

Do you think you are influenced by them? yes no

Do you think other people are influenced by them? yes no   If yes, who?

Copyright © Houghton Mifflin Company. All rights reserved.

SELECTED READINGS

Anderson, B. L. (1983). Primary orgasmic dysfunction: Diagnostic considerations and review of treatment. *Psychological Bulletin, 93*, 105–136.

Barlow, D. H. (1986). Causes of sexual dysfunction: The role of anxiety and cognitive interference. *Journal of Consulting and Clinical Psychology, 54*, 140–148.

Briere, J. (1992). Methodological issues in the study of sexual abuse effects. *Journal of Consulting and Clinical Psychology, 60*, 196–203.

Heiman, J. R., & LoPiccolo, J. (1988). *Becoming orgasmic: A sexual and personal growth program for women.* New York: Prentice-Hall.

Maletzky, B. M. (1991). *Treating the sexual offender.* Newbury Park, CA: Sage.

Rosen, R. C., & Leiblum, S. (Eds.) (1991). *Erectile failure: Diagnosis and treatment.* New York: Guilford.

Sattler, D., Shabatay, V., 7 Kramer, G. (1998). *Abnormal psychology in context: Voices and perspectives.* Boston, MA: Houghton Mifflin Company. Chapter 10, Sexual Dysfunctions and Disorders.

Clipson, C., & Steer, J. (1998) *Case studies in abnormal psychology.* Boston, MA: Houghton Mifflin Company. Chapter 10, Premature Ejaculation: Under Pressure to Perform. Chapter 11, Pedophilia: Predator of Youth.

VIDEO RESOURCES

Child Molesters: Facts and Fiction (16 mm, color, 30 min). This film uses a depiction based on actual case material to illustrate two different reactions: parents who overreact and terrorize the child, and those who react with more support. The effects on the child and the role of police and the courts are discussed. University of Kansas Audio Visual Center, 746 Massachusetts Street, Lawrence, KS 66044.

I Am Not This Body (16 mm, 28 min). Two transsexuals are interviewed: a man who is preparing for sex-change surgery and a woman who has already had the surgery. Misconceptions about transsexualism and homosexuality are attacked. Erickson Educational Foundation, P.O. Box 185, Kendall Post Office, Miami, FL 33156.

Michael: A Gay Son (16 mm, color, 27 min). An actual case; Michael works with a counselor to reveal his sexual orientation to his family. The film examines how society refuses to accept homosexuality and how this attitude affects the issue of "coming out." Filmmakers Library, Inc., 133 E. 58th Street, Suite 703A, New York, NY 10022.

Overcoming Erection Problems (16 mm, color, 21 min). This film is an explicit look at one man's erectile dysfunction. It traces Masters and Johnson therapy from initial assessment to sensate focus exercises and then to increasingly greater genital-to-genital contact. University of California, Los Angeles Instructional Media Library, Powell Library, Room 46, Los Angeles, CA 90024.

Pedophile (Child Molester) (16 mm, color, 20 min). This film examines the underlying causes of pedophilia and the various types of molesters that exist. The material is augmented by an examination of methods molesters use to prevent being detected. AMS Media Inc., 626 Justin Avenue, Glendale, CA 91201.

Copyright © Houghton Mifflin Company. All rights reserved.

Rape: A Preventive Inquiry (16 mm, color, 17 min). Presents information about reducing the chances of being raped by examining circumstances in which four women were victims. Police and convicted rapists discuss their experiences. Psychological Cinema Register, Pennsylvania State University, University Park, PA 16802.

Dear Mom and Dad, I am Gay (VHS, color, 28 min.). This video looks at what happens when a family discovers they have a homosexual child or adolescent. Films for the Humanities and Sciences. 1-800-257-5126.

Gay Couples: The Nature of Relationships (VHS, color, 50 min.). This video looks at one gay and one lesbian couple and their lives. Films for the Humanities and Sciences. 1-800-257-5126.

Recovery from Sexual Abuse (VHS, color, 47 min.). This video follows five teenagers as they work to recover and heal from sexual abuse. Films for the Humanities and Sciences. 1-800-257-5126.

Scared Silent: Incest (VHS, color, 22 min.). Oprah Winfrey explores how sexual abuse moves through the generations. Fanlight Productions. 1-800-937-4113.

Sexual Disorders (VHS, color, 60 min.). This video covers the various sexual disorders. Annenberg/CPB. 1-800-LEARNER.

Pedophiles: Preying on Our Children (VHS, 45 min) This program looks at the cyclical nature of child abuse from the eyes of an abuser, as well as considering issues of false accusations and the effects on community. Films for the Humanities and Sciences, P.O. Box 2053, Princeton, NJ 08543-2053, 1-800257-5126

Multiple Genders: Mind and Body in Conflict (VHS, 40 min) This fascinating film looks at a range of human sexuality that includes not only homosexuality (and the right of gays and lesbians to adopt), but also transsexuals, hermaphrodites, and transvestites. An important discussion revolves around whether infants should have operations that make the physical body consistent with their chromosomal structure and who should make such decisions; a clergyman discusses his church's views that seem somewhat surrealistic in the context of these very talented people with multiple genders. Films for the Humanities and Sciences, P.O. Box 2053, Princeton, NJ 08543-2053, 1-800257-5126

ON THE INTERNET

http://www.cdspub.com/ is the Creative Design Services (CDS) Transgender Forum and Resource Center.

http://www.mcsp.com/smcop/toc.html is the sadomasochists home page, which provides information on sadomasochism.

http://www.gmu.edu/facstaff/sexual/rapesas.html is the Rape and Sexual Assault Information Page, which has a large listing of links on rape and sexual assault

http://www2.impotent.com/ is the Online Guide to Impotence which provides an eight-item screening quiz, information about impotence and its treatment, and a physician's referral list for evaluation and treatment.

http://www.qrd.org/QRD/orgs/NAMBLA/journal.and.research.reports is a text-only site that includes an extensive longitudinal study on pedophilia in Germany.

Copyright © Houghton Mifflin Company. All rights reserved.

http://www.genderweb.org/medical/psych/ contains diagnostic information on transsexualism, gender identity disorder, and transvestic fetishism.

This is http://www.goaskalice.columbia.edu/index.html "Go Ask Alice" a sexual health question and answer service by Columbia University.

Copyright © Houghton Mifflin Company. All rights reserved.

CHAPTER 11
Mood Disorders

CHAPTER OUTLINE

I.   Mood disorders: disturbances in emotion that cause discomfort or hinder functioning

    A.   Prevalence

        1.   Rank among the top 10 causes of worldwide disability

            a.   a leading cause of absenteeism and diminished productivity in workplace

            b.   prevalence for all mood disorders is 15 percent for males, 24 percent for females

        2.   Depression (intense sadness, feelings of futility and worthlessness, withdrawal from others) is the most common complaint among those seeking help:

            a.   yearly prevalence in United States is 10 million people, 100 million worldwide;

            b.   lifetime prevalence: 10 to 25 percent for women, 5 to 12 percent for men

        3.   Mania (characterized by elevated mood, expansiveness, or irritability, often resulting in hyperactivity)

        4.   Likelihood of recurrence of depression is 50 percent after one episode, 70 percent after two, 90 percent after three

II. Symptoms of depression and mania

    A.   Symptoms of depression

        1.   Affective symptoms

            a.   Feelings of sadness, dejection, worthlessness

            b.   Crying, not necessarily connected to specific situation

            c.   Anxiety

        2.   Cognitive symptoms

            a.   Feelings of futility, self-denigration; loss of interest and energy

            b.   Poor concentration; difficulty making decisions

            c.   Cognitive triad (Beck): negative views of self, outside world, and future

        3.   Behavioral symptoms

            a.   Unkempt appearance, masklike face, slowed movements (psychomotor retardation)

            b.   Social withdrawal

            c.   Low energy is key symptom distinguishing between depressed and nondepressed

        4.   Physiological symptoms

            a.   Loss of appetite and weight (although some gain weight)

            b.   Constipation

            c.   Sleep disturbance (insomnia, early waking, nightmares)

       d.   Disrupted menstrual cycle

       e.   Aversion to sexual activity

   5.   Culture influences experience and expression of symptoms

   6.   Children more likely to express somatic complaints, irritability, social withdrawal; adolescents and adults more likely to have psychomotor retardation, hypersomnia, and delusions

  B. Symptoms of mania

   1.   Affective symptoms

       a.   Elevated, expansive, irritable mood

       b.   Boundless energy and enthusiasm

   2.   Cognitive symptoms

       a.   Fast, disjointed speech

       b.   Uncontrolled attention, poor judgment

   3.   Behavioral symptoms

       a.   Hypomania: overactive in behavior but no delusions

       b.   Mania: more disruptive grandiosity, incoherent speech; hallucinations and delusions possible

   4.   Physiological symptoms

       a.   High arousal and decreased need for sleep

       b.   Weight loss

III.   Classification of mood disorders

  A. Depressive disorders include major depressive disorder, dysthymic disorder, and depressive disorder not otherwise specified

   1.   Major depression

       a.   No history of mania

       b.   Lasts two weeks or more and represents change from earlier functioning

       c.   The earlier the onset, the more likely the recurrence

   2.   Dysthymic disorder

       a.   Impairment less than in major depression, but chronic condition of longer duration (most of the day, more days than not for two years or more)

       b.   Each year 10 percent of those with dysthymic have a major depressive episode

       c.   Lifetime prevalence 6 percent

  B. Bipolar disorders (one or more manic or hypomanic episodes)

   1.   Mania must last one week; hypomania must last four days

   2.   Bipolar I: mania episode (with or without depression); lifetime prevalence .8 percent

   3.   Bipolar II: one or more major depressive episodes and at least one hypomanic (no mania); lifetime prevalence .5 percent

   4.   Cyclothymic disorder: chronic mood swings but less than hypomania or depression

       a.   Lasts more than two months

       b.   Lifetime prevalence 0.4 to 1.0 percent (greater than bipolar, less than dysthymic)

       c.   Risk of becoming bipolar is 15 to 50 percent

  C. Other mood disorders

   1.   Due to general medical condition

Copyright © Houghton Mifflin Company. All rights reserved.

2. Substance induced

D. Symptom features and specifiers

  1. Symptom features: accompany disorders but not criteria for diagnosis (melancholia and catatonia, for depression)

  2. Course specifiers: cyclic, seasonal, postpartum, or longitudinal pattern of disorder (rapid cycling bipolar, seasonal affective disorder, postpartum depression)

E. Comparison between depressive and bipolar disorders

  1. Bipolar more genetically based

  2. Bipolar much less common

  3. Onset of bipolar earlier (late twenties) than unipolar (mid-thirties)

  4. Bipolar displays psychomotor retardation and more suicide attempts

  5. Bipolar responds to Lithium

IV. The etiology of mood disorder

A. Psychological or sociocultural approaches to depression

  1. Psychoanalytic explanations

    a. Loss (physical or symbolic) with anger and guilt

    b. Incomplete mourning; current rejection symbolic of earlier loss; anger turned inward

  2. Behavioral explanations

    a. Reduced reinforcement reduces activity

    b. Sympathy reinforces depression (secondary gain)

    c. Drive others away and lose social reinforcement

    d. Lewinsohn et al.: number of reinforcing events, availability of reinforcers, low social skills, stress

    e. In bipolar, biogenic factors dominant but rewards for euphoria continue until negative reactions bring on depression

  3. Cognitive explanations

    a. Primary disturbance in depression is negative thinking and low self-esteem

    b. Beck: schema (cognitive set) predisposes depression

    c. Arbitrary inference

    d. Selected abstraction

    e. Overgeneralization

    f. Magnification/minimization

    g. Depressives remember negative events

    h. Pessimism may be result, not cause of depression

  4. Cognitive-learning approaches: learned helplessness and attributional style

    a. Learned helplessness: depressive believes skills no longer effective in reaching goals

  5. Pessimistic attributional style

    a. Explain negative events in terms of internal, global, and stable factors

    b. Measured with Attributional Style Questionnaire and CAVE (content analysis of verbal expression)

    c. Attributional style related to achievements, health, and depression

Copyright © Houghton Mifflin Company. All rights reserved.

       d. Internality and externality may relate to different forms of depression

  6. Response style

  7. Sociocultural explanations

       a. Higher rates for Native Americans and Southeast Asians in United States; Chinese have more somatic complaints

  8. Stress and depression

       a   Diathesis (vulnerability) triggered by stress; one severe stress more likely to cause depression than several minor stressors; stress and depression have bi-directional relationship

       b. Gender and depression: women twice as likely as men to become depressed; differences may appear real or differences are real; Nolen-Hoeksema concludes women ruminate over moods; men minimize dysphoria

B. Biological perspectives on mood disorders

  1. Role of heredity

       a. Twin studies: MZ concordance rate 72 percent for bipolar, 40 percent for unipolar; DZ concordance rate 14 percent for bipolar, 11 percent for unipolar

       b. One study finds specific area of chromosome (not replicated); probably polygenetic

  2. Neurotransmitters and mood disorders

       a. Catecholamines (norepinephrine, serotonin, dopamine) insufficient due to excessive enzyme breakdown or excessive re-uptake

       b. May be problem in reception of neurotransmitter

  3. Abnormal cortisol levels

       a. Too-high level measured by dexamethasone suppression test

       b. Cortisol-depression relationship may be bi-directional

  4. REM sleep disturbance: rapid onset and increased level in depressives

C. Evaluating the causation theories

  1. Three developments added to understanding

       a. Prospective studies of events and depression

       b. Technological advances in psychophysiology

       c. Awareness that depression is heterogeneous

  2. Psychoanalytic difficult to test

  3. Cognitive has become more complex

  4. Behavioral and learned helplessness well-grounded in research

  5. Interaction of environment and biology

V. The treatment of mood disorders

A. Biomedical treatments for depressive disorders

  1. Medications

       a. Tricyclic antidepressants

       b. Monoamine oxidase (MAO) inhibitors

       c. Fluoxetine SSRI (Prozac)

  2. Electroconvulsive therapy (ECT)

       a. Voltage to brain for one-half second or less to induce convulsion and short coma

Copyright © Houghton Mifflin Company. All rights reserved.

      b. Improvement after four treatments; one in a thousand chance of serious complications

  B. Psychotherapy and behavioral treatments for depressive disorders

    1. Interpersonal psychotherapy: short-term, psychodynamic eclectic

      a. Focus on conflicts in current relationships

      b. Linked to past life experiences and traumas

    2. Cognitive-behavioral therapy

      a. Identify negative thoughts

      b. Link to depression

      c. Examine negative thought and decide if it can be supported

      d. Replace distorted negative thoughts with realistic ones

      e. Steps: monitor thoughts and substitute logical interpretations; increase activity level; improve social skills

      f. Evaluation

        1. Reduces risk of relapse compared to those treated with drugs

        2. Both interpersonal psychotherapy and cognitive-behavioral effective

        3. Cognitive therapy as effective as antidepressants

        4. Cognitive-behavioral skills can prevent depression

        5. Combination of medication and psychotherapy most advantageous

  C. Treatment for bipolar disorders

    1. Lithium

      a. Effective

      b. Side effects and compliance problems

LEARNING OBJECTIVES

1. Describe the mood disorders and distinguish them from normal mood changes. Recall prevalence rates for these disorders. (pp. 347-348)

2. Describe the symptoms of depression, including the affective, cognitive, behavioral, and physiological domains. (pp. 348-351)

3. Describe the symptoms of mania. Differentiate the two levels of manic intensity. (pp. 351-352)

4. Describe and differentiate among the following mood disorders and the symptom features that may accompany these disorders: major depressive disorder, dysthymic disorder, the bipolar disorders, cyclothymic disorder, and mood disorders associated with a medical condition or substance use. (pp. 352-355)

5. Describe and differentiate course specifiers including cycling type, seasonal, postpartum, and longitudinal patterns of mood disorders. Compare unipolar and bipolar disorders. (pp. 355-356)

6. Contrast the various theories of depression, including psychodynamic, behavioral, and Lewinsohn's comprehensive view of depression. (pp. 356-360)

7. Discuss the cognitive and cognitive-learning approaches to depression. Give examples of the logical errors depressives make and the pessimistic attributions they might use. (pp. 360-365)

8. Describe various sociocultural explanations for mood disorders, including cross-cultural differences, the role of stress, and social support in depression. (pp. 365-368; Mental Health & Society)

Copyright © Houghton Mifflin Company. All rights reserved.

9. Describe what is known about sex differences and depression and the explanations for any differences. (pp. 368-369).

10. Describe the biological theories of mood disorders, including genetic and neurotransmitter theories, the role of cortisol and REM sleep in depression. (pp. 369-373)

11. Evaluate the strengths and weaknesses of the various causal theories of depression. (p. 373)

12. Indicate the kinds of biological therapies that have been used to treat depression, including medication and electroconvulsive therapy (ECT). Discuss the effectiveness of these treatments and their side effects. (pp. 373-376; Mental Health & Society; Critical Thinking)

13. Describe psychological treatments for mood disorders, including interpersonal psychotherapy and cognitive-behavioral therapy. Evaluate the effectiveness of these treatments. (pp. 376-380)

14. Describe the use of lithium and its problems in treating bipolar disorders. (pp. 380)

CLASSROOM TOPICS FOR LECTURE AND DISCUSSION

1. Exogenous depressions are related to the experience of stressful life events. Both Lewinsohn's and Seligman's theories assume that negative events play a role in the development of depression, and research supports this idea. However, the availability and quality of social support can provide a buffer against depression. Support appears to have two key aspects: intimacy and integration in the community. Marital relationships are particularly important for intimacy. Major depression occurs twice as often in those who live alone than those who live with someone else (Weissman et al., 1991). Those with poor marital relationships report more signs of depression than those with better ones (Menaghan & Lieberman, 1986). Wives who rated their husbands as more supportive were less likely to be depressed one year later than wives who rated their husbands as less supportive (Monroe et al., 1986). It is unclear, however, whether poor support causes depression or the other way around. A depressive spouse can contribute to the deterioration of marital relations (Beach, Sandeen, & O'Leary, 1990). These researchers suggest that marital counseling be a routine part of the treatment of depressives who are married.

People who have few friends and who are involved in few social activities are more prone to being depressed (Barnett & Gotlib, 1988). Lack of social integration reduces the opportunities for engaging in pleasant events, reduces the number of sources of help, and allows people who ruminate on their distress to become further withdrawn and depressed.

Discuss with students the circumstances that have surrounded depression in their own lives and the roles that family members, friends, and other help providers have played in reducing or exacerbating depressive symptoms. How have their relationships been affected? What level of social integration did they experience before, during, and after the depressive episode?

Sources: Barnett, P. A., & Gotlib, I. H. (1988). Psychosocial functioning and depression: Distinguishing among antecedents, concomitants and consequences. *Psychological Bulletin, 104*, 97–126.

Beach, S. R. H., Sandeen, E. E., & O'Leary, K. D. (1990). Depression in marriage: A model for etiology and treatment. In D. H. Barlow (Ed.) *Treatment manuals for practitioners.* New York: Guilford Press.

Menaghan, E. G., & Lieberman, M. A. (1986). Changes in depression following divorce: A panel study. *Journal of Marriage and the Family, 17,* 319–328.

Monroe, S. M., Bromet, E. J., Connell, M. M., & Stener, S. C. (1986). Social support, life events, and depressive symptoms: A 1-year prospective study. *Journal of Consulting and Clinical Psychology, 54,* 423–431.

Copyright © Houghton Mifflin Company. All rights reserved.

Weissman, M. M. et al. (1991). Affective disorders. In L. N. Robins & D. A. Regier (Eds.) *Psychiatric disorders in America: The Epidemiological Catchment Area Study*. New York: The Free Press, pp. 53–80.

2.   To indicate the spectrum of mood disorders, draw a long horizontal line on the blackboard and label the poles "Psychotic Depression" and "Delirious Mania". At this point, explain what psychosis means. Then indicate a region toward the middle of the continuum that represents normal fluctuations in mood. Make only dotted lines to indicate the hazy boundaries separating "normal" behaviors and clinical disorders. On the depression side, label *neurotic* depression and explain that this term, though useful, is no longer part of the DSM terminology. Ask students to describe mild to moderate depression and list the affective, cognitive, behavioral, and physiological symptoms they suggest. In this region of the diagram, note dysthymia (based on closeness to "normal" and duration) and both exogenous and endogenous major depressions. Further toward the psychotic end, list the symptoms of psychotic depression. On the mania side of normal, describe hypomania and then acute and delirious mania. The area from neurotic depression to hypomania can then be linked by a double-headed arrow to show cyclothymia. Finally, the bigger mood swings of bipolar disorder can be indicated by an even larger double-headed arrow.

Many students don't understand the difference between Bipolar I and Bipolar II disorders. The key difference is that in Bipolar II a hypomanic episode (never reaching manic proportions) alternates with major depression. Bipolar I accounts for all other kinds of manic episodes.

Internet Site: http://www.health-center.com/english/brain/symptoms/mood.htm. Discusses mood symptoms.

3.   The mood disorders are divided into many subcategories. It may be helpful to students to organize these categories in the following way: First is the psychotic versus neurotic dimension. Unlike many other forms of disorders, the mood disorders raise the issue of continuity (from "neurotic" conditions to psychotic ones). Second is the unipolar versus bipolar dimension. Third, particularly with the depressions, are the exogenous and endogenous explanations. Fourth, some disorders are mild and prolonged (cyclothymia and dysthymia), whereas others are severe and perhaps more acute (major depression and bipolar disorders). Finally, some mood disorders are primary (unaccompanied by other mental disturbances), whereas many are secondary (the outgrowth or a concomitant feature of some other disorder). You should remind students that the categorization of disorders is often overly neat and tidy. Many people with drinking or other substance abuse problems experience serious depressive episodes. If a person is both depressed and drug dependent, must the diagnostician decide which is the "real" problem? A diagnosis of secondary depression may be more accurate, but figuring out which came first is a very difficult proposition.

4.   You can illustrate Lewinsohn's theory with a downward spiral drawn on the board. The spiral includes poor social skills, reduced reinforcement, lowered activity, and worsening depressive symptoms. Treatment argues that an upward spiral of increased activity, increased reinforcement, and increased social skill and mood is also possible. What appears to be missing are the cognitive components that Beck stresses. You can add to the Lewinsohn diagram the depressive's illogical and negative thoughts, which help to explain why events such as reduced reinforcement produce lowered activity. This more integrated model of depression mirrors the work of most cognitive behavioral therapists to change both the client's activity and his or her normal way of interpreting events.

Copyright © Houghton Mifflin Company. All rights reserved.

CLASSROOM DEMONSTRATIONS & HANDOUTS

1.   The reasons for the reported sex differences in depression are many and controversial. One reason is that men and women are socialized to express emotions differently and are taught to expect different reactions from others when they are distressed. The following exercise may reveal to students norms for experiencing depression and coping with it.

Set up small groups (six to eight per group) with even numbers of males and females. Then say the following:

> Think of a time when you were quite sad and depressed. Fix this time in your mind. Try to visualize where you were, what you were doing, and how others were responding to you. Using the incident you have in mind, answer the following questions as honestly as you can.

Then ask each student to write down on the handout his or her honest responses to the following questions below:

1.   In what ways did you behave differently during this time than you usually do?

2.   In what ways were your patterns of thinking different during this time than they usually are?

3.   In what ways did your body react differently during this time than your body usually reacts?

4.   During this time, what things did you do to cope with your feelings?

Finally, ask the students to write down how they think the *average* male and female student would answer the question about coping.

Then ask group members to read aloud their expectations for the opposite sex and compare these with the actual experiences. Caution students that they need not reveal any more than they feel comfortable revealing. The aim of the exercise is to see whether real differences occur in the behavior and expectations of men and women when "depressed." If Nolen-Hoeksema's (1991) conclusions about the gender difference in depression are supported, women will be more likely to analyze and track their depressed moods; men will be more likely to distract themselves from such emotions. Whether members of the opposite sex will expect such differences in coping methods is unknown.

If time permits, groups can report to the rest of the class whether they found actual sex differences in cognitive, behavioral, and affective symptoms and in predictions for the opposite sex. Students may discover that stereotypic differences in emotional expression and coping are exaggerated.

2.   Depression can be as exasperating as it is common. The responses of friends and family members to a depressed individual often range from sympathy to anger or avoidance. Some researchers even suggest that depression is a contagious disorder, since those who strive to alter the depressive often wind up depressed themselves. The following role-play exercise may illustrate this.

Have students pair off and ask each pair to decide who will play the role of a moderately depressed person first. This person is to talk negatively throughout the exercise. All suggestions from the "helper" are to be met with brief, "yes-but" responses or claims that the "depressed" person is too tired, too worthless, or not interested. The helper is assigned the role of the caring friend. This person should use the strategies that he or she has actually used with depressed friends or that he or she is expected to use. Ask each pair to imagine a series of encounters between the still-depressed individual and the helper-friend so that a condensed version of several days' or a week's contact is played out. You can assist by announcing to the class every three or four minutes that a day has gone by and the helper should try again to get the depressed person "undepressed."

Copyright © Houghton Mifflin Company. All rights reserved.

After the students have role-played four or so encounters, have the partners exchange roles. Ask the new helpers to use what they have learned from the first set of interactions to do a better job of dealing with the depressive.

After the second set of exchanges, ask partners to report to the class the sequence of strategies the first helpers tried. Write on the board whether the strategy was sympathy, questioning to determine the cause, cajoling and suggesting, anger and resentment, avoidance and defeat, or some other approach. Ask the helpers how they felt during the exercise and how they have felt in actual experiences dealing with depressives. How many of them feel defeated and depressed at the end? Link this to Lewinsohn's idea that sometimes the "help" of friends and family unwittingly reinforces depression.

Finally, ask whether they learned any lessons as to what are effective or self-protective ways of responding to depression. Discuss with students the need to educate the public about these strategies to prevent burnout and contagious depression in helpers.

Internet Site: http://www.health-center.com/mentalhealth A site that lists the DSM-IV-TR criteria for depression.

3.   This quick review will help students remember Beck's four errors in logic, all of which typify the negative schema that keeps depressives depressed. Present the short vignettes below and ask students to decide whether each best illustrates selective abstraction, magnification/ minimization, arbitrary inference, or overgeneralization. The overlap in these errors is considerable, but it is worthwhile clarifying the differences.

Tom is being interviewed for a job. He has seven years' work experience in a related field. The interviewer asks him a standard set of questions, including: "What would you say are your strengths and weaknesses?" This is Tom's answer:

> Well, it's a lot easier for me to talk about my weaknesses than my strengths. I guess my strength is that I'm pretty old and experienced. My problem is that I don't follow through on things, I make other people uncomfortable, I make silly mistakes, and I really don't have many creative ideas.

[Tom's response best illustrates magnification/minimization: The depressive exaggerates his/her limitations while minimizing his/her strengths. In a job interview, this negative schema is a serious problem.]

Gina handed in a 12-page term paper that included one page that was upside down. When her instructor flipped through the paper, he saw the upside-down one and said, "Oops." This is what Gina thought to herself:

> I'm such an incompetent, I can't even get all the pages going in the right direction. I'm sure he thinks I'm a fool. If I can't put 12 pages together and staple them correctly, how do I ever hope to be a lawyer? What a hopeless case I am.

[Gina's thinking best illustrates overgeneralization. She takes one mistake and generalizes it to mean that she is incompetent, foolish, and hopeless.]

Barry is the father of a three-year-old boy. On Halloween night, after the excitement of dressing up and eating candy, the boy cried and fussed about going to bed and, despite Barry's best efforts, was still awake one hour after his bedtime. Barry's explanation for his son's crying is as follows:

Copyright © Houghton Mifflin Company. All rights reserved.

I must be an incompetent parent, and he hates me. He probably thinks I'm as evil as I think I am. I have no sensitivity, no skills. When his wife wonders, Don't you think he might be crying for other reasons? Barry says flatly, No.

[Although this vignette could illustrate generalization, it best illustrates arbitrary inference, since Barry is unable to think of any alternative explanation for why his son was crying and draws conclusions that are unsupported by evidence. It does not dawn on him that his son might have been overtired, too excited to wind down, or even that, as a father, he helped his child have an enjoyable evening.]

Nancy painted her kitchen yesterday. She had picked out a very attractive color, bought the right brushes, and did an exceptionally neat job. However, a small dab of paint got on the tile floor despite her careful use of a drop cloth. When her husband saw the kitchen he was delighted and raved about how improved it looked. At one point he looked down, noticed the small dab of paint, and innocently tried to rub it off with the toe of his shoe. When he did this, Nancy said:

I completely missed that spot. Why can't I ever get things right? I'm sorry about the paint spill. I just can't seem to be careful even when I try. People are going to see that mistake on the floor as soon as they come into the room. My carelessness ruined everything.

[Nancy is taking one minor incident and blowing it up, while taking it out of context. Her husband was praising her, but she could only select out what she perceived as a negative and use it as proof that she "always ruins everything." This example best illustrates selective abstraction.]

4.   In this classroom exercise, give students only the shortest of descriptions for a person who may be suffering from one of many disorders, but who most likely has unipolar or bipolar disorder. The students' job is to think of the questions they would ask or the observations they would make as clinicians to decide which diagnosis is correct. Make clear to them that we do not know what the individual is really suffering from; the exercise is to get them thinking about the alternatives and introduce them to the process of ruling certain diagnoses in while ruling other diagnoses out.

Tell students to take out a fresh sheet of paper. At the top of the page, have them write *Bipolar disorder* on the left side and *Major depressive disorder* on the right. Then read them this brief description of a new client to an outpatient treatment facility:

Mrs. S. came to the clinic with her husband. Mrs. S. is 35, but looks much older. Her hair was unkempt, and she walked slowly and with a stooped posture, as though she were carrying a heavy burden. Her face showed little expression although there were tears in her eyes. Her answers to questions were given in a low voice in one- or two-word sentences. Clearly, Mrs. S. could have a mood disorder, but what kind? What information would rule in bipolar disorder? What information would rule it out? What would rule in unipolar depression? What would rule it out? What other disorders could Mrs. S. be suffering from?

Have students write out the questions they would ask or the observations they would make and the answers that would rule in or rule out the diagnoses. This can take the form of a flowchart in which each question has a yes or no answer which serves to confirm or deny a particular diagnosis.

Here are some of the observations and answers to questions that would support a diagnosis of bipolar disorder.

1.   Does she experience mood swings including sudden periods of elation, grandiosity, or irritability?   yes

2.   Has she had periods of high energy and sleeplessness before a period of depression?   yes

3.   Has she had several of these mood swings?   yes

Copyright © Houghton Mifflin Company. All rights reserved.

4. Is this the first episode of such a mood disorder?   no

5. Has she ever been successfully treated with lithium?   Yes

6. Did the mood disorder start without there being a clear precipitating event?   yes

7. Does anyone else in her family have a history of mood swings?   yes

8. Does she look especially anxious?   no

9. Does she worry constantly while in the depressed state?   no

10. When she is depressed, do her movement and speech slow down a great deal?   yes

Here are some of the observations and answers to questions that would support a diagnosis of unipolar disorder.

1. Did an undesirable or uncontrollable event precede the onset of the depressive episode?   yes

2. Has she had mood swings involving sudden periods of elation, grandiosity, or irritability? no

3. Is this the first episode of such a mood disorder?   yes

4. If she has been treated for this problem before, were antidepressants effective?   yes

5. Does she look especially anxious?   yes

6. Does she worry constantly while in the depressed state?   yes

7. Do these symptoms coincide with having recently given birth?   yes   (This answer suggests postpartum depression.)

8. Do these symptoms coincide with a specific season of the year?   yes   (This answer suggests seasonal affective disorder.)

Mrs. S. might be diagnosed as having other, nonmood disorders, such as a medical condition that leads to slowed movement (a thyroid condition, for example), a substance-related disorder involving depressants or withdrawal from stimulants, an organic brain dysfunction, or a schizoaffective or catatonic form of schizophrenia. To make matters even more confusing (just like real life!), many clients have two or more psychological or physiological conditions simultaneously. For example, the reported rates of personality disorders in depressed patients range from 30 to 40 percent; one study of a nonpatient sample found that 47 percent of those with a history of major depression had a personality disorder (Shea et al., 1992).

Make clear to students that diagnosis is done over a period of time and observations. Additional, noninterview information, such as psychological testing and medical tests (the dexamethazone suppression test, for example) can be brought to bear so the clinician can adequately test his/her hypotheses about the client. However, the efficient diagnostician does not ask questions whose answers fail to discriminate among possible diagnoses. For instance, it would not be helpful to ask if Mrs. S. is feeling depressed, since both bipolar and unipolar clients would say yes. Considering her gender or socioeconomic status would not add any relevant information.

Source: Shea, M. T., Widiger, T. A., & Klein, M. H. (1992). Comorbidity of personality disorders and depression: Implications for treatment. *Journal of Consulting and Clinical Psychology, 60,* 857–868.

Copyright © Houghton Mifflin Company. All rights reserved.

5.   This activity helps students see how positive moods and reinforcing activities are related in their own lives. It illustrates the main point that Peter Lewinsohn and his colleague at the University of Oregon make about depression: If you are not engaged in reinforcing activities, your mood tends to become more depressed, and as you become more depressed you engage in fewer activities. One handout helps students monitor their daily moods; the other is a shortened version of the Pleasant Events Schedule Lewinsohn developed, listing reinforcing actions. Students should check off all the items on the schedule that are pleasant for them and add others that are missing from the list. Before going to bed each day for two weeks, students should fill out the daily mood form and list the number of pleasant activities in which they took part that day. At the end of two weeks, have students average their daily mood scores and the number of activities they took part in. You can then perform a correlational analysis of the data supplied (anonymously) by the class. If Lewinsohn's work is supported, you should find a reasonably strong positive correlation. If not, consider with students other explanations. These might include ceiling effects on both mood and activities, cognitive factors that affect mood, ill health, and others.

Source: The idea for this demonstration comes from Nevid, J. S., Rathus, S. A., & Greene, B. (1994). *Abnormal psychology in a changing world* (2nd ed.). Prentice-Hall. Reprinted by permission.

6.   The handout for this demonstration is a quick screening test for depression. It is taken from the Online Depression Screening Test developed by the New York University Department of Psychiatry http://www.med.nyu.edu/Psych/screens/depres.html. The cutoff scores are NOT PROVIDED. Therefore, this demonstration is mostly aimed at critiquing the screening device rather than doing a depression screening of students in the class. Remind students that any such screening device is incapable of diagnosing a condition and that a full, face-to-face evaluation is needed for diagnosing depression.

Discuss the strengths and shortcomings of such self-report measures. Provide a list of the affective, cognitive, physiological, and behavior symptoms of depression from the text. Then ask students if they could improve on this measure. Are some symptoms overrepresented? are others underrepresented? Note with them that some questions cover multiple issues: Question 2, for instance, asks about both energy and inability to concentrate, so which symptom is the individual to rate? Discuss issues of social desirability, denial, and attention seeking. Finally, discuss the problem of finding an appropriate cutoff score. Remind students of the problems of false negatives (failing to detect real depressive symptoms) and false positives (seeing depressive symptoms when none exist). Which do they think is the more serious error?

If students still want to have their responses to the screening device scored and evaluated, you can provide the Internet address above. It is wise to remind them again of the need for further evaluation even if results come back suggesting they show depressive symptoms. You may also want to make yourself available for consultation if you use this demonstration.

Internet Site: http://www.med.nyu.edu/Psych/screens/depres.html. An online depression screening test developed by the New York University Department of Psychiatry.

7.   This demonstration is designed to introduce the students to depression and the media. Have each student watch one network news program, one local news program, one local newspaper and one major popular magazine. The student is to rate each news item as either negative or positive. Use an overhead transparency to track the individual responses from the students. Did the network news receive more negative or more positive ratings? Did any news medium receive more negative or more positive ratings than the others? In large classes you can compare the ratings for ABC, CBS, CNN, FOX, and

Copyright © Houghton Mifflin Company. All rights reserved.

NBC by making columns on the overhead transparency. Discuss the effects of various news media on one's mood. Ask the students for examples of when the media has influenced their mood.

8.   Have the student form small groups of 4-7 individuals depending on your class size and space limitations. Ask each group to develop a list of symptom of mood disorders with the most salient examples first. Each group could then have a spokesperson deliver a short talk about the best examples. You could provide a blank overhead transparency to each group at the beginning of this demonstration. Have each group conduct a discussion about why depression is so common in college and university environments. List reasons on an overhead transparency. Further, discuss which factors are the most common in the lives of college students.

9.   Invite a guest speaker who is a psychologist or psychiatrist specializing in treatment of mood disorders. Have the students develop questions during the class period before the guest lecturer is scheduled.

10.   Bring the DSM-IV-TR to class, and prepare an overhead transparency or PowerPoint slide ahead of time for your lecture on mood disorders. Describe the in-depth material from the DSM-IV while using the transparency or PowerPoint slide as an outline. Lead a discussion on the differences between different mood disorders. Encourage student input about individuals they have known with these symptoms.

Copyright © Houghton Mifflin Company. All rights reserved.

HANDOUT FOR DEMONSTRATION 1:
WAYS OF COPING WITH DEPRESSING SITUATIONS

Think of a time when you were quite sad and depressed. Fix in your mind the situation, what led up to it, and how you coped. After you are clear on the circumstances, answer the following questions as honestly as you can. You need not reveal your answers to others if you do not wish to.

1. In what ways, if any, did you behave differently during this time than you usually do?

2. In what ways, if any, were your patterns of thinking different during this time than they usually are?

3. In what ways, if any, did your body react differently during this time than your body usually reacts?

4. During this time, what things did you do to cope with your feelings?

How do you think the *average female* student would answer question 4?

How do you think the *average male* student would answer question 4?

HANDOUT FOR DEMONSTRATION 5:
DAILY MOOD RECORD

For a two-week period you are to fill out this daily mood form. Make seven copies of this form and cut them in half. Be sure to complete it at the same time each day, preferably before you go to sleep. Review the day and your feelings. Rate your overall mood for the day on a scale from 1 to 10 (1 = severely depressed, very much down in the dumps; 10 = best possible mood, absolutely elated). Do not miss a day! Be honest!

_____ Rating (from 1 to 10) for your overall mood for today: _____
   Today's date

Any reasons for your mood today?

_____

_____

_____

How many activities from the Pleasant Events Schedule did you do today? _____

_____ Rating (from 1 to 10) for your overall mood for today: _____
   Today's date

Any reasons for your mood today?

_____

_____

_____

How many activities from the Pleasant Events Schedule did you do today? _____

Copyright © Houghton Mifflin Company. All rights reserved.

HANDOUT FOR DEMONSTRATION 5: PLEASANT EVENTS SCHEDULE

Put a check mark next to each of the items that you find pleasant. Add any that are not on this list.

_____ 1. Wearing expensive clothes

_____ 2. Talking about sports

_____ 3. Meeting someone new

_____ 4. Going to a rock concert

_____ 5. Playing baseball, football, or basketball

_____ 6. Buying things for yourself

_____ 7. Going to the beach

_____ 8. Doing artwork

_____ 9. Rock climbing

_____ 10. Reading the Scriptures

_____ 11. Playing golf

_____ 12. Redecorating a room

_____ 13. Going to a sports event

_____ 14. Going to the races

_____ 15. Reading novels, plays, magazines

_____ 16. Sailing or canoeing

_____ 17. Camping

_____ 18. Playing cards or board games

_____ 19. Doing puzzles

_____ 20. Having lunch with friends

_____ 21. Driving long distances

_____ 22. Being with animals

_____ 23. Ice skating or skiing

_____ 24. Going to a party

_____ 25. Playing pool or billiards

_____ 26. Gardening

_____ 27. Dancing

_____ 28. Shopping in the city

_____ 29. Lying in the sun

_____ 30. Talking about philosophy

_____ 31. Having friends come to visit

_____ 32. Photography

_____ 33. Fishing

_____ 34. Writing a diary

_____ 35. Swimming

_____ 36. Making love

_____ 37. Knitting

_____ 38. Talking about politics

_____ 39. Doing yoga

_____ 40. Going to a restaurant

_____ 41. Attending a play

_____ 42. Going to a bar

_____ 43. Cooking meals

_____ 44. Getting a massage

_____ 45. Other _____

_____ 46. Other _____

Copyright © Houghton Mifflin Company. All rights reserved.

HANDOUT FOR DEMONSTRATION 6:
DEPRESSION SCREENING TEST

For more than two weeks:

1. Do you feel sad, blue, unhappy, or "down in the dumps"?
   A. Never
   B. Rarely
   C. Sometimes
   D. Very often
   E. Most of the time

2. Do you feel tired, have little energy, unable to concentrate?
   A. Never
   B. Rarely
   C. Sometimes
   D. Very often
   E. Most of the time

3. Do you feel uneasy, restless, or irritable?
   A. Never
   B. Rarely
   C. Sometimes
   D. Very often
   E. Most of the time

4. Do you have trouble sleeping or eating (too little or too much)?
   A. Never
   B. Rarely
   C. Sometimes
   D. Very often
   E. Most of the time

5. Do you feel that you are not enjoying the activities that you used to?
   A. Never
   B. Rarely
   C. Sometimes
   D. Very often
   E. Most of the time

6. Do you feel that you have lost interest in sex or are experiencing sexual difficulties?
   A. Never
   B. Rarely
   C. Sometimes
   D. Very often
   E. Most of the time

7. Do you feel that it takes you longer than before to make decisions or that you are unable to concentrate?
   A. Never
   B. Rarely
   C. Sometimes
   D. Very often
   E. Most of the time

Copyright © Houghton Mifflin Company. All rights reserved.

8. Do you feel inadequate, like a failure, or that nobody likes you anymore?
   A. Never
   B. Rarely
   C. Sometimes
   D. Very often
   E. Most of the time

9. Do you feel guilty without a rational reason, or put yourself down?
   A. Never
   B. Rarely
   C. Sometimes
   D. Very often
   E. Most of the time

10. Do you feel that things always go or will go wrong no matter how hard you try?
    A. Never
    B. Rarely
    C. Sometimes
    D. Very often
    E. Most of the time

Copyright © Houghton Mifflin Company. All rights reserved.

SELECTED READINGS

Barnett, P. A., & Gotlib, I. H. (1988). Psychosocial functioning and depression: Distinguishing among antecedents, concomitants, and consequences. *Psychological Bulletin, 104,* 97–126.

Coyne, J. C., & Gotlib, I. H. (1983). The role of cognition in depression: A critical appraisal. *Psychological Bulletin, 94,* 472–505.

Dobson, K. S . (1989). A meta-analysis of the efficacy of cognitive therapy for depression. *Journal of Consulting and Clinical Psychology, 57,* 414–419.

Kolata, G. (1986). Manic-depression: Is it inherited? *Science, 232,* 575–576.

Wender, P. H. et al. (1984). Psychiatric disorders in the biological and adoptive families of adopted individuals with affective disorders. *Archives of General Psychiatry, 43,* 923–929.

Sattler, D., Shabatay, V., & Kramer, G. (1998). *Abnormal psychology in context: Voices and perspectives.* Boston, MA: Houghton Mifflin Company. Chapter 4 Mood Disorders.

Clipson, C., & Steer, J. (1998) *Case studies in abnormal psychology.* Boston, MA: Houghton Mifflin Company. Chapter 5, Major Depressive Disorder. Chapter 6, Bipolar Disorder.

VIDEO RESOURCES

Depression: Recognizing It, Treating It (filmstrip and audiocassette, 42 min). How depression differs from normal mood changes. Psychoanalytic and cognitive behavioral perspectives on depression as well as biological theories of cause and methods of treatment. Harper & Row Media, 10 East 53rd Street, New York, NY 10022.

Depression: The Shadowed Valley (16 mm, color, 60 min). This film examines various forms of depression. Interviews with patients reveal the origins of problems and biological changes that occur during depression. A range of treatment methods is presented. Bristol-Myers Company, 345 Park Avenue, New York, NY 10022.

Depression: A Study in Abnormal Behavior (16 mm, color, 26 min). The stages in the development of depression in a 29-year-old woman are presented, including the issue of suicide. Electroshock treatment and other methods are depicted. CRM Educational Films, 1011 Camino Del Mar, Del Mar, CA 92014.

Four Lives: Portraits in Manic Depression (video, 60 min). Four individuals being treated for bipolar disorders are interviewed as well as their families. A segment showing a support group emphasizes the need for understanding and empathy from others. Fanlight Productions, 47 Halifax Street, Boston, MA 02130.

"Mood Disorders" (8) from *The World of Abnormal Psychology* series (video, 60 min). This segment describes major depression, bipolar disorder, the causal factors in depression and bipolar disorders, and both drug, ECT, and psychotherapies. Annenberg/CPB Collection, Dept. CA94, P.O. Box 2345, S. Burlington, VT 05407-2345; to order, call 1-800-532-7637.

Copyright © Houghton Mifflin Company. All rights reserved.

One Man's Madness (16 mm, color, 32 min). Nonfiction account of a manic-depressive writer's symptoms and the effect on his family. Shows swings in mood from mania to severe depression. Time-Life Multi-Media, 100 Eisenhower Drive, Paramus, NJ 07652.

Through Madness (video, 30 min). A documentary about three people who have either schizophrenia or bipolar disorder helps demystify students' perceptions of these psychotic disorders. The man with bipolar disorder remains married, and the interview with him and his wife is especially relevant to this chapter's material. Filmakers Library, 124 East 40th Street, Suite 901, New York, NY 10016.

Breaking the Dark Horse: A Family Copes with Manic Depression (VHS, color, 32 min.). The story of a woman with manic depression and how it affects her family and friends. Fanlight Productions. 1-800-937-4113.

Depression and Manic Depression (VHS, color, 28 min.). Covers depression and manic depression. Includes people such as Mike Wallace and Kay Red field James, author of *An Unquiet Mind*. Films for the Humanities.

Four Lives: A Portrait of Manic Depression (VHS, color, 60 min.). Portrays the lives of four patients with manic depression and their families. Medical and psychotherapeutic treatments are discussed. Flight Productions. 1-800-937-4113.

ON THE INTERNET

http://www.psycom.net/depression.central.genetics.html is Depression Central an extremely thorough clearinghouse for information on all mood disorders.

http://www.health-center.com/mentalhealth/symptoms/mood.htm describes a change in mood as a common complaint of many individuals. If your mood is interfering with your life, it may be due to one of the problems discussed at this site.

http://www.med.nyu.edu/Psych/screens/depres.html is an on-line depression screening test.

http://www.health-center.com/mentalhealth a site with information about mental health illnesses and issues

Copyright © Houghton Mifflin Company. All rights reserved.

CHAPTER 12
Suicide

CHAPTER OUTLINE

I. Problems in the study of suicide

    A. Possible reasons: loss of family life, pressure to excel, perceived poor quality of life, for a greater good or cause (more than just depression)

    B. Suicide now recognized as serious threat to public health

    C. Reasons for separate chapter

        1. Psychiatric symptoms usually associated with suicidal person, but suicidal ideation may represent separate clinical entity

        2. Increasing interest in suicide, which is the eighth leading cause of death in the United States

        3. Society increasingly open about discussing death

        4. Suicide is irreversible, but suicidal person often ambivalent

II. Correlates of suicide

    A. Cannot ask successful suicides about their motives

    B. Psychological autopsy: case records and survivor interviews to understand suicide

    C. Suicide notes rare (12 to 34 percent of cases)

    D. Attempters more likely to be white female housewives in 20s and 30s experiencing marital difficulties and use barbiturates; most likely to succeed are white males in 40s or older, who suffer ill health or depression and shoot or hang themselves

    E. Facts about suicide

        1. Frequency

            a. More than 31,000 in United States yearly actual number of suicides may be 25 to 30 percent higher)

            b. Eight to ten attempts for each completion

        2. Children and young people as victims

            a. Persons under age 25 accounted for 15 percent of suicides in 1997

            b. 12,000 children between ages five and fourteen admitted to hospitals for suicidal behavior yearly

            c. Rate among 15 to 24 age group up 40 percent in past decade

            d. 20 percent of college students think of suicide during college career, but college students half as likely as non-college student age peers to attempt suicide

        3. Suicide publicity and identification with victims

Copyright © Houghton Mifflin Company. All rights reserved

4. Gender: men succeed three to four times more often than women; women attempt three times more often than men

5. Marital status: lowest incidence amongst married people, highest among divorced

6. Occupation: high rates among physicians, lawyers, law-enforcement personnel, and dentists

7. Socioeconomic level: across all groups, but loss of wealth related to suicide

8. Choice of weapon

   a. over 60 percent of suicides are with firearms, 70 percent of attempts are drug overdose

   b. Men choose firearms

   c. women use poison and asphyxiation via barbiturates, but are increasingly using firearms and explosives

   d. Children jump from buildings or run into traffic

   e. Adolescents use hanging and drug overdoses

9. Religious affiliation lowest among Catholics and Arabs where suicide is condemned; highest were religious sanctions re suicide are weak or absent (Scandinavia and Eastern Europe)

10. Ethnic and cultural variables: highest among American Indians, lowest among

    Asian Americans

11. Jails and prisons: suicide is most frequent cause of death in U.S. jails, ranging from 90 to 230 per 1000,000 (16 times higher than in general population)

12. Historical period: decline during warfare and natural disasters; high during shifting norms

13. Communication of intent: two-thirds of those who commit suicide signal intent

    within three months of act; fewer than 5 percent unequivocally wish to die

14. Other important facts

    a. highest rate in spring and summer

    b. about one in six persons completing suicide leave notes

    c. rates in U.S. highest in Western mountain states, especially Nevada

F. Hopelessness and depression

   1. High correlation between suicide and depression, but not at depths of depression when too low in energy

   2. Hopelessness may be more catalyst than depression; supported with research

G. Alcohol consumption

   1. Successful suicide without alcohol consumption is rare

   2. Alcohol-implicated suicide 27 times higher than rate in general population

   3. Alcohol foreshortens thinking and makes solution seem all-or-none

H. Other psychological factors: many who commit suicide have DSM-IV-TR disorder; 15 percent of those with mood disorders, schizophrenia, or substance abuse attempt to kill themselves; separation and divorce, academic pressures, unemployment, and serious illness contribute

III. Theoretical perspectives

A. Sociocultural (Durkheim) suggests three categories

   1. Egoistic suicide: inability to integrate with society

   2. Altruistic suicide: for group's greater good

Copyright © Houghton Mifflin Company. All rights reserved.

3. Anomic suicide: sudden change in individual's lifestyle

4. Attributing suicide to a single sociological factor is simplistic and mechanistic, omit psychological dimension of person's struggle, don't explain why only certain group members commit suicide

B. Psychodynamic explanations focus

1. Self-destruction is hostility directed inward against interjected love object

2. Freud proposed thanatos: death instinct antagonistic to life instinct

C. Biological explanations

1. Low-5HIAA (indicating low serotonin activity) related to violent suicide

2. Low-5HIAA in suicidal individuals without history of depression

3. Genetics also implicated

IV. Victims of suicide

A. Children and adolescents

1. Prevalence

a. percent of suicides for age group 15-24 are by white males but most rapid rise in rates is black males

b. Suicide is second leading cause of teenage deaths (accidents are number 1, but some of those may actually be suicides)

c. Gallup poll of teens: 6 percent attempted suicide, 15 percent have come close to trying; estimate is that 8 to 9 percent of teens have engaged in self-harm behavior

2. Characteristics of childhood suicides

a. Attempters are female, fluctuating affect and hostile, occurs at home with parent nearby, during winter by drug overdose; families under economic stress; chaotic lives with parental chemical abuse

b. Family instability significant correlate

c. Need for early detection and treatment, including education of parents; teens using more lethal methods

3. Copycat suicides

a. Not common, but may be caused by colorful media portrayal

b. Grief and mourning not the culprits inducing copycat behavior

c. Need for suicide prevention program when suicide occurs in school; 41 percent of schools polled have suicide prevention programs

B. Elderly people

1. Stresses: physical changes, life events, and reduced income lead to depression associated with "feeling old"

2. High-risk groups

a. Elderly white males have highest rate of all

b. highest group for both genders is first generation Asian-Americans

V. Preventing suicide

A. Assessing lethality

1. Know factors correlated with suicide

2. Determine probability of person acting on wish

3. Implement appropriate actions

Copyright © Houghton Mifflin Company. All rights reserved.

B. Clues to suicidal intent

1. Demographics and previous history

2. Details about threat

3. Verbal signals

4. Behavioral clues (gestures)

C. Crisis intervention

1. Educate staff at mental health facilities and schools about signs

2. Crisis intervention program may include hospitalization and intensive care followed by more traditional therapy

D. Suicide prevention centers: first established in 1958 in Los Angeles, now widespread

1. Telephone crisis intervention

a. Staffed 24 hours per day by paraprofessionals

b. Techniques used: maintain contact and establish rapport; obtain necessary information; evaluate suicidal potential; clarify nature of stressor; assess strengths; recommend and initiate action plan

2. The effectiveness of suicide prevention centers

a. 95 percent of callers to suicide prevention centers do not use service again: either it was helpful/no further treatment needed, or not helpful and useless to call again

b. only 2 percent who kill themselves contact a center

c. studies of effectiveness contradictory and inconclusive

E. Community prevention programs

1. Collaborative response by psychologists and others in community

2. Methods (in case involving an elementary school teacher)

a. Faculty meeting to share feelings

b. Reassurance of children; individual sessions as needed

c. Education of parents on suicide prevention

F. The Surgeon General's call to action to prevent suicide: In 1999, Surgeon General David Satcher proposed the AIM program with three areas for reducing suicide: awareness, intervention, and methodology

VI. The right to suicide: moral, ethical, and legal implications

A. Suicide illegal and a sin (against Catholic canonical law)

B. Some states provide for "living will" to protect physicians who comply with request to stop life support; California narrowly voted down Death With Dignity Act allowing physicians to end lives of terminally ill

C. Thomas Szasz outspoken against suicide prevention centers; against coercive methods used by mental health professionals to stop client's action

D. Prolongation of life leads to prolonged dying

1. Hemlock Society provides manual for successful suicide

2. Dr. Jack Kevorkian uses "suicide machine" to assist suicide

E. Problems with right to suicide

1. Suicide not necessarily a rational act; patients may be coerced by relatives or others to choose to die

a. overburdening loved ones

b. medical cost control, particularly an issue for poor and disadvantaged

Copyright © Houghton Mifflin Company. All rights reserved.

    F.   Ethics of life quality versus preservation of life

        1. "Quality of life" and "quality of humanness" are subjective terms

        2. Therapist confronted with suicidal client must think through

        3. Werth summarized basic criteria for terminating life: hopeless condition, free of coercion, sound mind/rational decision, decision is consistent with patient's values

        4. Therapist has responsibility to prevent suicide if possible; failure to do so can result in legal liability

LEARNING OBJECTIVES

1. Explain why suicide is a serious concern in the United States and the problems involved in studying it. (pp. 384-387)

2. Identify some of the possible reasons for suicide and discuss the relationships among hopelessness, depression, and suicide. (pp. 387-391; Table 12.2)

3. Discuss the relationship between suicide and other psychological factors, including alcohol abuse and other DSM-IV disorders. (pp. 381-392; Mental Health & Society)

4. Describe the sociocultural factors in suicide, including egoistic, altruistic, and anomic suicide. (pp. 392-393)

5. Describe the psychodynamic and biological factors related to suicide and the different types of suicide notes. (pp. 393-394)

6. Describe and discuss research on child and adolescent suicide, including characteristics of suicidal children, family issues, and copycat suicides. (pp. 394-395)

7. Describe and discuss research on child and adolescent suicide, including characteristics of suicidal children, family issues, copycat suicides, and the elderly. (pp. 395-398)

8. Discuss suicide among special populations, including the elderly and among Asian Americans. (pp. 398-399)

9. Describe clues to suicide intent and crisis intervention efforts to prevent it. (pp. 399-402; Table 12.3)

10. Describe the methods used by workers in suicide prevention centers and the effectiveness of these efforts. (pp. 402-405; Mental Health & Society)

11. Describe how community prevention programs may help to reduce the stress of suicide on survivors, with a focus on school-based interventions. (pp. 405-406)

12. Discuss the moral, ethical, and legal implications of the right to suicide. Clarify your own position on the legality of doctor-assisted suicide. (pp. 406-409; Critical Thinking)

CLASSROOM TOPICS FOR LECTURE AND DISCUSSION

1.   The question of whether suicide can be a rational act is a good one for discussion. On the board, draw a line indicating a continuum of "rationality." At one end, give the reasons for committing suicide that could be expected if one were psychotic (I am cursed by Satan to bring evil to the world; I must die). At the other end, challenge students to describe the most rational suicide they can imagine. Now attempt to fill in the middle areas. As each suggestion is made, ask the student what aspects of the person's decision to end his or her life represent rationality. Some of the issues you can highlight are the length of time for which suicide is contemplated, the person's accuracy in predicting future happiness versus future sadness, and the impact of the suicide on survivors. Raise the issue that, if psychologists often have difficulty differentiating the psychologically disturbed from the "normal," this decision is made even more difficult when it occurs in the context of such an emotionally charged issue as suicide.

Copyright © Houghton Mifflin Company. All rights reserved.

Internet Site: http://www.suicideinfo.ca The Suicide Information and Education Center, which is a good source for the topic of suicide and suicide prevention.

2.   Student suicide will produce a good deal of interest. A discussion of what to look for in a potentially suicidal peer can be extremely beneficial. Given the subtlety of many clues to suicide, it is important to caution students against a form of medical student syndrome. They should be encouraged to consult with student mental health service professionals if they are concerned about a peer's behavior or comments.

It is also worthwhile to discuss methods of unobtrusively monitoring friends who may be suicidal. Offering to study silently in the room with such a student is a good strategy. Maintaining contacts with the potentially suicidal individual's social network is another. Reassure students that saying the word *suicide* to the person they are concerned about will not put a new idea into his or her head, and it may open the door to discussion of the person's concerns and plans.

Internet Site: http://www.suicideinfo.ca The Suicide Information and Education Center, which is a good source for the topic of suicide and suicide prevention.

3.   Elisabeth Kübler-Ross's three-stage model of adjustment to suicide can be discussed at several levels. Challenge the data on which these ideas are based. Kübler-Ross's ideas about death and dying have become very popular and are reported as "the truth" despite the fact that research fails to corroborate any such stage model. A second concern with Kübler-Ross's model is that it implies that, once a letting-go occurs, the problem of adaptation is largely solved. Suggest to students that, to the contrary, future situations dredge up the suicide. When survivors are honest with others about the cause of their loved one's death, they may suffer negative reactions. Anniversaries of the death often generate bouts of guilt and anger. The main points to make are that the accuracy of Kübler-Ross's proposed stage model is still unclear and that adaptation probably continues for a long time.

4.   Clients who voice suicidal thoughts have a strong influence on psychotherapists. A recent survey of 750 psychologists (Pope & Tabachnik, 1993) found that the most widespread fear therapists have is that a client will commit suicide. Ninety-seven percent reported having this experience at least once. Over half reported feeling so afraid about a client that their own sleeping, eating, and concentration were affected. These findings should put to rest students' impression that psychologists can compartmentalize their professional life so as to have no emotional response to their clients. For trainees, the experience of a client suicide seems even more traumatic, leading to stress levels usually found in patients who are in the process of bereavement (Kleespies et al., 1990).

Suicidal clients are an occupational hazard that students thinking about training in the helping professions should be aware of. Fears about suicide and coping when it actually occurs takes its toll.

Sources: Kleespies, P. M., Smith, M. R., & Becker, B. R. (1990). Psychology interns as patient suicide survivors: Incidence, impact, and recovery. *Professional Psychology: Research and Practice, 21,* 257–263.

Pope, K. S., & Tabachnik, B. G. (1993). Therapists' anger, hate, fear, and sexual feelings: National survey of therapist responses, client characteristics, critical events, formal complaints, and training. *Professional Psychology: Research and Practice, 24,* 142–152.

Copyright © Houghton Mifflin Company. All rights reserved.

CLASSROOM DEMONSTRATIONS & HANDOUTS

1.   You can effectively highlight the quality of life debate by dividing students into two groups: (1) the family members of a terminally ill person, who are fighting to terminate life support systems, and (2) the patient's physicians and nurses, who argue that life must be sustained. Provide ten minutes or so for group members to develop arguments for their position. Then pass out the Handout for Demonstration 1, which depicts relevant characteristics of the patient, his or her illness, and the family. Continue by asking, "At what point does the quality of life override the need to prolong life?"

2.   Staff members of your community's local suicide prevention center or hot line would be happy to make a presentation to your class. Invite both a professional staffer and a telephone volunteer to come to class. The speakers can give information about several important issues: recruiting volunteers (this can also lead to a request for student paraprofessionals), training telephone answerers, handling difficult calls, emotional effects of such work on the paraprofessional, and evidence for the center's effectiveness.

After the presenters leave, you can discuss with the class the degree to which the behavior of this center's volunteers matches that suggested by Heilig (1970) and listed in the text. (Be sure to announce the telephone number of the local hot line to your class.)

3.   Hand out the Revised Facts on Suicide Quiz (Hubbard & McIntosh, 1992). Then have students score their responses. For the true-false section, correct answers alternate true and false; for multiple-choice, the correct answers alternate a, b, and c. If time permits, poll students to record the questions that were missed by the largest percentage. The quiz is reproduced below with the percentage of the original 331 undergraduates in an introductory psychology class who answered each question correctly given in brackets after each item. This test should start a discussion of the origins of misconceptions about suicide and the damage that such misconceptions can bring. The quiz also shows the multidisciplinary nature of the study of suicide, since there are issues touching psychiatry, social work, and public health, as well as psychology.

T F ?   1.   The tendency toward suicide is not genetically (i.e., biologically) inherited and passed on from one generation to another. [46]

T F ?   2.   People who talk about suicide rarely commit suicide. [73]

T F ?   3.   The suicidal person neither wants to die nor is fully intent on dying. [38]

T F ?   4.   If assessed by a psychiatrist, everyone who commits suicide would be diagnosed as depressed. [57]

T F ?   5.   Suicide rarely happens without warning. [63]

T F ?   6.   If you ask someone directly, "Do you feel like killing yourself?" it will likely lead that person to make a suicide attempt. [95]

T F ?   7.   A time of high suicide risk in depression is when the person begins to improve. [47]

T F ?   8.   A suicidal person will always be suicidal and entertain thoughts of suicide. [76]

T F ?   9.   A person who has made a past suicide attempt is more likely to attempt suicide again than someone who has never attempted it. [80]

T F ? 10.   A person who commits suicide is mentally ill. [70]

T F ? 11.   Suicide is among the top ten causes of death in the United States. [83]

T F ? 12.   Nothing can be done to stop people from making the attempt once they have made up their minds to kill themselves. [92]

T F ? 13.   Most people who attempt suicide fail to kill themselves. [74]

T F ? 14.   Motives and causes of suicide are readily established. [58]

T F ? 15.   There is a strong correlation between alcoholism and suicide. [68]

Copyright © Houghton Mifflin Company. All rights reserved.

Chapter 12

T F ? 16. Those who attempt suicide do so only to manipulate others and attract attention to themselves. [64]

T F ? 17. Suicide seems unrelated to the phases of the moon. [49]

T F ? 18. Oppressive weather (e.g., rain) has been found to be very closely related to suicidal behavior. [26]

19. What percentage of suicides leave a suicide note? [40]
   a) 15 to 25%
   b) 40 to 50%
   c) 65 to 75%

20. With respect to sex differences in suicide attempts [65]
   a) males and females attempt at similar levels.
   b) females attempt more often than males.
   c) males attempt more often than females.

21. Suicide rates for the United States as a whole are _____ for the young. [8]
   a) lower than
   b) higher than
   c) the same as

22. Suicide rates among the young are _____ those for the old. [7]
   a) lower than
   b) higher than
   c) the same as

23. Men kill themselves in numbers _____ those for women. [67]
   a) similar to
   b) higher than
   c) lower than

24. The season of highest suicide risk is [11]
   a) winter.
   b) fall.
   c) spring.

25. Suicide rates for the young since the 1950s have [97]
   a) increased.
   b) decreased.
   c) changed little.

26. The most common method(s) employed to kill oneself in the United States is (are) [28]
   a) hanging.
   b) firearms.
   c) drugs and poison.

27. Suicide rates for non-whites are _____ those for whites. [35]
   a) higher than
   b) similar to
   c) lower than

28. The day of the week on which most suicides occur is [60]
   a) Monday.
   b) Wednesday.

Copyright © Houghton Mifflin Company. All rights reserved.

    c)   Saturday.

29.   Compared to other western nations, the United States suicide rate is [21]
    a)   among the highest.
    b)   moderate.
    c)   among the lowest.

30.   The ethnic/racial group with the highest suicide rate is [15]
    a)   Whites.
    b)   African Americans.
    c)   Native Americans.

31.   Which marital status category has the lowest rates of suicide? [59]
    a)   Married
    b)   Widowed
    c)   Single, never married

32.   The most common method(s) in attempted suicide is (are) [63]
    a)   firearms.
    b)   drugs and poison.
    c)   cutting one's wrists.

33.   The risk of death by suicide for a person who has attempted suicide in the past is _____ that for someone who has never attempted it. [80]
    a)   lower than
    b)   similar to
    c)   higher than

34.   On the average, when young people make suicide attempts, they are _____ to die compared to elderly persons. [41]
    a)   less likely
    b)   just as likely
    c)   more likely

35.   As a cause of death, suicide ranks _____ for the young when compared to the nation as a whole. [86]
    a)   the same
    b)   higher
    c)   lower

36.   The region of the United States with the highest suicide rate is the [36]
    a)   east.
    b)   midwest.
    c)   west.

Source: From "Integrating Suicidology into Abnormal Psychology Classes: The Revised Facts on Suicide Quiz," by R. W. Hubbard & J. L. McIntosh, *Teaching of Psychology*, 19, 1992, pp. 163–166. Copyright © 1992. Used with permission from Lawrence Erlbaum Associates, Inc., and the authors.

4.   Rich, Warstadt, and Nemiroff (1991) collected information from medical and police records as well as from interviews with the relatives and professionals who knew 204 suicide victims. The aim of the study was to find relationships concerning suicide among different age groups and the stressors that preceded the suicide. Over 95 percent of the suicides had one or more stressors prior to the suicide. Ask students what they think are the suicide-risk stressors for various ages in the life cycle. Conflict,

Copyright © Houghton Mifflin Company. All rights reserved.

separation, and rejection are the most common type of stressors in suicides until the age of sixty. Legal difficulties are a primary cause for people in their twenties and thirties. Economic problems were commonly reported for those in their forties. Illness and bereavement are the key stressors for suicides in the seventy and eighty age groups. Illness influenced 48 percent of suicides in their seventies and 57 percent in their eighties.

More recent research (Carney, Rich, Burke, & Fowler, 1994) indicates that suicides among those older than sixty are less likely to have financial problems as stressors than those under age sixty. They also seem to talk about suicide less than the younger groups.

An alternative to having students complete the handout in class is to have them survey one individual from each of the age groups. This task has the benefit of exposing traditional-age students to people from other age groups and registering their concerns. It also moves away from the students' perceptions to those of others. A combination of both sets of data, student perceptions and reports from surveyed individuals, would be even more comprehensive and thought provoking.

Sources: Carney, S. S., Rich, C. L., Burke, P. A., & Fowler, R. C. (1994). Suicide over 60: The San Diego study. *Journal of the American Geriatrics Society*, 42, 174–180.

Rich, C. L., Wassradt, R. A., Nemiroff, R. A., et al. (1991). Suicide stressors and the life cycle. *American Journal of Psychiatry*, 148, 524–527.

5.   Have the students form small groups of 4-7 individuals depending on your class size and space limitations. You could provide a blank overhead transparency to each group at the beginning of this demonstration. Ask the groups to discuss several questions related to suicide and depression like the ones found below. Each group could then have a spokesperson deliver a short talk about the best examples.

•   What are some of the reasons why people who are depressed don't seek help?

•   Does society place stigma on a person with depression? If so, what could be done to change this idea?

•   Should doctor-assisted suicide be made legal? Why? Why not?

6.   Discuss the accuracy of statistics on suicide. Ask the class if some national statistics might be adjusted to account for cultural beliefs and values? Ask students for cultural or religious examples. You can develop a list on an overhead transparency.   How often are deaths listed as accidents instead of suicides to spare mourners?   Can the class provide examples of some accidents called intentional suicides?

7.   Have the students form small groups of 4-7 individuals depending on your class size and space limitations. You could provide a blank overhead transparency to each group at the beginning of this demonstration. Ask the groups to discuss several questions related to suicide and depression like the ones found below. Each group could then have a spokesperson deliver a short talk about the best examples. Pose this question: "What is the role of rock lyrics in suicides among teenagers?" Do your students think that a rock group could be held responsible for a death that occurred after a young person had repeatedly listened to their morbid, suicide-praising lyrics? What role might video games play in suicides among children and adolescents? How has the film industry influenced younger children? Finally, ask how students would or should control the media.

Copyright © Houghton Mifflin Company. All rights reserved.

HANDOUT FOR DEMONSTRATION 1:
QUALITY OF LIFE

1. James is the patient. A devout Catholic, James always said that life was precious and something in God's control. However, James is now in a coma that doctors are 90 percent sure is irreversible. He suffered for several years with a painful form of cancer that has now invaded his brain. His family has seen him suffer terribly, and they want to let him die now.

2. Barbara is the patient. This 43-year-old woman suffered massive brain damage in a car accident, and doctors are 90 percent sure it is irreversible. She is unaware of her surroundings, but may live for many years. The family's savings have already been used up to provide her with care; three children who were planning to attend college have had to forego their education and take jobs. Her family wants her to be allowed to die now.

3. Verna, who is 77 years old, had always said she wanted to die if she were ever a burden to others. She has Alzheimer's disease, a progressive and incurable brain disorder in which memory and personality gradually erode. It is a terminal illness, but death usually occurs three to five years after diagnosis. Verna was diagnosed one year ago and is already unable to remember where she is or to whom she is speaking. Her family wants her to be allowed to die to avoid becoming the burden she feared she would become.

Copyright © Houghton Mifflin Company. All rights reserved.

HANDOUT FOR DEMONSTRATION 3:
THE REVISED FACTS ON SUICIDE QUIZ

Circle the answer you believe is most correct for each question.

T = true   F = false   ? = don't know

T F ? 1. The tendency toward suicide is not genetically (i.e., biologically) inherited and passed on from one generation to another.

T F ? 2. People who talk about suicide rarely commit suicide.

T F ? 3. The suicidal person neither wants to die nor is fully intent on dying.

T F ? 4. If assessed by a psychiatrist, everyone who commits suicide would be diagnosed as depressed.

T F ? 5. Suicide rarely happens without warning.

T F ? 6. If you ask someone directly, "Do you feel like killing yourself?" it will likely lead that person to make a suicide attempt.

T F ? 7. A time of high suicide risk in depression is when the person begins to improve.

T F ? 8. A suicidal person will always be suicidal and entertain thoughts of suicide.

T F ? 9. A person who has made a past suicide attempt is more likely to attempt suicide again than someone who has never attempted it.

T F ? 10. A person who commits suicide is mentally ill.

T F ? 11. Suicide is among the top ten causes of death in the United States.

T F ? 12. Nothing can be done to stop people from making the attempt once they have made up their minds to kill themselves.

T F ? 13. Most people who attempt suicide fail to kill themselves.

T F ? 14. Motives and causes of suicide are readily established.

T F ? 15. There is a strong correlation between alcoholism and suicide.

T F ? 16. Those who attempt suicide do so only to manipulate others and attract attention to themselves.

T F ? 17. Suicide seems unrelated to the phases of the moon.

T F ? 18. Oppressive weather (e.g., rain) has been found to be very closely related to suicidal behavior.

Copyright © Houghton Mifflin Company. All rights reserved.

19. What percentage of suicides leave a suicide note?
    a) 15 to 25%
    b) 40 to 50%
    c) 65 to 75%

20. With respect to sex differences in suicide attempts
    a) males and females attempt at similar levels.
    b) females attempt more often than males.
    c) males attempt more often than females.

21. Suicide rates for the United States as a whole are _____ for the young.
    a) lower than
    b) higher than
    c) the same as

22. Suicide rates among the young are _____ those for the old.
    a) lower than
    b) higher than
    c) the same as

23. Men kill themselves in numbers _____ those for women.
    a) similar to
    b) higher than
    c) lower than

24. The season of highest suicide risk is
    a) winter.
    b) fall.
    c) spring.

25. Suicide rates for the young since the 1950s have
    a) increased.
    b) decreased.
    c) changed little.

26. The most common method(s) employed to kill oneself in the United States is (are)
    a) hanging.
    b) firearms.
    c) drugs and poison.

27. Suicide rates for non-whites are _____ those for whites.
    a) higher than
    b) similar to
    c) lower than

28. The day of the week on which most suicides occur is
    a) Monday.
    b) Wednesday.
    c) Saturday.

Copyright © Houghton Mifflin Company. All rights reserved.

29. Compared to other western nations, the United States suicide rate is
    a) among the highest.
    b) moderate.
    c) among the lowest.

30. The ethnic/racial group with the highest suicide rate is
    a) Whites.
    b) African Americans.
    c) Native Americans.

31. Which marital status category has the lowest rates of suicide?
    a) Married
    b) Widowed
    c) Single, never married

32. The most common method(s) in attempted suicide is (are)
    a) firearms.
    b) drugs and poison.
    c) cutting one's wrists.

33. The risk of death by suicide for a person who has attempted suicide in the past is _____ that for someone who has never attempted it.
    a) lower than
    b) similar to
    c) higher than

34. On the average, when young people make suicide attempts, they are _____ to die compared to elderly persons.
    a) less likely
    b) just as likely
    c) more likely

35. As a cause of death, suicide ranks _____ for the young when compared to the nation as a whole.
    a) the same
    b) higher
    c) lower

36. The region of the United States with the highest suicide rate is the
    a) east.
    b) midwest.
    c) west.

Source: From "Integrating Suicidology into Abnormal Psychology Classes: The Revised Facts on Suicide Quiz," by R. W. Hubbard & J. L. McIntosh, *Teaching of Psychology, 19,* 1992, pp. 163–166. Copyright © 1992. Used with permission from Lawrence Erlbaum Associates, Inc., and the authors.

Copyright © Houghton Mifflin Company. All rights reserved.

HANDOUT FOR DEMONSTRATION 4:
SUICIDE STRESSORS QUESTIONNAIRE

For each age group indicate the stressors that would most commonly cause or trigger suicide.

Ages 5 to 19   1. _____   2. _____
                   3. _____   4. _____

Ages 20 to 29   1. _____   2. _____
                   3. _____   4. _____

Ages 30 to 39   1. _____   2. _____
                   3. _____   4. _____

Ages 40 to 49   1. _____   2. _____
                   3. _____   4. _____

Ages 50 to 59   1. _____   2. _____
                   3. _____   4. _____

Ages 60 to 69   1. _____   2. _____
                   3. _____   4. _____

Ages 70 to 79   1. _____   2. _____
                   3. _____   4. _____

Age 80 and over   1. _____   2. _____
                   3. _____   4. _____

Copyright © Houghton Mifflin Company. All rights reserved.

SELECTED READINGS

Blumenthal, S. J., & Kupfer, D. J. (Eds.) (1988). *Suicide over the life cycle: Risk factors, assessment and treatment of suicidal patients.* Washington, DC: American Psychological Association.

Bongar, M. (Ed.) (1992). *Suicide: Guidelines for assessment, management, and treatment.* New York: Oxford University Press.

Colt, G. H. (1991). *The enigma of suicide.* Summit, NJ: Summit Books.

Leenaars, A. A. et al. (Eds.). (1993). *Suicidology: Essays in honor of Edwin S. Shneidman.* Northvale, NJ: Jason Aronson, Inc.

Lester, D., & Yang, B. (1992). Social and economic correlates of the elderly suicide rate. Special Issue: Suicide and the older adult. *Suicide and Life-Threatening Behavior, 22,* 36–47.

Sattler, D., Shabatay, V., &Kramer, G. (1998). *Abnormal psychology in context: Voices and perspectives.* Boston, MA: Houghton Mifflin Company. Chapter 5, Suicide.

VIDEO RESOURCES

Born Dying (16 mm, color, 20 min). Presents the dilemma faced by parents of a newborn with multiple handicaps and examines the quality-of-life issue from several perspectives. Peter M. Robeck Company, Inc., 23 Park Avenue, New York, NY 10017.

Do I Really Want to Die? (16 mm, 31 min). This film presents interviews with individuals who attempted suicide. They reveal their motivations for their attempts and their current feelings. Polymorph Films, 331 Newbury Street, Boston, MA 02115.

Elderly Suicide (video, 28 min). Examines the reasons suicide is becoming an increasingly popular choice for the elderly. Psychology Video Catalogue, Fall, 1993.

Fragile Time (VHS, color, 30 min). Three young people provide cases illustrating teen depression and suicide; shows the warning signs of suicide and intervention strategies for prevention. Perennial Education, 930 Pitner, Evanston, IL 60602.

Suicide: A Teenage Crisis (16 mm, color, 10 min). Emphasizes the magnitude of the problem and community and school programs that can prevent suicide or reduce the impact on survivors. Film Rental Library, University of Kansas, Lawrence, KS 66045.

Suicide: But Jack Was a Good Driver (16 mm, color, 14 min). Classmates of a boy who died in a car accident reflect on his activities and conversations before his death. Understanding motivations for suicide and detecting the subtle signs of suicidal intent are stressed. A good discussion starter. CRM Educational Films, 1011 Camino Del Mar, Del Mar, CA 92014.

Copyright © Houghton Mifflin Company. All rights reserved.

Teenage Suicide (VHS, color, 16 min). Points out warning signs of suicide attempts using lives and deaths of four teens who committed suicide. Emphasis placed on parents' ability to listen. Also looks at suicide prevention centers. Audio-Visual Services, Pennsylvania State University, University Park, PA 16802.

Teenage Suicide: The Ultimate Dropout (VHS, color, 29 min). Explores feelings and circumstances that led a 14-old girl to attempt suicide. Looks at help-seeking by parents and provides advice to families facing a potential suicide crisis. Audio-Visual Services, Pennsylvania State University, University Park, PA 16802.

ON THE INTERNET

http://www.rochford.org/suicide/ is a general information page that answers some frequently asked questions about suicide.

http://www.save.org/ is the Suicide Awareness/Voices of Education home page.

http://crystal.palace.net/~llama/psych/ contains information about self-injury programs.

http://www.helpline.org is a suicide help line on the Internet.

http://www.psycom.net/depression.central.suicide.html provides an extensive listing of links for research information, help lines, bibliographies, and other resources concerning suicide

Copyright © Houghton Mifflin Company. All rights reserved.

CHAPTER 13

Schizophrenia: Diagnosis and Etiology

CHAPTER OUTLINE

I. Schizophrenia

   A. Group of disorders involving severely impaired cognitive processes, personality disintegration, and social withdrawal

   B. Lifetime prevalence in United States is 1 percent (males and females equally)

     1. Onset later in females probably due to protective factor of estrogen

     2. African American lifetime prevalence twice that of general population, probably due to lower socioeconomic status and higher divorce rates

     3. Hispanic American prevalence slightly lower, probably due to underreporting and less likely to seek help

     4. DSM-IV-TR presents unitary picture but evidence suggests heterogeneous syndrome with different etiologies and outcomes

   C. History of the diagnostic category and DSM-IV-TR

     1. Emil Kraepelin

       a. Names it "dementia praecox" (early insanity)

       b. Sees it as organic and incurable

     2. Eugen Bleuler suggests it is a group of disorders with different causes, including environment interacting with genetics; four A's

       a. Autism (complete self-focus)

       b. Associations (unconnected ideas)

       c. Affect (inappropriate emotions)

       d. Ambivalence (uncertainty over actions)

     3. When diagnosed according to international standards, 50 percent of patients get other diagnoses

     4. DSM-IV-TR uses more restrictive definitions consistent with international standards; increases diagnostic reliability and validity of research, but makes comparison with previous research difficult

   D. DSM-IV-TR and the diagnosis of schizophrenia

     1. Delusions; hallucinations; or marked disturbances of speech, thinking, or affect

     2. Deterioration from previous functioning

     3. Disorder lasted six months at some point in life, currently present for one month

     4. Must rule out organic causes and affective disorders

II. The symptoms of schizophrenia

   A. Types of symptoms

1. Positive symptoms: hallucinations; delusions; and disorganization of speech, affect, behavior

2. Negative symptoms: associated with poor premorbid functioning and prognosis

    a. Flat affect (little emotional expression)

    b. Alogia (lack of meaningful speech)

    c. Avolition (inability to take action or become goal-oriented)

B. Positive symptoms

1. Delusions: firmly held beliefs inconsistent with evidence or logic

    a. Delusions of grandeur

    b. Delusions of control

    c. Delusions of thought broadcasting

    d. Delusions of persecution

    e. Delusions of reference

    f. Thought withdrawal

    g. Capgras's syndrome: belief in existence of identical doubles who coexist or replace others or themselves

    h. Variability in how firmly delusions are held

    i. Develop beliefs on basis of too little information

    j. Therapists have some success challenging delusions and hallucinations

2. Perceptual distortions: perceptions not directly attributable to environmental stimuli

    a. Hallucinations are sensory perceptions not directly attributable to environmental stimuli (differ from delusions, which are false intellectual experiences)

    b. Not pathognomonic (distinctive) to schizophrenia

    c. Auditory most common

    d. Schizophrenic attributes to sources outside self

    e. Delusions and hallucinations can be extremely distressing to schizophrenic

    f. Can be challenged by therapist

    g. Coping strategies include distraction, ignoring, selective listening, settling limits

3. Disorganized thought and speech

    a. A primary characteristic of schizophrenia

    b. Found in deaf as well as hearing

    c. Loosening of associations? cognitive slippage? is continual shifting from topic to topic without apparent logical or meaningful connection between thoughts

    d. Schizophrenic may respond to words or phrases in concrete manner, demonstrate difficulty with abstractions

    e. Inability to inhibit contextually irrelevant information

4. Disorganized motor disturbances

    a. Hyperactive or inactive, odd postures, gestures, grimaces

    b. Maintaining odd position: sign of catatonic

C. Negative symptoms: flat affect, avolition, alogia

1. Primary (arise from schizophrenia itself)

2. Secondary (response to medication or hospitalization)

3. Associated with poor prognosis and may be related to structural abnormality in brain

Copyright © Houghton Mifflin Company. All rights reserved.

    D. Associated features

        1. Anhedonia (inability to experience pleasure)

        2. Lack of insight

        3. Other comorbid disorders;

        4. Approximately 11 percent commit suicide: risk factors include severe depression, younger age, traumatic stress

    E. Cultural issues

        1. Culture may affect how symptoms are displayed or interpreted

        2. Ethnic group differences also found

        3. May cause problems with diagnostic errors and clinician bias; diagnostic system based on white middle-class norms

III. Types of schizophrenia

    A. Paranoid schizophrenia: the most common form, persistent delusions, usually persecution or grandeur (or both)

        1. Differentiate from delusional disorder, where delusions are less bizarre and behavior is functional

        2. Delusional disorder often stems from suspicious personality exacerbated by lack of corrective feedback

    B. Disorganized schizophrenia (formerly called hebephrenic): severe regression, incoherence, and inappropriate affect without delusions; childish; bizarre

    C. Catatonic schizophrenia: quite rare; extreme excitement or profound withdrawal; waxy flexibility during withdrawal

    D. Undifferentiated and residual schizophrenia

        1. Undifferentiated: when the person's behavior shows prominent psychotic symptoms that do not meet criteria for the other three types

        2. Residual: those who have had at least one previous schizophrenic episode but currently have an absence of prominent psychotic features

            a. continuing evidence of two or more symptoms (e.g., marked social isolation, peculiar behaviors)

            b. symptoms not strong enough nor prominent enough to warrant classification as one of the other types

    E. Psychotic disorders once considered schizophrenia

        1. Brief psychotic disorder: duration under one month

        2. Schizophreniform disorder: duration between one and six months

        3. Both have better prognosis than schizophrenia

        4. Two-thirds of those with schizophreniform later diagnosed with schizophrenia

    F. Other psychotic disorders

        1. Shared psychotic disorder: person with close relationship with delusional individual comes to accept delusions

        2. Schizoaffective disorder: both mood disorder and psychotic symptoms for at least two weeks without prominent mood symptoms

IV. The course of schizophrenia

    A. Premorbid personality usually impaired

    B. Prodromal phase: withdrawal and peculiar actions or talk

    C. Active phase: full-blown symptoms

Copyright © Houghton Mifflin Company. All rights reserved.

    D. Residual phase: symptoms no longer prominent although full recovery rare

    E. Long-term outcome studies

        1. Newer definition requiring six months duration should reduce percentage with positive outcome

        2. Prognosis favorable in over 50 percent of cases in one study

V. Etiology of schizophrenia

VI. Heredity and schizophrenia

    A. Meehl (1962): identify schizophrenic by a finding person whose identical twin has been diagnosed

    B. Problems in interpreting genetic studies

        1. Several types of the disorder may have different causes and varying degrees of genetic influence

        2. Psychological condition of both parents must be considered

        3. Studies based on patients with severe and chronic cases may inflate estimates of genetic influence

        4. Researchers may use differing definitions of concordance

        5. Bias in interviewers of relatives

    C. Studies involving blood relatives

        1. General finding: the closer the blood relationship, the higher the risk among relatives of schizophrenics

        2. Environment confounded with genetics

    D. Twin studies

        1. Concordance rates for schizophrenia should be higher for MZ twins than for DZ twins

        2. Discrepancy in concordance rates likely due to methodological differences in what is considered "concordant"

            a. early studies included schizophrenia spectrum (those genetically related to schizophrenia): "latent or borderline" schizophrenia, acute schizophrenic reactions, schizoid an inadequate personality

    E. Adoption studies: still difficult to separate effects of heredity from effects of environment

        1. In Heston (1966) study, zero of fifty controls become schizophrenic, versus five of forty-seven in at-risk group

            a. Mother's status and antipsychotic drug use may confound results

            b. At-risk group who do not get sick are more creative

        2. Families of adoptive parents whose children developed schizophrenia show no schizophrenia; only biological relatives of adoptive child who became schizophrenic show the disorder

        3. No increase in rate of disorder when adoptive family shows schizophrenic symptoms

    F. Studies of high-risk populations: developmental studies following children of schizophrenic parents

        1. Mednick's study

            a. Fifteen of high-risk group (whose mothers had schizophrenia) diagnosed as schizophrenic

            b. Risk factors: severely disturbed mothers, more at-birth complications, aggression; slow to habituate to arousing stimuli

        2. The Israeli study

Copyright © Houghton Mifflin Company. All rights reserved.

  a. High- and low-risk children raised either on kibbutz (collective farm) or in suburban home with biological parents

  b. When high-risk groups are in their thirties, diagnosis of schizophrenia in five people (no more in kibbutz than in town); none from control group were schizophrenic

  c. Most high-risk individuals do not show severe psychopathology

  d. Quality of parenting important; none of high-risk children with "adequate" parenting developed schizophrenia

 3. Conclusions and methodological problems

  a. Reasonably strong support for involvement of heredity

  b. Childhood and adolescence are especially vulnerable periods

  c. Schizophrenia is due to interaction of predisposition and environment

  d. Most high-risk children do not develop disorder

  e. Questions about control groups (should have other forms of psychopathology), choice of variables (should assess parent-child interaction), use of DSM-IV criteria

VII. Physiological factors in schizophrenia

 A. Biochemistry: dopamine hypothesis (excess dopamine activity)

  1. Evidence

   a. Effective drugs (phenothiazines) reduce dopamine activity by blocking receptor sites

   b. L-dopa converts to dopamine and can produce schizophrenia-like symptoms

   c. Amphetamines produce or intensify schizophrenic symptoms

  2. Problems

   a. Minority (25 percent) of schizophrenics unresponsive to drugs

   b. Specific brain areas may be sensitive to either excess or deficiency of dopamine

   c. Effectiveness of Clozapine (works on serotonin) points to other neurotransmitters

 B. Neurological findings

  1. Abnormal neurological findings

   a. Neuronal loss (ventricles larger) related to negative-symptom schizophrenia

   b. Decreased frontal lobe functioning in schizophrenics

   c. Cerebral blood flow decreased only in identical twins with schizophrenia

  2. Conclusions

   a. Differences in neuronal loss too small to have significance in diagnosis

   b. Many contradictions in findings as summarized by Heinrichs (1993)

VIII. Environmental factors in schizophrenia

 A. Infections during fetal period a possibility

 B. Stress related to schizophrenic diagnosis and relapse

 C. Family influences

  1. Theoretical constructs: negative family environments

   a. Schizophrenogenic mother (cold and overprotective)

   b. Double-bind theory (contradictory messages for which any response is punishing) produce thought disturbance

  2. Problems with earlier research

Copyright © Houghton Mifflin Company. All rights reserved.

        a.   Earlier research lacked control groups

        b.   Observation made after diagnosis

    3.   Expressed emotion: critical comments and emotional over involvement

        a.   Predicts relapse

        b.   May be effect rather than cause of disorder (bidirectional)

        c.   Not pathognomic for schizophrenia; more evident in western societies

  D. Effect of social class

    1.   Most prevalent in lower SES

        a.   Stress of poverty causes (breeder hypothesis)

        b.   Those with disorder cannot work (downward-drift hypothesis)

        c.   Evidence for both

  E. Cross-cultural comparisons

    1.   Many cultures have discrepancies in the perception of symptoms and treatments.

    2.   Symptoms often mirror culture's norms (Japanese more rigid, compulsive, passive)

    3.   U.S. African Americans show more severe symptoms than Whites

        a.   Race-related misdiagnosis another explanation

IX. The treatment of schizophrenia

  A. Early warehousing has been replaced

  B. Antipsychotic medications (neuroleptics such as Thorazine and Clozapine)

    1.   Highly effective with positive symptoms, not very good for negative symptoms, and not a cure

    2.   Side effects seem like neurological disorders

    3.   Relatively large group does not benefit from medication

    4.   Need for monitoring drugs

    5.   Clinicians unaware of motor and psychological side effects (tardive dyskinesia)

    6.   The right to refuse medication

    7.   Reduced dosage decreases side effects but increases relapse rate

  C. Psychosocial therapy: both medication and therapy

    1.   Institutional approaches

        a.   Milieu therapy: patients involved in ward decision-making

    2.   Cognitive-behavioral therapy

        a.   Positive and negative symptoms targeted to reduce frequency and severity; coping skills enhanced to allow patient management of symptoms

        b.   Help patients critically evaluate irrational beliefs

        c.   Social skills training emphasizes communication skills and assertiveness

        d.   Cultural sensitivity incorporates cultural values, may include family and other social support networks

  D. Interventions focusing on family communications and education (over 50 percent of recovering patients live with families)

    1.   Normalizing the family experience

    2.   Educating family about schizophrenia

    3.   Identifying strength of family and patient

    4.   Developing skills in problem solving

Copyright © Houghton Mifflin Company. All rights reserved.

5. Learning to cope with symptoms
6. Recognizing early signs of relapse
7. Creating a supportive family environment
8. Meeting needs of all family members
9. Family approaches and social skills training more effective in preventing relapse than drug treatment alone

Copyright © Houghton Mifflin Company. All rights reserved.

LEARNING OBJECTIVES

1. Discuss the general characteristics of schizophrenia (pp. 413-414).

2. Discuss the history of the diagnostic category known as schizophrenia and the current DSM-IV-TR criteria. (pp. 414-415; Table 13.1)

3. Describe the symptoms of schizophrenia, including positive and negative symptoms, delusions, and perceptual distortions. (pp. 415-419; Mental Health & Society)

4. Describe the problems of communication and thought disturbance seen in schizophrenia, including loosening of associations. (p. 419)

5. Describe the motoric disturbances and negative symptoms, and associated features seen in schizophrenia, as well as the role of culture in interpreting symptoms. (pp. 420-423)

6. Differentiate between the various subtypes of schizophrenia, including the paranoid, disorganized, catatonic, undifferentiated, and residual types of schizophrenia. (pp. 423-425)

7. Describe the psychotic disorders once considered schizophrenia including delusional disorder, brief psychotic disorder and schizophreniform disorder, and differentiate them from schizophrenia. Differentiate delusional disorder from paranoid schizophrenia. Describe shared psychotic disorder and schizoaffective disorder. (pp. 426-427; Table 13.2)

8. Describe the three phases of schizophrenia, then discuss research on long-term outcomes of schizophrenia, including studies in developing and developed countries (pp. 427-429; Critical Thinking)

9. Consider the usefulness of combining hereditary and environmental influences for understanding the origins of schizophrenia, then discuss and evaluate the genetic studies, including blood relatives, twin research, adoption and high-risk population studies, and the methodological issues involved with each type of study. (pp. 430-436)

10. Describe the biochemical theories of schizophrenia, including the dopamine hypothesis of schizophrenia and research results that strengthen and weaken this hypothesis. (pp. 436-438; Table 13.4)

11. Describe the neurological impairments, cognitive, and information-processing deficits believed to be associated with schizophrenia. Evaluate the usefulness of a neurological explanation of schizophrenia. (pp. 438-440)

12. Discuss environmental factors in the development of schizophrenic symptoms, including the family environment theories, methodological problems with this research, and the role pf expressed emotion in schizophrenia. (pp. 440-443)

13. Discuss the social class and cross-cultural aspects of schizophrenia (pp. 443-446)

14. Discuss the use of antipsychotic medications in the treatment of schizophrenia and the problems in using these drugs in treatment. Discuss changes in patients' rights to refuse medication. (pp. 446-449; Mental Health & Society; Critical Thinking)

15. Describe the psychosocial therapies including institutional approaches, cognitive-behavioral therapy, Integrated Psychological Therapy, and interventions targeted at relapse prevention by reducing expressed emotion. Discuss the effectiveness of these treatments. (pp. 449-452)

CLASSROOM TOPICS FOR LECTURE AND DISCUSSION

1. Schizophrenia is a difficult disorder to treat successfully when it occurs alone, but when it is accompanied by substance abuse, patients are frequently condemned to lives of instability, terror, and treatment without effect. Unfortunately, the prevalence of "dual diagnosed" schizophrenics with

Copyright © Houghton Mifflin Company. All rights reserved.

substance-related disorders is very high. Mueser, Bellack, and Blanchard (1992) thoroughly tell the grim story. The range of lifetime prevalence of co-morbid schizophrenia and drug abuse is enormous—from 10 percent to 65 percent, the differences probably due to sampling and diagnostic criteria. However, in the large-scale, national Epidemiological Catchment Area program lifetime prevalence of alcohol diagnosis in the schizophrenic population was 33.7 percent (compared to 13.5 percent in the general population); drug diagnosis in the schizophrenic population was 27.5 percent (compared to 6.1 percent in the general population).

The high-risk groups for dual diagnosis are males, young adults, those with low education, and those with early hospitalization and poor treatment compliance. In inner city psychiatric hospitals, dual diagnosis is so common that clinicians seeing young male schizophrenics assume there is an alcohol or drug problem unless evidence contradicts them. Unfortunately, once dual diagnosed, these patients usually receive less outpatient care, since mental health workers see them as less desirable and more difficult to treat (Solomon, 1986).

Why should schizophrenics be so likely to have alcohol and drug problems, too? The most prominent explanation is that individuals suffering from auditory hallucinations and anxiety self-medicate, and they use alcohol because it is so available. But there is no consistent evidence that those with the most symptoms or the most pronounced symptoms are most likely to use drugs. An alternative reason is that drug use is largely a social phenomenon and develops out of social reinforcement or peer pressure. Further, genetics and/or parenting may play a role, since schizophrenics who abuse drugs are more likely to come from families in which there is a history of substance abuse.

The effects of combining alcohol or other drugs with schizophrenia are devastating. Chronic drug use amplifies the cognitive deficits of schizophrenia. Substance abuse generates the kind of family arguments that heighten the schizophrenic's arousal level (a kind of drug-induced expressed emotion), making relapse more likely.

However, the substance-abuse and psychiatric camps have different treatment philosophies. Substance-abuse treatment in the United States usually subscribes to a 12-step (Alcoholics Anonymous) approach that stresses confrontation, assumed personal responsibility, and abstinence from all drugs (often including psychotropic ones). This orientation is a poor match with a schizophrenic patient who is vulnerable to heightened arousal and who may need medication to think straight. Psychiatric treatment tends to be more tolerant and accepting. This approach may be a poor match with the substance abuser, who is expert at distorting the truth and hiding symptoms. Despite a huge need for coordinated treatment, most communities treat dual-diagnosed schizophrenic/substance abusers separately, with contradictory treatment messages and poor relapse prevention (Minkoff, 1991).

Sources: Minkoff, K. (1991). Program components of a comprehensive integrated care system for seriously mentally ill patients with substance disorders. In K. Minkoff & R. E. Drake (Eds.) *Dual diagnosis of major mental illness and substance disorder*. San Francisco: Jossey-Bass, pp. 13–28.

Mueser, K. T., Bellack, A. S., & Blanchard, J. J. (1992). Comorbidity of schizophrenia and substance abuse: Implications for treatment. *Journal of Consulting and Clinical Psychology, 60*, 845–856.

Solomon, P. (1986). Receipt of aftercare services by problem types: Psychiatric, psychiatric/substance abuse, and substance abuse. *Psychiatric Quarterly, 87*, 180–188.

Internet Site: http://www.erols.com/ksciacca/. A site on dual diagnosis.

2.   The word *schizophrenia* is so widely misused that you should spend some time differentiating schizophrenia from multiple personality disorder. A short history of terminology, from Kraepelin's dementia praecox to Bleuler's schizophrenia, would be useful. It is important to convey that the split in schizophrenia is within a personality—between emotion and thinking—rather than between complete

Copyright © Houghton Mifflin Company. All rights reserved.

personalities. Finally, a listing of Bleuler's four A's (what he considered to be the fundamental symptoms of the schizophrenic spectrum disorders) helps to dispel the idea that schizophrenics are anything like the three faces of Eve. The four A's are association (thought disorder), affect (inappropriate or blunted), ambivalence (indecisive in carrying out daily activities), and autism (withdrawal into self).

Internet Site: http://www.health-center.com/mentalhealth A major site for the diagnosis and treatment of psychological disorders: link to schizophrenia for in-depth information and resources.

3.   Many students have difficulty imagining what a psychotic existence might be like. This inability to empathize makes intolerance more likely. You can link psychotic experiences to more everyday ones while discussing the symptoms of schizophrenia. Most people have experienced problems in thinking clearly during times of great stress; when severely fatigued; when drugged, intoxicated, or suffering from a fever; or even when first awakening. Hallucinations occur every night in our dreams and, for some people, every day during daydreams. Furthermore, we have all experienced auditory hallucinations, hearing music or our parents' voices when there is no actual source for the sounds. In fact, musicians train themselves to hear the music written on the paper before them. (Beethoven could not have composed most of his symphonies without this ability to hallucinate.) Finally, most of us have had odd and disturbing (and incorrect) thoughts at one time or another that we were unwilling to relinquish.

What best differentiates the schizophrenic's subjective experience from ours is the degree of control we have over these states and our understanding of what causes them. Ask students to think about how they would feel if their problems in thinking were not transitory and were not easily explainable by, for instance, intoxication. Students may see that even the most bizarre forms of abnormal behavior occur on a continuum of human experience.

Internet Site: http://www.health-center.com/mentalhealth A major site for the diagnosis and treatment of psychological disorders: link to symptoms for a discussion of the positive symptoms of schizophrenia.

4.   An intriguing experiment by Cohen, Nachmani, and Rosenberg (1974) gives students an appreciation of when loosening of associations occurs and what it looks like. A group of normal subjects and a group of people with schizophrenia were given the task of looking at two colored disks and then describing one of them in such a way that a person looking at the two disks would be able to pick out the one being described.

This task requires the speaker to find accurately descriptive words or associations to convey the right color. When the colors were quite dissimilar, the descriptive ability of normals and people with schizophrenia was the same. For instance, when one disk was blue and the other was purple, both normals and schizophrenic people said "purple" or "violet."

However, when the discrimination task became more difficult, the normal speakers refined their first efforts and found a way to convey the color they meant. The schizophrenic subjects "fell apart" and a torrent of loose associations came forth. Here are the verbatim comments made by two normal subjects and two people with schizophrenia when the two colors were very similar hues of pinkish-red.

Normal subject: My God this is hard. They are both about the same, except that this one might be a little redder.

Normal subject: They both are either the color of canned salmon or clay. This one here is the pinker one.

Schizophrenic subject: This is a stupid color of a shit ass bowl of salmon. Mix it with mayonnaise. Then it gets tasty. Leave it alone and puke all over the fuckin' place. Puke fish.

Copyright © Houghton Mifflin Company. All rights reserved.

Schizophrenic subject: Make-up. Pancake make-up. You put it on our face and they think guys run after you. Wait a second! I don't put it on my face and guys don't run after me. *Girls* put it on them.

When the task is difficult, the schizophrenic subjects seem to become confused and the first association they make, even if it is not helpful in identifying the color, becomes the starting point for chains of associations that they cannot control. Make-up becomes pancake make-up, which leads to personal references to women, guys, and, perhaps, fears of being thought of as a homosexual.

Source: Cohen, B. D., Nachmani, G., & Rosenberg, S. (1974). Referent communication disturbances in acute schizophrenia. *Journal of Abnormal Psychology, 83,* 1–13.

Internet site: http://www.health-center.com/mentalhealth A major site for the diagnosis and treatment of psychological disorders: link to negative symptoms for exercise.

5.   The DSM-IV-TR gives the impression that schizophrenia is a single disorder and that, despite its many forms, it represents a syndrome. Your text suggests that schizophrenia stems from both biogenic and psychogenic factors. Heinrichs (1993) asserts that schizophrenia is a brain disease, but one that is very hard to understand.

Heinrichs argues that three criteria must be met in order to understand the neuropsychology of schizophrenia: (1) a core set of features that makes the disorder distinct from others and internally consistent; (2) evidence of brain damage that is consistently associated with the behavioral dysfunction; and (3) linkages between the brain damage and behavior that make neurological sense. Unfortunately, present evidence fails to meet any of the three criteria, although the problem of heterogeneity (standard 1) is the biggest obstacle.

Heinrichs notes that people with schizophrenia show positive symptoms at some points in the illness and negative symptoms at others. Some schizophrenics have neurological abnormalities, whereas others do not. A large minority of patients do not respond to antipsychotic medication. These factors make researching schizophrenia as a singular entity quite difficult, but subdivision into separate disorders is not warranted either.

Curiously, neuropsychological testing (for example, Halstead-Reitan) results usually indicate that people with schizophrenia have signs of brain damage, but only one-half of patients show abnormality on common imaging techniques (for example, CAT scans). The type of abnormality is not consistent among schizophrenics nor is it strongly related to behavior. Some schizophrenics have enlarged ventricles, but many do not. Some schizophrenics have decreased metabolic activity in the prefrontal lobes, others have increased activity, and others show no difference from normals. What's worse is that the relationships between schizophrenic behavioral deficits (memory, language, and perceptual distortions) do not match up with behavioral deficits seen in traditional neurological patients. In short, schizophrenia—devastating and life-long for many—remains a difficult scientific puzzle.

For there to be progress, Heinrichs suggests that the heterogeneity issue be faced. "To make progress in reducing heterogeneity, neurobiologists need to join forces with behavioral researchers: thus it will be possible for some researchers to work 'up' from the neurobiological level, while others work 'down' from behavior to the brain" (p. 230).

Source: Heinrichs, R. W. (1993). Schizophrenia and the brain: Conditions for a neuropsychology of madness. *American Psychologist, 48,* 221–233.

6.   Schizophrenia is as much a social problem as it is a psychological one. The revolution in antipsychotic medication has helped people function well enough to be discharged quickly. The problem is that adequate support for these people is not available. A frequent consequence of this is the

Copyright © Houghton Mifflin Company. All rights reserved.

revolving-door syndrome of treatment and relapse. In discussion, you can take this issue in at least three directions.

First, the financial and social costs of "dumped" mental patients in cities and other communities create problems. Although the percentage of homeless people who are mentally disturbed has been inflated in the media, far too many people who are released become impoverished, abandoned, and abused. Students can be challenged to devise alternative plans for dealing with discharged schizophrenic patients in an era of shrinking budgets.

Second, discuss what it feels like to be on the staff of a mental hospital where patients repeatedly return for treatment. Burnout and frustration are significant contributors to staff apathy and turnover. These facts make treatment less effective, so the cycle perpetuates itself.

Third, the family of the schizophrenic needs support and education. Falloon et al.'s (1984) method of intervention to reduce expressed emotion is being used to slow or stop the revolving door. Less extensive intervention efforts may also be helpful. For instance, concerned family members can learn strategies to ensure that discharged patients continue taking medication (slipping Thorazine concentrate in the patient's morning orange juice). The role of social support in the recovery of schizophrenics is detailed in several articles in a 1981 issue of *Schizophrenia Bulletin* (Vol. 7, No. 1).

Source: Falloon, I. R. H., Boyd, J. L., & McGill, C. W. (1984). *Family care of schizophrenia*. New York: Guilford Press.

7.   Token economies are a key treatment method in inpatient and halfway house environments. In explaining token economies, show how operant theory is applied to treatment. Token economies require clear communication of expectations, consistency, and constant monitoring. Unfortunately, most hospital staffs are not equipped to provide such attention to detail. Further, there is a tendency to be softhearted with some patients and, in that way, undermine the system. Share with students the difficulties of being a helper while simultaneously withholding the tokens that might lead to the patient's happiness.

Two related issues are also good discussion topics. Although token economies are very effective in shaping desirable behaviors and reducing or eliminating undesirable ones, the problem of generalization of behavior to unstructured environments is a significant one. Clinicians who use token economies should fade reinforcements prior to discharge so that desirable behaviors are more resistant to extinction. (This concept is another way of applying operant theory to a treatment method.) A second way of improving generalization is to use cognitive behavioral methods so that rewarding self-statements are given along with physical tokens and social reinforcements. If a discharged patient is equipped with a new set of self-statements that reinforce appropriate behavior, he or she is better able to cope in a hostile or uncaring world outside.

Internet Site: http://www.health-center.com/mentalhealth A major site for the diagnosis and treatment of psychological disorders: link to section on therapy.

8.   In about 75 percent of cases, the symptoms of schizophrenia are greatly reduced with neuroleptic medication. However, for 25 percent of schizophrenic clients, major symptoms such as hallucinations, delusions, and social withdrawal remain despite trials with different types and doses of medication. The clinician and the client both seek relief. What else is available?

Christison et al. (1991) provide a review of alternative somatic treatments for these refractory cases. They list eight alternatives:

1.   Clozapine (Clozaril)
2.   Lithium

Copyright © Houghton Mifflin Company. All rights reserved.

3. Benzodiazepines (Valium, Xanax)
4. Reserpine
5. Carbamazepine
6. Propanolol
7. Electroconvulsive therapy (ECT)
8. L-dopa

Based on double-blind, placebo studies, Christison et al. (1991) suggest that Clozapine, Lithium, and benzodiazepines be tried on refractory patients, and in that order. Clozapine is the drug of first resort because it can have such dramatic effects on otherwise refractory patients. Evidence for Lithium is the next-most promising.

For clients whose symptoms are most negative (amotivational, mutism), L-dopa is the only treatment that has even weak evidence of being helpful. L-dopa exacerbates positive symptoms. In patients with the opposite form of symptoms—impulsive aggressiveness—Clozapine and Lithium are better medications than benzodiazepines because sometimes the benzodiazepines increase outbursts by disinhibiting behavior. Carbamazepine has been useful in reducing aggressiveness, but in only one controlled trial to date (Neppe, 1983).

The other treatments, Reserpine, Propanolol, and ECT have been largely ineffective, usually after an initial burst of enthusiasm for their benefits in treating schizophrenia.

Sources: Christison, G. W., Kirch, D. G., & Wyatt, R. J. (1991). When symptoms persist: Choosing among alternative somatic treatments for schizophrenia. *Schizophrenia Bulletin, 17,* 217–245.

Neppe, V. (1983). Carbamazepine as adjunctive treatment in nonepileptic chronic inpatients with EEG temporal lobe abnormalities. *Journal of Clinical Psychiatry, 44,* 326–331.

Internet Site: http://www.health-center.com/mentalhealth.   A major site for the diagnosis and treatment of psychological disorders: link to medications.

9.   Is schizophrenia related to viral infection? Present students with this puzzling finding: More people with schizophrenia are born in the late winter and early spring than in any other time of the year (although the difference in timing is rather small). Why might this be? Evidence is growing that influenza or other viral infections contracted during pregnancy may account for the disorder. Rather than seeing a virus as directly causing schizophrenia, researchers hypothesize that a virus either interferes with neural development late in the fetal period or induces a deficiency in the immune system. A review of this work is provided in O'Reilly (1994).

Source: O'Reilly, R. L. (1994). Viruses and schizophrenia. *Australian and New Zealand Journal of Psychiatry, 28,* 222–228.

10.   Could we spot early signs of schizophrenic deterioration in home movies? Research suggests we could (Walker & Lewine, 1990). The researchers collected home movies from four families in which one of the siblings developed schizophrenia and others did not. Experienced clinicians and graduate students in psychology, blind as to which child later developed schizophrenia, viewed segments of children interacting and were asked to identify the "preschizophrenic" individual. The viewers' judgments were correct 80 percent of the time, significantly better than chance (50 percent). The criteria the viewers used were atypical emotional expressions and movements, especially poor eye contact, poor motor coordination, and less facial responsiveness. However, it is not at all clear these differences are pathognomonic for schizophrenia; they may be precursors of other disorders. Replication with larger samples is certainly needed.

Copyright © Houghton Mifflin Company. All rights reserved.

The prospects of using home videos to investigate the cognitive, emotional, and behavioral markers of schizophrenia are quite impressive. This method also allows, over time, a way of seeing how family interaction styles may cause or be caused by schizophrenic symptoms. With the increased availability and use of camcorders, larger and larger samples of adult-onset cases can be investigated for early signs.

Source: Walker, E., & Lewine, R. J. (1990). Prediction of adult-onset schizophrenia from childhood home movies of the patients. *American Journal of Psychiatry, 147,* 1052–1056.

CLASSROOM DEMONSTRATIONS & HANDOUTS

1.   Most students believe that they can detect "craziness" rather easily. To test this belief, you can read aloud excerpts from works by several twentieth-century writers, such as e. e. cummings, James Joyce, and Gertrude Stein, that illustrate a writing style called stream of consciousness. Among these writings, intersperse recitations of case transcripts that illustrate loosened associations in schizophrenics. (Transcripts can be obtained from several of the sources in the "Selected Readings" section.) Tell students that some of the sources represent published authors (presumably not schizophrenics) and some represent chronic schizophrenics. Ask students to judge which is which. Poll the class to see how accurate their judgments are. Then ask what factors influenced their decisions.

2.   The diagnosis of paranoid schizophrenia and delusional disorder is much more difficult than students might suspect. To demonstrate the problem, relate the following vignettes and ask whether these beliefs are signs of a disorder. If students conclude that they are not, ask them at what point the belief would go "over the line" into the realm of delusion.

A 13-year-old girl is convinced that her English teacher is trying to embarrass her in front of the class. She claims the teacher calls on her to read a passage out loud even though the teacher knows she has a speech impediment. Each time she recites, her classmates snicker.

A 50-year-old man is devoutly religious and claims that he was chosen by God to form a new church. He hears the voice of God when he goes for walks in the woods and believes his mission is to cleanse others of wickedness and heal them of both psychological and physical illness.

A policeman is certain that drug dealers in the city where he works have developed a conspiracy to burn his house down and kidnap his children for ransom. He claims that several drug dealers he has arrested have threatened to get even, and he has seen the same car repeatedly driven in front of his house at night.

Internet Site http://www.mentalhealth.com/book/p45-para.html. This site discusses paranoia.

3.   Osberg (1992) suggests reading (or, better yet, memorizing and delivering) a monologue that contains examples of the key qualities of schizophrenic thought, according to the DSM-IV-TR. Osberg argues that such a monologue has more impact if given without warning. Students may be distressed, depending on your acting ability, but the monologue will break up the routine, generate lively discussion, and give a concrete example of schizophrenic symptoms. Then distribute the handout that lists the types of schizophrenic thought disturbances and the portions of the monologue that illustrate each. Osberg reports that 100 percent of his students have recommended he use the demonstration in future classes. It takes about ten to fifteen minutes of class time. The monologue follows:

Okay, class, we've finished our discussion of mood disorders. Before I go on, I'd like to tell you about some personal experiences I've been having lately. You see I've (pause) been involved in highly abstract (pause) type of contract (pause) which I might try to distract (pause) from your gaze (pause) if it were a new craze (pause) but the sun god has put me into it (pause) the planet of the

Copyright © Houghton Mifflin Company. All rights reserved.

lost star (pause) is before you now (pause) and so you'd better not try to be as if you were one with him (pause) because no one is one with him (pause) always fails because one and one makes three (pause) and that is the word for thee (pause) which must be like the tiger after his prey (pause) and the zommon is not common (pause) it is a zommon's zommon.

But really, class, (holding your head and pausing) what do you think about what I'm thinking right now? You can hear my thoughts, can't you? I'm thinking I'm crazy and I know you (point to one student) put that thought in my mind. You put that thought there! Or could it be that the dentist did as I thought? She did! I thought she put that radio transmitter in my brain when I had the novocaine! She's making me think this way and she's stealing my thoughts! (Osberg, 1992, p. 47).

Source: From "The Disordered Monologue: A Classroom Demonstration of the Symptoms of Schizophrenia" by T. M. Osberg, *Teaching of Psychology, 19*, 1992, pp. 47–48. Copyright © 1992. Used with permission from Lawrence Erlbaum Associates, Inc., and the author.

4.   An important goal of Chapter 13 is to convey the humanity of people who suffer from schizophrenia. Nothing accomplishes this goal better than first-person accounts of what the disorder is like. The National Institute of Mental Health publication *Schizophrenia Bulletin* has a continuing series called "First Person Accounts" at the back of every issue. The accounts are from people with schizophrenia as well as their siblings, parents, and other family members. If you read excerpts aloud to your class, students may be surprised by the articulateness of the authors, by the continuing struggle they face, and by their successes in the world despite their psychological impediments. Finally, their pleas for understanding may touch your students and increase their tolerance for people who have severe mental illness.

The handout for this demonstration contains an abbreviated first-person description of schizophrenia and recovery. Have students read the account and see how many behaviors relate to the DSM-IV criteria for schizophrenia (also supplied in a handout). They might also make links to depression. In fact, an argument can be made that Alison is misdiagnosed; psychotic depression or schizoaffective disorder are at least as reasonable diagnoses as schizophrenia. This real case will show the complexities of diagnosis and the inadequacy of contemporary care for psychotic disturbances. Ask students what they think led most to Alison's recovery. Do they think she will relapse?

Internet Site: http://www.schizophrenia.com/. The Schizophrenia Home Page. This site contains links to chat rooms and sites for families of affected individuals and for individuals with schizophrenia.

5.   Schizophrenia is such a devastating and mysterious disorder that it has an especially strong and negative effect on siblings of the person with the disorder. The National Alliance for the Mentally Ill has a Sibling and Adult Children Network for discussion of the disorder's impact on other children in the family. A handout provides an abbreviated list of the common concerns siblings experience, the things parents can do, and the things parents cannot do. Ask students to comment on whether the issues listed seem specific to schizophrenia or general to other forms of psychopathology. You might want to distribute the handout to students at the end of one class and ask if any students who have dealt with a sibling having a chronic mental or physical condition are willing to discuss their experience with the class. This activity will show students that such difficulties happen in their peers' lives and that material in the book "lives."

Internet Site: http://www.nami.org/. The home page for the National Alliance for the Mentally Ill.

6.   Perhaps no other psychological term is so misused as *schizophrenic*. Even well-educated people mistake the term for what psychologists call *multiple personality disorder* or *dissociative identity disorder*. An out-of-class data-gathering project can quantify the degree to which the term *schizophrenic* is

Copyright © Houghton Mifflin Company. All rights reserved.

misunderstood. Have each student survey two or three people who are not in the class and who have not taken a class in abnormal psychology. Students can use the Handout for Demonstration 6.

You can modify the handout questions to test a number of hypotheses. The current version tests whether taking a course in introductory psychology or abnormal psychology affects the way people understand certain terminology. Other testable hypotheses are that respondents who have had experience in the social service field (paid or volunteer work) or people who have had family members in psychological care are more accurate in their use of the terms.

Have students return the survey data and, in front of the class, read off some of the responses. You or the students can classify answers (right, mostly right, mostly wrong, wrong) and use chi-square analyses to informally test your hypotheses.

7.   This would be a good opportunity to invite mental health personnel from the local community mental health center to guest-lecture in class about day-treatment programs and other services available for individuals diagnosed with schizophrenia and other chronic mental illnesses.

8.   Have the students form small groups of between 4-7 individuals depending on your class size and space limitations. Ask each group to develop a list of symptom of schizophrenic disorders with the most salient examples first. Each group could then have a spokesperson deliver a short talk about the best examples. You could provide a blank overhead transparency to each group at the beginning of this demonstration.

Then ask each groups to discuss the term "nervous breakdown" as it is sometimes used to describe an individual who has experienced a psychotic episode. Many times this term is used for affluent individuals who are in private mental hospitals. Ask each group to define a nervous breakdown in their own terms. Summarize the results to see if most responses include schizophrenic symptoms. Ask each group to discuss the question, "Why do affluent individuals have a nervous breakdown while poor individuals are classified as schizophrenic?"

9.   Communication problems are a major etiological component in schizophrenia. To get students to appreciate how chaotic such communications can be, ask them to write out several double-bind statements. Have one or two students read or act out what they have written. You can exaggerate some of these and point out the mixed nonverbal signals that make double-bind communications so emotional. A second feature of the communications in dysfunctional families is the tendency to speak tangentially and over another person (failing to take turns listening). An impromptu role-play of such a family conversation can illustrate how frustrating this would be for a child. Finally, explain that in these families the child cannot escape from the confusion (nor does the child know that any other existence is possible). Verbatim transcripts of such poor communication are available in Susan Sheehan's brilliant nonfiction account of a schizophrenic woman's life, *Is There No Place on Earth for Me?*

Make clear that faulty communications may not be the cause of the disorder. Emphasize the bidirectionality of confusing communications. Studies with the families of schizophrenic children have shown that parents communicate poorly only with the schizophrenic child, not the nonschizophrenic children. Engage students in a discussion of how the odd behaviors and thoughts of schizophrenic children could influence the communication patterns of others and how their frustration and emotional responses might exacerbate symptoms.

Internet site: http://www.health-center.com/mentalhealth link to schizophrenia, then to symptoms, then to negative symptoms for a discussion of the negative symptoms associated with schizophrenia

10.   A major stumbling block to long-term recovery from schizophrenia is the general public's intolerance and fear. This obstacle is particularly crucial in work settings, because discharged patients

Copyright © Houghton Mifflin Company. All rights reserved.

must have some way of keeping busy as well as supporting themselves. The following exercise might sensitize students to the need to improve work environments for treated schizophrenics.

Divide the class into small groups (four or five per group) and assign each group the task of developing methods of changing the work climate of a small business (perhaps a fast-food restaurant or gift shop) so that co-workers and customers would be more accepting of newly discharged schizophrenic patients. Ask them to brainstorm what skills the former patient needs, what information the co-workers need, and how the work roles can be designed so that former patients can experience success.

Have each group report the results of their brainstorming to the whole class. After you list the ideas on the board, ask the students what keeps business people from being more involved in the rehabilitation of mental patients. Suggest that greater exposure to the information made available through your course may increase tolerance and decrease the fears of the general public, especially of powerful people like employers.

11.   This classroom exercise is suitable for both Chapters 13 and 14. Give students the briefest possible descriptions of people who may be suffering from one of the schizophrenic-spectrum disorders. The students' job is to think of the questions they would ask or the observations they would make as clinicians to decide which diagnosis is correct. Make clear that we do not know what the individual is really suffering from; the exercise is to get them thinking about the alternatives and introduce them to the process of ruling certain diagnoses in while ruling other diagnoses out. A secondary goal is to have them formulate a treatment plan for the person they have "diagnosed."

Distribute the Handout for Demonstration 3. Then read aloud this brief description of a new client in an outpatient treatment facility:

> Wendy is in her mid twenties and has become less and less able to perform her work at a local bank. She complains that her thoughts are unconnected and uncontrollable. She hears things that other people do not hear. She looks confused.

Instruct students to list questions or observations that, when answered, would support a diagnosis for each of the three schizophrenia-spectrum disorders.

Students should consider Wendy's behavior brief reactive psychosis if she has had thought disturbance that has interfered with social or other functioning for less than one month. The only difference between brief reactive psychosis and the others is duration. A diagnosis of positive symptom schizophrenia requires evidence of hallucinations (is she hearing voices that no one else can?), delusions, bizarre behavior, and loose associations. Negative symptom schizophrenia involves an absence of facial expression, speaking in very short sentences, and an inability to feel pleasure or motivation to do anything. In both positive and negative symptom schizophrenia, the symptoms must have lasted for six months. Questions should be asked to rule out substance-related disorders and mood disorders.

You could follow up this exercise by giving more information about Wendy, suggesting that she is in the active stage of paranoid schizophrenia (she believes her parents are trying to poison her and that she is Christ). Tell students that she has come to their mental hospital and have them write down a treatment plan for Wendy on the handout. Encourage students to think of a treatment plan involving several components—medication, cognitive therapy, social skills training, family therapy, and so forth.

12.   Depending on your acting skills, you can demonstrate the side effects of excessive or prolonged neuroleptic medication. The extrapyramidal and Parkinsonian side effects of phenothiazines makes clients walk with a slow shuffle, rub their thumbs and forefingers against each other in what is termed *pill rolling*, keep their arms rigidly at their sides while shuffling, and, because of dry mouth, swallow frequently. Tardive dyskinesia involves thrusting out the tongue, smacking the lips, or making facial

Copyright © Houghton Mifflin Company. All rights reserved.

grimaces. In more extreme cases, the head is jerked to one side or arms and shoulders have tic like movements. About 20 percent of patients receiving antipsychotic medications over a long time develop tardive dyskinesia, especially elderly women who have been institutionalized many times (for whom the prevalence may be 50 percent).

13.   The deinstitutionalization of schizophrenics was seen as a major breakthrough made possible by the introduction of antipsychotic medications. Unfortunately, this breakthrough has not been a success. Many patients are admitted and discharged from state hospitals over and over again, some going through this process more than a hundred times.

Have the students form small groups of 4-7 individuals depending on your class size and space limitations. Ask each group to develop a list of problems associated with deinstitutionalization with the most salient examples first. Each group could then have a spokesperson deliver a short talk about the best examples. You could provide a blank overhead transparency to each group at the beginning of this demonstration.

Then ask the groups to discuss:

Who is responsible to care for the mentally ill who are allowed to leave state mental hospitals without outside support?

Is the United States in a crisis with regard to the homeless mentally ill? What can be done?

Source: From Celler, J. L. (1992). A historical perspective on the role of state hospitals viewed from the era of the 'revolving Door.' *American Journal of Psychiatry, 149,* 1526-1533.

Internet Site: http://www.rwjf.org/publications/publicationsPdfs/anthology2000/chapt6.htm   This site discusses the trend of deinstitutionalization and the effects on the mental health field.

14.   Bring the DSM-IV-TR to class, and prepare an overhead transparency or PowerPoint slide ahead of time for your lecture on schizophrenic disorders. Describe the in-depth material from the DSM-IV while using the transparency or PowerPoint slide as an outline. Lead a discussion on the differences between different schizophrenic disorders. Encourage student input about individuals they have known with these symptoms.

Copyright © Houghton Mifflin Company. All rights reserved.

HANDOUT FOR DEMONSTRATION 3: SYMPTOMS OF SCHIZOPHRENIA

Clang associations:

"abstract/contract/distract"

"gaze/craze"

"makes three and that is the word for thee"

Perseveration:

"no one is one"

"and any one who tries to be one"

"fails because one and one"

Neologism:

"zommon"

Loose associations:

throughout the monologue

Thought broadcasting:

"You can hear my thoughts, can't you?"

Thought insertion:

"You put that thought in my mind. You put that thought there!"

Thought withdrawal:

"She's stealing my thoughts."

Delusions of being controlled:

"She put a radio transmitter in my brain."

Source: From "The Disordered Monologue: A Classroom Demonstration of the Symptoms of Schizophrenia" by T. M. Osberg, *Teaching of Psychology, 19,* 1992, pp. 47–48. Copyright © 1992. Used with permission from Lawrence Erlbaum Associates, Inc., and the author.

Copyright © Houghton Mifflin Company. All rights reserved.

HANDOUT FOR DEMONSTRATION 4: ALISON'S STORY OF RECOVERY

My illness became apparent when I was about 19 years old. I was depressed as a teenager but didn't have any really psychotic symptoms until I was in my second year at university; then I stopped going to classes and started daydreaming all the time and sleeping all day, just waking up for meals. I was living in a fantasy world where I was a super-special person, and yet I was depressed because I couldn't fulfill this role as a super-special person. One of my girlfriends suggested that, since I was missing classes, I speak to the women's counselor. So I spoke to her and told her my symptoms, and she told me to see a psychiatrist at the university. I went to see him, and I told him all my symptoms: I felt like people started looking like robots to me, my body seemed to be alien matter to myself, I seemed to be like from outer space somehow. He gave me some pills, some antidepressant pills and some antipsychotic pills, but he didn't give me any diagnosis at the time. He just wanted to see how my illness went on.

This lasted about two years, and I was quite suicidal for that period . . . because I didn't know what was going on and I was becoming more and more depressed as I could see my career slipping away . . . and living in this world that I had created and not having any idea what I was supposed to do with my life at that time, and I was very discouraged because nobody gave me any hope.

I ended up in the hospital twice while I was actively suicidal and I finally decided that some of the medications weren't working and I thought I would try another approach. I went to an orthomolecular psychiatrist. He started me on niacin and vitamin C, and it's either coincidence or it really worked, but for some reason or other I got better within a month or two and I was no longer depressed . . . I don't know to this day if they work, but I still take them.

I graduated in 1988, and then the following year I started to notice my depression coming back slowly. I couldn't find a job and I was hanging around my apartment all day. I did find a job and started working at it part-time, but then I started hearing screaming and becoming very agitated for no apparent reason . . . I couldn't go to work any longer . . . I went back to a psychiatrist, and he put me on Prozac and that helped a little bit but didn't help the psychosis part until I ended up in the hospital another time. I sort of became catatonic and they started me on Haldol. I was on Haldol for several months but had several bad side effects so I started on Loxapine after that. I was still a bit suicidal and not really depressed at being suicidal, but it was more of an elated feeling where I wanted to become an angel or something very special again. The doctor said, "Are you depressed?" and I said, "Not really, but I still want to die and I wish God would let me die by some natural cause."

I went to another day program and that helped me quite a bit. I was in that for four months and they taught me how to live on a budget . . . and social assertiveness techniques and I found that very helpful because that gave me a reason to get up in the morning. . . . I was in the hospital a few more times because I was suicidal again. My doctor . . . tried Risperidone for a few months. That seemed to work, but I seemed to be a bit flat on that so I went back on Loxapine and vitamins and I feel fairly good today. I'm not ready to look for a job . . . but at least I have the hope element in my life. I know that all my suffering was for a reason . . . I have since moved home with my parents because I became too lonely but I look forward to moving out again when I feel a lot better.

Copyright © Houghton Mifflin Company. All rights reserved.

DSM-IV-TR criteria for diagnosis of schizophrenia:

A. At least two of the following, lasting for at least one month in the active phase (exception: only one symptom if it involves bizarre delusions or if hallucinations involve a running commentary on the person or two or more voices talking with each other)

    1. Delusions

    2. Hallucinations

    3. Disorganized speech (incoherence or frequent derailment)

    4. Grossly disorganized or catatonic behavior

    5. Negative symptoms (flat affect, avolition, alogia, or anhedonia)

B. During the course of the disturbance, functioning in one or more areas such as work, social relations, and self-care has deteriorated markedly from premorbid levels (in the case of a child or adolescent, failure to reach expected level of social or academic development)

C. Signs of the disorder must be present for at least six months

D. Schizoaffective and mood disorders with psychotic features must be ruled out

E. The disturbance is not substance induced or caused by organic factors

Reprinted with permission from Internet Mental Health (www.mentalhealth.com)

Copyright © Houghton Mifflin Company. All rights reserved.

HANDOUT FOR DEMONSTRATION 5:
WHEN A SIBLING HAS A SEVERE MENTAL DISORDER

The are common concerns and reactions of siblings of the mentally ill. The following are some of the things the sibling of someone with mental illness may be thinking. By understanding these thoughts, you will be better able to deal with them.

1. He/she may try to escape, physically or emotionally, from the family. May establish rigid boundaries or barriers to separate self from others.

2. The healthy sibling may take sides with one or both parents or with the ill sibling. She/he may try to act as a mediator and may have conflicting feelings of feeling sorry for and angry with parents and the ill sibling.

3. The healthy sibling may feel the need to make up for the ill sibling's failings or to avoid creating more problems.

4. The healthy sibling may feel more "serious" about life. The atmosphere at home may be more serious and intense.

5. The healthy sibling may establish a more critical, realistic view of parents earlier; may also become closer to parents.

6. The healthy sibling may feel guilt because he/she is angry at the ill sibling.

7. The healthy sibling may feel embarrassment over the ill sibling's behavior and the reaction of the general public who know little about mental illness.

8. The healthy sibling may feel grief because of the loss of the sister or brother they once knew.

9. The healthy sibling may have concerns about whether or not to have children; worried about the genetics of mental illness.

10. The healthy sibling may have concern about becoming mentally ill, too.

What parents CAN do:

1. Be aware that all family members are profoundly affected.

2. Be aware of the coping stance the siblings adopt (for example, isolation and overinvolvement).

3. Talk about your feelings and encourage them to do the same.

4. Learn about mental illness to reduce family anxiety.

5. Do not make the ill family member the axis around which the family revolves.

What parents CANNOT do:

1. Take away the fact that the mental illness affects other siblings.

2. Lessen the impact by not talking about it.

3. Shield the siblings from their own feelings about the ill sibling.

4. Determine the coping style siblings may adopt.

5. Do the grieving and mourning for them.

6. Take away peer and social stigma.

From a handout prepared by Rex Dickens on behalf of the Alliance for the Mentally Ill/Friends and Advocates of the Mentally Ill, 432 Park Avenue South, New York, NY 10016. Phone: 212-684-3264. Reprinted by permission of the author.

Copyright © Houghton Mifflin Company. All rights reserved.

HANDOUT FOR DEMONSTRATION 6: SURVEY ON PSYCHOLOGICAL TERMS

First, make another copy of this form since you will be surveying two people.

The purpose of this exercise is to see how accurately people can define psychological terms. You should pick one male and one female respondent whom you do not know. Pick people from different age groups. Introduce yourself by saying, "May I have a moment of your time? I am doing a research project for a college class. We are interested in people's understanding of certain psychological terms. Are you willing to participate?" If the person says no, thank them for their time and find another person. If they say yes, mark down their gender.

_____ female _____ male

Ask the following questions:

What is your age? _____

Have you ever taken a high school or college-level introduction to psychology course?

_____ yes _____ no

If yes, how many psychology courses after introduction to psychology did you take?

_____ none (only introduction)   _____ one   _____ two   _____ three   _____ more than three

Were any of the psychology courses you took about abnormal psychology?   _____ yes _____ no

Introduce the next section by saying, "I will now name some psychological terms. Please define each of them to the best of your ability. This is not a quiz; I simply want to find out how people understand the meaning of these words." [Write down, word for word, the definition the respondent provides.]

  1. phobia

  2. psychopath

  3. schizophrenic

You should supply the correct answers for those who get the definitions wrong and want to hear the right ones. Here are the definitions from your textbook:

  phobia: an intense fear of some object or situation and its avoidance that causes great distress

  psychopath: a person with antisocial personality disorder (also called a sociopath) who chronically violates the rights of others without feeling remorse or shame

  schizophrenic: a person who has schizophrenia, a psychotic disorder marked by severe distortion and disorganization of thought, perception, emotions, and behavior and by social withdrawal (not a split personality)

Be sure to thank your respondents for their help in the research.

Copyright © Houghton Mifflin Company. All rights reserved.

HANDOUT FOR DEMONSTRATION 11: DIAGNOSIS AND TREATMENT OF SCHIZOPHRENIC-SPECTRUM DISORDERS

You have just listened to your instructor's description of a person who exhibits psychotic symptoms. Your job is to identify which type of psychosis it **MIGHT** be. No one, not even your instructor, knows what the correct diagnosis is because this is an incomplete and hypothetical case. For the purposes of this activity, we limit the potential diagnoses to three: Brief Psychotic Disorder, Paranoid Schizophrenia, and Schizophrenia (negative symptom). For each potential diagnosis, indicate the questions you would ask, the information you would gather, and the tests you would run to determine that the diagnosis was correct.

Brief Psychotic Disorder   **Information you need to choose this diagnosis**

Paranoid Schizophrenia   **Information you need to choose this diagnosis**

Schizophrenia (negative symptom)   **Information you need to choose this diagnosis**

Copyright © Houghton Mifflin Company. All rights reserved.

Your instructor has given you additional information about the person in the hypothetical case and has provided a diagnosis. Imagine that you are a psychologist or psychiatrist in a treatment facility that can offer comprehensive services for people with this form of mental disorder. Think about and write a treatment plan for your hypothetical person. You need to identify what you think are important treatment goals so you can choose therapeutic approaches to reach those goals. Consider in your treatment plan all the methods that might be effective with this person. What specific forms should these therapies take? What are the potential drawbacks of each?

Your treatment plan

Treatment goals

   1.

   2.

   3.

Specific treatment methods

   1.

   2.

   3.

Potential drawbacks

   1.

   2.

   3.

Copyright © Houghton Mifflin Company. All rights reserved.

SELECTED READINGS

Andreasen, N. C., & Flaum, M. (1991). Schizophrenia: The characteristic symptoms. *Schizophrenia Bulletin, 17,* 27–48.

Chapman, L. J., & Chapman, J. P. (1980). Scales for rating psychotic and psychotic-like experiences as continua. *Schizophrenia Bulletin, 6,* 476–489.

Fowles, D. C. (1992). Schizophrenia: Diathesis-stress revisited. *Annual Review of Psychology, 43,* 303–336.

Gray, J. A., Feldon, J., Rawlins, J. N. P., Hemsley, D. R., & Smith, A. D. (1991). The neuropsychology of schizophrenia. *Behavioral and Brain Sciences, 14,* 1–84.

Nicholson, I. R., & Neufeld, R. W. J. (1993). Classification of the schizophrenias according to symptomatology: A two-factor model. *Journal of Abnormal Psychology, 102,* 259–270.

Robbins, M. (1993). *Experiences of schizophrenia: An integration of the personal, scientific, and therapeutic.* New York: Guilford Press.

Sattler, D., Shabatay, V., & Kramer, G. (1998). *Abnormal psychology in context: Voices and perspectives.* Boston, MA: Houghton Mifflin Company. Chapter 7, Schizophrenia.

Clipson, C., & Steer, J. (1998) *Case studies in abnormal psychology.* Boston, MA: Houghton Mifflin Company. Chapter 7, Schizophrenia.

VIDEO RESOURCES

Anne (16 mm, color, 40 min). A portrayal of a woman in her mid-fifties who has spent most of the last twenty years in mental hospitals. The film presents her mental and physical illnesses, her perceptions of her situation, and the world both inside and outside the hospital. Psychological Cinema Register, Pennsylvania State University, University Park, PA 16802.

"Madness" (7) from *The Brain* series (VHS or 16 mm, color, 60 min). Actual case studies of acute and chronic schizophrenic individuals illustrate thought and behavior problems. Brain researchers discuss neurotransmitters and brain anomalies. WNET-TV, 356 W. 58th Street, New York, NY 10019.

Dialogues with Madwomen (video, 90 min). Seven women including the filmmaker describe their experiences with schizophrenia, bipolar disorder, and multiple personality disorder. They emphasize the creativity and symbolism of madness as well as their individual paths to recovery. Women Make Movies, 462 Broadway, 5th floor, New York, NY 10013.

Full of Sound & Fury: Living With Schizophrenia (video, color, 60 min). Three people with schizophrenia are interviewed. The video shows the daily struggle of living with mental illness, delusions, and social isolation. It examines the effectiveness of drugs and the need for compassion from others. Filmakers Library, 124 E. 40th Street, Suite 901, New York, NY 10016.

Interview with a Schizophrenic (video, color, 50 min). The interview explores the subjective experience of the schizophrenic: thought disturbance, hallucinations, and social withdrawal. Media Guild, 118 South Acacia, Box 881, Solana Beach, CA 92075.

"In Two Minds" from the *Madness* series (video, color, 60 min). This segment addresses the degree to which schizophrenia is a brain disease. Clients' behavior gives a good idea of what the schizophrenic

Copyright © Houghton Mifflin Company. All rights reserved.

experience entails and how the disorder can be treated in a variety of ways. PBS Video; to order, call 1-800-424-7963.

Jupiter's Wife (video, color, 78 min). This drama and documentary describes the life of a homeless and delusional woman who says she is Jupiter's wife. Over a two-year period, she is shown in and around New York's Central Park. We learn that she lost custody of her two children due to her mental illness. The video puts a human face on the issue of the psychotic homeless. Blackbridge Productions, 169 Mercer Street, New York, NY 10012.

Losing the Thread: The Experience of Psychosis (video, color, 54 min). This video is a portrait of a woman, Rachel Corday, who has had intermittent episodes of psychosis for twenty-five years. She explains how she feels before and during a psychotic episode, why simple objects become menacing, and how she loses her ability to recognize even close friends. The tape increases student understanding and empathy. Insight Media, 2162 Broadway, New York, NY 10024.

Mental Illness: Awareness and Hope (video, color, 14 min). Parents of mentally ill children and recovered victims discuss their lives and struggles. Mental health professionals describe how research efforts may lead to better understanding and reduced stigma concerning schizophrenia. American Mental Health Fund, 3299 Woodburn Road, Suite 334, Annandale, VA 22003.

Schizophrenia: The Shattered Mirror (16 mm, 60 min). The film presents the chief characteristics of schizophrenia through the examination of a young girl's behavior and feelings. Research on different treatment methods (drugs, psychotherapy, and ECT) are also described. Audio-Visual Center, Indiana University, Bloomington, IN 47401.

"The Schizophrenias" (video, color, 25 min) from *The Brain* series. This segment explores the case of a man with undifferentiated schizophrenia. The Annenberg/CPB Collection, Dept. CA94, P.O. Box 2345, S. Burlington, VT 05407-2345; to order, call 1-800-532-7637.

"The Schizophrenias" (9) from *The World of Abnormal Psychology* (video, color, 60 min). This tape shows patients suffering from chronic and acute schizophrenia, illustrates both positive and negative symptoms, and discusses current knowledge on causes and treatment. The Annenberg/CPB Collection, Dept. CA94, P.O. Box 2345, S. Burlington, VT 05407-2345; to order, call 1-800-532-7637.

Back from Madness: The Struggle for Sanity (VHS, color, 53 min.). This video follows four psychiatric patients for up to two years as they deal with severe mental illness, including manic-depression, schizophrenia, obsessive-compulsive disorder, and major depression. Films for the Humanities and Sciences. 1-800-257-5126.

Inside Schizophrenia (VHS, color, 33 min.). This video focuses on how the family of a schizophrenic is affected by the disorder. Fanlight Productions.

Pharmacotherapy of Schizophrenia (VHS, color, 75 min.). This video covers the current state of psychopharmacotherapy, including side effects. Insight Media. 1-800-233-9910.

Schizophrenia (VHS, color, 28 min.). Phil Donahue interviews Dr. E. Fuller Torrey, *the author of Surviving Schizophrenia: A Family Manual*. Films for the Humanities and Sciences.

The Schizophrenias (VHS, color, 60 min.). Interviews are conducted with individuals diagnosed with schizophrenia. One of The World #Abnormal Psychology series. Annenberg/CPB. 1-800-LEARNER.

Copyright © Houghton Mifflin Company. All rights reserved.

ON THE INTERNET

http://www.mentalhealth.com/fr20.html is a major site for the understanding of schizophrenia. This site contains many links on this topic.

http://www.health-center.com/mentalhealth a web site that consists of a thorough listing of offerings on mental health issues; check out those that apply to schizophrenia (antipsychotic medications, diagnosis and treatment, positive and negative symptoms, etc.) by linking as appropriate

http://www.schizophrenia.com is a massive site with many links to all aspects of schizophrenia

http://members.aol.com/leonardjk/USA.htm contains a listing of support organizations in the U.S. for people with schizophrenia and their families.

Copyright © Houghton Mifflin Company. All rights reserved.

CHAPTER 14
Cognitive Disorders

CHAPTER OUTLINE

I. Cognitive disorders: behavioral disturbances resulting from transient or permanent brain damage; Mohammed Ali is a contemporary example

    A. DSM-IV-TR major classifications

        1. Delirium

        2. Dementia

        3. Amnestic disorders

        4. Cognitive disorders not otherwise specified

    B. Prevalence

        1. Severe disorders: 1 percent; mild disorders: 6 percent

        2. 22 times more likely in people over age seventy-five than in those 18 to 24

        3. No gender difference

        4. More African Americans than Whites or Hispanics

II. The assessment of brain damage

    A. Neuropsychological tests assess memory, dexterity, and other functions

    B. Neurological tests: more direct monitoring of brain functioning and structure

        1. Electroencephalogram (EEG) measures electrical activity

        2. Computerized axial tomography (CAT) scan assesses brain damage via x-rays and computer technology

        3. Cerebral blood flow measurement

        4. Positron emission tomography (PET) monitors metabolism of glucose in brain

        5. Magnetic resonance imaging (MRI) radio waves produce pictures of brain

    C. Localization of brain damage

        1. Four lobes of cerebral cortex associated with certain functions

        2. Diaschisis: damage in one area disrupts distant, anatomically intact areas

        3. Redundancy ("unused" areas of brain) and plasticity (undeveloped areas) account for recovery

    D. Dimensions of brain damage

        1. Mild to moderate to severe

        2. Endogenous (within person) versus exogenous (outside agent)

        3. Diffuse versus specific

        4. Acute (not permanent) versus chronic (permanent)

Copyright © Houghton Mifflin Company. All rights reserved

    E. Diagnostic problems: similarity of functional and cognitive symptoms

      1. Depressed and schizophrenic individuals misdiagnosed

      2. Older people particularly vulnerable to inaccurate diagnosis

      3. Look for external cause or evidence of brain damage

III. Types of cognitive disorders

    A. Four major categories, then subdivided by causal agent (for example, delirium due to substance induced conditions)

    B. Dementia: deterioration of memory, language (aphasia), motor function (apraxia), failure to recognize or identify objects (agnosia), judgment affecting social functioning, and significant decline from prior level

      1. Major etiological categories

        a. General medical condition (Alzheimer's, stroke, Parkinson's, brain trauma)

        b. Substance induced

        c. Multiple etiologies (for example, medical condition and substance use)

        d. Not otherwise specified

      2. Prevalence

        a. Severe: 1.5 million Americans; mild to moderate: another 1 to 5 million

        b. Those over age 65: 5 to 7 percent have dementia, 2 to 4 percent have Alzheimer's

        c. Those over age 85: more than 20 percent have dementia

      3. Associated with range of causes (Alzheimer's, vascular disease, alcoholism, intracranial masses)

    C. Delirium: rapid-onset reduction in ability to attend, memory deficit, disorientation

      1. Sometimes reduced consciousness; sleep-wake cycle disturbed

      2. Those over age 65 who are hospitalized: about 10 percent have delirium on admission

    D. Amnestic disorders

      1. Inability to learn new or recall old information

      2. Most common causes include head trauma, stroke, and Wernicke's encephalopathy (alcohol-induced thiamine deficiency)

IV. Etiology of cognitive disorders

    A. Brain trauma: case of Phineas Gage; physical injury to brain (affects more than 1.9 million Americans per year)

      1. Concussion: mild injury caused by blow to head

        a. Dazed, headache, disoriented, temporary memory loss, nausea

        b. Symptoms usually persist for days; can persist for years

      2. Contusion: bruising of brain

        a. Symptoms similar, but more severe than those of concussion

        b. Lose consciousness for hours or days

      3. Laceration: tearing of brain tissue

        a. Usually due to object penetrating brain

        b. Most severe impact on functioning

      4. Consequences of serious brain trauma

        a. Permanent disability or death

Copyright © Houghton Mifflin Company. All rights reserved.

b. Closed-head injuries most common form

c. Epilepsy Epilepsy develops in about 5 percent of closed-head injuries and in more than 30 percent of open-head injuries in which train tissue is penetrated

d. One-third with severe injury return to employment, although new treatment shows higher success rate

B. Aging and disorders associated with aging

1. Aged a growing group in United States; predicted 20 percent of Americans over age 65 by 2030

2. Cerebrovascular accidents or strokes: sudden stoppage of blood flow to portion of brain, leading to lost function

   a. Afflict more than 400,000 Americans per year (third leading cause of death); one-fourth develop major depression

   b. Strokes caused by narrowing of blood vessels due to atherosclerosis (buildup of fatty material on interior walls) or block of blood vessels, resulting in cerebral infarction, death of brain tissue from decreased supply of blood

   c. A series of infarctions may lead to vascular dementia, characterized by uneven deterioration of intellectual abilities (some remain intact)

3. Memory loss in older people

   a. May mistake side effects of prescribed drugs for senile dementia

   b. Overlap between normal aging and disorders makes diagnosis difficult

   c. Fear of cognitive decline common concern, but only performance and fluid (problem-solving) intelligence diminishes with age in most

   d. Determine age-related cognitive deficit based on comparison with general population, age group, similar individuals, and previous functioning

C. Alzheimer's disease: brain tissue atrophies, leading to marked deterioration of intellectual and emotional functioning; accounts for 80 percent of dementia in older persons

1. Characteristics of Alzheimer's: irritability, cognitive impairment (memory loss), social withdrawal, neglect of personal hygiene, delusions

2. Alzheimer's disease and the brain: neurofibrillary tangles and senile plaques (degenerated nerve endings) in brain

3. Etiology of Alzheimer's: unknown but speculation about reduced acetylcholine, aluminum exposure, head injuries, infection, decreased blood flow; perhaps genetic (chromosome 21), especially in early onset

D. Other diseases and infections of the brain

1. Parkinson's disease: progressive tremors, stiff gait, flat affect, social withdrawal, depression, dementia

   a. Lesion in motor area of brain stem; low dopamine

   b. Treated with L-dopa

2. AIDS (acquired immunodeficiency syndrome)

   a. AIDS virus reaches brain and affects mental processes

   b. AIDS reduces immune function, allowing infection that causes neuropsychological problems

   c. Confusion and depression arise from knowing one has AIDS

3. Neurosyphilis (general paresis): delayed brain damage resulting from syphilis; occurs in 10 percent of untreated cases of syphilis

   a. Symptoms: euphoria, simple dementia, apathy, paralysis; then death

Copyright © Houghton Mifflin Company. All rights reserved.

      b. If syphilis treated early, clinical remission occurs; after five years of treatment more than half of patients with serious symptoms lose those symptoms

    4. Encephalitis: viral infection causes brain inflammation

      a. Symptoms: rapidly developing headache, sleep, delirium; agitated when awake

    5. Meningitis: inflammation of brain membrane by bacteria, virus, or fungus

      a. Symptoms: high fever, lethargy, stiff neck

      b. Residual effects: hearing loss, mental retardation

    6. Huntington's disease: genetic disorder producing twitching, dementia, and death

      a. Onset at between 25 and 55; death within 16 years of onset

      b. Gene now identified, but no treatment

  E. Cerebral tumors: abnormal tissue growing in brain (faster growing produce most mental symptoms)

    1. Symptoms: diminished attention; mild dementia

    2. Removal can produce dramatic results

  F. Epilepsy: general term for set of symptoms (intermittent and short periods of altered consciousness, sometimes seizures and excessive electrical discharge in brain), no specific cause

    1. Prevalence

      a. Most common neurological problem

      b. 1 to 2 percent of population at some point in lifespan

      c. Most frequently diagnosed in childhood

    2. Causes: alcohol, lack of sleep, fever, low blood sugar, brain injury, hyperventilation, flickering lights

    3. Controlled but not cured by medication

      a. 30 to 50 percent of people with epilepsy have psychological problems

    4. Types

      a. Tonic-clonic: aura before loss of consciousness; tonic (falls to ground), clonic (jerking movements), then coma

    5. Etiological factors: genetics, stress, personality, biochemical imbalances, head injury and physical illness

  G. Use of psychoactive substances

V. Treatment considerations

  A. Surgery

  B. Medication: drugs to control symptoms

  C. Cognitive and behavioral approaches

    1. Memory improvement techniques

    2. Stress inoculation

    3. Classical conditioning to prevent seizures

  D. Environmental interventions and caregiver support

    1. Preserve patient's sense of control

    2. Continued, short social contacts

    3. Diversions in low-arousal settings

    4. Tasks assigned to increase self-worth

Copyright © Houghton Mifflin Company. All rights reserved.

5. Caregivers need support (worry, guilt, parent-child role reversal)

VI. Mental retardation

A. Association for Retarded Citizens estimates that 75 percent of children with retardation can become self-supporting if given appropriate education and training

1. Decrease of people with mental retardation in institutions from 200,000 in 1967 to 110,000 by 1984

B. Diagnosing mental retardation

1. Prevalence: seven million or more in United States; have IQs of about 70 or less

2. Criteria

a. IQ of 70 or less

b. Deficiencies in adaptive behavior

c. Onset before 18

3. Characteristics: dependency, passivity, low self-esteem, depression, self-injurious behavior

C. Issues involved in diagnosing mental retardation

1. Validity of IQ tests: IQ predicts scholastic achievement in Whites but not in minorities

a. Issue has resurfaced

b. Alternative explanations for lower African American IQ scores

2. *Larry P. v. Riles* case

D. Levels of retardation

1. Mild (IQ 50–55 to 70)

2. Moderate (IQ 35–40 to 50–53)

3. Severe (IQ 20–25 to 35–40)

4. Profound (IQ below 20 or 25)

5. American Association on Mental Retardation no longer uses classification based on IQ scores; classifies the level of support needed

E. Etiology of mental retardation

1. Environmental factors

a. Absence of stimulation

b. Chronic stress and poverty

2. Genetic factors

a. Normal variation in genetics related to intelligence

b. Genetic anomalies (rare) leading to significant physical and intellectual impairment

3. Down syndrome (extra chromosome on 21(superscript: st) pair: trisomy 21)

a. physical characteristics: short incurving finger, short broad hands, slanted eyes, protruding tongue, flat broad face, harsh voice, incomplete or delayed sexual development (cosmetic surgery for tongue can help physical appearance and speaking/eating)

b. those who live past 40 are at risk for Alzheimer's because of the 21 (superscript: st) chromosome anomaly; also, greater intellectual decline than with other types of mental retardation

c. prenatal assessment via amniocentesis or chronic villus sampling; older mothers (older than 35) at higher risk for Down syndrome children

Copyright © Houghton Mifflin Company. All rights reserved.

       d.   other genetic anomalies that produce mental retardation: Turner's syndrome, Klinefelter's syndrome, phenylketonuria (PKU), Tay-Sachs disease, and cretinism

    4. Nongenetic biogenic facts

       a.   Prenatal: German measles, drugs, radiation, poor nutrition.

       b.   fetal alcohol syndrome (FAS): consumption of alcohol during pregnancy: small body size, microcephaly, mild retardation, academic and attentional difficulties, hyperactivity, behavioral deficits; exacerbated risk with smoking and poor nutrition; especially high among Native Americans

       c.   Perinatal (during birth) factors: birth trauma or asphyxiation

       d.   postnatal: head injuries, infections, tumors, malnutrition, ingesting toxic substance (e.g., lead), child abuse; small proportion of organically caused mental retardation

  F. Programs for people with mental retardation

    1. Early intervention: Head Start

    2. Employment programs

    3. Living arrangements ("least restrictive environment")

       a.   Group homes

       b.   "Normalized" homes

LEARNING OBJECTIVES

1. Define cognitive disorders and discuss their possible causes. Compare the prevalence rate for different population groups. List the DSM-IV-TR categories of cognitive disorders and differentiate these disorders from other disorders involving cognitive problems that are not part of the cognitive disorders group. (pp. 455-458)

2. Describe the methods for assessing brain damage and the problem of linking functional loss to a specific brain location. (pp. 458-460)

3. Describe the dimensions by which brain damage is categorized. (pp. 460-461; Table 14.1)

4. Describe how cognitive disorders are categorized by cause and the problems in diagnosing cognitive disorders. (pp. 461-462)

5. Describe and differentiate dementia and delirium and discuss the possible causes of these disorders. (pp. 462-465; Mental Health & Society)

6. Describe the amnestic disorders and differentiate them from dementia and delirium. (p. 465)

7. List and differentiate the types of brain traumas, their symptoms and aftereffects. (pp. 466-467)

8. Describe the health conditions that accompany old age, including the nature and effects of, and risk factors for, cerebrovascular accidents (strokes) and vascular dementia. (pp. 467-468)

9. Discuss the extent and reasons for memory loss in older people. Discuss the characteristics of Alzheimer's disease, brain abnormalities, and what is known about its cause. (pp. 469-472; Mental Health & Society)

10. Describe and differentiate among the following: Parkinson's disease, AIDS-related dementia, neurosyphilis (general paresis), encephalitis, meningitis, Huntington's chorea, cerebral tumors, and epilepsy. (pp. 472-478)

11. Describe methods of treating cognitive disorders, including medication and cognitive and behavioral approaches. (pp. 478-480)

12. Discuss the need for environmental interventions and methods of supporting the caregivers of individuals with cognitive disorders. (p. 480)

Copyright © Houghton Mifflin Company. All rights reserved.

13. Discuss the class of disorders known as mental retardation, including different forms of retardation, how mental retardation is diagnosed, the four levels of retardation, and the predisposing factors associated with mental retardation. (pp. 480-483; Table 14.3)

14. Explain the causes of mental retardation, including how environmental factors and nongenetic biogenic factors may be involved. (pp. 483-487)

15. Describe and discuss early intervention and employment programs and living arrangements for people with mental retardation. (pp. 487-488)

CLASSROOM TOPICS FOR LECTURE AND DISCUSSION

1.   There are so many different cognitive disorders and the names of some are so unfamiliar to students that they will appreciate a handout that lists the categories of disorders, their names, and their major symptoms. Students will quickly recognize a major problem for diagnosticians: the similarity of symptoms despite widely different causes. The Handout for Classroom Topic 1 organizes the various brain disorders by type and symptoms.

Internet Site: http://www.merck.com/pubs/mmanual. Consists of the DSM criteria.

2.   In most cases, stroke survivors leave the structured environment of the hospital and return home, often without much preparation given to the family. In Leeds, England, a transitional program is in place that seems to improve the psychological and physical adjustment of stroke survivors (Geddes & Chamberlain, 1989; Geddes et al. 1991). The Leeds Family Placement Scheme (FPS) is a community-based rehabilitation program in which stroke patients and their families get intensive support for about eight weeks after the patient is stabilized after the stroke. Substitute careers help the patient, and the rest of the family devises rehabilitation plans and provides information and assistance in the recovery process. Apparently, patients who learn to cope soon after the stroke develop greater motivation to continue their rehabilitation and have greater acceptance of their changed lifestyles. A comparison of ten stroke patients placed in the FPS with 61 controls showed no overall improvement in functioning among controls but significant improvements between three and twelve months poststroke for those in the FPS intervention.

Sources: Geddes, J. M., & Chamberlain, M. A. (1989). The Leeds Family Placement Scheme: An evaluation of its use as a rehabilitation resource. *Clinical Rehabilitation, 3*, 189–197.

Geddes, J. M., Chamberlain, M. A., & Bonsall, M. (1991). The Leeds Family Placement Scheme: Principles, participants, and postscript. *Clinical Rehabilitation, 5*, 53–64.

Internet Site: http://neurosurgery.mgh.harvard.edu. Provides an extensive list of national associations involved with stroke, paralysis, spinal cord injury, and other neurological conditions.

3.   Alzheimer's disease is a cruel disorder because it robs people of their memory so that they know that it is being stolen. Both the individual with the disorder and the family member who is caregiver experience an extended grieving process for the person who used to be. Even if the individual fights hard to retain memories and tantalizingly, on good days, recovers functioning, there is the inevitability of loss long before death itself occurs. The emotions this situation engenders are difficult to express. For some, writing about the experience is therapeutic.

Below is a poem written by a professional writer, Cris Cassidy, who is watching her highly educated mother lose her battle with Alzheimer's. It is taken from an Internet site (see "On the Internet" at the end of this chapter) where people can submit poetry concerned with neurological disorders. Read this poem

Copyright © Houghton Mifflin Company. All rights reserved.

and ask students to respond. Expect a discussion of the quantity versus the quality of life and a return to issues of suicide or family-assisted suicide. Ask if grief can be experienced while a person is still alive.

Death Before Dying

It isn't fair
that a woman who spoke four languages
and knew every word in Webster's dictionary
should be brought to this . . .
this death before dying.
She still remembers words
but strings them all together wrong.
On night wanderings she babbles in four languages.
"I can remember everything!" she cries,
and then she cries
because somewhere she knows
that everything does not remember her.

Source: The Neurology Web Forum run by Massachusetts General Hospital, Department of Neurology Ms. Cassidy can be contacted by e-mail at raycris@erols.com The poem by Cris Cassidy is reprinted by permission of the author.

Internet Site: http://www.sfcrc.com/html/alzheimers.htm . The San Francisco Alzheimer's and Dementia Clinic.

Copyright © Houghton Mifflin Company. All rights reserved.

HANDOUT FOR CLASSROOM TOPIC 1: REVIEW OF THE COGNITIVE DISORDERS

DEMENTIAS

Deterioration of brain tissue resulting in impaired intellectual ability including memory function and decreased judgment; impairs social and occupational functioning

Types	*Key Symptoms*
Caused by cerebrovascular accident	
Stroke (blood vessels rupture or narrowing of blood vessels)	Paralysis, aphasias, memory impairments, depression, and anxiety
Multi-infarct dementia (series of small strokes)	Uneven deterioration in intellectual functions, especially memory
Caused by Alzheimer's disease	Worsening short-term memory loss, delusions, poor judgment, eventual death
Caused by infection	
Neurosyphilis (general paresis)	Ten to fifteen years after syphilis infection, memory loss, delusions of grandeur, apathy
Caused by deteriorating conditions	
Parkinson's disease	Muscle tremors, shuffling walk, expressionless face, response to L-dopa
Huntington's chorea	Onset when 25 to 50 years old; twitches become jerky movements, dementia, irritability
Caused by brain trauma	
Concussion	Dazed, temporary loss of consciousness, confusion
Contusion	Similar to concussion but more severe
Laceration	Coma, followed by minor to major impairments or death

DELIRIUM

Types	*Key Symptoms*
Caused by infection	
Encephalitis (sleeping sickness)	Rapidly developing headache, prolonged sleep, fever, delirium, irritability
Meningitis	Great variance, but stiff neck, headache, seizures common

Copyright © Houghton Mifflin Company. All rights reserved.

Types	*Key Symptoms*
Caused by substance use	
Amphetamine psychosis	Paranoia, restlessness, thought disturbance
Intoxication from alcohol, narcotics, hallucinogens, and so on	Stuporous, confused, uncontrolled emotions

AMNESTIC DISORDERS

Types	*Key Symptoms*
Wernicke's encephalopathy	Inability to remember recent information; thiamine deficiency

THE EPILEPSIES

Types	*Key Symptoms*
Petit mal	Momentary dimming or loss of consciousness
Grand mal	Aura followed by intense muscular contractions and spasms, then coma
Jacksonian	Seizures spread from one area of body to another
Psychomotor	During spell, behavior appears normal, but no recollection when spell is over

Copyright © Houghton Mifflin Company. All rights reserved.

CLASSROOM DEMONSTRATIONS & HANDOUTS

1.   Neuropsychological tests have had a great impact on the field of cognitive assessment. The Halstead-Reitan and Luria-Nebraska tests, in particular, are frequently used. The following demonstrations can give students a window into the kinds of tasks that are used in such assessments without invalidating the tests.

A subtest of the Halstead-Reitan that screens for aphasia can be simulated in the following way. Cut out of cardboard several shapes, such as a triangle, square, and circle. Without allowing students to observe, place one shape in a brown bag. Ask a student volunteer to come forward and, without looking, place a hand into the bag. After allowing the volunteer to feel the shape, ask him or her to name it. Then ask the volunteer to draw the shape on the board. Finally, place all three shapes in the bag and ask the volunteer to take the correct shape out of the bag when the word for it is written on the board or said aloud. This test examines the comprehension of written and spoken words as well as the association between touch and language.

A second subtest, trail making, asks the test taker to link labeled circles in a certain sequence. Draw two sets of ten circles on separate areas of the board. Inside one set, write the Roman numerals I, II, III, and so on. In the first test, the volunteer must, as quickly as possible, draw lines linking the circles in the order labeled. In the second set, label some circles with the sequence 1, 2, 3, and so on, and the rest with A, B, C, and so on. Now instruct the volunteer to link the 1 to A, the A to 2, the 2 to B, and so on as quickly as possible. This tests both dexterity and the ability to shift categories.

Finally, ask students to tap their desk surfaces with their dominant-hand index fingers as rapidly as possible and count the number of taps over ten seconds. Repeat the task. Then ask them to tap with the index fingers of their nondominant hands for ten seconds. Repeat. Explain that the test indicates not only the speed of responding, but also whether there is a difference between dominant and nondominant brain hemispheres. A normal number of finger taps for the dominant hand is roughly 50. This subtest, more than others, can show how elderly, high-functioning individuals might perform poorly on neuropsychological tests.

Internet Site: http://www.cps.nova.edu/~cpphelp/HRNTB. This site describes the Halstead-Reitan Neuropsychological Battery

2.   Recent research suggests that it may be possible to identify early in life those individuals who will develop Huntington's disease in midlife. Given the fact that the disorder cannot be treated or cured, and that developing it represents a ten-year deterioration into psychosis and death, would people want to know their fate ahead of time? What are the implications for genetic counseling if more commonly occurring degenerative and incurable cognitive disorders such as Alzheimer's disease could be predicted?

To get students thinking about these issues, split the class into groups of four to five students each. Ask the students to discuss in the groups whether they themselves would want to know whether they would develop such a disorder. Ask them to discuss the advantages and disadvantages to the wider society of the ability to predict the development of incurable disorders. Finally, discuss the psychological counseling that might be necessary for both those who "learn of their fate" and their close family members. Have them report their deliberations to the whole class.

Internet Site: http://www.lib.uchicago.edu/~rd13/hd/index.html. This site has information on Huntington's chorea.

Copyright © Houghton Mifflin Company. All rights reserved.

3.   The odds are good that at least 10 percent of your students have a relative who suffers from dementia. Ask for a show of hands of those who are willing to describe the impact that this relative's dementia has had on them, their parents, or other caregivers. Students who have had contact with dementia can give others an appreciation of the specific forms the symptoms take, the degree to which symptoms come and go, and the physical and emotional toll on caregivers.

Internet Site: http://www.merck.com/pubs/mmanual. This site defines and discusses dementia, delirium, and depression in elderly populations.

4.   Traditional-age college students (18 to 22) often have difficulty empathizing with the situations older people face. Although it is important to underscore the fact that most older people remain in good health and do not face cognitive deterioration or depression, the reality is that life is often more trying for older individuals. With increasing age comes decreasing sensory and motor functions. If one has impaired eyesight, hearing, and flexibility of movement, many activities become more difficult to perform. Interpersonal life is strained and self-esteem can deteriorate. These problems may make depression, anxiety, and even disorientation more likely.

The following demonstration can increase students' awareness of the impact of sensory and motor impairments on behavior, emotion, and thought. You will need the following equipment: several pairs of the inexpensive reading glasses available at pharmacies, a jar of Vaseline petroleum jelly, a box of absorbent cotton, a roll of transparent tape, at least four unsharpened pencils, and four rolls of elastic (Ace) bandages. You will also want to have some water, dishwashing liquid, and tissues available.

Ask for at least two volunteers from the class to participate in an exercise to mimic some of the impairments experienced in older age. If the students wear glasses, ask if they are willing to have the lenses smeared with Vaseline, promising that they will be cleaned later. If they say no or do not wear glasses, supply them with reading glasses that you have already smeared with the jelly. This visual impairment will mimic that of cataracts, a common eye disorder of older people. Have the volunteers stuff their ears with absorbent cotton until quiet speech is muffled. Now put strips of tape on the second knuckle of each finger on their dominant hand and the thumb joint. This should give them some appreciation for joint stiffness experienced by those with arthritis, although we cannot convey the pain that is involved. To reduce mobility, you can put one pencil on each side of the knee joint when the leg is straight and wrap tightly with the Ace bandage. Repeat with the other leg.

Have the volunteers talk with each other in quiet voices while the rest of the class engages in normal conversation. In about a minute the volunteers will appreciate how little of their conversation they can understand and how much they ordinarily use visual cues to assist in their interactions. Because of the smeared lenses, they have few visual cues and may experience some of the frustration that older people feel when, in loud restaurants or other social settings, they cannot maintain interactions with others. After this portion of the demonstration, give the volunteers some lined paper and pens. Ask them to copy information from the course textbook in their best handwriting. They will struggle to see the words on the page, will not be able to manipulate the pen well, and will gain some empathy for those who suffer from arthritis. Finally, have them walk around the room, out into the hallway, and, preferably up and down a flight of stairs. For this last one, make sure an able-bodied person is close by to protect the volunteers from falling. You may want to create an obstacle course of sorts in the classroom, too. As the volunteers stumble or just feel unsure of themselves, they will begin to appreciate how disorienting, depressing, and isolating some of the physical disorders of the aged can be.

Encourage the volunteers to voice their awareness, emotions, and thoughts to the rest of the class. Help them understand that cognitive disorders that occur on this background of sensory and motor impairment are more difficult to treat. You could also indicate on the board how a vicious cycle can evolve: Physical impairments increase the likelihood of depression and isolation, which increase the

Copyright © Houghton Mifflin Company. All rights reserved.

likelihood of cognitive disorders. Ask if any of their relatives have gone through this progression. Finally, encourage the rest of the class to try some of these activities on their own and report their experiences to the class.

Remember to leave time at the end to clean up the glasses of volunteers. That's what the water, dishwashing liquid, and tissues are for.

5.   The fact that many cognitive disorders have similar symptoms and that these overlap with symptoms of noncognitive disorders presents problems for the diagnostician. Show students the thought processes that diagnosticians use to rule in or rule out various cognitive and affective disorders. Present this very sketchy portrait of a person who may have a cognitive disorder:

> Mrs. W. is 68 years old and lives alone. She moves very slowly and does not respond verbally to what others say. She sometimes mumbles to herself. Her face is expressionless. She seems confused by her surroundings. She is accompanied by her daughter, who is highly observant and an accurate reporter of Mrs. W.'s past medical and psychosocial history.

First, provide students with the handout so they can think through the potential cognitive and affective disorders that might be appropriate for Mrs. W. Assure them that *no one*, not even you, knows what disorder Mrs. W. really has. The object is to brainstorm for legitimate, likely cognitive and noncognitive disorders. These include Parkinson's disease, Alzheimer's disease, multi-infarct dementia, stroke, depression, and possibly negative symptom schizophrenia. Ask students to report the disorders they wrote down and put a list on the board.

Next, ask students what information they need to make a firm, differentiating diagnosis. Their first decision should be whether the disorder is cognitive or noncognitive. Have them write down the information they would want. If they need assistance, suggest that interviews, psychological testing, and neurological assessments might help. Observations and a medical and social history supplied by Mrs. W.'s daughter should be considered highly accurate information. When they have worked on the cognitive-noncognitive issue, ask them to refine their diagnoses to differentiate among the cognitive disorders. You can help by reminding them that some cognitive disorders involve dementia and that others involve delirium. Some are chronic, whereas others are acute. Have them think about the potential causes of the cognitive impairment, too. When they have finished this portion of the activity, ask for the information they listed for each of the disorders you have listed on the board. Correct any mistaken impressions and add your own thoughts on how to perform a differential diagnosis. Remember to mention that this task is extremely complex and difficult and that misdiagnosis is all too common.

As an example, ask how they would differentiate Alzheimer's disease from vascular dementia.. Alert them to the fact that many professionals are stumped by this question. Finally, discuss the value of making a specific diagnosis. In some cases (such as Alzheimer's disease versus multi-infarct dementia), there is little difference in treatment of the condition. In others (such as Alzheimer's versus depression), differential diagnosis makes a huge difference in appropriate treatment.

Internet Site: http://www.merck.com/pubs/mmanual. This site defines and discusses dementia, delirium, and depression in elderly populations.

6.   Screening for dementia can involve asking patients and their relatives for information on their recent cognitive, emotional, and behavioral functioning. A more standardized procedure is to ask questions from a mental status examination. A brief mental status exam developed by Glasko et al. (1990) is provided in the Handout for Demonstration 6. It will give students an idea of how to define *orientation* and the kind of short-term memory that is impaired by dementia. Caution students not to see this as a definitive diagnostic instrument. Further, since no cutoff scores or norms are provided, there is

Copyright © Houghton Mifflin Company. All rights reserved.

no way to evaluate responses. However, this screening device is available on the Internet at http://teri.bio.uci.edu/forms/short.html. Responses are scored and given in the form of probability that the patient is "normal." These results are not explained: "normal" goes undefined, there are no age-graded norms used, and the normative sample is not described. You can use this opportunity to discuss (again) the need for critical thinking when people are consumers of mental health materials.

Source: Glasko, D., Klauber, M. R., Hofstetter, C. R., Salmon, D. P., Lasker, B., & Thal, L. J. (1990). The mini-mental state examination in the early diagnosis of Alzheimer's disease. *Archives of Neurology, 47*, 49–52. Copyright © 1990, American Medical Association. Reprinted by permission.

Internet Site: http://www.merck./com/pubs/mm_geriatrics/figures/38fl.htm. A screen for dementia.

7.   The Alzheimer's Association developed a list of warning signs for the disease. Because normal forgetfulness and early dementia are not easily distinguished, mistaken worry about Alzheimer's is commonplace. Also common is ignoring the early signs of the disease. A handout is provided with the association's warning signs for Alzheimer's disease. Caution students that this information does not qualify them to engage in amateur diagnostics. Nevertheless, it can help them determine whether an impairment is of potential concern or not.

Source: The Alzheimer's Association, Inc., Chicago, Illinois. Reprinted by permission.

Internet Site: http://www5.biostat.wustl.edu/alzheimer/. The site is an educational service created and sponsored by the Washington University Alzheimer's Disease Research Center.

8.   Have the students form small groups of 4-7 individuals depending on your class size and space limitations. The task of the group is to develop suggested policies or laws related to doctor-assisted suicide. There should be at least one policy in favor of doctor-assisted suicide and one policy against doctor-assisted suicide. The students need to discuss whether there is a difference between doctor-assisted suicide and turning off life support systems. Should spouses who help their loved one commit suicide be prosecuted? In the process of developing the policies or laws, the students have to debate many issues related to doctor-assisted suicide.

9.   Invite an official from your local Council on Aging organization or Alzheimer's support group to talk to the class about the many problems that face the elderly in the areas of health and mental health. The speaker should also discuss the kinds of services available in your area for individuals with Alzheimer's and their families, as well as other services for the elderly.

Internet Site: http://www.sfcrc.com/html/alzheimers.htm. The San Francisco Alzheimer's and Dementia Clinic.

10.   The treatment of mental retardation usually involves some combination of psychoactive medication (phenothiazines and antidepressants, for the most part) and behavior therapy. Behavior therapy techniques have become widely used (and misused) in public institutions, group homes, sheltered workshops, and home environments. When used consistently and ethically, contingent positive reinforcement and modeling can help people with mental retardation control their emotions, learn self-care and daily living skills, and acquire job-related skills. Time out from reinforcement is the most common method of reducing inappropriate behavior, but it can be used inappropriately. Explain that behavioral principles are neutral—in the hands of staff members who want to work less or who have disdain for people with retardation, they can be abused. Capricious use of point systems, excessive time outs, and even the use of physical punishment are considered behavior therapy by those who do not truly value their patients. Unfortunately, behavior therapy, undoubtedly the most effective means of helping people with retardation when correctly employed, has acquired a bad reputation in some circles because it is so easily misused.

Copyright © Houghton Mifflin Company. All rights reserved.

Internet Sites: http://www.cet.fsu.edu/tree/NICHCY/MR/MR.html. This site includes links to organizations and resources on mental retardation.

http://TheArc.org/. The Association for Retarded Citizens home page has a search engine that allows the user to ask for information on any topic related to retardation.

11.   Mental retardation can serve as an excellent illustration of the social and political implications of incorrect diagnosis. Nowhere can we see the tragic effects of self-fulfilling prophecies more clearly than when a child is misdiagnosed as "retarded." An appropriate topic for discussion is the reliability and validity of assessment methods used to make these diagnoses. Remind students of the concepts of test-retest and interrater reliability and of both concurrent and predictive validity. Point out that although the psychometrics indicate that IQ tests have strong test-retest reliability for scores in the middle range of the distribution, reliability drops dramatically for extreme scores. Therefore, as retardation becomes more severe, the value of such numbers decreases. Ask students whether school performance (that which IQ scores predict) should be the sole (or even most important) criterion for intellectual ability. Finally, the accuracy and interrater reliability of social adaptation measures are rather weak. You can ask students what factors make the parents of a child suspected of having mental retardation somewhat unreliable reporters of their child's adaptive behavior. A final point to make: Diagnoses as important as mental retardation require multiple assessment methods reported by multiple sources over multiple points in time.

Internet Sites: http://www.cet.fsu.edu/tree/NICHCY/MR/MR.html. This site includes links to organizations and resources on mental retardation.

http://TheArc.org/. The Association for Retarded Citizens home page has a search engine that allows the user to ask for information on any topic related to retardation.

12.   The DSM-IV-TR has included in its definition of mental retardation the idea that other diagnoses are not excluded from consideration. This point confronts the common perception of those with mental retardation: that their intellectual impairment so overshadows other problems that the existence of other, independent disorders can be ignored or discounted. People with mental retardation can be expected to be depressed, for example. This may be a secondary depression stemming from their treatment by others. However, the depression could be a separate disorder. Whether primary or secondary, such problems as depression, alcohol or drug abuse, and anxiety disorders are quite prevalent in people with mental retardation, and they need to be acknowledged. This situation is what we mean by the term *dual diagnosis*. These problems, often overlooked, deserve treatment just as much as the symptoms of retardation. However, many treatment administrators and therapists feel constrained to place people either in institutions or programs that are focused on intellectual impairments or in institutions or programs that are focused on emotional problems. Instead, dual diagnosis should result in dual treatment.

Internet Sites: http://www.cet.fsu.edu/tree/NICHCY/MR/MR.html. This site includes links to organizations and resources on mental retardation.

http://TheArc.org/. The Association for Retarded Citizens home page has a search engine that allows the user to ask for information on any topic related to retardation.

13.   Invite an employee of the local developmental disabilities and rehabilitation services to class to discuss services available in the community for developmentally delayed adults.

Copyright © Houghton Mifflin Company. All rights reserved.

14.   Learning disabilities present significant difficulties for students. Some, by incredible hard work, do well enough to be considered by selective colleges; even so, they must deal with timed tests, such as the SAT and ACT. Students with dyslexia have an extremely difficult time completing these tests in the required amount of time. The College Board and the American College Testing Program do allow students to take un-timed, special administrations of these tests, which supposedly reflect more accurately the student's real academic achievement. It is possible for some students to be able to take the un-timed version of the tests by producing documentation of a diagnosis of a learning disability.

Have the students form small groups of 4-7 individuals depending on your class size and space limitations. Ask each group to develop this list with the most salient examples first. Each group could then have a spokesperson deliver a short talk about the best examples. You could provide a blank overhead transparency to each group at the beginning of this demonstration.

How do your students in each group feel about learning-disabled students taking un-timed tests? If the student cannot compete for admission on the same basis as everyone else, how can he or she compete in the classroom without enormous amounts of assistance? Do your students know of anyone who took the un-timed versions? Is it fair to have resources made available to them that are not available to other students? What kind of services are available on campus for students with disabilities? Ask the students to discuss these issues keeping in mind that they may have a learning-disabled classmate in the group with them.

Copyright © Houghton Mifflin Company. All rights reserved.

HANDOUT FOR DEMONSTRATION 5:
THINKING CLINICALLY: DIFFERENTIATING COGNITIVE
AND NONCOGNITIVE DISORDERS

You have heard a brief description of an older woman and her symptoms. Using only this information, indicate the potential cognitive and noncognitive disorders she might have and the reasons you think they might be accurate diagnoses. Then list the assessment information (interview questions for the woman or her daughter, psychological and neurological test results, observations, etc.) that would help differentiate one disorder from another.

Potential Cognitive Disorders	*Reasons for Initial Diagnosis*	*Additional Information Needed to Ensure This Is the Correct Diagnosis*
1.		
2.		
3.		

Potential Noncognitive Disorders

1.

2.

Copyright © Houghton Mifflin Company. All rights reserved.

HANDOUT FOR DEMONSTRATION 6: SCREENING TEST FOR DEMENTIA

This is a short-form mental-state examination developed to screen for Alzheimer's disease. Your instructor has purposefully not provided cutoff scores, so this test cannot be used to evaluate anyone. The point of this demonstration is to show you the questions used to identify dementia in its early stages.

Instructions:

1. Say: "I am going to ask you to repeat three words, and in a minute or two, I will ask you to recall those words on your own."

2. Say: "Repeat these three words: Apple, Table, Penny."

   - If needed, correct the patient until he/she has correctly said all the words without assistance.

   - Then say, "Repeat those three words again."

   Score: # of tries to obtain two correct repetitions of the three words _____

3. Say, "Recite the months of the year in reverse order, from December down to January."

   December November October September August July June May April March February January

   Score: # failed _____   # self-corrected_____   # completely correct _____

4. Say: "What state is this?"   correct   incorrect

5. Say: "What county is this?"   correct   incorrect

6. Say: "What city is this?"   correct   incorrect

7. Say: "What is the name of this place?"   correct   incorrect

8. Say: "What floor are we on?"   response _____   actual floor _____

9. Say: "What were the three words I asked you to remember?"

   Apple   Table   Penny

Source: Glasko, D., Klauber, M. R., Hofstetter, C. R., Salmon, D. P., Lasker, B., & Thal, L. J. (1990). The mini-mental state examination in the early diagnosis of Alzheimer's disease. *Archives of Neurology, 47,* 49–52. Copyright © 1990, American Medical Association. Reprinted by permission.

Copyright © Houghton Mifflin Company. All rights reserved.

HANDOUT FOR DEMONSTRATION 7: WARNING SIGNS YOU SHOULD KNOW FOR ALZHEIMER'S DISEASE

To help you know what warning signs to look for, the Alzheimer's Association has developed a checklist of common symptoms of Alzheimer's disease. (Some of them also may apply to other dementing illnesses.) Review the list and check the symptoms that concern you. If you notice several symptoms, the individual with the symptoms should see a physician for a complete examination.

1. **Memory loss that affects job skills:** It is normal to occasionally forget assignments, colleagues' names, or a business associate's telephone number and to remember them later. Those with dementia, such as Alzheimer's disease, may forget things more often and not remember them at all.

2. **Difficulty performing familiar tasks:** Busy people can be so distracted from time to time that they may leave the carrots on the stove and only remember to serve them at the end of the meal. People with Alzheimer's disease could prepare a meal and not only forget to serve it, but also forget they made it.

3. **Problems with language:** Everyone has trouble finding the right word sometimes, but a person with Alzheimer's disease may forget simple words or substitute inappropriate words, making his or her sentence incomprehensible.

4. **Disorientation of time and place:** It is normal to forget the day of the week or your destination for a moment. But people with Alzheimer's disease can become lost on their own street, not knowing where they are, how they got there, or how to get back home.

5. **Poor or decreased judgment:** People can become so immersed in an activity that they temporarily forget the child they are watching. People with Alzheimer's disease could forget entirely the child under their care. They may also dress inappropriately, wearing several shirts or blouses.

6. **Problems with abstract thinking:** Balancing a checkbook may be disconcerting when the task is more complicated than usual. Someone with Alzheimer's disease could forget completely what the numbers are and what needs to be done with them.

7. **Misplacing things:** Anyone can temporarily misplace a wallet or keys. A person with Alzheimer's disease may put things in inappropriate places: an iron in the freezer or a wristwatch in the sugar bowl.

8. **Changes in mood or behavior:** Everyone becomes sad or moody from time to time. Someone with Alzheimer's disease can exhibit rapid mood swings—from calm to fear to anger—for no apparent reason.

9. **Changes in personality:** People's personalities ordinarily change somewhat with age. But a person with Alzheimer's disease can change drastically, becoming extremely confused, suspicious, or fearful.

10. **Loss of initiative:** It is normal to tire of housework, business activities, or social obligations, but most people regain their initiative. The person with Alzheimer's disease may become very passive and require cues and prompting to become involved.

Source: The Alzheimer's Association, Inc. Taken from its Internet site at http://www.alz.org./.

Copyright © Houghton Mifflin Company. All rights reserved.

SELECTED READINGS

Gatz, M., & Smyer, M. A. (1992). The mental health system and older adults in the 1990s. *American Psychologist, 47,* 741–751.

Hantz, P., Caradoc-Davies, G., Caradoc-Davies, T., Weatherall, M., & Dixon, G. (1994). Depression in Parkinson's disease. *American Journal of Psychiatry, 151,* 1010–1014.

Mace, N. L., & Rabins, P. (1981). *The 36-hour day: A family guide to caring for persons with Alzheimer's disease, related dementing illnesses, and memory loss in later life.* Baltimore: Johns Hopkins University Press.

Sacks, O. (1985). *The man who mistook his wife for a hat and other clinical tales.* New York: Summit. This is a must read.

Weiner, M. F. (Ed.) (1995). *The dementias: Diagnosis, management, and research* (2nd ed.). Washington, DC: American Psychiatric Press.

Sattler, D., Shabatay, V., & Kramer, G. (1998). *Abnormal psychology in context: Voices and perspectives.* Boston, MA: Houghton Mifflin Company. Chapter 11, Cognitive Disorders.

Clipson, C., & Steer, J. (1998) *Case studies in abnormal psychology.* Boston, MA: Houghton Mifflin Company. Chapter 16, Dementia of the Alzheimer's Type: Descent into Darkness.

Zigler, E., & Hodapp, R. M. (1991). Behavioral functioning in individuals with mental retardation. *Annual Review of Psychology, 42,* 29–50.

Dorris, M., & Erdrich, L. (1990). *The Broken Cord.* Harper Collins Publishers. This poignant book, co-authored by Michael Dorris, his wife Louise Erdrich, with input from his adopted son, talks about the trials and tribulations of adopting and raising an FAS child. Michael Dorris, an anthropologist, became a single father when he adopted a Native American boy, not knowing the child's mother was an alcoholic and the child would encounter lifelong difficulties that ultimately led to his early death. The story is made sadder by knowing that Dorris himself later committed suicide.

VIDEO RESOURCES

"Aging" from *The Mind* series (video, color, 60 min). This tape debunks the idea that impairing diseases are the normal outcome of aging. Alzheimer's disease is given prominent discussion, as is the need for research on prevention and cure for this disease. PBS; to order, call 1-800-424-7963.

Alzheimer's Disease: The Long Nightmare (video, color, 19 min). The tape shows the limitations of current Alzheimer's research and points out recent advances in understanding protein production in the brain. Also discussed are the medical, financial, and emotional aspects of caring for those with Alzheimer's. Films for the Humanities and Sciences, New York, NY.

Brain and Behavior (16 mm, 22 min). Parts of the brain and their relationship to physical and psychological functioning. The film also shows patients with brain injuries. McGraw-Hill Films, 1221 Avenue of the Americas, New York, NY 10020.

Divided Brain and Consciousness (16 mm, 22 min). Illustrates the different effects of damage to the left and right hemispheres of the brain; split-brain research. Harcourt Brace Jovanovich, 7555 Cardwell Avenue, Chicago, IL 60648.

Copyright © Houghton Mifflin Company. All rights reserved.

"Organic Mental Disorders" from *The World of Abnormal Psychology* series (video, color, 60 min). This comprehensive tape shows the biological, psychological, and social aspects of cognitive disorders as well as their treatment and current topics in research.

Somebody Waiting (16 mm, color, 24 min). This film shows hospitalized children with severe cerebral dysfunctions who, as a result, are physically, emotionally, and mentally handicapped. The film includes a discussion and description of hospital staff experiences and personal growth amidst these tragic cases and a discussion of the need for environmental stimulation. University of California Extension Media Center, 2223 Fulton Street, Berkeley, CA 94720.

"The Two Brains" from *The Brain* series (video, color, 60 min). This tape focuses on split-brain research and the relationships between the hemispheres. Topics relevant to cognitive disorders include language and its relation to thought, and gender differences in brain function. PBS; to order, call 1-800-424-7963.

When the Brain Goes Wrong (video, color, 45 min). This video covers people with epilepsy, stroke, and closed-head injury as well as those with alcohol dependence, schizophrenia, and bipolar disorder. All are seen as having brain dysfunctions, so the differentiation of cognitive disorders may be blurred. However, the exploration of available treatments is good. Insight Media, 2162 Broadway, New York, NY 10024.

Maturing and Aging (VHS, color, 30 min.). Part of the Essential Themes in Psychology: Discovering Psychology series. Annenberg/CPB1-800-LEARNER .

Organic Mental Disorders (VHS, color, 60 min.). Part of The World of Abnormal Psychology series. Locks at organic and neurological disorders that affect the brain and its functioning. Annenberg/CPB. 1-800-LEARNER.

Behavior Modification: Teaching Language to Psychotic Children (16 mm, color, 15 min). This short film shows how mentally retarded individuals can be taught self-care and independent living skills through the application of operant conditioning techniques. Sensory Systems, 4314 Abbott Avenue, Minneapolis, MN 55459

David: A Portrait of a Retarded Youth (16 mm, 28 min). The case history of a Down syndrome adolescent is the focus of this film, which gives a balanced view of the challenges and successes in dealing with the disorder. Filmmakers Library, 124 E. 40(superscript: th) Street, Suite 901, New York, NY 10016

PKU: Preventable Mental Retardation (16 mm, color, 16 min). Preventable Mental Retardation (16 mm, 16 min) This film shows how mental retardation resulting from phenylketonuria can be prevented through early detection and diagnosis in infancy and through restricted diet. International Film Bureau, 332 South Michigan Avenue, Chicago, IL 60604

Through Different Eyes (16 mm, color, 15 min). This short film shows how training programs must match the method of training to the specific handicap of individual children with mental retardation. Media Sales, Pennsylvania State University, 118 Wagner Building, University Park, PA 16802.

When the Mind Fails: A Guide to Alzheimer's Disease. (VHS, 59 min). A guide for caregivers and Alzheimer's patients that discusses the first signs, diagnosis, middle stages, getting organized, coping, dealing with the day-to-day struggles, last stages, and hope for the future, which talks about the latest genetic research. Films for the Humanities & Sciences, P.O. Box 2053, Princeton, NJ 08543-2053. 1-800-257-5126.

Fetal Alcohol Syndrome: Life Sentence (VHS, 24 min). Consumption of alcohol during pregnancy can cause permanent brain damage for the child that results in learning disabilities, poor judgment, antisocial

Copyright © Houghton Mifflin Company. All rights reserved.

behavior, and alcohol addiction. Focus on early intervention is critical. Films for the Humanities & Sciences, P.O. Box 2053, Princeton, NJ 08543-2053. 1-800-257-5126.

ON THE INTERNET

http://www.alz.org./ is the official home page of the Alzheimer's association.

http://neurosurgery.mgh.harvard.edu provides an extensive list of national associations involved with stroke, paralysis, spinal cord injury, and other neurological conditions from The National Stroke Association.

http://www.stroke.org/ has a five-item quiz on the facts and risk factors involved in stroke.

http://teri.alz.uci.edu is the Institute for Brain Aging and Dementia, a collaborative effort of the University of Southern California and the University of California, Irvine.

http://www.mentalhealth.com/fr20.html includes descriptions, treatments, research references, books, magazine articles, and other links to the topic of dementia of the Alzheimer type.

http://www.sfcrc.com/html/alzheimers.htm is The San Francisco Alzheimer's and Dementia Clinic one of the institutions in the United States devoted to the investigation, diagnosis, treatment, and management of Alzheimer's.

Copyright © Houghton Mifflin Company. All rights reserved.

CHAPTER 15

Disorders of Childhood and Adolescence

CHAPTER OUTLINE

I. Range of childhood and adolescent disorders

    A. Almost 21 percent of children in the U.S. between ages nine and seventeen have a diagnosable mental or addictive disorder with at least minimal impairment; 11 percent have significant impairment; 5 percent has extreme impairment

    B. The disorders range from severe disturbance to those that are less severe

II. Pervasive developmental disorders: Severe disorders with qualitative impairments in verbal and nonverbal communications and social interaction; do not include hallucinations or delusions

    A. Autistic disorder: Kanner identified three behaviors of "infantile autism": extreme isolation/inability to relate to people; psychological need for sameness; significant difficulties with communication

        1. DSM-IV-TR: qualitative impairment in social interaction and/or communication; restricted, stereotyped interest and activities; delays or abnormal functioning in major area before age 3

        2. Prevalence: about two to twenty cases in 10,000 children; four to five times more common in boys than girls

        3. Impairments

            a. Social interactions (lack of interest in others is primary aspect of disorder); appear unaware of other people's identity; treat people as objects

            b. Verbal and nonverbal communication; half develop no speech; echolalia common in those who speak

            c. Activities and interests few; unusual repetitive habits (spinning things); minor changes produce rage

            d. Intellectual functioning; up to 75 percent have IQs below 70 (mental retardation); splinter skills (drawing, rote memory of calendars, song lyrics, math calculation); "autistic savants" as portrayed in the movie *Rain Man*

        4. Diagnosis

            a. Many different medical conditions can produce symptoms of autism

            b. Autistic profile found in those with and without neurological problems

            c. Shares communication and social problems with other disorders

            d. Wide range of symptoms

            e. Coexistence of mental retardation

        4. Research on autism

Copyright © Houghton Mifflin Company. All rights reserved

      a. Autistic children more interested in inanimate objects than in people

      b. Can match sound and drawing of nonhuman stimuli but not human

      c. Lack a "theory of mind": cannot recognize others' beliefs as mistaken, cannot appreciate others' mental states

  B. Other pervasive developmental disorders

    1. Prevalence: about 22 in 10,000

    2. Controversy about overlap with autistic disorder and neurological conditions

    3. Asperger's disorder: severe social and emotional impairments but no language deficits

    4. Childhood disintegrative disorder: normal development for at least two years followed by deterioration of social and language skills

    5. Rett's disorder: normal development between five and forty-eight months followed by deterioration of social and language skills; diagnosed only in females

    6. Pervasive developmental disorder not otherwise specified

  C. Etiology

    1. Rett's, Asperger's, and childhood disintegrative too new to have been researched

    2. Four etiological groups for autistic: familial, medical, nonspecific brain dysfunction, without family history or brain dysfunction

    3. Psychodynamic theories

      a. Kanner blamed cold, unresponsive parenting; described parents as cold, humorless perfectionists; later came to see autism as innate

      b. psychological factors no longer implicated in autism

    4. Family and genetic studies

      a. Increased risk in siblings

      b. 36 percent concordance in MZ twins, 0 percent in DZ; some of discordant twins have language impairment

    5. Central nervous system impairment

      a. Inherited brain dysfunction

      b. Left hemisphere (language)

      c. Smaller brainstem and cerebellum

      d. Inconsistent findings

    6. Biochemical studies: high serotonin and dopamine in some patients

  D. Prognosis: mixed (some show highly significant improvement; those with severe mental retardation have poorer outcomes)

  E. Treatment

    1. Drug therapy: results are mixed

      a. Haloperidol (Haldol): modest reduction in withdrawal and movements

      b. Fenfluramine: decreased hyperactivity and increased attention

    2. Behavior modification: used effectively

      a. Eliminates echolalia, self-destructiveness

      b. Increases attention, language, social play

      c. Intensive program had positive effect on IQ

      d. Social impairments harder to alter

III. Other developmental disorders

  A. Overview

Copyright © Houghton Mifflin Company. All rights reserved.

1. What constitutes a disorder is vague
2. Cultural differences in childhood problems

B. Problems with diagnosis

   1. Controversy over guidelines

   2. Clinicians must decide if problems behaviors are present, excessive, maladaptive, or inappropriate for developmental level; such judgments are difficult to make

IV. Attention deficit/hyperactivity disorders and disruptive behavior disorders

A. Prognosis: without intervention, they tend to persist

B. Attention deficit/hyperactivity disorder (ADHD)

   1. Symptoms

      a. Short attention span

      b. Low self-control and greater motor activity in two or more situations

      c. Academic impairment

      d. Poor peer relations

      e. Present before age seven and persists at least six months

   2. Three forms: predominantly hyperactive-impulsive; predominantly inattentive; combined

   3. Prevalence: 3 to 7 percent of school-age children; boys much more likely to receive diagnosis

   4. Prognosis: continues into adolescence, fewer problems if attention deficit only; increased likelihood of delinquency in adolescence, but not in adulthood; require structured situations; worse prognosis if other disruptive disorders

   5. Etiology

      a. Inconsistent findings on neurological cause

      b. No evidence for food additives or sugar as cause

      c. Family variables

   6. Treatment

      a. 75 to 90 percent of children with ADHD respond positive to stimulant medication

      b. Concerns about overmedicating

      c. Combine drugs and behavior therapy

      d. interventions based on functional behavior assessment almost completely eliminate aggressive behavior in those with high activity levels

C. Oppositional defiant disorder (ODD): negativistic, hostile

   1. Controversial: not in International Classification of Diseases and may be normal variation in child behavior

   2. DSM-IV-TR: the problem causes "significant impairment in social or academic functioning"

   3. Associated with parent-child conflict, espousing unreasonable beliefs, negative family interactions

D. Conduct disorders: consistent antisocial behavior over six months; prevalence from three to ten percent, four to five times more often in boys

   1. Two subtypes: childhood onset (prior to age ten); adolescent onset (after age ten)

   2. 83,000 juveniles in American correctional institutions; 1.75 million arrested in 1990; coexists with ODD and ADHD; prognosis poor, particularly with sexually aggressive

Copyright © Houghton Mifflin Company. All rights reserved.

behaviors, prognosis better for high IQ males whose parents do not have antisocial personalities and for females

    3. Etiology

        a. Psychodynamic perspective—underlying anxiety

        b. Biological perspective/genetic factors; little actually known about genetic influences

        c. Parental failure and lack of supervision

    4. Treatment

        a. Resist traditional psychotherapy

        b. Cognitive behavioral self-control treatment for child, role playing

        c. Parent management training; greatest success combines skill training and parent training

V. Anxiety disorders: exaggerated autonomic responses; internalizing or over controlled

    A. Prognosis is promising even without treatment

    B. Separation anxiety disorder: excessive anxiety when separated from parents or home [then continue with A ("constantly seek parents' company..."; 1-4 fine]

        1. Early temperament (shyness) interacts with parenting skill deficits

        2. School phobia subtype: 6 percent of females; 2.5 percent of males during lifetime

        3. Etiology: overdependence (psychodynamic); parental reinforcement (learning)

        4. Prognosis: for young children, very good; worse when symptoms develop in adolescence

VI. Reactive attachment disorder: extreme disturbance in relating to others socially

    A. Develops in infancy or early childhood from extreme abuse, neglect, institutional upbringing, or repeated changes in primary caregiver

        1. Result in inability to meet the child's physical or emotional needs that affect attachment formation.

    B. Therapy

        1. Rebirthing therapy ineffective; may put vulnerable children at risk

        2. These children need to feel they are in a safe and nurturing environment

        3. Caretakers should learn parenting skills, and children need to learn to set goals related to their specific symptoms.

VII. Mood disorders

    A. DSM-IV-TR does not list childhood depression under childhood disorders, but children and adolescents may suffer from any form of mood disorder

        1. Bipolar: children cycle more rapidly; hyperactive, irritable, shifting moods

        2. Most common form of depression: reactive, which lasts a limited period of time in response to specific stressful situation

    B. Prevalence: 2 to 7 percent of children; common in adolescents, especially girls

    C. Treatments include cognitive behavioral and skills training

VIII. Tic disorders

    A. Chronic tic disorder (lasts more than one year)

        1. Most common: eye blinks, jerking movements of head

        2. Transient tic disorder (lasts four weeks but less than one year)

            a. 15 to 23 percent of children have transient tics

            b. Can only be diagnosed in retrospect

Copyright © Houghton Mifflin Company. All rights reserved.

B. Tourette's syndrome: facial tics, grunting and barking, coprolalia (compulsion to shout obscenities)

    1. . Prevalence: 5 to 30 cases per 10,000 children; three to five times more frequent in boys than girls; 1 to 2 children per 10,00 continue to have symptoms in adulthood

    2. Course: varies from individual to individual; many suffer no significant distress and do not seek treatment

    3. Etiology and treatment

        a. Anxiety plays central role

        b. Avoidance response

        c. Nearly 50 percent meet criteria for ADHD

        d. Involves dopamine; some treatment success with Haloperidol, but there is a risk of negative side effects, such as tardive dyskinesia; fewer risks with clonodine

IX. Elimination disorders

A. Toilet training is a major focus of conflict

B. Enuresis

    1. Commonly seen in children as bed wetting

    2. Significant distress in social, academic everyday life for children with enuresis

    3. Both psychological and biological explanations

    4. Interventions involve medication to decrease depth of sleep or volume of urine; most successful psychological procedure are behavioral

        a. constant reinforcement form parents

        b. wake child to use toilet

        c. give child responsibility for making bed if accident occurs

        d. bedtime urine alarm treatment

C. Encopresis

    1. Less common that enuresis

    2. Defecating in clothes, on the floor or other inappropriate places

        a. Occurs in 1 percent of grade school children, boys far outnumbering girls; can persist for years

        b. seen with functional constipation; usually involuntary

    3. Amount of psychosocial impairment is in direct proportion to its effects on child's self-esteem: problems arise through shame, embarrassment, attempts to concel disorder; ostracism by peers, anger from caregivers, rejection; but most children with encopresis do not have serious psychological or behavior problems

    4. Treatment: medical evaluation, behavioral and family therapy, parent and child education re toileting regimens

LEARNING OBJECTIVES

1. Describe the characteristics of pervasive developmental disorders and identify the prevalence of behavior problems in children and adolescents. (pp. 491-493)

2. Indicate the prevalence of autistic disorder and describe the main impairments it entails. Describe diagnostic difficulties and research findings related to autism. Discuss the relation autistic disorder has to retardation and splinter skills. (pp. 493-496)

Copyright © Houghton Mifflin Company. All rights reserved.

3. Differentiate between autism and Rett's disorder, childhood disintegrative disorder, Asperger's disorder, and pervasive developmental disorder not otherwise specified. (pp. 496-497; Figure 15.2)

4. Discuss the etiology of autistic disorder, including psychodynamic, family, genetic, central nervous system impairment, and biochemical theories. (pp. 497-500)

5. Describe the prognosis and treatment for children with pervasive developmental disorders. Discuss drug therapy and behavior modification for these children. (pp. 500-501)

6. Discuss the problems with the diagnosis and classification of other developmental disorders. (pp. 501-503; Table 15.1)

7. Describe the symptoms, etiology, and treatment of the attention deficit/hyperactivity disorders. Discuss the difficulty involved in making an ADHD diagnosis accurately. (pp. 503-508; Mental Health & Society)

8. Define and differentiate oppositional defiant disorder and conduct disorder and discuss the prevalence, etiology, and treatment of conduct disorders. (pp. 508-512)

9. Consider the question of whether school violence is a "sign of the times." (p. 510; Critical Thinking)

10. Contrast the anxiety-related disorders of childhood, including separation anxiety disorder and school phobia. Discuss how they can be treated. (pp. 512-513)

11. Describe reactive attachment disorder and how to deal with it. (pp. 513-514)

12. Describe the prevalence, symptoms, and treatment of childhood depression. (pp. 514-515; Mental Health & Society)

13. Describe the symptoms, etiology, and treatment of chronic and transient tic disorders, including Tourette's syndrome. (pp. 515-519)

14. Discuss the various elimination disorders, including enuresis and encopresis. (pp. 519-520)

CLASSROOM TOPICS FOR LECTURE AND DISCUSSION

1. Recent research and clinical interest has focused on the children of dysfunctional families. Much has been written in the popular press about children of alcoholics and children of divorced parents. Some research (see Judith Wallerstein's longitudinal research on children of divorce) indicates the likelihood of both immediate and long-delayed effects of growing up with conflict, parental absence, and emotional tension related to the noncustodial parent. Clinicians who work with alcoholic families assert the existence of designated roles for children from these homes: the overachieving mini-parent (the "hero"), the black sheep who is the psychological lightning rod (the "scapegoat"), the tension-breaking comedian (the "mascot"), and the depressed invisible child (the "lost child"). Unfortunately, this assertion is based on scant evidence. Furthermore, there is every reason to believe that some of these roles are played by children in any dysfunctional family in which parents fail to act responsibly. You can use this topic to stress the need for skepticism and replicable findings based on well-designed research before accepting sweeping assertions about the effects of alcoholism on children.

2. Most students are eager to know about the prognosis for treated autistic children. McEachin et al. (1993) present follow-up results of an extremely comprehensive and well-controlled comparison of intensive behavior therapy with a control group getting less intensive behavior therapy. The original intervention occurred when most of the children were about three-and-one-half years old or less. The experimental group (N = 19) received forty or more hours of one-to-one behavior therapy per week for two or more years. Controls (N = 19) got ten hours per week or less. Lovaas (1987) provides details about this treatment and the first evaluation of it.

At a mean age of eleven and one-half, the children getting the intensive program (out of treatment for an average of five years) showed substantially better adjustment than the controls (who averaged three years, posttreatment). Average IQ scores for those getting intensive treatment was 84.5; average for the

Copyright © Houghton Mifflin Company. All rights reserved.

controls was 54.9. Vineland Adaptive Behavior scores averaged 71.6 for experimentals, 45.7 for the controls. Furthermore, the nine experimental subjects with the best outcomes were, on the basis of IQ (average score = 108), indistinguishable from normal children. The best-outcome subjects also had Personality Inventory for Children scores that were within the normal range for all scales.

Despite the limitations of small samples and the absence of replication by other researchers, these results are heartening. Given early and intensive work with children having autistic disorder, long-term outcome can be quite positive.

Sources: Lovaas, O. I. (1987). Behavioral treatment and normal educational and intellectual functioning in young autistic children. *Journal of Consulting and Clinical Psychology, 55,* 3–9.

McEachlin, J. J., Smith, T., & Lovaas, O. I. (1993). Long-term outcome for children with autism who received early intensive behavioral treatment. *American Journal on Mental Retardation, 97,* 359–372.

Internet Site: http://www.autism-society.org the web site fro the Autism Society of America

3.   As the United States becomes a more culturally diverse country, teachers, nurses, pediatricians, and mental health professionals who come in contact with children will have to be increasingly aware of cultural differences in parental expectations. Childhood psychopathology is defined not by children, but by the adult authorities in their lives. Those authorities can hold quite different views about the acceptability of such childhood behaviors as opposition to parents and fighting with peers. As defined by parents, what is deviant in one culture is normative in another (Lambert et al., 1992).

Weisz et al. (1988) investigated the impact of cultural norms on perceptions of children's problems. Vignettes of children were shown to parents, teachers, and psychologists in Thailand and the United States. Each person viewed two videos, one depicting a child who was disobedient and aggressive, the other showing a fearful, shy youngster. Viewers then rated how worrisome and serious they thought the children's behavior was, and whether they thought the children's behavior would improve without professional help. Ask students what they think the results would be. You can help here by putting a graph on the board with "average problem perception" on the vertical axis and, on the horizontal axis, six places indicating Thai parents, teachers, and psychologists and U.S. parents, teachers, and psychologists.

The results show that psychologists from both cultures gave quite similar ratings (4.72 and 4.82 on a seven-point scale for the Thai and U.S. psychologists, respectively). The Thai parents and teachers gave much lower ratings of problems (4.43 and 4.25) than did U.S. parents and teachers (5.63 and 5.82). Now ask students why they think such dramatic differences exist. Weisz et al. (1988) suggest that Buddhist values tolerate a wide range of childhood behaviors and assume that behavior will change for the better. Parents are socialized to relax about their children's behavior and expect that, with time, they will mature out of their foolishness. Americans are socialized to believe that childhood patterns are signposts of future behavior and that there is a relatively narrow range of acceptable behavior for children. What other explanations might there be?

In addition, Weisz and his colleagues looked at the types of problems that parents typically see in children in the two countries. Problems of overcontrol—anxiety, sleeplessness, somatic complaints including headaches and stomachaches—were more common than problems of undercontrol in Thai society; American children tended to have the opposite kinds of problems. Even among the "undercontrolled" children in Thailand, children showed more control than in the United States. Rather than hitting other children undercontrolled Thai children tend to harm animals or simply not pay attention to parents' requests. (Weisz, et al., 1993). These results suggest that sociocultural norms dictate not only how problems are seen but also the nature of the symptoms involved. Thailand is like many other Asian nations where a high premium is put on the individual's ability to control selfish desires in favor of the group. Harmony is more important than individuality. One could argue that Americans place more emphasis on independence and creativity than they do on group cohesion and collaboration.

Copyright © Houghton Mifflin Company. All rights reserved.

As it is argued for adult disorder, so it is for childhood disorders: Symptoms are mirrors of the culture's norms.

Sources: (The first portion of this discussion is taken from Nevid, J. S., Rathus, S. A., & Greene, B. (1994). *Abnormal psychology in a changing world* (2nd ed.). Englewood Cliffs, NJ: Prentice-Hall).

Lambert, M. C., et al. (1992). Jamaican and American adult perspectives on child psychopathology. Further exploration of the threshold model. *Journal of Consulting and Clinical Psychology, 60,* 64–72.

Weisz, J. R., et al. (1988). Thai and American perspectives on over- and undercontrolled child behavior problems: Exploring the threshold model among parents, teachers, and psychologists. *Journal of Consulting and Clinical Psychology, 56,* 601–609.

Weisz, J. R., et al. (1993). Behavioral and emotional problems among Thai and American adolescents: Parent reports for ages 12–16. *Journal of Abnormal Psychology, 102,* 395–403.

4.   Bedwetting is a common occurrence for young children, especially before age five, and is not really considered a problem unless it continues page age six or seven. Some issues to explore with your students might be: what are the appropriate steps for toilet training a child and how early should this start? what problems might a child encounter if she or he has not acquired bladder control by age five or six? what causes enuresis (psychological and physiological causes)? what would be the differences between the etiology of voluntary versus involuntary enuresis? what are the different ways that enuresis is treated, and which seems to have the best outcome?

More of a problem, particularly emotionally, is encopresis, or defecating at inappropriate times in inappropriate places. Explore the following with your students: how does encopresis differ in severity from enuresis? what causes encopresis? how would parents know if their child has encopresis? why is encopresis a concern? in terms of behavior, how might voluntary encopresis differ from involuntary encopresis? what are the best treatments for encopresis?

Based on what the students have learned from the text and by using other resources, have them develop a community plan to educate parents and children about the elimination disorders.

Internet sites: http://www.aafp.org/afp/990415ap/2171.html Treatment Guidelines for Primary Nonretentive Encopresis and Stool Toileting Refusal, on the American Family Physician website

http://www.bedwetting.ferring.ca is a web site sponsored by Ferring Pharmaceuticals, a Canadian company that produces DDAVP (desmopressin), a drug used to treat enuresis

http://www.medicine.uiowa.edu/uhs/enco.cfm is the University of Iowa's Health Care Center for Disabilities and Development, which offers information about the causes and treatment of encopresis

http://www.wetbuster.com a site for parents and children (as well as adults with enuresis) who experience problems with bedwetting

CLASSROOM DEMONSTRATIONS & HANDOUTS

1.   Behaviors that are considered disorders in childhood change with the age of the child and the norms of the wider culture. Distribute the handout for this demonstration and ask students to rate each short description on a five-point scale, with 1 indicating no indication of a problem and 5 being a strong indication of a problem. Remind students that in each case a 10-year-old child is engaging in the behavior today. Ask students to re-rate the items while imagining that the child is 15 years old. Have them turn in their handouts; before the next class period, tabulate and average their ratings for the 10-

Copyright © Houghton Mifflin Company. All rights reserved.

year old and the fourteen-year-old. If you can, calculate the standard deviations as well. Display the averages on the board and ask if students are surprised by any of the ratings. Ask people who were tolerant (mostly gave 1s and 2s) to explain their thinking. Compare and contrast this attitude with the opinions of those who gave mostly 4s and 5s. Also ask students whether the same behaviors would have been seen as problematic if they themselves had engaged in them as 10- and 14-year-olds.

This exercise illustrates how diverse our standards may be and how expectations of normative development influence definitions of abnormality. If your students represent a diverse set of cultures (international students, rural versus urban, white versus people of color), ask if social expectations influenced their ratings. Finally, you will get a rousing discussion of differences in the behaviors parents allow from first-born and last-born children. Birth order is yet another factor that muddies the waters when childhood behavior is rated as problematic or not.

Internet Site: http://www.aacap.org/publications/factsfam The American Academy of Child and Adolescent Psychiatry provides up-to-date information on issues that affect youngsters

2.   Many students have strong opinions about how parents should interact with their children in order to foster self-esteem and open communication. Divide the class into small groups or engage in a round table discussion of the following themes:

1. What methods did your parents use in rearing you that you are going to use in raising your own children?

2. What child-rearing methods will you use as a parent that your parents failed to use?

3. How much is the person you are today the direct result of the way your parents communicated with you?

4. To what extent should a parent be a child's "best friend"?

This topic can spark heated discussion about the do's and don'ts of parenting. It is a good idea to interject questions about how research can evaluate assertions of the "right" method. You can also note that different subcultures may have different right ways of being parents and that there are many parenting styles, all (none?) of which can be effective.

3.   Although the text did not include a section on learning disorders (there is a limit to how much can be included in any textbook!), they present significant difficulties for students that extend into adulthood. Some, by incredible hard work, do well enough to be considered by selective colleges; even so, they must deal with timed tests, such as the SAT and ACT. Students with dyslexia have an extremely difficult time completing these tests in the required amount of time. The College Board and the American College Testing Program do allow students to take un-timed, special administrations of these tests, which supposedly reflect more accurately the student's real academic achievement. It is possible for some students to be able to take the un-timed version of the tests by producing documentation of a diagnosis of a learning disability.

Have the students form small groups of 4-7 individuals depending on your class size and space limitations. Ask each group to develop this list with the most salient examples first. Each group could then have a spokesperson deliver a short talk about the best examples. You could provide a blank overhead transparency to each group at the beginning of this demonstration.

How do your students in each group feel about learning-disabled students taking un-timed tests? If the student cannot compete for admission on the same basis as everyone else, how can he or she compete in the classroom without enormous amounts of assistance? Do your students know of anyone who took the un-timed versions? Is it fair to have resources made available to them that are not available to other students? What kind of services are available on campus for students with disabilities? Ask the students

Copyright © Houghton Mifflin Company. All rights reserved.

to discuss these issues keeping in mind that they may have a learning-disabled classmate in the group with them.

4.   Have the students form small groups of 4-7 individuals depending on your class size and space limitations. Ask your students in the groups to discuss the difference between the laws related to special education in the public schools and the Americans with Disabilities Act, which affects higher education. Have the students develop a list of similarities and a list of differences.

Copyright © Houghton Mifflin Company. All rights reserved.

HANDOUT FOR DEMONSTRATION 1:
WHEN IS CHILDHOOD BEHAVIOR A SIGN OF A PROBLEM?

For each of the following descriptions, imagine that the child involved is 10 years old and lives in your hometown. Rate each behavior from 1 to 5, with 1 indicating no behavior problem and 5 indicating a definite problem.

Behavior	*No Problem*				*Definite Problem*

1. The child stays up until 10:30 P.M. watching PG-13-rated video rentals on school nights.

   1 2 3 4 5

   Suppose the child was 14 years old. How, if at all, would your rating change?

2. The child sometimes goes into stores in the mall and shoplifts shirts, jewelry, or other items.

   1 2 3 4 5

   Suppose the child was 14 years old. How, if at all, would your rating change?

3. The child spends the summertime sitting alone in his or her room reading books rather than playing outside or interacting with other children.

   1 2 3 4 5

   Suppose the child was 14 years old. How, if at all, would your rating change?

4. The child is so nervous before taking a test in school that he or she gets only three hours of sleep the night before and throws up after breakfast.

   1 2 3 4 5

   Suppose the child was 14 years old. How, if at all, would your rating change?

5. During a party thrown by adults, the child sneaks three or four drinks of beer.

   1 2 3 4 5

   Suppose the child was 14 years old. How, if at all, would your rating change?

6. Whenever the child's parents want to go out for the evening, the child begs the parents to stay.

   1 2 3 4 5

   Suppose the child was 14 years old. How, if at all, would your rating change?

7. Afraid of being embarrassed by the teacher, the child fakes being ill in order to stay home from school.

   1 2 3 4 5

   Suppose the child was 14 years old. How, if at all, would your rating change?

8. Whenever a parent asks the child to help with household chores, the child screams and refuses.

   1 2 3 4 5

   Suppose the child was 14 years old. How, if at all, would your rating change?

Copyright © Houghton Mifflin Company. All rights reserved.

SELECTED READINGS

Dodge, K. A. (1993). Social-cognitive mechanisms in the development of conduct disorder and depression. *Annual Review of Psychology, 44,* 559–584.

Kazdin, A. E. (1990). Psychotherapy for children and adolescents. *Annual Review of Psychology, 41,* 21–54.

Meisels, S. J., & Shonkoff, J. P. (Eds.) (1990). *Handbook of early childhood interventions.* New York: Cambridge University Press.

Quay, H. C., Routh, D. K., & Shapiro, S. K. (1988). Psychopathology of childhood: From description to validation. *Annual Review of Psychology, 38,* 491–532.

Sattler, D., Shabatay, V.,& Kramer, G. (1998). *Abnormal psychology in context: Voices and perspectives.* Boston, MA: Houghton Mifflin Company. Chapter 12, Disorders of Childhood and Adolescence, Mental Retardation, and Eating Disorders.

Clipson, C., &Steer, J. (1998). *Case studies in abnormal psychology.* Boston, MA: Houghton Mifflin Company. Chapter 14, Attention-Deficit Hyperactivity Disorder: All Wound Up and Out of Control.

Christophersen, E. R., & Mortweet, S. L. (2001). *Treatments that work with children.* Washington, DC: American Psychological Association.

VIDEO RESOURCES

Behavior Modification: Teaching Language to Psychotic Children (16 mm, color, 43 min). This classic film shows the self-destructive behavior of psychotic children and how contingent punishment can suppress it. The step-by-step operant conditioning methods developed by Ivar Lovaas to increase attending behavior and vocalization and to teach the functional use of speech are illustrated. Prentice-Hall Media, Inc., 150 White Plains Road, Tarrytown, NY 10591.

A Boy Named Terry Egan (16 mm, color, 53 min). The case study of a nine-year-old autistic boy who progresses in language use and social interaction through the efforts of his parents, doctor, and teachers. Interviews with parents illustrate the doubts, confusion, and guilt of parents who wonder how their child could have such desperate problems. Carousel Films, 1501 Broadway, New York, NY 10036.

Chrysalis '86 (video, color, 32 min). This video follows the process of a therapy group of adolescent girls at a summer residential camp for disturbed children. The focus is on three girls with problems ranging from cerebral palsy to depression following years of sexual abuse. It shows how an intensive group experience helps change behavior and self-perception. Penn State Audio-Visual Services, Special Services Building, University Park, PA 16802.

Edge of Awareness (16 mm, 27 min). This film illustrates procedures that can help autistic children develop greater awareness of other people and open the door for greater communication. Cognitive Development Designs, Inc., 25 Huntington Avenue, Boston, MA 02116.

Genetic Defects: The Broken Code (16 mm, 87 min). This film shows how genetic diseases are passed on to future generations and discusses genetic counseling and the moral questions this counseling raises. Indiana University, Audio Visual Center, Bloomington, IN 47401.

Copyright © Houghton Mifflin Company. All rights reserved.

Harry: Behavioral Treatment of Self-Abuse (16 mm, 38 min). This award-winning documentary film illustrates behavioral techniques used in helping a year old develop self-control skills. Research Press, Box 317740, Champaign, IL 61820.

Headbangers (16 mm, color, 30 min). This film unflinchingly examines the self-destructive behavior of severely retarded individuals and treatment programs to protect them from themselves. The persistent, cooperative efforts of the staff and the therapist are viewed as the primary treatment mode. U.S. National Audio-Visual Center, Audiovisual Archives Division National Archives and Records Service, 7th and Pennsylvania, NW, Washington, DC 20408.

Hyperactive Child (16 mm, color, 14 min). Part of a CBS news report on the symptoms of attention deficit hyperactivity disorder, its effects on parents and teachers, and the use of drug therapy. The Feingold diet is also discussed. Carousel Films, Inc., 1501 Broadway, New York, NY 10036.

Behavior Disorders of Childhood (VHS, color, 60 mm.). Explores the DSM-IV disorders first found in childhood. Annenberg/CPB. 1-800-LEARNFR.

Secret Shame: Bullied to Death (VHS, color, 28 mm.). Looks at how aggressive bullies embarrass and torment other children. Films for the Humanities and Sciences. 1-800-257-5126

Teen and Child Depression (VHS, color, 19 mm.). Looks at depression and bipolar disorders in children and adolescents. Films for the Humanities and Sciences. 1-800-257-5126.

Childhood Depression (VHS, 28 min) This program discusses the prevalence of depression, especially among adolescent girls, and emphasizes the importance of early diagnosis and treatment.

Silence of the Heart is an excellent, moving movie (now on video) starring a young Charlie Sheen and Chad Lowe dealing with issues of suicide and its effects on family and friends; delves into copycat suicides. Check it out on Amazon.com.

ON THE INTERNET

http://www.chadd.org/ is the web page of Children and Adults with Attention Deficit Disorder (CHADD).

http://www.autism-society.org is the web site for the Autism Society of America

http://www.bedwetting.ferring.ca is a web site sponsored by Ferring Pharmaceuticals, a Canadian company that produces DDAVP (desmopressin), a drug used to treat enuresis

http://www2.health-center.com/mentalhealth provides a link to ADHD where you can learn more about Attention Deficit Hyperactivity Disorder, a problem usually diagnosed in children but that can last throughout adolescence into adulthood

http://www2.health-center.com/pharmacy to check out the types of medication prescribed for ADHD

http://www.medicine.uiowa.edu/uhs/enco.cfm is the University of Iowa's Health Care Center for Disabilities and Development, which offers information about the causes and treatment of encopresis

http://www.wetbuster.com a site for parents and children (as well as adults with enuresis) who experience problems with bedwetting

Copyright © Houghton Mifflin Company. All rights reserved.

CHAPTER 16
Eating Disorders

CHAPTER OUTLINE

I. Eating Disorders

   A. Prevelance:

      1. 13.4 percent of girls and 7.1 percent of boys have engaged in disordered eating patterns

      2. More than 5 million Americans have eating disorders, characterized by physically and/or psychologically harmful eating patterns

      3. 15 percent of young women having "substantially disordered" eating attitudes and behaviors

   B. Anorexia nervosa: refusal to maintain a body weight above the minimum normal weight for one's age and height; an intense fear of becoming obese that does not diminish with weight loss; body image distortion; and (in females) the absence of at least three consecutive menstrual cycles otherwise expected to occur.

      1. Prevalence

         a. ranges from 0.5 to 1 percent of females

         b. peak years: 15 to 19

         c. increase in early onset (ages 8 to 13)

      2. Subtypes:

         a. restricting type loses weight through dieting or exercising;

         b. binge-eating/purging type loses weight through self-induced vomiting, laxatives, or diuretics.

      3. Physical complications: cardiac arrhythmias, low blood pressure, lethargy, and irreversible osteoporosis

      4. Associated characteristics: obsessive-compulsive behaviors and certain personality characteristics

      5. Course and outcome

         a. approximately 44 to 50 percent of individuals treated for anorexia recover completely

         b. mortality rate primarily from cardiac arrest or suicide ranges from 5 to 20 percent

   C. Bulimia nervosa: recurrent episodes of binge eating high caloric foods at least twice a week for three months, during which the person loses control over eating.

      1. Differs from binge-eating/purging anorexia: for anorexia, weight is under minimally expected levels

      2. Subtypes

         a. purging type: individual regularly vomits or uses laxatives, diuretics, or enemas

         b. nonpurging type: excessive exercise or fasting are used to compensate for binges.

Copyright © Houghton Mifflin Company. All rights reserved

3.   Prevalence rate is 3 percent of women in the United States; few males exhibit the disorder.

4.   Physical complications: erosion of tooth enamel, dehydration, swollen parotid glands, and lowered potassium, which can weaken the heart and cause arrhythmia and cardiac arrest

5.   Associated features

    a.   comorbid mood disorders are common

    b.   characteristics of borderline personality.

6.   Course and outcome

    a.   onset generally later than for anorexia (late adolescence or early adulthood)

    b.   follow-up studies tend to find almost 70 to 75 percent remission

D.   Binge-eating disorder (BED): a diagnostic category "provided for further study" in DSM-IV-TR; consumption of large amounts of food over a short period of time, accompanying feeling of loss of control, and marked distress over the binges; lacks the compensatory behaviors of bulimia (e.g., vomiting).

1.   Prevalence

    a.   one and one-half times more likely for females than males

    b.   range estimated at from 0.5 to 5 percent

    c.   African American women are as likely as European American women to have the disorder, but have fewer attitudinal concerns

    d.   prevalence rates for American Indian women are as high as 10 percent

2.   Associated characteristics: comorbid features include major depression, obsessive-compulsive personality disorder, and avoidant personality disorder.

3.   Course and outcome

    a.   onset typically late adolescence or early adulthood

    b.   most individuals make a full recovery even without treatment, but weight is likely to remain high

E.   Eating disorder not otherwise specified: DSM-IV-TR includes the category for those that do not meet all the criteria for anorexia or bulimia nervosa.

II.   Etiology of eating disorders

A.   Determined by social, gender, psychological, familial, cultural, and biological factors.

B.   Societal influences: social desirability of thinness in women in western culture

C.   Family and peer influences

1.   Family influences:

    a.   family interactions characterized by parental control, emotional enmeshment, and conflicts and tensions not openly expressed

    b.   maternal over-protectiveness, parental rejection

    c.   these findings problematic: case studies, and may be reaction to eating problem, not its cause

2.   Peers or family members criticize weight, encourage dieting, glorify ultra-slim models

3.   Peer relationships can serve as buffer to eating disorders or produce pressure to lose weight

D.   Cultural factors

1.   Culture-bound syndrome

2.   Eating disorders are rare in Asia

Copyright © Houghton Mifflin Company. All rights reserved.

3. African Americans ignore white media messages equating thinness with beauty, more likely than white American women to be satisfied with their body shape and to feel that beauty stems from personality not thinness

4. White women in their twenties have especially high standards of thinness

E. Other suggested etiological factors in eating disorders

1. Poor self-esteem, depression, and feelings of helplessness

2. Anorexics are often described as perfectionistic, obedient, good students, excellent athletes, and model children; emphasis on weight allows them to have control over an aspect of their lives.

3. Sexual abuse may be indirectly related to eating disorders

F. Genetic influences: concordance rates were 22.9 for MZ twins and 8.7 percent for DZ twins for bulimia

III. Treatment of eating disorders

A. Prevention programs in schools: aimed at reducing the incidence of eating disorders and disordered eating patterns.

B. Anorexia nervosa

1. Focus on weight gain (by feeding tube, contingent reinforcement for weight gain, or both

2. Cognitive-behavioral and family therapy sessions common after weight gain, but relapse and continued obsession with weight are common.

C. Bulimia nervosa

1. Initially assessed for conditions that may have resulted from purging, including cardiac and gastrointestinal problems.

2. Treatment: psychotherapy, cognitive-behavioral treatment, and antidepressant medications

3. Combination of cognitive-behavioral therapy and medications most effective

4. Even with treatment, only about 50 percent recover fully

5. Treatments for anorexia and bulimia involve interdisciplinary teams that include physicians and psychotherapists

D. Binge-eating disorder

1. Similar to those for bulimia, including weight reduction strategies

2. Fewer physical complications for BED

3. Cognitive therapy: clients identify impact of societal messages regarding thinness, encourage development of healthier goals and values, develop normal eating patterns, a more positive body image, and healthier ways to deal with stress learning objectives

LEARNING OBJECTIVES

1. Describe the prevalence and characteristics of eating disorders. (pp. 523-526.

2. Discuss the symptoms and subtypes of anorexia nervosa. (pp. 526-528)

3. Consider the physical complications that can arise from anorexia nervosa and why it is difficult to overcome. (pp. 528-529; Mental Health & Society)

4. Delineate other characteristics and mental disorders that are associated with anorexia nervosa. (pp. 529-530)

5. Describe the course and outcome of anorexia nervosa. (p. 530)

Copyright © Houghton Mifflin Company. All rights reserved.

6. Discuss the characteristics of bulimia nervosa, as well as its physical complications, associated features, and course and outcome. (pp. 530-532)

7. Discuss the characteristics of binge-eating disorder, as well as its associated features, and course and outcome; briefly describe the eating disorders not otherwise specified that are categorized in DSM-IV-TR. (pp. 532-534)

8. Describe the risk factors for and etiology of eating disorders and evaluate the degree to which society creates eating disorders. (pp. 534-543)

9. Compare the attitudes toward weight of European American and African American females. (pp. 540-542)

10. Compare the treatments for anorexia nervosa, bulimia nervosa, and binge-eating disorder. (pp. 543-546)

CLASSROOM TOPICS FOR LECTURE AND DISCUSSION

1.   A major irony of anorexia nervosa and bulimia nervosa are that they occur in times and places of relative affluence (consider the "vomitoria" of ancient Rome where wealthy Romans would go to purge after binging on lavish feasts). Such a pattern would logically suggest that these eating disorders are socially and culturally influenced. However, research on rats suggests that two hormones influence appetite. A team of investigators at the Howard Hughes Medical Institute and the University of Texas Southwestern Medical Center isolated the hormones, which they call orexin A and orexin B (orexis eans "appetite" in Greek). Although the researchers aren't sure that these hormones act the same way in humans as they do in rats, they are exploring how orexins interact with other appetite-related hormones in an attempt to develop treatments both to increase hunger in anorexics and to reduce cravings in binge-eaters and the obese.

Leutwyler, K. (1998, March 2). Treating eating disorders. Scientific American.

Internet site: http://www.sciam.com/explorations/1998/030298eating/index.html for a copy of this Scientific American article.

2.   What happens when you encounter a friend or relative who clearly has a problem, such as an eating disorder, and clearly doesn't want to talk about it? Do you back off? Do you push ahead and offer advice? Do you offer to listen and wait for the person to come to you for help? How would you feel if you "just waited" and the person died? Anorexia and bulimia are difficult disorders to deal with, even for professionals; typically waiting it out is not an option, while insisting that the person get help is likely to result in withdrawal. You're stuck between that proverbial "rock and a hard place."

The National Association of Anorexia Nervosa and Associated Disorders provides some guidelines on how to confront someone with anorexia or bulimia, which they call:

The Plan: "CONFRONT"

Concern The reason you are doing the confronting. You care about the mental, physical, and nutritional needs of the person.

Organize Decide WHO is involved, WHERE to confront, WHY concern, HOW to talk, WHEN is a convenient time.

Face The actual confrontation. Be empathetic, but direct. Do not back down if the problem is initially denied.

Respond By listening carefully.

Copyright © Houghton Mifflin Company. All rights reserved.

Offer Help and suggestions. You may want to encourage the person to contact you when there is the need to talk to someone.

Negotiate Another time to talk and a time span to seek professional help.

Time Remember to stress that recovery takes time and patience. However, there is a lot to gain by the process and a lot to lose if the choice is made to continue the existing behaviors.

What type of response would you expect with this plan? What factors would be relevant in terms of how effective this might be? What plan could you come up with?

Internet Site: http://www.anad.org/confront.htm is the web site for ANAD National Association of Anorexia Nervosa and Associated Disorders

3.   Chapter 18 discusses legal and ethical issues involved in providing therapy to persons who do not want to accept treatment. This is a critical issue for someone with anorexia nervosa (and often bulimia nervosa) when the individual's life may be threatened by the disease. As discussed in the chapter, the first step in treating anorexia is weight gain, and often this means use of a feeding tube to force feed the patient. The insidious nature of anorexia creates strong resistance to weight gain and all strategies to promote weight gain, even in the face of permanent, lifelong physical ailments and even death.

Considering this dilemma (and perhaps jumping ahead to Chapter 18 to look at the issues involved in a patient's right to refuse treatment), do you believe that someone has the right to refuse force feeding? What issues are involved? How would you go about dealing with a situation like this? If you were the anorexic patient, how would you react? If you were that patient's parent, what would you do? What role do you believe a physician or therapist should play? What other options might be available?

CLASSROOM DEMONSTRATIONS & HANDOUTS

1.   One of the major influences on body image in the U.S. and other western nations are the media, particularly television and movies, but also magazines, music videos, and various forms of advertising. In small groups, have students put together presentations that demonstrate the effect of the media on body image and eating disorders, then have them present a plan to counteract these powerful forces. After completing the presentations, the class as a whole, could design an intervention to present to junior high school and high school classes to educate students about the problem and prevention.

2.   Have your students develop and administer a weight satisfaction survey in which they collect data from males and females ranging in age from preteen to early adulthood, from different ethnic/cultural groups. Referring to information in the text, they should include questions concerning respondents' views of "ideal weight for males," "ideal weight for females," respondents' self-perceptions concerning their own weight, body image, how they feel about themselves when looking in the mirror at their faces and in the nude, what they consider to be their "best" feature and their "worst" feature, how they feel about themselves in comparison to others (and whether/how often they compare themselves with others), and other questions that seem relevant.

Responses from the entire class can be analyzed statistically and compared with research presented in the text. The results of the survey and data analysis can be used to develop presentations for local schools and other community organizations.

Copyright © Houghton Mifflin Company. All rights reserved.

3.   Eating disorders are always a topic of strong interest and concern. A large-scale (N = 3,175) survey of middle-school children found that more than 40 percent reported feeling fat and wishing to lose weight. Among girls, whose average age was 12, 43 percent had dieted, 11 percent had fasted, and 6 percent had made themselves vomit to lose weight (Childress et al., 1993).

Restrained eating (Herman & Polivy, 1975) is an associated concept. It involves a tendency to restrain oneself from eating for fear of gaining weight. People with clinical eating disorders and "normal" people can be restrained eaters. They diet frequently and, when feeling susceptible to stress or negative emotions, binge rather than eat normally. The 10-item Eating Restraint Scale is presented as a handout. Scoring instructions are on the handout. A high score (14 points or more) indicates a tendency to restrain eating. Let students know that the Eating Restraint Scale is not a clinical indicator. It is useful in helping students look at their attitudes and behaviors relevant to eating, but many other sources of information are needed before concluding that high scorers have a problem. Students may approach you for additional information. If a student become distressed about his or her eating patterns, you should make a referral to your school's counseling center.

Sources: Childress, A. C., Brewerton, T. D., Hodges, E. L., & Jarrell, M. P. (1993). The kid's eating disorders survey (KEDS): A study of middle school students. *Journal of the American Academy of Child and Adolescent Psychiatry, 32,* 843–850.

Eating Restraint Scale from "Anxiety, Restraint, and Eating Behavior" by C. P. Herman, & J. Polivy, *Journal of Abnormal Psychology, 84,* pp. 666–672. Copyright © 1975 by the American Psychological Association. Reprinted with permission from the American Psychological Association and the author.

Internet Site: http://www.health-center.com/mentalhealth   This site discusses the major categories of eating disorders.

Copyright © Houghton Mifflin Company. All rights reserved.

HANDOUT FOR DEMONSTRATION 3:
EATING RESTRAINT SCALE

Circle one response for each item.

Item		*Scoring*
	(Points)	

1. How often are you dieting?

Never	0
Rarely	1
Sometimes	2
Often	3
Always	4

2. What is the maximum amount of weight (in pounds) that you have ever lost within one month?

0 to 4 pounds	0
5 to 9 pounds	1
10 to 14 pounds	2
15 to 19 pounds	3
20 pounds or more	4

3. What is your maximum weight gain within a week?

0 to 1 pounds	0
1.1 to 2.0 pounds	1
2.1 to 3.0 pounds	2
3.1 to 5.0 pounds	3
5.1 pounds or more	4

4. In a typical week, how much does your weight fluctuate?

0 to 1 pounds	0
1.1 to 2.0 pounds	1
2.1 to 3.0 pounds	2
3.1 to 5.0 pounds	3
5.1 pounds or more	4

5. Would a weight fluctuation of five pounds affect the way you live your life?

Not at all	0
Slightly	1
Moderately	2
Very much	3

6. Do you eat sensibly in front of others and splurge alone?

Never	0
Rarely	1
Often	2
Always	3

Copyright © Houghton Mifflin Company. All rights reserved.

7. Do you give too much time and thought to food?

Never	0
Rarely	1
Often	2
Always	3

8. Do you have feelings of guilt after overeating?

Never	0
Rarely	1
Often	2
Always	3

9. How conscious are you of what you are eating?

Not at all	0
Slightly	1
Moderately	2
Extremely	3

10. How many pounds over your desired weight were you at your maximum weight?

0 to 1 pounds	0
2 to 5 pounds	1
6 to 10 pounds	2
11 to 20 pounds	3
21 pounds or more	4

Scoring instructions. Add your total points: If your total score is 14 or more points, you have a tendency to be a restrained eater.

From "Anxiety, Restraint, and Eating Behavior" by C. P. Herman & J. Polivy, *Journal of Abnormal Psychology, 84*, pp. 666–672. Copyright 1975 by the American Psychological Association. Reprinted with permission from the American Psychological Association and the author.

Copyright © Houghton Mifflin Company. All rights reserved.

SELECTED READINGS

Clipson, C., & Steer, J. (1998) *Case studies in abnormal psychology*. Boston, MA: Houghton Mifflin Company. Chapter 15, Bulimia Nervosa: The Self-Destructive Diet..

Hall, L., & Ostroff, M. (1998). *Anorexia nervosa: A guide to recovery*. Gurze Designs & Books.

Kazdin, A. E. (1990). Psychotherapy for children and adolescents. *Annual Review of Psychology, 41*, 21–54.

Meisels, S. J., & Shonkoff, J. P. (Eds.) (1990). *Handbook of early childhood interventions*. New York: Cambridge University Press.

Porter, T. (2002). *A dance of sisters*. Joanna Cotler Books.

Sattler, D., Shabatay, V.,& Kramer, G. (1998). *Abnormal psychology in context: Voices and perspectives*. Boston, MA: Houghton Mifflin Company. Chapter 12, Disorders of Childhood and Adolescence, Mental Retardation, and Eating Disorders.

VIDEO RESOURCES

Diet unto Death: Anorexia Nervosa (VHS, color, 50 min). This documentary shows interviews with four anorexic adolescent girls who describe their self-starvation and their attempts to overcome their obsession with thinness. MTI Teleprograms, 3710 Commercial Avenue, Northbrook, IL 60062.

Dying to Be Thin (VHS, color, 28 mm.). Provides information about anorexia and follows a young women as she battles anorexia. Films for the Humanities and Sciences. 1-800-257-5126

Eating Disorders (VHS, 15 min) Explains anorexia nervosa and bulimia nervosa through the eyes of two women suffering from these eating disorders and an expert who discusses treatment. Shows the devastating effect on the women and their families. Films for the Humanities & Sciences, P.O. Box 2053, Princeton, NJ 08543-2053. 1-800-257-5126.

Media Impact (VHS, 28 min) Looks at the seductive nature of visual media that constantly impact us, whether actual reality or manufactured reality, and how the media popularize unhealthy or antisocial behaviors. Films for the Humanities & Sciences, P.O. Box 2053, Princeton, NJ 08543-2053. 1-800-257-5126.

ON THE INTERNET

http://nationaleatingdisorders.org is the web site for the National Eating Disorders Association, which among other things offers advice on "listening to your body" and links to other resources

http://www.apa.org is the web site for the American Psychological Association, where a search can be performed for the various eating disorders

Copyright © Houghton Mifflin Company. All rights reserved.

http://www.edauk.com is the web site for the Eating Disorders Association (EDA) in the United Kingdom; it presents a great deal of information as well as how to get help and poetry written by young people with eating disorders

http://www.mentalhealth.org is the web site for The Center for Mental Health Services; this site, which is under the United States Department of Health and Human Services, offers a variety of resources, including search capability to learn about eating disorders

http://www.raderprograms.com overtureindex.htm discusses the eating disorders presented in the text, as well as other related issues and solutions (the site is sponsored by Rader Programs, which specializes in treating eating disorders)

http://www2.health-center.com mental health and link to eating disorders

Copyright © Houghton Mifflin Company. All rights reserved.

CHAPTER 17
Psychotherapeutic Interventions

CHAPTER OUTLINE

I. Biology-based treatment techniques

  A. Electroconvulsive therapy

    1. History: first use of shock was insulin shock; Meduna (1930s) believed that schizophrenia could be reduced through seizures; Cerletti and Bini (1938) introduced ECT

    2. Procedure: 65 to 140 volts for 0.1 to 0.5 seconds, now applied to one hemisphere

    3. Effective with depression; may alter cortisol levels; concern over side effects; drugs used instead

  B. Psychosurgery: brain surgery performed to correct severe mental disorder

    1. Moniz (1930s): destroying certain brain connections (particularly in frontal lobes) could disrupt psychotic thought patterns and behaviors

    2. Procedures include prefrontal and transorbital lobotomy, lobectomy (removal of portions of frontal lobe), electrical cauterization; videolaserscopy operates on extremely small areas

    3. Scientific and ethical objections; abandoned except for tumors; drugs used instead

  C. Psychopharmacology: study of drug effects on mind and behavior

    1. Antianxiety drugs (minor tranquilizers)

      a. Barbiturates: serious side effects, addiction

      b. Meprobamate (Propanediol) and benzodiazepines (Librium, Valium): block synaptic transmission; safer, but still cause addiction, overreliance

    2. Antipsychotic drugs (major tranquilizers)

      a. Chlorpromazine (Thorazine) and other drugs reduce schizophrenic symptoms, increase interactions

      b. Drugs allow release of thousands of chronic patients

      c. Concern about side effects (Parkinson-like symptoms, sensitivity to light, dry mouth, tardive dyskinesia—involuntary movements of mouth, tongue, extremities)

    3. Antidepressants

      a. Monoamine oxidase (MAO) inhibitors

      b. Tricyclics

      c. SSRIs; Fluoxetine (Prozac), Paxil (Paroxetine), and Zoloft (Sertraine)

    4. Antimanic drugs (for bipolar disorder)

      a. Lithium effective but has limitations—only preventative, toxic dosage must be monitored

Copyright © Houghton Mifflin Company. All rights reserved

5.　Psychopharmacological considerations

　　a.　Specific drugs for specific subtypes of disorder and individuals

　　b.　Reduce symptoms but do not cure, do not teach skills

　　c.　Controls people

II.　Psychotherapy

　A.　Definition: systematic application of techniques derived from psychological principles by professionals for purpose of aiding psychologically troubled people

　B.　Many variations but four common characteristics

　　1.　Opportunity for relearning

　　2.　Development of new, emotionally important experiences

　　3.　Provides a therapeutic relationship

　　4.　Clients have motivations and expectations, anxiety and hope

　C.　Mental health services can be made culturally appropriate for ethnic minorities

III.　Insight-oriented approaches to individual psychotherapy

　A.　Psychoanalysis: uncovering repressed material to achieve insight; inappropriate for children and for nonverbal and schizoid adults

　　1.　Free association and dream analysis: manifest and latent content

　　2.　Analysis of resistance

　　3.　Transference; avoid countertransference

　　4.　Interpretation

　　5.　Modern psychodynamic therapy: loosened therapeutic techniques

　　6.　Effectiveness of psychoanalysis

　　　a.　Impossibility of operational definitions makes confirmation difficult

　　　b.　Questions about symptom substitution in nonanalytic therapies

　　　c.　Declining use in future is predicted

　B.　Humanistic–existential therapies: focus on qualities of "humanness"

　　1.　Person-centered therapy (Rogers): acceptance, empathy, unconditional positive regard; emphasis on relationship

　　2.　Existential analysis: philosophical encounter; case studies but little empirical support for effectiveness

　　3.　Gestalt therapy (Perls): totality of here-and-now, exaggeration of feelings, dream analysis

IV.　Action-oriented approaches to individual psychotherapy

　A.　Classical conditioning techniques

　　1.　Systematic desensitization (Wolpe): anxiety reduction through relaxation paired with steps in anxiety hierarchy; highly effective

　　2.　Flooding and implosion: anxiety induced and then extinguished in real life (flooding) or imagination (implosion)

　　　a.　Developers claim they are effective

　　　b.　Some clients find procedures traumatic

　　3.　Aversive conditioning: undesirable behavior (such as smoking or alcohol use) paired with noxious stimulus

　　　a.　Rapid smoking produces nausea and avoidance

Copyright © Houghton Mifflin Company. All rights reserved.

      b. Covert sensitization (imagined disgusting scenes associated with unwanted behavior)

  B. Operant conditioning techniques

    1. Token economies: tokens for desirable behavior exchanged for reinforcers; used in institutional settings

    2. Punishment: suppresses self-destructive behavior

      a. Electric shock to suppress self-destructive behavior

      b. Ethical issues led to decline in use

  C. Observational learning techniques (modeling)

  D. Cognitive-behavioral therapy: change irrational thoughts, teach coping skills and problem-solving techniques

    1. Rational-emotive therapy (Ellis): confront irrational beliefs

    2. Beck's cognitive-behavioral therapy: gradual assessment of validity of client's assumptions

    3. Meichenbaum's stress inoculation therapy

    4. Effectiveness: better than drugs for certain depressions

  E. Health psychology: goal of changing lifestyles to prevent illness or to enhance quality of life

    1. Biofeedback: information about autonomic functions and reward for changing functions in desired direction

    2. Relationship between Type A and heart disease

    3. General strategies

      a. Establish priorities

      b. Avoid stressful situations

      c. Take time out for yourself

      d. Exercise regularly

      e. Eat right

      f. Make friends

      g. Learn to relax

V. Evaluating individual psychotherapy

  A. Controversies between action-oriented and insight-oriented therapists

    1. Recent survey suggests movement toward integration and cognitive, away from psychoanalysis and transactional analysis

  B. Eysenck's criticisms of psychotherapy

    1. Therapy ineffective

    2. Methodological flaws invalidate claim

    3. Do outcome studies accurately reflect psychotherapy? Persons (1991): outcome studies do not represent current models of psychotherapy; theory-based assessment of clients not done; in actual therapy, assessment and treatment are inseparable; studies have standardized treatment but real treatment is individualized

  C. Meta-analysis and effect size (large number of studies analyzed by looking at effect size? treatment-produced change)

    1. Meta-analysis is controversial? it has supporters and detractors

    2. 79 percent of those in treatment better off than those untreated; largest gains in first few months

Copyright © Houghton Mifflin Company. All rights reserved.

3. Empirically supported treatments (ESTs) specify psychological treatments shown to be efficacious in controlled research with specific populations and demonstrate that they benefit clients

   a. cognitive-behavioral treatment for anxiety and depression

   b. interpersonal therapy for depression and bulimia

   c. behavioral therapy for sexual dysfunctions

   d. other therapies may be effective, but have not been rigorously studied

D. Important characteristics of therapists and therapies

  1. Demographic characteristics, e.g., age, gender, ethnicity

  2. Overall reputation

  3. Experience with clients who have similar problems

  4. Therapeutic orientation

  5. Interpersonal style

  6. Values and beliefs

VI. Group, family, and couples therapy

A. Group therapy

  1. Wide range of formats, theoretical perspectives, purposes

  2. Commonalities of group therapy

   a. Social situation

   b. Interpersonal response in real-life context

   c. Develop new communication and social skills

   d. Reduce isolation and fear

   e. Provide strong social support

  3. Little substantial research on effectiveness

  4. Disadvantages: lack of individual attention; group pressures

B. Family therapy

  1. Assumptions

   a. Economical and logical to see family

   b. "Identified patient" only shows family's symptoms

   c. Therapist should modify relationships

  2. Communications approach (Satir, Haley)

   a. Identify present patterns

   b. Work for changes in communication

  3. Systems approach (Minuchin)

   a. Emphasis on interlocking roles, including "sick role"

   b. Create flexible roles to foster positive relationships

C. Couples therapy

  1. Normal for conflicts to develop

  2. Clarify and improve communications and role relationships

  3. Not designed to save the marriage

VII. Systemic integration and eclecticism

Copyright © Houghton Mifflin Company. All rights reserved.

    A. Therapeutic eclecticism: process of selecting concepts, methods, and strategies from a variety of current theories that work

        1. Lazarus' early "technical eclecticism" has been modified into multimodal behavior therapy, which is behavioral in basis but embraces cognitive and affective concepts also

        2. Openness and flexibility; but can encourage indiscriminate, haphazard, inconsistent use of therapeutic techniques and concepts

    B. Goal to find therapies that work best with specific clients who have specific problems under specific conditions

VIII. Culturally diverse populations and psychotherapy

    A. Western psychology and mental health concepts characterized by assumption that they are universal, that human condition is governed by universal principles, and members of groups that don't fit those standards are deficient

        1. Surgeon General's Report on Mental Health: using European American standards to judge normality and abnormality is fraught with dangers, may result in denying appropriate treatment to minority groups, may oppress culturally different clients, it is important to recognize and respond to cultural concerns of other groups

        2. Few studies exist on empirically supported treatments with minority populations

    B. Guidelines are suggested for working with particular groups, but they should not be adhered to rigidly.

        1. African-Americans: bring up issue of racial differences between the client and the white therapist; to try to understand client's worldview; see client's suspiciousness/reluctance to self-disclose as a survival mechanism; assess client's positive assets; problem-solving approaches are useful for external problems.

        2. Asian Americans and Pacific Islanders: be aware of potential social stigma of seeing a therapist; psychological conflicts may be expressed via somatic complaints and/or other socially acceptable issues; reluctance to self-disclose/ express feelings may be due to cultural factors, not psychopathology; explain purpose, expectations, and process of therapy, and use action-oriented, problem-solving approach.

        3. Latino or Hispanic Americans: engage client in a warm, respectful manner while maintaining a formal persona; linguistic misunderstandings are possible; discuss therapy goals; watch for misinterpretations, e.g., differences in body language; consider client's positive assets and resources, including the nuclear and extended family.

        4. Native Americans: patience is important; basic needs should be addressed first; client's communal environment is important; sensitivity to differences in communication styles, especially body language; consider consulting with indigenous healers.

IX. Community psychology

    A. Managed health care: reforms needed to make care accessible and affordable

        1. Changes: shift to HMOs, short-term treatment, reliance on master's (less expensive) level providers, increased accountability, and quality assurance

        2. Criticisms: reduce costs and reduce quality

        3. American Psychological Association endorses principle of properly trained psychologists prescribing medication

        4. Use of treatment manuals to make care more systematic

        5. Increased use of computer programs to provide psychotherapy to clients

    B. Prevention of psychopathology

        1. Primary prevention: reduce the number of new cases of disorders

           a. Head Start is one example

Copyright © Houghton Mifflin Company. All rights reserved.

      b.   Munoz and colleagues (1995) report communitywide effort to prevent depression

      c.   Interventions to prevent juvenile delinquency

  2. Secondary prevention: shorten duration of mental disorders, but problems exist

      a.   traditional diagnostic methods are often unreliable, provide little insight into which treatment procedures to use; more specialized diagnostic techniques are needed

      b.   once detected, it may be difficult to decide what therapy is most effective for the specific disorder and patient

      c.   prompt treatment often unavailable

  3. Tertiary prevention: facilitate readjustment to community life of people hospitalized for mental disorders

LEARNING OBJECTIVES

1. Discuss the various biological therapies, including electroconvulsive therapy (ECT) and psychosurgery, and their use and effectiveness in treating mental disorders. (pp. 549-551)

2. Define psychopharmacology. Describe and evaluate the use of antianxiety, antipsychotic, antidepressant, and antimanic medications. (pp. 551-555)

3. Define psychotherapy and describe its basic characteristics. Discuss why traditional psychotherapy may not be effective with individuals from non-Western cultures and ethnic minority groups. (pp. 555-556)

4. Describe the goals and techniques of psychoanalysis and post-Freudian psychoanalytic therapy. Evaluate the effectiveness of psychoanalytic therapy. (pp. 556-559)

5. Describe the therapies based on the humanistic/existential perspective, including person-centered therapy, existential analysis, and gestalt therapy. (pp. 559-560)

6. Describe the therapeutic techniques based on classical conditioning, including systematic desensitization, flooding and implosion, and aversive conditioning. (pp. 560-562)

7. Describe the therapeutic techniques based on operant conditioning, including token economies and punishment. (pp. 562-563)

8. Describe observational learning techniques and cognitive-behavioral therapies. (pp. 563-564)

9. Discuss the goal of health psychology and describe the techniques used to promote lifestyle changes, including biofeedback. (pp. 564-566)

10. Discuss research on the effectiveness of individual psychotherapy. (pp. 566-569)

11. Describe the common components and types of group therapy; evaluate the effectiveness of group therapy. Describe the functions of couples and family therapy, and the different emphases of the communications and systems approaches. (pp. 569-573)

12. Evaluate the factors involved in choosing a therapist. (p. 570; Critical Thinking)

13. Discuss the movement toward systematic integration and eclecticism. (pp. 573-574)

14. Consider the issues raised with respect to culturally diverse populations and psychotherapy. (pp. 574-579)

15. Discuss the changes in mental health service delivery caused by managed health care. (pp.579-581)

16. Describe primary, secondary, and tertiary prevention and give examples of each. (pp. 581-583)

Copyright © Houghton Mifflin Company. All rights reserved.

CLASSROOM TOPICS FOR LECTURE AND DISCUSSION

1.   Family therapy usually captures the attention and interest of students. Several family therapy tactics are provocative and unique. One is the development of a family genogram. Draw on the board a three- or four-generational diagram of a hypothetical family in which one or two current family functions or traits ("alcohol-abusing black sheep" or "workaholic, distant parent") can be traced from previous generations. The genogram also clarifies the "sides of the family" issue in most marriages and the tendency for traits or problems to skip generations because children use their parents as a negative reference.

A second family therapy stratagem is paradoxical instructions. Many family theorists (for example, Jay Haley and Paul Watzlawick) suggest that two things occur when a symptom is described to a family: The family is challenged with an entirely original reappraisal of its experience, and it is influenced by the change agent. If the family accepts the therapist's suggestion, the influence of this change agent is clear, and it can be used for future interventions. If the family resists the suggestion, the family shows itself its own power and moves toward health. Either way, the therapist wins! Students will react strongly to the manipulative aspects of this strategy. You should accept concerns that acceptance of the paradoxical instruction ("Go home and beat your children; it's how you show your love") can be dangerous. However, an analogue study shows that although students find paradoxical interventions less acceptable than nonparadoxical ones, they do not negatively influence the perceptions of the therapist's expertness or trustworthiness (Betts & Remer, 1993).

Source: Betts, G. R., & Remer, R. (1993). The impact of paradoxical interventions on perceptions of the therapist and ratings of treatment acceptability. *Professional Psychology: Research and Practice, 24,* 164–170.

2.   A series of articles in *Psychological Bulletin* illustrates the difficulties in performing therapy-effectiveness research. It also shows students how researchers from different viewpoints can interpret the same information differently. Bowers and Clum (1988) performed a meta-analysis on 69 studies comparing behavior therapy with placebo and nonspecific treatment conditions to assess the value of behavior therapy for a wide range of conditions. The meta-analysis yielded an effect size (ES) relative to placebo conditions of .55, a strong indication that behavior therapy is far better than placebo. Several years later Brody, (1990) argued that the meta-analysis gave a misleading picture. Brody noted that a wide range of behavior therapies (systematic desensitization, meditation, social-skill training, and so forth) and patient problems (test anxiety, schizophrenia, anorexia, and so forth) were lumped together. Brody took the ten studies that involved "neurotic" conditions such as agoraphobia and anorexia and did a simple box-score to see if behavior therapy was more effective than placebo conditions. Brody concluded that there was no evidence for the superiority of behavior therapy. Further, Brody argued that few, if any, of the studies had long-term follow-ups. Therefore, the outcome studies and the meta-analysis on which they were based did not yield clinically significant information. Clum and Bowers (1990) agreed that longer follow-ups were needed but calculated the median ES (eliminating the chance of the mean being influenced by extreme scores) for the same ten studies. They report an ES of .63, even stronger than the average for the entire analysis of 69 studies. The same data prove both that behavior therapy is superior and is not superior to placebo treatment conditions; the result depends on the method of analysis.

Sources: Bowers, T. G., & Clum, G. A. (1988). Relative contribution of specific and nonspecific treatment effects: Meta-analysis of placebo-controlled behavior therapy research. *Psychological Bulletin, 103,* 315–323.

Brody, N. (1990). Behavior therapy versus placebo: Comment on Bowers & Clum's meta-analysis. *Psychological Bulletin, 107,* 106–109.

Copyright © Houghton Mifflin Company. All rights reserved.

Clum, G. A., & Bowers, T. G. (1990). Behavior therapy better than placebo treatments: Fact or artifact? *Psychological Bulletin, 107,* 110–113.

Internet Site: www.apa.org/journals/bul.htm. The home page for the *Psychological Bulletin.*

3.   The ethics of methodologically sound psychotherapy-effectiveness research is a good topic for discussion. Ask students to suggest an appropriate control group for a study of treated individuals. If they respond, "people who do not receive treatment," point out the possibility that people who ask for help (and get it) may be different in some outcome-relevant way from people who do not ask for help. Further, how can we be sure that untreated people do not get some other form of help (for example, read a self-help book) that might be much like therapy? These questions highlight the problem of random assignment, a key component of true experiments. A second kind of control group, the waiting-list control, includes random assignment but has its own problems. Ask students how they feel about the ethics of arbitrarily placing people in distress on a waiting list. Do the merits of the study outweigh the possible harmful effects? A third option is a pseudotherapy control group—the psychological equivalent of a placebo pill. But one wonders whether any treatment can be considered "inert." Conclude by proposing that anyone placed on a waiting list or in a pseudotreatment control group should be given free access to the treatment if it proves to be effective. However, the economics of many (most?) treatment facilities makes this proposal difficult to implement.

Internet Site: http://www.apa.org/ethics/code.html. The American Psychological Association site for ethical principles of psychologists which also defines the code of conduct.

4.   The common components of psychotherapy mentioned in the text are reasonable and accurate. Jerome Frank's view of psychotherapy—and, in fact, of all forms of healing and persuading—can be added to the discussion. Frank, in his classic book, *Persuasion and Healing,* argues that the social aspects of the therapeutic relationship overwhelm any technical or theoretical considerations. According to him, the three active ingredients in the change process are (1) a socially sanctioned healer whose powers and status are respected by the sufferer, (2) a sufferer who seeks relief from symptoms, and (3) a fairly structured set of contacts (with their own rituals) that convinces the sufferer to change his or her attitudes and behavior. Key to this last process is the sufferer's need to have mysteries explained by the healer and to feel that there is hope for improvement by relying on the expert. Ask students whether the same analysis can be applied to faith-healing evangelists or voodoo doctors.

Imagine out loud this "therapy" with your students: A charismatic person writes a book and appears on television talk shows arguing that depression and fatigue are the result of certain allergens and toxic chemicals seeping into people's bloodstreams through their clothes. The offending chemicals, this person asserts, come from polyesters and other synthetic fabrics and from modern laundry detergents. The cure is for people to throw away all their garments except for 100 percent natural cottons and wools and to wash only with "pure" soap. Given the mystery of depression and fatigue, the desperation of some, the status afforded television appearances, and the effort involved in the treatment, it is fairly likely that such a "therapy" could catch on (and be successful) with some sufferers.

5.   The most common form of community psychology activity is mental health consultation, a form of secondary prevention in which mental health professionals provide information to non–mental health professionals about a disorder, its causes, symptoms, and ways to make referrals. The professionals most often involved have frequent contact with troubled individuals but are not specifically trained to interact with them. For example, school teachers, police officers, and emergency room nurses often come in contact with distressed individuals and need to know how to best interact with them and make referrals to professionals when necessary. Ask students to think of other professions that have this kind of frequent contact with distressed individuals. Some examples are funeral directors, clergymen, general practice physicians, bartenders, hairdressers, and divorce attorneys. The consultant-consultee

Copyright © Houghton Mifflin Company. All rights reserved.

relationship is a unique one. It is a contracted arrangement in which the mental health professional listens to the consultee's difficulties and provides advice. It is not a form of therapy. The consultee is seen as just as much a professional as the consultant: the consultant never tells the consultee how to do his/her job. Neither does the consultant have direct contact with the consultee's clients. The relationship involves only indirect coaching; the consultant has no specific supervisory role.

Gerald Caplan (1970) laid out a scheme that indicates the range of mental health consultations that are possible. Three of Caplan's consultation types deserve description. The most common is case-centered, consultee consultation. In these consultations the mental health professional (MHP) works on a case-by-case basis with the consultee to assist in job-related problem solving. For example, the MHP might meet weekly with kindergarten teachers. One week, a teacher might mention the problems she has had with a boy who is suspected of having attention deficit hyperactivity disorder. Perhaps the boy is distracting other children. The consultant might provide tips on how to structure the environment to reduce the boy's impact or how to set up a reward system so he stays on task longer. Another week, the focus might be on a student who is excluded from play activities because she is intensely shy. Consultees usually feel most comfortable asking for help when the focus is on cases, not on their own difficulties.

However, Caplan notes that sometimes consultees reveal, indirectly and over time, that they have emotional blind spots that interfere with their ability to relate to clients. For instance, if one of the kindergarten teachers repeatedly described herself as losing her temper with children and storming out of the room, the focus of consultation might have to change to what Caplan calls "consultee-centered consultation." Here, the consultant helps consultees develop skills to overcome their emotional blind spots. Care must be taken not to imply that the consultee has a psychological problem because this form of consultation can come dangerously close to therapy.

A third type, called administrative consultation, focuses on the administration of a program. For instance, if a teacher wanted to establish a parent-teacher coordination program so that homework was more frequently checked and turned in, the consultant could act as a sounding board for ideas on how to approach parents, teachers, and administrators to get support for the program. Like case-centered consultations, the consultant would provide information (in this case about organizational behavior and persuasion) that would augment the consultee's professional knowledge.
These consultations can become politically complicated, especially if the program's goals or methods are at odds with others in the organization or in the wider community.

Source: Caplan, G. (1970). *The theory and practice of mental health consultation.* London: Tavistock.

CLASSROOM DEMONSTRATIONS & HANDOUTS

1.   If your training has prepared you to do so, model the style of various therapy strategies by asking a student volunteer to either think up a fictitious problem or discuss an actual, but not very significant, personal concern (for instance, trouble getting to sleep at night). Ask the volunteer to leave the classroom while you inform the rest of the class that during the first four to five minutes of the interview you will play the role of a Rogerian therapist and then, without warning, you will change roles and play an operant-conditioning-oriented therapist. The object will be to see whether the student volunteer notices that any change occurred and whether one or the other pattern of therapist behavior was preferred.

Copyright © Houghton Mifflin Company. All rights reserved.

When the student volunteer returns, spend the first four to five minutes mirroring statements of the student's feelings and thoughts (for example, "Sounds like getting to sleep frustrates you"). Then the questions should abruptly take a decidedly behavioral turn (for example, "What exactly are the circumstances that precede sleepless nights?"). After ten minutes of interviewing, ask the volunteer whether he or she noticed any shift in the therapist's behavior. Can he or she identify the therapeutic orientations? Was it easier to respond to one than to the other?

This exercise should keep student interest and illustrate the differences in therapeutic strategies as well as their impact on the client.

2.   This activity helps students see how the theoretical orientation of a psychologist guides the development of a treatment plan. The experience also gives you a chance to correct any misperceptions the students may have about the techniques used in the various treatment approaches.

The first step in this activity is for you to find some casebooks (the DSM-IV-TR casebook is excellent) or other sources from which you can take a case study illustrating a mental disorder. In order for the activity to be relevant to a range of therapeutic orientations, choose an adult, nonpsychotic condition such as an anxiety disorder, mood disorder, or form of substance abuse. Duplicate the case study for the class.

Divide the class into four groups. Each group will be responsible for one therapeutic approach: drug treatment, psychoanalytic psychotherapy, behavior therapy (you can stipulate classical conditioning, operant conditioning, or modeling or allow them to use their own judgment), and cognitive behavioral (rational emotive or Beck's cognitive) therapies. Have each group develop a treatment plan using the specific techniques of the therapeutic approach they were assigned. Also have the groups examine the potential barriers to successful treatment and their estimation that the client would be successfully treated.

Ask each group to report to the whole class the results of their discussions and list their ideas on the board. Clarify and correct as necessary. At the end of the activity, encourage students to think about integrative treatments that might use the best of each approach. Underscore the fact that most therapists approach problems with this kind of eclecticism. You might also suggest that other treatment approaches not discussed—group therapy, family therapy, humanistic-existential—might have been just as valuable.

Internet site: http://www.appi.org/dsm.html to order the DSM-IV-TR casebook from the APA (American Psychiatric Publishing, Inc.); it can also be ordered from http://www.amazon.com

3.   One way to increase student involvement in the class and the material is to have them role-play different therapies. Ask students to volunteer to be therapists. You will need at least four therapists, one each for psychoanalysis, behavior therapy, humanistic-existential therapy, and cognitive therapy. You will also need four volunteers to play clients. It is a good idea to supply the clients with guidelines on what their problems are. On the Handout for Demonstration 3 is an example of these guidelines. Having some uniformity in the problems the clients present will foster discussion of how different therapies compare and contrast.

To add to the entertainment value of this activity, assign the "therapists" to their therapeutic approach in private and tell them not to disclose what form of treatment they will be using. This way, the rest of the class can be involved in trying to guess the kind of therapy being demonstrated. Tell the therapists they should allot five minutes or so to conduct therapy. Pair up the clients and therapists randomly and have them perform one after the other before the class. After all the therapy sessions end, ask those in the audience to guess which therapist was demonstrating which form of treatment. Discuss whether the principles of each approach were adhered to and whether techniques were left out because of time constraints. Interview the clients and find out how the exercise felt for them. Participants and audience can discuss what they think would be most helpful to the client, including integrative combinations of the approaches. Finally, students will probably want to voice opinions about the therapy they would

Copyright © Houghton Mifflin Company. All rights reserved.

personally be most comfortable with. Point out that comfort and effectiveness may not come in the same therapeutic approach. Also, indicate that outcome research suggests that nontheoretical factors (the interpersonal quality of the therapist, the therapist's professional experience, or the client-therapist match) may have more to do with positive outcomes than the techniques used in treatment.

4.   Many psychoactive drugs are used to treat people with emotional and behavioral disorders. Develop a list on the board that indicates each general category of drug, when it is prescribed, the generic and brand names for the more commonly used ones, and the side effects or contraindications for each. An abbreviated example is given in the Handout for Demonstration 4. Stress that each drug has many side effects, some of which are serious but exceedingly rare. One way to illustrate this point is to bring the *Physician's Desk Reference* to class and look up the contraindications and side effects segments on several commonly used drugs, such as Mellaril or Librium. Students are often shocked at the number and variety of possible side effects.

The irresponsible prescription of psychoactive drugs is a serious concern. Note on the board that each drug is therapeutic in a range of dosages (dependent on weight, age, health status, and condition of the patient). Above this range the drug becomes toxic; below this range the drug is ineffective. A commonly suggested way of treating mental disorders biologically is to increase the drug dosage to the patient until the toxic (side effects) level is reached and then back off the dosage. The danger to the patient is that the side effects may be serious or the doctor may not be consulted for a reduction in dosage. In the case of lithium carbonate, the therapeutic range is very narrow. Only a small change in dose or diet can effect a toxic overdose. Further, some drugs are prescribed to treat the side effects of other drugs, and they themselves have side effects. Cogentin and Artane are trade names for anti-Parkinsonian drugs given when schizophrenics are on phenothiazines. But because these drugs tend to cause a drying out of tissues in patients, other drugs are given to offset this effect. Warn students that some psychiatrists go overboard when using drugs to treat behavioral and emotional problems.

Internet Site: http://www.mentalhealth.com/fr30.html. An extensive list of drugs used in the treatment of psychological disorders, including dosage, warning, effects, and side effects.

5.   Ask students to recall portrayals of psychotherapy from television and movies. Although there are relatively few television portrayals, the movies *Ordinary People*, *Prince of Tides*, and others show a dramatized version of psychoanalytic therapy. Point out that therapy is usually much less immediately helpful than is shown in the media; as in most other things, therapy is usually a process of two steps forward and one step back. Alternatively, therapy is shown to be clichéd and ineffective as in *What About Bob?*, *Nuts*, and the old Bob "Newhart Show" of the 1970s.

Only a very small sample of the psychotherapies is shown in the media. Challenge students to recall any portrayals of behavior or cognitive therapy. The only example I can recall is the damning one in the movie *A Clockwork Orange*, which showed behavior therapists in the future depriving the protagonist of his only enjoyment (listening to Beethoven) for the good of the state—not a very accurate or positive reflection of behavior therapy.

6.   This demonstration heightens students' awareness of the role of nonverbal messages in counseling and psychotherapy. What therapists say with their bodies can be as important as what they say with words, particularly in initial sessions. The experienced therapist knows that the client will reveal more when the therapist conveys, verbally and nonverbally, an attitude of openness, attention, and concern.

Gerard Egan (1982), a noted writer on the subject of training clinicians, suggests that *physical attending*—the nonverbal signals that tell clients they are being listened to—has five components, which can be remembered with the acronym SOLER. S stands for squarely facing the other person so you convey that you are available to that person. O stands for adopting an open posture, with arms unfolded and legs uncrossed. L stands for leaning slightly forward at times to underscore the idea that you are listening and empathizing with the other person. E stands for eye contact that avoids staring but tells the other person you are interested. And R stands for remaining relatively relaxed so as to model an attitude of

Copyright © Houghton Mifflin Company. All rights reserved.

trust. You should cover the five components, model them, and show the opposite of good posture or gesture for each so that students can learn how not to do it.

When you think students understand what SOLER stands for, have class members pair up. Tell them they will be interviewing each other on a specific topic for about six minutes. One topic might be what they think of the different therapies that are discussed in your text. The topic is really irrelevant; it just needs to be something on which all participants can voice an opinion. Each pair must decide who will interview first. Now instruct the interviewers that during the first several minutes they should adopt good nonverbal attending postures but, at your signal, violate every SOLER principle they can. They should slouch, avert eye contact, fiddle with pens, and so on while continuing the interview. Those who are being interviewed should keep track of how they felt and what they thought during the two parts of the interview.

Tell the students to begin interviewing. At about three minutes, say loudly, "Switch to bad nonverbal postures!" At about six minutes, stop the interviewing and ask for comments from both the interviewers and interviewees. Was it harder for interviewers to remember what was said when they were physically distant? How did the interviewees feel during the two parts of the interview? If you have enough time, have the pairs switch roles and do the interviews again.

When the exercise is over, suggest that, as homework, students note the quality of nonverbal communications in their daily conversations during the next several days. Have them write down their observations and ask for them in the next class period. This exercise makes students aware of the generally poor quality of listening that characterizes day-to-day interactions and points up the special quality of therapeutic ones.

Source: Adapted from *Exercises in Helping Skills,* Second Edition by Gerard Egan. Copyright © 1982, by Wadsworth, Inc. Adapted by permission of Brooks/Cole Publishing Company, Pacific Grove, CA 93950.

7.   Community psychology emphasizes the potential for community resources to be used for the prevention of psychological and other problems. To that extent, it is a field that must be optimistic about the ability of people to work collaboratively and consistently for the common good. It is interesting to poll students on their optimism for social change. The 1980s were characterized by a general pessimism that government or any other community agency could reduce suffering and prevent problems. The 1990s may be showing a small swing in the pendulum toward social activism. The author has polled students in the way described in the Handout for Demonstration 7 for some 15 years and has seen a small increase in optimism lately. Some conditions, however, are seen as unalterable: mental retardation and addictions among them.

Survey your students using the Handout for Demonstration 7. Give feedback to the class about the issues that were seen as likely to be eradicated and the ones that are seen as unchangeable. Ask students why they feel as they do. Probe the kinds of research and interventions that would be necessary to prevent social problems. Clarify for them the difference between primary and secondary prevention approaches.

8.   Ask the students to conduct their own Internet research into the common psychotropic medications listed in the text. The students should gather information concerning the situations in which these medications are most commonly prescribed, recommended dosage, side effects, possible drug interactions, and any other information of interest. Use the Internet site below as a reference or baseline for this demonstration.

Internet Site: http://www.mentalhealth.com/fr30.html. An extensive list of drugs used in the treatment of psychological disorders, including dosage, warning, effects, and side effects.

9.   Have the students form small groups of 4-7 individuals depending on your class size and space limitations. Ask each group to develop this list based on the following topic with the most salient

Copyright © Houghton Mifflin Company. All rights reserved.

examples first. Ask the students to discuss which type(s) of therapy they liked the best for the lecture and text book. Which type of therapy would be the most useful for most people? What are the barriers for people who don't seek some form of therapeutic treatment when it is needed? Can anything be done to change this?

Copyright © Houghton Mifflin Company. All rights reserved.

HANDOUT FOR DEMONSTRATION 3: A CASE FOR ROLE-PLAYING THERAPY

You and another person in the class will role-play a short therapy session. You are to play the role of the client. The following paragraph presents background information about the character you will play. Feel free to add details to this basic description. Please memorize the information so that when you are interviewed you will not need to look at this handout.

You are a 20-year-old college student with symptoms of both anxiety and depressive disorders. For the past six weeks you have had trouble sleeping—you wake up at 3 or 4 A.M. and cannot get back to sleep. You have had recurring nightmares in which you are threatened by a large man who snickers at your fear of him. During the day, you are fatigued and apathetic; you push yourself through the day. You have never before experienced such a feeling. Formerly you enjoyed conversations with friends and family; now it is a chore to be around them. Avoiding people you know is hard to do, but you try. You find it hard to study because you have trouble concentrating. You often worry about both major and minor things. For instance, you are concerned about your financial situation: Your part-time job was eliminated and you have many bills to pay. More distressing, you are preoccupied with how unfriendly your friends seem to be and whether you have offended them in small ways. You also feel that college isn't what you really want to be doing, but you do not know what is. You have always been something of a perfectionist, so recent inadequacies in academic, social, and job-related situations have you doubting your worth.

Copyright © Houghton Mifflin Company. All rights reserved.

HANDOUT FOR DEMONSTRATION 4: A SAMPLE OF DRUGS USED TO TREAT MENTAL DISORDERS, USUAL DOSAGE, AND THEIR SIDE EFFECTS[*]

Antianxiety drugs

Benzodiazepines

diazepam	Valium	2–40 mg/day	drowsiness, dizziness, confusion

Triazolobenzodiazepine

alprazolam	Xanax	0.75–4 mg/day	drowsiness, dizziness, confusion

Antidepressants

Tricyclics

imipramine	Tofranil	75 mg/day initially	changes in blood pressure and heart rate, anxiety, dry mouth

Serotonin-specific reuptake inhibitors

fluoxetine	Prozac	20–80 mg/day	anxiety, drowsiness, insomnia

Antipsychotic drugs

Phenothiazines

chlorpromazine	Thorazine	30–1,000 mg/day	drowsiness, jaundice, tremors, light sensitivity, dry mouth

Butyrophenones

haloperidol	Haldol	1–6 mg/day	drowsiness, jaundice, tremors, light sensitivity, dry mouth

Antimanic drugs

lithium	Eskalith	must be individualized	tremor, thirst, nausea

[*]Underlined term = category of drug, italic term = drug class. Under each class is the generic and trade name.

Copyright © Houghton Mifflin Company. All rights reserved.

HANDOUT FOR DEMONSTRATION 7: SURVEY ON SOCIAL PROBLEMS

Many of our society's problems are listed below. For each, indicate the degree to which you think the problem could be eliminated within your lifetime if adequate money and other resources were put to work to prevent it.

Within your lifetime, given adequate resources, how likely is it that this problem will be eliminated?

Problem	Very Likely	Likely	Unlikely	Very Unlikely
1. Illiteracy	4	3	2	1
2. Homelessness	4	3	2	1
3. Sexually transmitted diseases	4	3	2	1
4. Mental retardation	4	3	2	1
5. Domestic violence	4	3	2	1
6. Schizophrenia	4	3	2	1
7. Child abuse	4	3	2	1
8. Suicide	4	3	2	1
9. Cigarette smoking	4	3	2	1
10. Unwanted pregnancies	4	3	2	1
11. Gang violence	4	3	2	1
12. Depression	4	3	2	1
13. Heroin addiction	4	3	2	1
14. Coronary heart disease	4	3	2	1
15. Cancer	4	3	2	1

Copyright © Houghton Mifflin Company. All rights reserved.

SELECTED READINGS

Andreason, N. C. (1986). *The broken brain: The biological revolution in psychiatry.* New York: Harper & Row.

Bergin, A. E., & Garfield, S. L. (Eds.) (1994). *Handbook of psychotherapy and behavior change* (3rd ed.). New York: Wiley.

Freedheim, D. K. (Ed.) (1992). *History of psychotherapy: A century of change.* Washington, DC: American Psychological Association.

Schreter, R. K., Sharfstein, S. S., & Schreter, C. A. (Eds.) (1994). Allies and adversaries: The impact of managed care on mental health services. Washington, DC: American Psychiatric Press.

Sue, D. W., & Sue, D. (1990). Counseling the culturally different: Theory and practice. New York: Wiley.

Sattler, D., Shabatay, V., & Kramer, G. (1998). *Abnormal psychology in context: Voices and perspectives.* Boston, MA: Houghton Mifflin Company. Chapter 13, Individual and Group Therapy.

VIDEO RESOURCES

Asylum (video, color, 51 min). An outstanding documentary about St. Elizabeth's Hospital in Washington, D.C., traces the history of psychiatric treatment. It gives credit to underpaid and overworked psychiatric staff. An excellent debate on the pros and cons of the asylum concept, and long-term care is a highlight. Director Cinema Limited, P.O. Box 69899, Los Angeles, CA 90069.

Awareness (16 mm, color, 27 min). Dr. Frederick (Fritz) Perls shows how the gestalt method can teach individuals to increase their potential and to understand the idea of suffering. Films, Inc., 1144 Wilmette Avenue, Wilmette, IL 60091.

Behavior Therapy: An Introduction (16 mm, color, 29 min). Demonstrates the three forms of behavior therapy—classical conditioning, operant conditioning, and observational learning—and includes an interview with Joseph Wolpe. Pennsylvania State University Film Center, University Park, PA 16802.

Demonstration of Gestalt Therapy (16 mm, color, 38 min). This film shows factors that speed up the therapeutic process and demonstrates gestalt therapy by working with a man's recent fantasy. Emphasizes the importance of self-realization in therapy. Human Development Institute, 20 Executive Park West, Atlanta, GA 30329.

Electroconvulsive Therapy (ECT): The Treatment, the Questions, the Answers (video, color, 16 min). This short video gives a clear, calm, and objective description of ECT without sidestepping the problems. The film uses real patients and interviews them about the experience. It discusses the benefits of unilateral ECT. University of Michigan Medical Center R-4440 Kresge 1, Box 56, Ann Arbor, MI 48109-0010.

Group Psychotherapy—The Dynamics of Change (16 mm, color, 32 min). This film presents six patients and a psychiatrist in a portion of a group psychotherapy session. It shows one patient who achieves a significant breakthrough toward self-understanding. Association Films, Inc., 512 Burlington Avenue, La Grange, IL 60525.

Madness and Medicine: Parts I and II (16 mm, color, 21 and 28 min). Part I examines a mental institution and patients' feelings about institutional life. Doctors and patients discuss medications used in therapy.

Copyright © Houghton Mifflin Company. All rights reserved.

Part II deals with issues in ECT and psychosurgery. Patients, family members, and doctors are interviewed, and reentry into community life is discussed. CRM Educational Films, 1011 Camino Del Mar, Del Mar, CA 92014.

"An Ounce of Prevention" (13) from *The World of Abnormal Psychology* series (video, color, 60 min). This segment examines community-based projects (mostly primary prevention) at different points in the lifespan of the person: one for infants, one for adolescents, and one for middle-aged people. Each provides skills to participants but also examines environmental factors that produce disorders. To order, call The Annenberg/CBP Collection at 1-800-532-7637.

Psychotherapy (16 mm, color, 26 min). This film depicts three phases in the therapist-client interaction (building trust, self-awareness, and working through) that are found in most psychotherapies. CRM Educational Films, 1011 Camino Del Mar, Del Mar, CA 92014.

"Psychotherapy" (22) from the *Discovering Psychology* series (video, color, 28 min). Shows the relationships among theory, research, and practice and how cultural and social forces influence the treatment of psychological disorders. To order, call The Annenberg/CPB Collection at 1-800-532-7637.

"Psychotherapies" (12) from *The World of Abnormal Psychology* series (video, color, 60 min). This segment demonstrates the three major forms of psychotherapy—psychodynamic, experiential, and cognitive-behavioral—and explains how they can be useful in individual and group work. To order, call The Annenberg/CBP Collection at 1-800-532-7637.

Rational Emotive Therapy (16 mm, color, 30 min). This film shows Dr. Albert Ellis in practice. He explains his paradigm in which irrational beliefs determine the effect of events on feelings, and he presents alternatives to irrational self-talk. Research Press, Box 317740, Champaign, IL 61820.

Social Network Therapy (video, color, 11 min). This very short video describes a unique approach to treatment: the coaching and convening of schizophrenics and their family and friends for the purpose of reducing social isolation and mobilizing continuing care. Actors enact situations; founder of the therapy, Ross Speck, narrates. Because of its brevity, the video glosses over the complexities of network therapy. Mental Health Library, 331 Dundas Street, East Toronto, Ontario Canada M5A 2A2.

Token Economy (16 mm, color, 20 min). This film illustrates the use of tokens in an inpatient treatment program, and B. F. Skinner explains the approach. CRM Educational Films, 1011 Camino Del Mar, Del Mar, CA 92014.

ON THE INTERNET

http://www.appi.org is a brief descriptions of articles in recent issues of the *American Journal of Psychiatry, Psychiatric News,* and *Journal of Psychotherapy: Practice and Research.*

http://www.rebt.org is the web site for the Albert Ellis Institute, which contains information on rational emotive behavior therapy

http://www.mentalhealth.com/fr30.html which provides an extensive list of drugs used in the treatment of psychological disorders, including dosage, warnings, effects, and side effects

http://helping.apa.org/brochure/index.html offers helpful information about when you might need a therapist and how to choose one

Copyright © Houghton Mifflin Company. All rights reserved.

CHAPTER 18

Legal and Ethical Issues in Abnormal Psychology

CHAPTER OUTLINE

I. Mental health concerns can become legal and ethical issues

   A. Several example of the interaction of psychology and the legal system

   B. Tarasoff case concerns limits of confidentiality

   C. Ethics of therapist-client relationships

II. Criminal commitment: the incarceration of an individual for having committed a crime

   A. Criminal law assumes free will and personal responsibility for actions

   B. Insanity defense: legal term (not psychological) arguing that defendant who admits to committing a crime is not guilty because of being mentally disturbed at the time

      1. Martin Ome cleverly deduced that Kenneth Bianchi was faking multiple personality

      2. Legal precedents

         a. M'Naghten Rule (England, 1843): at time of act, defendant did not know right from wrong or know what he or she was doing (purely cognitive)

         b. Irresistible impulse test: lacked will power to control behavior

         c. Durham standard (United States, 1954): products test (actions were the product of mental disease or defect)

         d. American Law Institute (ALI) Code (United States, 1962): "as a result of mental disease or defect he lacks substantial capacity either to appreciate the criminality of his conduct or to conform his conduct to the requirements of the law" (does not include antisocial personality as mental disease or defect)

         e. Diminished capacity: in some jurisdictions, often in sentencing phase; Dan White "Twinkies defense"

      3. Guilty, but mentally ill: adopted after John Hinckley verdict; Insanity Reform Act (1984) bases insanity solely on ability to understand what one did

      4. Thomas S. Szasz against insanity defense and involuntary commitment

   C. Competency to stand trial: defendant knows nature of proceedings and can assist in own defense (not mental state at time of crime)

      1. Much more common than insanity issue

      2. *Jackson v. Indiana* (1972)

         a. Prevents indefinite incarceration for incompetence without trial

         b. Protects due process

III. Civil commitment: involuntary confinement of a person judged to be a danger to himself, herself, or others, even though the person has not committed a crime

Copyright © Houghton Mifflin Company. All rights reserved

A. Negative effects: lifelong social stigma, lowered self-esteem, lost civil liberties

B. Criteria for commitment

   1. Clear and imminent danger to self or others

   2. Unable to care for self & without communal support (most common reason)

   3. Unable to make responsible decisions

   4. In unmanageable state of panic

C. Assessing dangerousness (the person's potential for doing harm to self or others): difficult to predict

   1. Clinicians usually overpredict dangerousness

   2. Mistakes due to rarity of the event (fewer than 10 percent of psychotic patients are assaultive), dangerousness situation-specific, best predictor is past conduct or history of violence

D. Procedures in civil commitment

   1. Voluntary commitment preferred

   2. Involuntary (temporary action or longer detention after court hearing)

      a. Court hears testimony of two independent professionals as well as others

      b. Length of treatment usually finite (generally six to twelve months)

   3. Protection against involuntary commitment

      a. Critics argue that criminals have more rights than mentally ill (liberty denied in anticipation of actions)

      b. Opposite view: committed incapable of decision, will be grateful later

   4. Rights of mental patients

      a. Level of proof (*Addington v. Texas*, 1979): "clear and convincing evidence" (75 percent sure)

      b. Least restrictive environment

   5. Right to treatment (constitutional right)

      a. *Wyatt v. Stickney* (1972): stipulates treatment, environmental standards if committed

      b. *O'Connor v. Donaldson* (1975): cannot confine nondangerous person capable of independent or supervised living

      c. *Youngberg v. Romeo* (1982): allows mental health professionals to define "treatment"

   6. Right to refuse treatment

      a. *Rennie v. Klein* (1978): people have constitutional right to refuse drug medication

      b. *Rogers v. Okin* (1979): supports Rennie

      c. Application to psychotherapy unclear

IV. Deinstitutionalization: shifting responsibility for care of mental patients from large central institutions to agencies within local communities

A. Produced a 75 percent decrease in average daily number of committed patients

B. Reasons for deinstitutionalization

   1. Hospital may hinder recovery

   2. Patient rights; belief that mainstreaming in community can be accomplished by outpatient service or halfway house

   3. Insufficient state funds to treat

Copyright © Houghton Mifflin Company. All rights reserved.

    C. Impact of deinstitutionalization

       1. Dumping; homeless mentally ill

       2. Lack of family and friends support system

       3. Criminalization

       4. Often low-quality care in nursing homes, group residences

       5. Alternative community programs have more positive outcomes

V. The therapist-client relationship

    A. Confidentiality and privileged communication

       1. Confidentiality an ethical standard to protect clients from disclosure without their consent

          a. Disclose only as required by law

          b. Important in therapeutic relationship

       2. Privileged communication a narrower legal concept

          a. Client holds privilege of privileged communication

          b. Exemptions from privileged communication: civil or criminal commitment; client sues therapist; client under 16 and victim of crime; criminal action involved; client dangerous

       3. Exceptions from privileged communications

          a. Civil and criminal commitment

          b. Defense in a civil action

          c. Client is younger than sixteen or is a dependent elderly person who the therapist believes has been the victim of a crime

          d. Client is a danger to self or others

    B. The duty-to-warn principle (Tarasoff v. Board of Regents, 1976)

       1. Therapist must warn intended victim and others who might be with the victim

       2. *Jaffee v. Redmond*

       3. Criticism of the duty-to-warn principle

    C. Sexual relationships with clients

       1. Always unethical, according to every mental health organization

       2. Nationwide survey: 5.5 percent of male, 0.6 percent of female therapists admit to having had intercourse with clients

       3. Fosters dependency, objectivity is lost, client open to exploitation

          a. 90 percent of clients who had sexual involvement with therapist were adversely affected

          b. Committee on Women in Psychology of APA says sexual relationship between therapy and client is never the fault of the client

       4. Processes for revoking license of therapist for misconduct exist

VI. Cultural and pluralism and the mental health profession

    A. Cultural bound concepts of mental health and mental disorders (specific to middle-class, white, highly individualistic, ethnocentric population) result in misdiagnosis and inappropriate treatments that often victimize ethnic-minority clients

    B. Similar problems extend to other marginalized groups (women, homosexuals, the disabled)

    C. APA Code of Conduct

Copyright © Houghton Mifflin Company. All rights reserved.

1. Working with culturally different clients is unethical unless the mental health professional has adequate training and expertise in multicultural psychology

2. Guidelines for Providers of Psychological Services to Ethnic, Linguistic, and Culturally Diverse Populations (APA, 1993) and Guidelines for Psychotherapy with Lesbian, Gay, and Bisexual Clients (APA, 2000) : moral and professional responsibility to become culturally competent if working with diverse clientele

3. DSM-IV-TR acknowledges the importance of culture in diagnosis and treatment of mental disorders

4. APA Divisions 17, 44, and 45 of APA submitted document in 2001: "Guidelines for Multicultural Counseling Proficiency for Psychologists: Implications for Education and Training, Research and Clinical Practice" to ensure adequate training and expertise of therapists to deal with diversity

LEARNING OBJECTIVES

1. Describe the range of legal and ethical issues relevant to abnormal psychology. (pp. 587-590; Table 18.1)

2. Define criminal commitment processes and discuss criminal law's position on free will. (pp. 590-591)

3. Discuss the rationale for the insanity defense and the legal precedents that have shaped the current standing of the insanity defense, including the M'Naghten Rule, the irresistible impulse test, the *Durham* standard, the American Law Institute (ALI) Model Penal Code, and diminished capacity. (pp. 591-594)

4. Discuss the arguments for and against the plea "guilty, but mentally ill," including Thomas Szasz's arguments against the insanity defense and involuntary commitment. (pp. 594-597; Mental Health & Society)

5. Describe the criteria for finding a defendant competent to stand trial and the procedures involved in determining it, including due process. (pp. 595-596)

6. Describe the concept of civil commitment and the criteria by which individuals are committed. Explain why the assessment of dangerousness is difficult. (pp. 596-599)

7. Explain the rationale for civil commitment, the procedures involved, and the protections that exist against its abuse. Outline the criticisms of civil commitment. (pp. 599-601; Mental Health & Society)

8. Discuss the key legal rulings concerning the rights of mental patients, including the level of proof necessary for commitment (*Addington v. Texas),* the least restrictive environment principle, and the right to treatment (*Wyatt v. Stickney , O'Connor v. Donaldson,* and *Youngberg v. Romeo). (pp. 601-603)

9. Discuss the legal rulings concerning the right to refuse treatment (*Rennie v. Klein* and *Rogers v. Okin)* and the arguments for and against this right. Define the term *least intrusive treatment.* (p. 603)

10. Discuss the reasons for and the impact of the deinstitutionalization of mental patients. Evaluate the present living conditions of many ex–mental hospital patients and the prospects for mainstreaming and alternative community programs. (pp. 603-605)

11. Distinguish between the concepts of confidential and privileged communications. Discuss when therapists may disclose confidential information and where there are exemptions to privileged communications. (p. 605-606)

12. Describe the duty-to-warn principle, the legal rulings related to it (*Tarasoff v. Board of Regents of the University of California*), and the criticisms of the duty-to-warn principle. (pp. 606-609; Critical Thinking

Copyright © Houghton Mifflin Company. All rights reserved.

13. Identify the position of professional organizations on the issue of sexual intimacies between therapist and client. Discuss the research on the impact of therapists' sexual involvement with clients. (pp. 609-610)
14. Discuss how mental health professionals need to accommodate the changes in the ethnic profile of Americans. Describe the ethical guidelines for working with culturally different clients and the information in DSM-IV that deals with multicultural influences. (pp. 610-611)

CLASSROOM TOPICS FOR LECTURE AND DISCUSSION

1.   Pope and Tabachnick (1993) report the results of a national survey of 285 clinical and counseling psychologists, equally divided among men and women and those over and under the age of 45. From the 67-item survey, here are some thought-provoking results. In the table below is the percentage of psychologists who responded "rarely" or more often to each item. This survey is the source of the textbook authors' comment that having sexual fantasies about clients is not uncommon, but losing control of behavior is extremely uncommon.

Item	Percentage responding "Rarely," "Sometimes," "Often," or "Most Always"
A client hugs you	89.1
Feeling sexually attracted to a client	87.3
A client flirts with you	87.0
You hug a client	81.1
A client tells you that he/she is sexually attracted to you	73.3
You hold a client's hand	60.4
Feeling sexually aroused while in the presence of a client	57.9
A client seems to become sexually aroused in your presence	48.4
A client kisses you	24.2
You flirt with a client	19.6
Client files a complaint against you (for example, malpractice, ethics)	11.6
You kiss a client	5.6
Talking with a current client about sharing a sexual relationship after termination of therapy	2.1

Psychologists' theoretical orientation had an effect on ratings. Psychodynamic therapists were more likely to experience clients flirting, clients becoming sexually aroused, and the therapist suggesting the client tell about sexual fantasies. Psychodynamically oriented therapists were *less* likely than others to hug, be hugged, or hold a client's hand.

Gender also had strong effects. Male therapists were more likely than female therapists to have had a client file a complaint (17 percent versus 6 percent). Female clients were more likely than male clients to have been hugged and seen as physically attractive by their therapists.

Source: Pope, K. S., & Tabachnick, B. G. (1993). Therapists' anger, hate, fear, and sexual feelings: National survey of therapist responses, client characteristics, critical events, formal complaints, and

Copyright © Houghton Mifflin Company. All rights reserved.

training. *Professional Psychology: Research and Practice, 24,* 142–152. Copyright © 1993 by the American Psychological Association. Reprinted with permission

2.   A flowchart diagram either drawn on the board or distributed as a handout can help students understand the general procedures in civil commitment and criminal cases, including competency hearings and the insanity defense. Because there are considerable differences between states, it is not possible to present such a flowchart here. (Consult with an attorney familiar with civil and criminal commitment who can describe correctly the specific procedures in your state.)

A general map of the civil commitment terrain indicates that once someone (police, family, or social service agency) petitions the court for commitment, there are psychological evaluations, a hearing with counsel, and either release or confinement for a specific period or an indefinite period during which there is periodic review. Let students know that some variance often occurs between the process as described on paper and as it occurs in real life. For instance, although people who face civil commitment have the right to counsel, some studies show that attorneys meet and discuss the case with their clients for only a few minutes before the commitment hearing.

In criminal cases the prosecution or defense (and often both) can question defendants' competency—their ability to understand the proceedings and assist rationally in their defense. Following psychological examinations, the court will either find the defendant competent, which leads to a trial, or find the dependent not competent, which leads to the same kind of confinement as in civil commitment. However, charges can be dropped and the person freed at this point. If, after a period of involuntary treatment, experts feel the person will not regain sufficient mental stability to be competent, either the defendant is released or a petition for civil commitment ensues. If the person is found competent to stand trial, the person may choose to plead not guilty by reason of insanity (NGBRI). If the verdict is NGBRI, the person is confined in a mental hospital until mental health experts report to the court that the person is no longer dangerous. There is no definite sentence or provision of parole or time off for good behavior. If the verdict is guilty, a sentencing hearing ensues at which time more psychological evidence is presented to determine the length of sentence in a penal facility.

Emphasize to students the number of points in these procedures where mental health experts are asked to make evaluations, judgments, and predictions. At virtually every step in the process, expert testimony is requested. However, because the legal system is an adversarial one, the testimony is often conflicting and sometimes diametrically opposed. Coupled with the reliability problems in assessment mentioned in Chapter 3 and the time constraints due to the vast number of cases that must be processed, students should begin to see the opportunities for error that exist in the process. Still, the situation is far better than it was 50 years ago when a person could be committed to a psychiatric facility for an indefinite period without any form of due process. Despite their comic value, you might mention the grim side of such movies as *Arsenic and Old Lace* and *Harvey* in this context.

Internet site: http://www.nami.org the site of the National Alliance for the Mentally Ill, to check out issues concerning civil commitment

3.   Federal Judge Frank Johnson made a landmark decision in *Wyatt v. Stickney*. This class action suit was brought against the Commissioner of Mental Health in Alabama (Stickney) on behalf of Ricky Wyatt and other mentally retarded patients at a state hospital and school. Not only did Johnson declare that the state had failed to provide treatment, he described what adequate treatment entailed. You can contrast the dehumanizing conditions that existed in this facility with the requirements that Johnson stipulated.

Before *Wyatt,* the state hospital housed patients in barnlike structures that had no privacy. There were no partitions between bathroom stalls, patients wore tattered clothing, and the wards were dark and filthy. The kitchens were unsanitary and the food was inedible—the state spent less than 50 cents a day on food per patient. The patient-to-psychologist ratio was 1,000 to 1!

Copyright © Houghton Mifflin Company. All rights reserved.

Johnson required at least two psychiatrists, one doctoral-level psychologist, and two master's-level social workers per 250 patients. No more than six patients were to be housed in a room, and screens or curtains had to be provided to afford privacy. No more than eight patients were to share one toilet facility, and separate stalls had to be provided to ensure privacy. Below is a more complete, but still partial, listing of patients' rights Johnson specified:

1. Right to privacy and to be treated with dignity

2. Right to visitation and telephone privileges unless special restrictions apply

3. Right to treatment under the least restrictive conditions that meet the purposes commitment was intended to serve

4. Right to regular exercise and opportunities to spend time outdoors

5. Right to suitable opportunities to interact with the opposite gender

6. Right to refuse potentially hazardous treatments such as lobotomy, ECT, and aversive behavioral treatments

7. Right to nutritionally balanced diets

8. Right to wear their own clothing and keep personal possessions unless doing so proved to be dangerous or inappropriate to the treatment program

9. Right not to be subject to experimental research unless their rights to informed consent are protected

10. Protection from being kept in restraints or in isolation unless in emergency conditions where their safety or that of others is threatened

11. Protection from being required to do work that is performed for the sake of maintaining the facility

This ruling became the model for reforms nationwide and, to a great extent, is responsible for the infinitely better treatment that committed patients now receive. It is not too much to say that Judge Johnson was the Philippe Pinel of our age.

Source: *Wyatt v. Stickney*, 334 F. Supp. 1341 (1972).

CLASSROOM DEMONSTRATIONS & HANDOUTS

1.   The following demonstration can spark discussion about the value of the insanity defense. After each well-publicized insanity case hits the TV news, there is a strong emotional response from the public. One goal of this demonstration is to sensitize students to their own reactions to the insanity defense.

In small groups (five to six people), have students read the Handout for Demonstration 1 and consider, individually, their responses to the situations. Then have them discuss their reactions with one another and explain their responses. Groups should then try to arrive at a consensus for each of the situations and report them to the rest of the class; these responses should also be listed on the board. Discuss whether levels of responsibility exist and whether the severity of a crime has any place in these

Copyright © Houghton Mifflin Company. All rights reserved.

deliberations; discuss the amount of emphasis that should be placed on expert testimony (particularly given the inevitable disagreements between prosecution and defense experts).

As a final jolt, ask students whether their tolerance for the behavior of mental patients would change if, in each of the situations described in the handout, the victim were their mother!

2.   Divide the class into small groups, and instruct the groups that they have been asked by their local government to brainstorm ways of dealing with the problems of the discharged chronic mental patient. Each group must outline the following:

1. What should mental hospitals do to increase the likelihood of successful patient adjustment in the community?

2. What kinds of community supports are needed to increase the likelihood that former patients will develop stable living arrangements (either with family, independently, or with supervision)?

3. What needs to be done to increase the community's acceptance of discharged mental patients?

4. What can be done to overcome the barriers discussed in question 3?

This exercise will probably take an entire class period, but it can get students to appreciate the dilemmas that communities and professionals face in dealing with deinstitutionalization. It should also bring to the foreground the fact that money is a central issue in any of these debates.

3.   The success of therapy may be determined by ethnic and other cultural similarities or at least a willingness on the part of the therapist to modify interventions to accommodate cultural styles. This issue promises to become more widespread as the United States becomes more culturally diverse. Ask for student volunteers to role-play an assessment interview in which a therapist is all wrong for the client, being insensitive about gender issues as well as racial and social concerns. Ask the class to identify the problem areas and recommend specific changes that might make the interaction more successful. Then ask either the original volunteers or others to reenact the interview with greater cultural sensitivity. Finish the activity by asking if such sensitivity is a moral responsibility or simply a "nice thing to do." Note that the textbook authors consider cultural sensitivity a moral and ethical obligation.

4.   The Ellie Nessler case was a very famous case in the national media and is appropriate for a group discussion activity.   To review, Ellie Nessler, 41, shot and killed Daniel Driver in a Jamestown, California, courtroom on April 2, 1993. She smuggled the weapon into the courtroom and shot Driver five times. Driver had been on trial for molesting Nessler's six-year-old son.

Divide the class into groups of eight to twelve members. Distribute the two-page handout for this activity. Each person should read the facts of the case and then decide Nessler's guilty or insanity using the four tests for insanity. You may need to remind students of the legal language used for each test. You can put this information on the board, ask them to look it up in the text, provide a handout, or tell them verbally. Be sure they understand the differences. Like jurors, after they vote individually, they should discuss their reasoning and the group should attempt to arrive at a consensus. You may even want to have them assign a jury foreperson who will report the group's "deliberations and verdict" to the class.

Record on the board similarities and differences in judgments by each group. Ask for explanations of differences. Clarify any misconceptions students have about the four standards. Tell students that the jury in the case found Nessler guilty of voluntary manslaughter (she killed in the heat of passion, not after deliberation as in first-degree murder). She was found legally responsible for her actions, but the jury conceded that some mental disorders existed and that they hoped Nessler would receive

Copyright © Houghton Mifflin Company. All rights reserved.

psychological therapy. Point out the subjective judgments that are made in these cases. Note also that the M'Naghten standard is used exclusively at the federal level, whereas the states have various standards and, in a few, there is no insanity defense at all.

Internet site: http://www.wisecounty.com/themuse/Column24.htm to read a press release on the Ellie Nessler case

5.   An ethical question that students should consider is summed up in the acronym NIMBY, which stands for "Not In My Back Yard." At the end of a course in abnormal psychology, students are often more aware of the problems of people with mental disorders. They appreciate the need for more humane and community-based treatment and prevention services. However, are they ready to have direct contact with such people?

Ask students to imagine that a halfway house for individuals with problems is to be located on their street at home. You can vary the clientele of the halfway house, from clearly innocent victims (abused children) to more "dangerous" individuals (alcoholic women or adults with mental retardation) to very "dangerous" individuals (ex-prison inmates). Ask students how the neighborhood would react, how their parents would react, and how they would feel. In what neighborhoods would such halfway houses be acceptable? for what kind of clients? Discuss with students the problem of citing community services in unsafe areas. Suggest that, having taken this course, they can help dispel myths about the dangerousness and incurability of people with mental disorders.

6.   Have the students form small groups of 4-7 individuals depending on your class size and space limitations. Ask each group to develop a list of examples on the following topic, with the most salient examples first. Discuss the role of managed care in mental health services as a controversial issue. Ask the students how they would feel if their insurance provider chose to limit the number of visits they are allowed to see a therapist. Ask the students to discuss what other barriers to mental health treatment exist. What would the members of the discussion group do to make mental health services available for all who need them?

7.   The following demonstration can spark discussion about the value of the insanity defense. After each well-publicized insanity case hits the TV news, there is a strong emotional response from the public. One goal of this demonstration is to sensitize students to their own reactions to the insanity defense.

Have the students form small groups of 4-7 individuals depending on your class size and space limitations. Ask each group to develop a list of examples on the following topic with the most salient examples first. Each group could then have a spokesperson deliver a short talk about the best examples. You could provide a blank overhead transparency to each group at the beginning of this demonstration.

Discuss whether levels of responsibility exist for the defendant and whether the severity of a crime has any place in courtroom deliberations. Then discuss the amount of emphasis that should be placed on expert testimony (particularly given the inevitable disagreements between prosecution and defense experts). Use the most recent national or regional court case as an example to start the discussion.

Copyright © Houghton Mifflin Company. All rights reserved.

HANDOUT FOR DEMONSTRATION 1: THE INSANITY DEFENSE

For each of the situations described, decide how you would feel about the defendant's being found not guilty by reason of insanity (NGBRI). Be as honest as you can be.

1. A woman sitting in a fast food restaurant is shot in the back and paralyzed for life. The person who fired the shot is John, a mentally retarded young man who says he found the loaded gun and was playing with it in the restaurant. "I just wanted to see what would happen if I pulled the trigger," he says. Psychological assessments indicate that he is moderately retarded and did not know that what he was doing was against the law.

   Is John responsible for his actions (NGBRI fails)?

Definitely Not Guilty	Probably Not Guilty	Not Sure	Probably Guilty	Definitely Guilty
1	2	3	4	5

2. A woman sitting in a fast food restaurant is shot in the back and paralyzed for life. The person who fired the shot is Bill, a chronic schizophrenic young man who says he had seen the woman looking at him the way the devil does. "I must protect myself from demons—and she was one," he says. Psychological assessments indicate that, at the time of the crime, Bill's delusions prevented him from acting in any other way.

   Is Bill responsible for his actions (NGBRI fails)?

Definitely Not Guilty	Probably Not Guilty	Not Sure	Probably Guilty	Definitely Guilty
1	2	3	4	5

3. A woman sitting in a fast food restaurant is shot in the back and paralyzed for life. The person who fired the shot is Pete, a chemically dependent young man who says he was drunk and high when he saw a woman who looked like his ex-girlfriend. "I was so out of my mind on drugs that she looked like my old lady," he says. Psychological assessments indicate that, at the time of the crime, Pete was suffering from a chemically induced organic brain syndrome called delirium.

   Is Pete responsible for his actions (NGBRI fails)?

Definitely Not Guilty	Probably Not Guilty	Not Sure	Probably Guilty	Definitely Guilty
1	2	3	4	5

Copyright © Houghton Mifflin Company. All rights reserved.

HANDOUT FOR DEMONSTRATION 4: DECIDING WHETHER ELLIE NESLER WAS NOT GUILTY BY REASON OF INSANITY

Ellie Nesler, 41, shot and killed Daniel Driver in a Jamestown, California, courtroom on April 2, 1993. She smuggled the weapon into the courtroom and shot Driver five times. Driver had been on trial for molesting Nesler's six-year-old son.

The defense argued that Nesler was insane at the time of the crime. Here are the defense's arguments:

1. Nesler had lived in violent family environments. Her alcoholic father often battered her mother, she was attacked when she tried to shield her mother and two younger sisters from her father, and she was molested at the age of three and was sexually abused by at least three other men. As a child she had thoughts of suicide. She, therefore, had a history of trauma that made her psychologically vulnerable.

2. Nesler discovered that her six-year-old son had been molested by Daniel Driver, a man Nesler trusted but did not know was a convicted child molester. She was racked with guilt knowing she had entrusted her son to this man. During the three years when Driver was sought by law enforcement for the molestation, the son (Danny) lived in constant fear that Driver would find and harm him.

3. Nesler saw "secret signs" from the routine comments of friends and relatives that ordered her to kill Driver. These caused her to smuggle a pistol into the courtroom and kill Driver.

4. Several mental health professionals evaluated Nesler and, although their diagnoses varied, one included brief reactive psychosis and another posttraumatic stress disorder.

The prosecution argued that Nesler did not act like an insane person and should be found guilty of the crime. Here are the prosecution's arguments:

1. Nesler's behaviors leading up to the crime were planned and deliberate. She admitted that she wanted to see if Driver would be remorseful before shooting him. She wanted to see if he would "cop a plea" (accept a level of guilt for his actions rather than plead not guilty).

2. She checked to see if a deputy whom she had befriended would get in trouble if Driver was killed.

3. She made sure no children were present in the courtroom so they would not witness the shooting.

4. Several mental health professionals with credentials equal to the defense's evaluated Nesler and argued that she had the ability to distinguish right from wrong.

Consider all the information presented here and decide individually, Was Ellie Nesler insane at the time she shot Daniel Driver? Next, individually, check for each test of insanity on the next page whether Nesler was guilty or not guilty by reason of insanity. Be prepared to defend your judgments.

Now reveal your verdicts to others in your group. See if, like real juries, you can come to a consensus on Nesler's guilt or insanity. Would it differ or remain the same for each of the four insanity tests? Be prepared to report your group's decision and its rationale to the rest of the class.

Copyright © Houghton Mifflin Company. All rights reserved.

	M'Naghten Rule	Irresistible Impulse	Durham Rule	ALI Guidelines
Verdict				
Guilty	_____	_____	_____	_____
Not Guilty	_____	_____	_____	_____

Rationale for M'Naghten Rule:

Rationale for Irresistible Impulse:

Rationale for Durham Rule:

Rationale for ALI Guidelines:

Copyright © Houghton Mifflin Company. All rights reserved.

SELECTED READINGS

Appelbaum, P. A. (1994). *Almost a revolution: Mental health law and the limits of change.* New York: Oxford University Press.

Corey, G., Corey, M. S., & Callanan, P. (1993). *Issues and ethics in the helping professions* (4th ed.). Pacific Grove, CA: Brooks/Cole.

McNeil, D. E., & Binder, R. L. (1986). Violence, civil commitment, and hospitalization. *Journal of Nervous and Mental Disease, 174,* 107–111.

Nietzel, M. T., & Dillehay, R. C. (1986). *Psychological consultation in the courtroom.* New York: Pergamon.

Wrightsman, L. S. (1987). *Psychology and the legal system* (2nd ed.). Pacific Grove, CA: Brooks/ Cole.

VIDEO RESOURCES

Bitter Welcome (16 mm, 35 min). This film shows the effects of labeling on a newly discharged mental patient and his efforts to overcome community stigmatization. Psychological Cinema Register, Pennsylvania State University, University Park, PA 16802.

Bold New Approach (16 mm, 59 min). This film from the mid-1960s depicts the dream of deinstitutionalization: community facilities available to all mental patients. Offers an interesting counterpoint to current concerns about unsupported chronically mentally ill patients. Psychological Cinema Register, Pennsylvania State University, University Park, PA 16802.

Interrupted Lives (video, color, 60 min). This video describes the problems of people with chronic mental illness who have neither hospital nor community resources available. It argues for community integration. Boston University Center for Rehabilitation, Research, and Training in Mental Health, 1019 Commonwealth Avenue, Boston, MA 02215.

Operation Reentry (16 mm, 30 min). Demonstrates the successful rehabilitation of mental patients in the Palo Alto, California, VA hospital. Shows former patients as advisors to those preparing for independent living. Indiana University Audio-Visual Center, Bloomington, IN 47405.

Storefronts (16 mm, 28 min). Documentary film that shows the community mental health services offered in Harlem as an extension of Lincoln Hospital. Contemporary Films, McGraw-Hill Book Company, 1221 Avenue of the Americas, New York, NY 10020.

Back from Madness: The Struggle for Sanity (VHS, color, 53 mm.). Follows four psychiatric patients from the time they are admitted to Massachusetts General Hospital and for several years afterward. Films for the Humanities and Sciences. 1-800-257-5126.

Committed in Error: The Mental Health System Gone Mad (VHS, color, 64 mm.). The story of a man incarcerated and forgotten in a mental health institution for sixty-six years. Films for the Humanities and Sciences. 1-800-257-5126.

The Psychopathic Mind (VHS, color, 27 mm.). Describes the characteristics of a psychopath and how they are classified. Films for the Humanities and Sciences. 1-800-257-5126.

Copyright © Houghton Mifflin Company. All rights reserved.

ON THE INTERNET

http://www.fbi.gov/ includes the FBI's "Ten Most Wanted" list of fugitives, as well as employment opportunities and general information on the FBI.

http://www.priory.com/forpsy.htm is useful for the study of forensic psychiatry with a number of links to articles on topics associated with the field.

http://www.geocities.com/Athens/7429/psychlaw.htmlis a large resource page with many links, court cases, and journal references.

 http://www.tandf.co.uk/journals/titles/09585184 is *The Journal of Forensic Psychiatry*, which provides a leading forum of communication for professionals working in this field: psychiatrists, psychologists, lawyers, social workers, criminologists, and sociologists.

http://www.aapl.org/ethics.htm is the Web site for the American Academy of Psychiatry and the Law, which is dedicated to the highest standards of practice in forensic psychiatry.

Copyright © Houghton Mifflin Company. All rights reserved.